Microsoft® Office

Excel® 2007
for Project Managers

Microsoft® Office

Excel® 2007
for Project Managers

Kim Heldman
William Heldman

BICENTENNIAL
1807
WILEY
2007
BICENTENNIAL

Wiley Publishing, Inc.

Acquisitions Editor: Maureen Adams
Development Editors: Maureen Adams and Tom Cirtin
Technical Editor: Vanessa L. Williams
Production Editor: Sarah Groff-Palermo
Copy Editor: Judy Flynn
Production Manager: Tim Tate
Vice President and Executive Group Publisher: Richard Swadley
Vice President and Executive Publisher: Joseph B. Wikert
Vice President and Publisher: Neil Edde
Book Designer: Judy Fung
Compositor: Laurie Stewart, Happenstance Type-O-Rama
Proofreader: Ian Golder
Indexer: Ted Laux
Anniversary Logo Design: Richard Pacifico
Cover Designer: Archer Design

Acknowledgments

We'd like to thank all the people who helped make this book possible. Writing a book meets the definition of a project, and as with most projects, it takes the dedication and hard work of many team members to bring it to a successful conclusion.

Thank you to Maureen Adams, our acquisitions editor, for suggesting this book and for asking us to write it. It's always a delight to work with her. We'll miss her and we wish her well in her new endeavors.

Thanks also to Vanessa Williams, our technical editor, for checking and rechecking the Excel and MOSS references. Her suggestions were invaluable and helped make some of our examples even better.

Thanks to Sarah Groff-Palermo and Judy Flynn, our production editor and copyeditor, respectively, who are experts at quality assurance! We appreciate their thoroughness and eye for detail.

There are many others behind the scenes at Sybex who also worked hard to make this book the best product it could be. Thanks to Laurie Stewart and Ian Golder. We also want to thank the book distributors and merchants for getting our books on the shelves and into your hands.

Another big thanks goes to all of the instructors and consultants out there who've used Kim's other project management books for classroom and corporate instruction—Terri Wagner and Claudia Baca in particular.

Most of all, thanks to you, our readers, for buying this book. We hope you find it helpful for managing your next project.

About the Authors

Kim Heldman, the chief information officer for the Colorado Department of Natural Resources, has more than 16 years of project management experience in the information technology field. She's managed small, medium, and large projects over the course of her career and shares her breadth of experience and knowledge in her books through examples, stories, and tips.

Kim is the best-selling author of several other project management books, including *PMP Project Management Professional Study Guide, Third Edition* (Sybex, 2005); *Project Manager's Spotlight on Risk Management* (Sybex, 2005); and *Project Management JumpStart* (Sybex, 2005). You can learn more about Kim at her website: `KimHeldman.com`.

Bill Heldman is a computer technology instructor at a Career and Technical Education (CTE) high school in Lakewood, Colorado, where he teaches 11th- and 12th-graders on a variety of topics, including programming (application and game), networks, A+, project management, security, databases, and TCP/IP. Bill has 20 years of experience in the computer technology field, starting with mainframe computing and working through programming, networks, and enterprise application software. He has worked as a technician, supervisor, and mid-manager in both public and private-sector information technology organizations.

Bill has written numerous certification study guides for Sybex. He is also a frequent contributor to *Microsoft Certified Professional (MCP) Magazine* and its cousin, *Redmond Magazine*, as well as *Windows IT Pro* magazine. You can learn more about Bill at his website: `BillHeldman.com`. You can view his class outline along with other academic information at `www.ctfp.org`.

Contents at a Glance

Contents

Introduction

We have written this book for those of you who have some experience in project management and are looking for a quick and efficient way to manage your projects. When combined, Excel 2007 and Microsoft Office SharePoint Server (MOSS)—two components of the Office 2007 initiative that Microsoft has developed—are great for managing all phases of a project, creating templates, collaborating on planning processes, tracking project progress, and sharing information with all interested parties.

The project management field has grown exponentially over the last decade. Run a query on your favorite job-hunting site and you'll see that project management experience is a requirement (or at a minimum, a desired skill set) for tens of thousands of job postings. In addition, many of you have upwards of half a dozen to a dozen independent projects running at the same time. This book will show you how to organize the management of those projects using templates we've built for Excel 2007 and how to take advantage of the power of SharePoint to communicate and share that information with team members and stakeholders.

If you find that this topic interests you and project management seems like a career worth pursuing, we strongly recommend that you consider obtaining your Project Management Professional (PMP) certification through the Project Management Institute (PMI). PMI is the de facto standard in project management methodologies. You will find that many organizations now require a PMP certification for positions related to project management.

This book is based on the project management guidelines recommended by PMI, and many of the terms, concepts, and processes you'll read about in this book are based on PMI's publication, *A Guide to the Project Management Body of Knowledge (PMBOK Guide), Third Edition.*

 For a more detailed exploration of the PMP certification, pick up a copy of *PMP Project Management Professional Study Guide, Third Edition,* by Kim Heldman (Sybex, 2005).

Whether you choose to pursue certification or not, solid project management practices are required to achieve success on your projects. Using the processes, templates, and communication methods we've outlined in this book will help you achieve that success.

Who Should Read This Book

This book was written for those of you who have some understanding of project management but would like to further that understanding and apply some solid principles to your next project. It's for those of you who manage the day-to-day projects that keep your organization running. Excel 2007 is a great tool for managing those types of projects. This doesn't mean you'll have to implement a rigorous discipline that will take as long to set up and administer as it will to complete the project itself. Project management really boils down to a handful of basic principles that can be scaled to meet the complexity of each project. Excel 2007 and

SharePoint can help you set up those processes and this book will show you how. You'll find the templates and checklists included in this book immediately applicable to your next project.

Your knowledge and practice of the principles outlined in this book will help assure employers that you understand how to bring a project to a successful closure. If you're interested in managing projects using a proven approach that's efficient, easy to use, and not excessively burdensome, this book is for you.

What This Book Covers

This book walks you through a project life cycle from beginning to end and shows you step-by-step how to set up templates to manage the process and how to share project information using SharePoint. We've included many useful examples, tips, and hints that will help you solve common project management dilemmas. Here's a high-level overview of what this book entails:

Chapters 1 and 2   These chapters lay the foundation of project management, Excel 2007, and SharePoint Server Fundamentals and delve into definitions, project life cycles, and the skills all good project managers need for success.

Chapters 3 and 4   This section deals with the Initiating and Planning phases of the project. Here you'll find templates for initiating projects and documenting the scope of the project, and we'll discuss how to set project goals and document the requirements. We'll also walk through how to publish these documents to the SharePoint server.

Chapters 5 and 6   These chapters walk you through acquiring resources, building strong teams, managing contracts, and identifying and planning for risks. There are a host of templates for you to use and or modify for projects.

Chapters 7 and 8   These chapters discuss the quality management processes, breaking down the work of the project into manageable components, and creating the project schedule. You'll also determine schedule and budget estimates and create the project budget, all using Excel 2007.

Chapters 9 and 10   A large part of the planning work is done. In these chapters, we'll discuss procedures for managing changes to the project, assessing change impacts, monitoring the performance of the project, taking corrective action, accepting the final project, and documenting lessons learned. We'll also show you how to publish and archive this information on SharePoint.

Appendix   The Appendix covers the more esoteric elements of Excel 2007 such as pivot tables, publishing to MOSS, automating Excel, and Excel functions. While some of these features may have been prevalent in previous versions of Excel, they have been updated for Excel 2007. And, of course, if you've never ventured into these advanced areas, the Appendix walks you through so that you have the ability to utilize these tremendously helpful features in your project management efforts.

Making the Most of This Book

At the beginning of each chapter, you'll find an introduction that highlights all the topics covered in the chapter. In addition, some special elements highlight important information:

    Notes provide extra information and references to related information.

    Tips are insights that help you perform tasks more easily and effectively.

Appendix A discusses many of the built-in functions Excel 2007 contains that are useful in everyday project management.

All the templates you'll encounter throughout the book can be downloaded from www.sybex.com/go/excelpm.

Chapter 1

Establishing Project Management Fundamentals

This chapter will start us off with the fundamentals of project management. We want to make sure that your understanding of project management is in line with ours, because after all, there is more than one way to manage a project. If your experience is like ours, you probably tried several approaches until you found one that worked for you. For some, the process of managing a project, organizing data, and communicating with stakeholders and team members comes naturally. For others, let's just say there were a few knocks along the way and finding a system that works is still somewhat of a struggle. No matter how you manage a project or what your understanding of project management processes is, we're going to set the foundation here and walk you through a process that incorporates sound project management principles with the benefits of Excel 2007 (and other Office 2007 products) to manage your projects and project data more efficiently.

Project Management Institute

Project management brings together a set of tools and techniques that describe, organize, and monitor the activities and work of the project. Project management is performed by people, and you probably have experience doing just that whether you call it project management or not.

As we mentioned, there are several established project management processes you could use to manage a project. We will be using the principles outlined by the Project Management Institute (PMI) in *A Guide to the Project Management Body of Knowledge (PMBOK Guide), Third Edition*. PMI sets the standard in project management today. It is the most widely recognized organization regarding project management and it has successfully promoted project management best practices around the globe. PMI offers two certifications, the Project Management Professional (PMP) and the Certified Associate in Project Management (CAPM). If you're interested in learning more about these certifications, please visit www.pmi.org. If you have not yet obtained the PMP certification, we encourage you to do so. You'll find that this certification is now a requirement for many project management job postings and other positions, particularly in the information technology field, where project management is a significant function and responsibility of the role.

If you're thinking about taking the PMP exam offered through PMI, be sure to get a copy of Kim Heldman's *PMP Project Management Professional Study Guide, Third Edition* (Sybex, 2005). Thousands of people world-wide have used Kim's book to study for and pass the PMP exam.

As you progress through this book, you may find that you've used the processes and procedures outlined but perhaps called them by another name. Others may be new to you. That's okay—follow along and you'll learn some of the terms and processes found in *A Guide to the PMBOK* and how to make the best use of Excel 2007 functions and features to make your project a success.

First we'll look at what a project is and some of the ways they come about.

What Is a Project?

We can't think of a better place to lay our foundation than by defining the term *project*. It may seem odd to have to explain what a project is, but people frequently confuse projects with ongoing operations. Projects have definite beginning and ending dates and produce a unique product or service. Ongoing operations don't typically have start or end dates and usually the same process is used to produce the same result. (We'll look more closely at these definitions in the next section).

The focus of this book is on projects. Projects follow a specific process from start to finish, and that process is repeatable for any project you undertake. For example, all projects start with a request (produced in the Initiating process). Each project requires proper planning and monitoring techniques to ensure that the goals of the project are met and that they satisfy stakeholder expectations. We'll examine these processes as we proceed through the remaining chapters of this book.

Projects versus Ongoing Operations

Asking your spouse to install new shelving and clean and organize the garage may evoke a statement like, "I don't have time for a project like that right now." Cleaning and organizing the garage may be a project. But how do you know for sure? As we said in the previous section, projects have a definite beginning and ending date, they're limited in duration, and at their conclusion a unique product or service is produced. In this case, cleaning out the garage meets the definition of a project. There's a clear start and end date, and when you're finished, a new result is produced because the shelves are installed and scattered items are now neatly organized and categorized.

The purpose of a project is to meet its goal and conclude. The purpose of ongoing operations is to keep the organization functioning.

Now suppose you have company coming for dinner. If you're like us, there's a mad rush 20 minutes before the guests arrive to tidy up and run the vacuum to get all those dark fuzzies off the carpet. Is this a project? No. It doesn't fit the definition. Vacuuming is an ongoing operation. Sure, you start and stop at a specified time (hopefully before the doorbell rings), but there isn't a unique product or service produced at the end. Every time you vacuum, you use the same process and get the same result. And it's seemingly a never-ending chore. Vacuuming must occur every few days or so and it's almost always performed in the same way. That describes an ongoing operation. There is no clear start and end date, the tasks are repetitive in nature, and generally the same result is produced over and over.

Ongoing operations may or may not follow a specific process, and they can take on a million different forms. The process for one operation isn't necessarily the same as it is for another. This doesn't mean that you can't use the templates and spreadsheets presented in this book for tracking ongoing operations or organizing other data or tasks. In fact, you may find several of the forms and spreadsheets in this book useful for other applications, so feel free to modify them and incorporate them into your routine.

Perhaps your boss approaches you with the following scenario: She'd like to consolidate the four disparate networks in your organization into one network and clearly define the roles and responsibilities for each of the team members under the new scenario. Is it a project? Yes. It has a definite start and end date and it produces a unique product or service at its conclusion. However, when this project is over and the networks are successfully consolidated, the process of monitoring and fine-tuning the network becomes an ongoing operation. This scenario tends to occur quite often in the information technology field. A project is completed and then assimilated into the ongoing, everyday work of the organization. For example, a new software program is written to monitor customers' buying patterns. When the software is tested and implemented, another team of specialists takes over the day-to-day tasks of monitoring the software and helping users work through problems.

In other industries, projects may come to a conclusion without being assimilated into ongoing operations. The construction and manufacturing industries are some examples that come to mind. Once you've constructed a building or produced a new product, it's turned over to the consumer. Table 1.1 recaps the characteristics of projects and ongoing operations.

TABLE 1.1   Projects versus Ongoing Operations

Projects	Ongoing Operations
Definite beginning and ending.	No definitive beginning and ending.
Temporary.	Ongoing.
Produces a unique product or service.	Produces the same product or service over and over.
Resources are dedicated to the project.	Resources are dedicated to operations.
Ending is determined by specific criteria.	Processes are repeated over and over.

How Projects Come About

The authors have over 40 years combined experience working on or managing projects. It never ceases to amaze us how new projects come about. We've seen them announced at team meetings, mentioned in the hallway, scribbled down on a lunch napkin, and turned over to us in the restroom. The topper is the one that came about when one of our coworker's bosses told a newspaper reporter about a project his organization was undertaking. The trouble was our coworker hadn't heard a word about the project until he read the article in the Sunday paper. You probably have a few stories of your own like these.

On a serious note, there are several reasons a project comes about. Understanding the reason will help you clarify the goals and scope of the project. For example, if you know the project came about due to a new law or mandatory regulation, you'll know there are specific requirements that must be met and certain aspects of the project that cannot be compromised. The new law may have strict specifications and those specifications must be incorporated as part of the requirements for your project.

Organizations are always examining ways of creating business, staying competitive, gaining efficiencies, and serving their customers in new and creative ways. Projects may result from all of these needs. Business requirements, opportunities, or problems may also bring about a new project. According to *A Guide to the PMBOK,* most projects come about as a result of one of the following six needs or demands. We'll briefly examine each next.

Market demands   Market demands often drive new project requests. Changes in the economy, changes in consumer habits, and changes in supply and demand are all examples of market demands that can bring about a new project. For example, spikes in utility prices or interruptions in oil supplies and reserves may bring about projects to create alternative energy sources.

Business needs   Business needs such as improving efficiency, reducing costs, and increasing inventory churn are often reasons for project creation. An example business need might involve implementing an enterprise resource planning system that improves the customer ordering and fulfillment process while providing the organization with up-to-the-minute revenue information.

Customer requests   Customer requests are an endless source of project creation. We usually think of customers as external to the organization. Keep in mind that there are also internal customers. Typically the information technology, human resources, and accounting divisions have internal customers within the organization that they serve. Customer requests, both internal and external, may drive many projects. For example, the folks in the human resources department might decide to implement an automated system for tracking all human resource transactions. They want to track job applications, promotions, terminations, and so on online rather than in file drawers.

Legal requirements   Legal requirements primarily come about as a result of government action. For example, the Food and Drug Administration requires an extensive testing process for new medical devices before they can be introduced to the marketplace and used on us mere humans. Those processes may drive a project or drive the need for additional requirements for an existing project. The legal requirements category may also include industry regulations imposed to ensure safety, accountability, environmental protection, and so on.

Technological advances   This one happens to be the authors' favorite category. Without technological advances, we wouldn't have the iPod, cell phones, personal digital assistants, digital cameras, or myriad other devices we could not live without. Today it seems that technological advances come about almost overnight. It especially seems that way after you've just purchased what you thought was the latest and greatest only to find the next latest and greatest introduced the week after you purchased your model.

Social needs   Projects driven by social needs may include things like preventing infectious disease, purifying drinking water, and creating educational programs for underprivileged children. Social needs may come about due to customers or concerned citizens.

Each category represents opportunities, business requirements, or problems that need solved. Management generally decides how to respond to needs and demands, and those decisions will likely bring about a new project.

Overview of the Project Process Groups

Most project management methodologies have a series of processes through which projects progress. Most methodologies start with an initiating process and continue through to closing. Since we're basing our methodologies on *A Guide to the PMBOK* standards, we'll look at the five project management process groups they promote:

- Initiating
- Planning

- Executing
- Monitoring and Controlling
- Closing

A number of individual processes collectively make up each group. For example, the Initiating process group includes two individual processes, Develop Project Charter and Develop Preliminary Project Scope Statement.

These groups, along with their individual processes, make up the project management process. A project starts off in the Initiating group and proceeds through each of the groups until it is either completed successfully and closed out or cancelled.

 Often during the course of a project, you'll find that you need to revisit a process group (most likely the Planning group) to update or add information that changes assumptions made previously. Project management is an iterative process in that you discover information as you get further along in a project. This may require changes and tweaking to previous work to keep documents, plans, and the work of the project on track with the goals.

Next let's take a look at a high-level definition of each of the process groups.

Initiating   The Initiating process is where the project comes to life. Initiating officially acknowledges that a project should begin. It also indicates that resources (both human and financial) should be encumbered for the project. The project manager is usually named here and is authorized to begin work on the project. The first project documentation gets created in this group in the form of the project charter. This document describes the goals of the project, the business reason or justification for the project, a high-level description of the project's product or service, and more. The following are some of the accomplishments for this process group:

- Determining the major goals of the project
- Assigning the project manager
- Documenting and publishing the project charter

Planning   The Planning process group is where a great deal of the project management work of the project occurs. Here you'll further define the goals of the project, discover and document deliverables and requirements, formulate communication plans, highlight risks that may occur on the project, determine quality metrics, and more. The Planning processes are critical to the functions of the remaining process groups. In project management terms, Planning is more than likely the most important process group of all. The accomplishments for this process group include the following:

- Documenting and publishing the project scope statement
- Establishing a project budget

- Defining project activities
- Developing a project schedule
- Determining resource needs, skills, and talents

Executing The Executing process is where the work of the project happens. The project manager coordinates and directs project resources and oversees the completion of the project plan. This process also ensures that future project work stays in alignment with the project goals. Approved changes to the project plan are typically implemented here. Sometimes the changes require a trip back through the Planning processes to adjust plans or schedules to keep the project on track. The following list includes some of the accomplishments for this process group:

- Forming and motivating the project team
- Directing and leading the project team
- Obtaining other project resources
- Communicating project information
- Conducting project status meetings

Monitoring and Controlling Monitoring and Controlling, as the name implies, is where the work of the project is measured, verified, and accepted or where action is taken to correct work that is not in line with the project plan. Performance measurements are taken and evaluated during these processes to determine if variances exist between the work results and the project plan. If variances are discovered, corrective action is taken to once again get the work of the project in line with the plan. This might mean another pass through the Planning process group to adjust project activities, resources, schedules, budgets, and so on. Here are some of the accomplishments for this process group:

- Measuring project performance against the plan
- Taking corrective actions when needed to bring performance measures within limits
- Evaluating the effectiveness of corrective action measures
- Ensuring that the project progresses according to the plan
- Reviewing and implementing change requests

In practice, the Executing and Monitoring and Controlling processes are often combined and performed together—or very close together. As work results are produced (Executing), they're verified and accepted or adjustments are made to correct the work and produce results in line with the plan (Monitoring and Controlling). If you find it easier to combine these processes (as these authors do), stay alert to changes and make certain not to skip the important steps within either process group.

Closing   The Closing process group brings a formal, orderly end to the project. In this group, final acceptance of the project occurs, project documents are gathered and archived, contracts are closed out, lessons learned are documented, and more. Closing is the most often skipped process. Once the work of the project is complete, project teams have a tendency to jump right into the next project. Taking the time to collect and archive documents will really pay off when you undertake a new project that's similar in size and scope to the project you've completed. You can review the documents, reuse templates, and save time by reviewing risks, plans, and so on to speed up the Planning processes in particular. Here are some of the accomplishments for this process group:

- Obtaining acceptance of the deliverables
- Documenting lessons learned
- Archiving project records
- Formalizing project closure
- Releasing project resources

 If you're working on a large project or a project that contains multiple sub-projects, the Closing process group will become an input to the Initiating process group. For example, imagine you're working on a construction project that is extending a university campus and adding several new buildings. New buildings, roads, and other infrastructure components make up the overall project. At the completion of each phase of the project (building A, building, B, building C, and so on), the closing process becomes an input into the next phase. Therefore, Initiating can signal not only the beginning of a project but also the beginning of the next phase of a project.

As we stated earlier, these processes are iterative. Planning, Executing, and Monitoring and Controlling are the most often repeated processes. Also, the outputs of one process group (Initiating, for example) become the inputs to another process group (Planning, for example). It's important to be as detailed and accurate as you can as you progress through the processes because you'll be building on the documentation and work you've done previously. Figure 1.1 shows the inputs and outputs and the iterative nature of these processes.

We'll cover each of the process groups as we progress through the remaining chapters of this book, with the most emphasis on the Planning processes. Planning is probably the most important process group of all and is likely the place where Excel 2007 and the other Office products will get the heaviest use. You'll continue to use Excel throughout the remainder of the project, but the largest effort will be spent up front establishing templates, forms, and processes that you'll fill in and update as the work of the project progresses. Next we'll take a look at the key skills every good project manager should possess.

FIGURE 1.1   Project management process groups

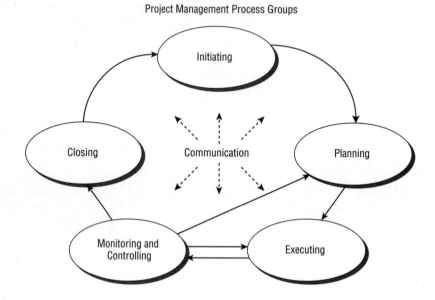

Project Management Process Groups

Key Project Management Skills

When this author (Kim) started her career in project management, the field wasn't even called project management. We were known by a host of names: analysts, implementation specialists, engineers, integrators, hey you, and so on. Several times before the term *project manager* became commonplace, my coworkers and managers would describe us as "those organized people with a mix of technical, business, and people skills—you know, the 'do everything' kind." In reality, this description wasn't, and still isn't, far from the truth. Project managers must have a wide variety of skills and they must have high competency levels in those skill sets. Four cornerstones frame the skill set of every good project manager:

- Leading
- Communicating
- Team building and motivating
- Negotiating and problem solving

From these skills, the project management house is constructed. Project management skills form the next floor. General management skills, technical skills, organizational skills, business skills, industry-specific skills, and so on all build upon this foundation. We will look at each of the foundational skills later in this section with the exception of team building. We'll cover that topic in Chapter 5, "Planning and Acquiring Resources."

The four cornerstone skills, known as "soft" skills, are the most important set of skills you have as a project manager. And of the four, leadership is the foundation stone you'll lay first. If you aren't good at leading, your project and your project team will likely suffer for it. Technical skills are important, but without a mastery of the soft skills, the technical skills aren't a lot of help. Think of it as having a set of stairs in a 20-story building. The trip to the top floor is possible, but it's a lot of hard work and you'll likely lose team members along the way. An elevator would make the journey a lot more pleasant.

> Whether you believe soft skills are intertwined with our personalities and styles or you believe they can be learned, it's safe to say none of us knows everything and there's always opportunity to learn new information and add a few new tips and tricks to your tool bag.

Mastering the four foundation skills is even more important today than it was in the past because the field of project management has grown up within the organization. We'll look at how that's happened next.

Project Management Maturity

As the project management profession has grown and matured, so has its place in the typical organization. For example, in the early days of our careers, we wielded notebooks full of spreadsheets, checklists, and documentation for each project we were assigned. The positions we held were buried several layers deep in the organization—usually somewhere in the customer service or information technology departments.

Today, many organizations take a much more holistic approach to project management. Sure, we still have the spreadsheets and checklists, but project management has moved from the tactical, buried eight levels deep in an obscure department to the strategic. Project management offices (PMOs) have cropped up everywhere. The PMO is responsible for the management of all the major projects within an organization (also known as portfolio or program management), and its director often holds a high-level management position. We're even beginning to see "C" level job postings—Chief Project Management Officer—to head up those PMOs.

Project management is no longer a matter of how to take a project from step 1 to step 10—although the tactical aspects will never go away. Project management has now taken a seat at the executive table. Today project management is strategic as well as tactical. Where once an organization may have decided to implement a technology product to improve workforce efficiency, for example, that same project is now examined from the perspective of the overall value it adds to the organization. It's weighed against the strategic direction of the organization and other projects of similar importance. Return on investment is investigated, as is the value to the customer or end user. Global business implications are determined. And the list goes on. The factors today are considered from an organizational perspective rather than a departmental perspective.

Project management has matured from the tactical to the strategic. It still requires tactical skills to manage the day-to-day activities of project work, but increasingly, projects are viewed from the perspective of the organization as a whole and the value they add to the organization or its customers.

Because of this maturity from the tactical to the strategic, it's more imperative than ever that project managers have a well-rounded set of skills. As we said, a project manager's skills are first and foremost built upon leadership abilities. Without solid leadership skills, it's difficult to impart vision, gain support for that vision, and inspire project teams to perform at their best. We'll look at leadership skills in the next section.

Leadership Skills

What's your definition of a leader? Is a leader a leader because they hold a position of authority? Do you know leaders who don't hold a managerial title? Our guess is your answer to this last question is yes. Leaders don't necessarily have a position of authority in the organization. Nonetheless they are leaders in their own right. These are the go-to folks in the organization. They're the ones likely to inspire project team members to say, "I wonder what [fill in the blank] thinks of that idea," and to follow their opinion on the topic.

Leadership is more than getting people to do what you want them to do. Dictators don't have any trouble performing this feat, but their followers aren't usually happy about it. Successful project managers know that certain key aspects of leadership are important.

- Imparting a vision of the project's value to the organization
- Imparting a vision of the product or service of the project (the project's end result)
- Gaining consensus on the goals and deliverables of the project and other issues that arise as the project progresses
- Establishing direction and a clear plan for meeting the goals of the project
- Managing the expectations of stakeholders, management, and team members
- Inspiring others to perform at their best
- Backing the team and their actions when it's appropriate
- Removing obstacles from the project team's path
- Managing conflict
- Building trustworthy relationships

Most of these factors probably seem obvious. At a minimum, they make sense. However, don't fall into the trap of thinking that you've accomplished these things, as we've seen many project managers do. They lull themselves into believing "everyone" knows the plan or that everyone knows you're there to help with issues and conflicts as they arise. Make it a habit to ask. Ask your team members. Ask your stakeholders. Ask questions such as these: Do you know the goal of this project? Are there any problems I should be aware of? Don't assume anything. Institute an open-door policy and stand behind it (the policy, that is). You'll be surprised what people will tell you when they see your leadership qualities and you have gained your trust and respect.

Project management processes are important, but people are even more important. Members of high-performing teams have a high level of respect and trust for their leader and for each other. Strong leadership skills along with clear communication will go a long way toward building that trust.

Leadership involves many aspects and it's beyond the scope of this book to go into everything leadership entails. Mastering the skills listed previously and remembering to actively engage your team members and stakeholders will help your project progress along the successful path.

Communicating Successfully

A very close second to leadership skills is communication skills. Actually, we don't know how you can be a leader without being a good communicator. It's possible to communicate without being a leader—we've all got our war stories about bosses like that—but being a leader without being an effective communicator isn't really possible. So let's examine some of the key skills needed for effective communication in the project management arena.

Senders

Communication at its basic level is an exchange of information. Notice the word *exchange* in that definition. Communication requires a sender, a transmission of the message, and a receiver. Yes, the project manager can speak and no one may listen, but according to our definition, that isn't communication. We won't go into the mechanics of the communication model, but keep in mind that information that is distributed but isn't read or acknowledged by the receiver hasn't accomplished anything. If, for example, you know before opening an email that you're likely to get sucked into a 20-minute reading marathon to try to find the point, you may not read it. At best, you'll skim through it and may miss the point. So how can project managers avoid some common communication blunders? We're glad you asked. Here are a few tips on making your communication as effective as possible when you are the sender:

- Write clear and concise documents and stay on topic.

- Create communication that's appropriate for the audience. Executives like bullet points—use them.

- Rehearse important topics or meetings beforehand. Ask someone to critique your rehearsal if needed.

- Make certain you define terms that are not familiar to the receiver.

- Leave negative emotions at your desk but take passion with you.

- Communicate the right information and the right amount of information to avoid receivers tuning you out.

Receivers

On the receiving end of communication is listening. We're certified marriage counselors in our spare time (no, we never sleep). Based on several years of helping couples with their martial woes, we can safely say that a large percentage of issues are communication issues. And of those, listening tends to be the problem. When you ask one of the spouses to repeat what they just heard the other say, what's repeated is often different than what was stated. That's because the listener puts their own perspective and interpretation on what was stated without having *really* listened to what was said. Sure enough, we've experienced this same phenomenon in the workplace. One team member "hears" what a stakeholder or another team member has to say. When you get them both in the same room and have each of them restate the issue, you usually discover there was some misinterpretation or misunderstanding on one or both of their parts. Guard against adding your own seasoning to what you hear and practice active listening with the following techniques:

- Ask clarifying questions.

- Paraphrase what you heard in your own words and ask the speaker if you've understood the issue correctly.

- Show genuine interest by nodding in agreement or asking questions about the topic.

- Maintain eye contact.

- Do not interrupt; wait for the speaker to finish.

Making Connections

If you've recently attended a child's birthday party, you may have played the gossip game. All the kids stand in a circle and someone whispers a secret into the ear of the first child. They repeat the secret to the child next to them and so on until it goes around the circle. The last child tells everyone the secret. As you know, it's usually nothing at all like the original version. This illustrates not only the importance of active listening, but also the importance of limiting the number of participants in the circle, or meeting as may be the case. The more people in the communication chain, the more likely misinterpretations will occur.

Figure 1.2 illustrates the lines of communications among 8 participants.

If you counted all the lines in the figure, you'd come up with 28 lines of communication among the 8 participants. That amounts to 28 places for misunderstanding and misinterpretation. If you prefer to do this mathematically, you can calculate the lines of communication as follows:

$n(n-1)/2$ = total lines of communication

FIGURE 1.2 Lines of communication

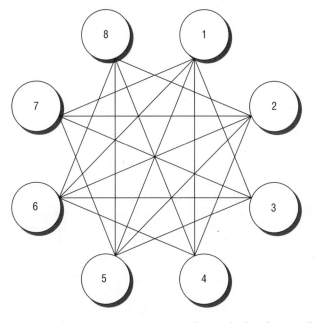

As you can see, the more participants you have, the harder you'll have to work to make certain everyone hears and understands the message. This doesn't mean the project meetings become an exclusive club with only a handful of members. It's most important to consider the number of people in meetings where decisions need to be made. Once you go over 10 or 11 participants, the lines of communication become unwieldy. Again, it doesn't mean you can't be successful, but decision-making meetings are much more effective with fewer participants. In fact, some of the research going on regarding successful projects shows that small teams are much more successful than large teams, so whenever you can, limit the participants to those who are critical to the task at hand.

 The Project Management Institute states that project managers spend 90 percent of their time communicating. Based on our experience, that's a correct statement. If you aren't spending the majority of your day talking (or otherwise communicating) with team members, stakeholders, and others about the project, get started now. Hang out at the water cooler if you have to. Practice both good sending and receiving skills.

Communications, like leadership, is a topic that could fill several books all on its own. It's beyond the scope of this book for us to go into all the details, but we're hoping you'll put the pointers we've given you to good use on your next project. Next we'll stir up a little conflict and reveal some helpful negotiating and problem-solving techniques.

Negotiating and Problem-Solving Skills

Negotiating and problem-solving skills make up another foundation stone of successful project management. Along with leadership and communication, you will use negotiating and problem-solving skills almost daily. We'll look at the typical project management situations where negotiation skills are needed next and follow up with an overview of five conflict resolution techniques.

Negotiating Skills

Usually when we think of negotiation, we think of contracts or complex disputes that need resolved. While that's true, negotiation occurs on a much smaller scale as well. You will often have to negotiate for team members with other managers in the organization, you'll negotiate for additional time or money, you'll negotiate costs and delivery times with vendors, and there's usually a never-ending stream of project issues that require negotiation to resolve. These issues can range from the very minor up to and including a decision to kill the project.

As a project manager, you may find yourself in a situation where you do not necessarily have ultimate authority over the project decisions. For example, you may have several divisions within your organization that have pooled their resources, both budget and people, to execute a project. That means the stakeholders from each of the participating divisions have an equal say in decisions or where and how money will be spent. Like the Survivors who use extreme measures to fight their way into the last-person-standing position, this calls for extreme negotiating skills. Only in this example, you don't want to be the last person standing; you want all the others to come along with you. This means you'll have to go beyond simple compromise. You'll need to establish effective relationships with the stakeholders and understand their needs and issues. You'll have to do a little personality sleuthing and determine how best to communicate and work with each individual. And you'll have to have genuine concern for their stake in the project and the competing needs they face within their own divisions. As the project manager, it's your job to bring these issues to light and help the entire group understand them. You should also present and discuss alternative solutions and bring the group to consensus on a resolution.

Conflict Resolution

But what happens when you can't reach consensus on a resolution and end up with a conflict on your hands? Conflict is when the desires, needs, or goals of one person or group are not in agreement with another. You could throw in the towel and go home, but that's not recommended. In all seriousness, withdrawal is a conflict resolution technique—just not a very effective one. There are five conflict resolution techniques that use different approaches to solving the issue at hand: forcing, smoothing, compromise, problem solving, and withdrawal. Of them, problem solving is the best approach and should be used whenever possible. However, there are times when this technique may not work or may not be appropriate. It's also handy to understand these techniques because you'll be able to easily spot which one other participants are using and try to steer them into the problem-solving technique. Let's look briefly at each of them next.

Forcing   Forcing is just as it sounds. One person forces a solution on the other parties. This typically occurs when one of the stakeholders has more authority than the others or more power to exert their influence. While this is a permanent solution, it isn't necessarily the best one. People will go along with it because, well, they're forced to go along with it, but it doesn't mean they agree with the solution.

Smoothing   Smoothing is where one of the parties attempts to make the conflict appear less important than it is. Everyone looks at each other and scratches their head and wonders why they thought the conflict was such a big deal anyway. As a result, a compromise is reached and everyone feels good about the solution until they get back to their desk and start thinking about the issue again. When they realize that the conflict was smoothed over and really is more important than they were led to believe, they'll be back at it and the conflict will resurface.

Compromise   Compromise is achieved when each of the parties involved in the conflict gives up something to reach a solution. Everyone involved decides what they will give on and what they won't give on, and eventually through all the give and take, a solution is reached. Neither side wins or loses in this situation, and it could result in apathy from all the participants. If compromise must be used, make certain firm commitments to the resolution are made by all parties to help assure that the solution is permanent.

Confrontation   This technique is also called problem solving and is the best way to resolve conflict. A fact-finding mission results in this scenario. The thinking here is that one right solution to a problem exists and the facts will bear out the solution. Once the facts are uncovered, they're presented to the parties and the decision will be clear. Thus the solution becomes a permanent one and the conflict expires. This is the conflict resolution approach project mangers use most often and is an example of a win-win conflict resolution technique.

Withdrawal   Withdrawal occurs when one of the parties gets up and leaves and refuses to discuss the conflict. This never results in resolution. It's probably the worst of all the techniques because nothing gets resolved. Withdrawal is a lose-lose technique.

General Management Skills

General management skills, as mentioned earlier, involve accounting, marketing, procurement, human resources, international business, and so on. From a project management perspective, they involve what *A Guide to the PMBOK* calls the nine knowledge areas. These are specific areas of knowledge that bring together information and processes by commonalities. For example, the Cost Management knowledge area involves budgeting, estimating, and cost control. The nine knowledge areas are as follows:

Project Integration Management   This knowledge area involves identifying and defining the work of the project and combining, unifying, and integrating the appropriate processes to complete that work. The information developed and documented in this knowledge area includes the project charter, the project scope statement, and change control processes.

Project Scope Management   Project Scope Management is concerned with defining the work of the project and is highly interactive. It also concerns defining both project scope and product scope. Project scope involves managing the work of the project, whereas product scope concerns defining the characteristics of the product. Some of the activities in this knowledge area are creating the scope statement, creating the work breakdown structure, and controlling project scope throughout the project.

Project Time Management   This knowledge area is concerned with estimating the duration of the project plan activities, devising a project schedule, and monitoring and controlling deviations from the schedule. Collectively, this knowledge area deals with completing the project in a timely manner. Time management concerns keeping the project activities on track and monitoring those activities against the project plan to ensure that the project is completed on time. Some of the accomplishments achieved in this knowledge area are defining activities, estimating activity durations, creating the project schedule, and controlling the project schedule.

Project Cost Management   The activities in the Project Cost Management knowledge area establish cost estimates for resources and keep watch over those costs to ensure that the project stays within the approved budget. This knowledge area is primarily concerned with the costs of human resources, but other costs should be considered as well. The activities in this knowledge area include estimating costs, developing the project budget, and controlling costs.

Project Quality Management   The Project Quality Management knowledge area assures that the project meets the requirements it was undertaken to produce. Some of the activities in this knowledge area are creating the quality management plan, measuring performance, monitoring project results, and comparing them to the quality standards to ensure that the customer will receive the product or service they thought they purchased.

Project Human Resource Management   Project Human Resource Management involves all aspects of people management, including leading, coaching, dealing with conflict, performance appraisals, and more. This knowledge area ensures that the human resources assigned to the project are used in the most effective way possible. Some of the activities you'll perform in this knowledge area are acquiring project teams, team building, and managing and motivating teams.

Project Communications Management   Project Communications Management makes certain that all project information, including project plans, risk assessments, meeting notes, and more, is collected, documented, archived, and disposed of at the proper time. This knowledge area also ensures that information is distributed and shared with stakeholders, management, and project members at appropriate times. When the project is closed, the information is archived and used as a reference for future projects. This is referred to as historical information in several project processes. The information you'll gather, document, and report in this knowledge area includes communication plans, performance measurements, status reports, and more.

Project Risk Management   Risks include both threats and opportunities to the project. This knowledge area is concerned with identifying, analyzing, and planning for potential risks, both positive and negative, that may impact the project. This means minimizing the probability and impact of negative risks while maximizing the probability and impact of positive risks. Some of the documents you'll create in this knowledge area are a risk management plan, a risk identification list, a risk register, risk responses, and more.

Project Procurement Management   This knowledge area is concerned with purchasing goods or services from vendors, contractors, suppliers, and others outside the project team. The activities and documents you'll perform in this knowledge area include planning for purchases, preparing bids and requests, selecting vendors, and writing contracts.

There is a lot of information covered in each of these knowledge areas and we'll discuss each throughout the remainder of this book. For example, the Project Integration Knowledge area covers the project charter and project scope statement. We'll talk about the project charter later in this chapter and jump into the scope statement in Chapter 4, "Determining Project Requirements."

Organizing Time and Information

Another skill that project managers should have in their tool bag is solid time management and organization skills. Each of us has eight hours or so every workday to accomplish our tasks. It seems some people accomplish twice the amount of work in that period of time than others. Time management is a process that you use to control the priorities in your day so that you can work on the most important items. Organizational skills are particularly useful in project management terms when it comes to organizing project documentation, organizing meetings, and organizing teams.

Microsoft Outlook is an effective time management tool. It contains a calendar, a task list, and a contact list all in one place. Most of you are probably familiar with its capabilities or have used a product similar to it. You can set recurring project meetings, for example, create tasks and give them specific due dates, and so on. One of the new features of Outlook 2007 allows you and each of your team members to publish your calendars to the Office Server, making it available to others. This is helpful when setting up meetings or when checking on someone's availability. We'll talk more about scheduling team members' activities and setting up resource calendars in Chapter 8, "Constructing the Project Schedule and Budget."

Task lists are another feature of Outlook. You can set up customized views to see the status of tasks by owners and due date and percent complete and so on. However, we find tasks lists easier to create and manage in Excel. For example, in your role as a project manager, you will have multiple team members and tasks to track. These tasks will roll up into project deliverables. Again, we'll look more closely at task lists in Chapter 8.

Tips for Managing Time

Remember that project managers spend up to 90 percent of their time communicating. This means talking to people and writing project documentation and status updates and so on. If you don't schedule time to perform these functions, they may not happen. And talking to your team members should rank high on your priority list. Keep these tips in mind when managing your time:

- Schedule time on your calendar every day to talk to team members so your calendar shows that time as "busy."

- Schedule time to update project documentation. Again, block out 30 minutes or whatever time it will take so that no one else schedules you for a meeting during that time.

- Don't forget to add travel time before and after offsite appointments.

- Set project status meetings, change control meetings, stakeholder updates, and so on as recurring appointments.

- Review your calendar and task list first thing every morning and again before you leave the office. At the end of the day, determine what tasks need carried over to the next day and review upcoming appointments. You'll wish you had remembered this one the first time you show up to work and realize you have an important stakeholder meeting on the schedule but you wore your grubby clothes that day.

- Handle every piece of information you see (email, regular mail, voicemail, memos, and so on) preferably only once but as few times as possible. Read it, answer it, file it, or delete it as soon as you're finished.

If you find yourself always feeling rushed or find that your day manages you rather than you managing your day, you should invest in a time management course that can offer more information than we have the space for here.

Tips for Managing Information

Managing time and managing information have a lot in common. In fact, if you're effective at managing information, you'll save time. How many times have you found yourself wondering where you put an email or stashed a file on your hard drive? Thank goodness for search engines—but there is a better way. Developing an effective filing system and sticking with it will cut down on the number of times you'll need to call upon a search engine. Keep in mind there's no right way to do this. We'll offer you a few suggestions, but you should use what works best for you. Feel free to modify these ideas to fit your style.

Often project managers manage more than one project at a time. Therefore, it makes sense to create folders for each project. For example, suppose you have a project titled Web Redesign and one titled Retail Feasibility Study. Create an electronic folder for each project. Then within each folder, you might consider subfolders with names that describe the types of information they hold, such as, for example, project status reports, budget, vendor list, project schedule, stakeholder communication, and so on. If your project will extend over several months, consider creating another set of subfolders within each of these that are date based. For example, the project status folder would have subfolders called Jan 2008, Feb 2008, and so on.

As you will discover later, using portal software such as Windows SharePoint Services (WSS) or SharePoint Portal Server (SPS) allows you to enhance the abilities you have to store documents. For example, using SPS (now called Microsoft Office SharePoint Server – MOSS), you can add metadata ("data about the data") to a spreadsheet file as well as create different views of the data for various users.

It's also helpful to follow a consistent naming convention for your files so that if you do have to search for them, you at least know what they're called. Staying with the project status reports example, you may consider naming the files with the date followed by the name. For example if you have weekly status reports, name them something like 01-11-08 Status Report. Or if you have monthly status reports, Jan-08 Status Report will work.

If you require individual team members to provide you with status reports (this is a good idea), you could name them similarly and file them in a subfolder under Project Status called Team Status Reports. In this case, use the date and the team member's name.

You might want to consider creating an Excel spreadsheet to track where and when information was filed, especially if you are managing a very large project that will likely collect mounds of documentation or you're managing multiple projects. This is especially helpful if you have a collection of documents, some electronic and some hard copy, that are filed in two different places. Figure 1.3 shows a sample portion of a project file tracking spreadsheet.

We often hear the term *information overload* today. You can manage project information overload by following some of the tips we outlined in these last two sections. Keeping yourself and your team organized will save you time. Writing things down helps prevent loss and also protects the project from delays when a key team member leaves with all the information "in their head."

FIGURE 1.3   Sample file tracking log

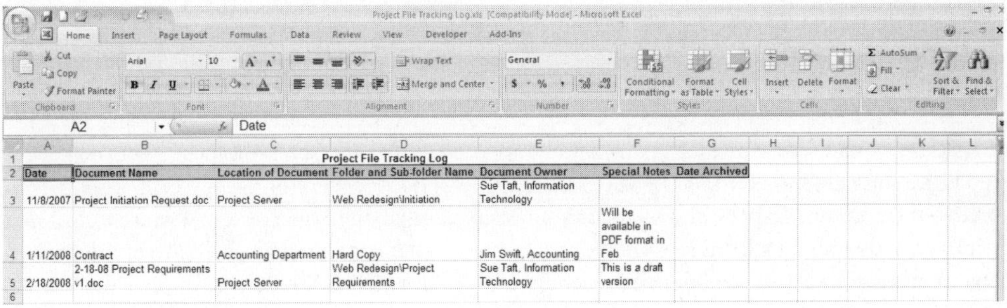

	Date	Document Name	Location of Document	Folder and Sub-folder Name	Document Owner	Special Notes	Date Archived
1			Project File Tracking Log				
2	Date	Document Name	Location of Document	Folder and Sub-folder Name	Document Owner	Special Notes	Date Archived
3	11/8/2007	Project Initiation Request.doc	Project Server	Web Redesign\Initiation	Sue Taft, Information Technology		
4	1/11/2008	Contract	Accounting Department	Hard Copy	Jim Swift, Accounting	Will be available in PDF format in Feb	
5	2/18/2008	2-18-08 Project Requirements v1.doc	Project Server	Web Redesign\Project Requirements	Sue Taft, Information Technology	This is a draft version	
6							

Professional Responsibility

Certified project managers are required to adhere to a code of professional conduct. Certified or not, it's still a great idea. As in most professions, honesty and integrity should be your number one priority. Honesty builds credibility with your team members and stakeholders. When you hit those bumps in the project road, stakeholders may not like the news you have to deliver but they'll know you're telling the truth if you've practiced honesty and integrity all along.

Project managers are often in positions in which they have a lot of interaction and contact with vendors, stakeholders, and outside boards or commissions. These people may have influence over your career or have the ability to reward you in other ways. Your personal gain, whether a promotion or a golf trip to Arizona, should never be taken into account when making project decisions. Don't allow vendors or stakeholders to pressure you into making decisions that sound right for you personally but might be a disaster for the project.

You'll also want to avoid conflict-of-interest situations. A conflict of interest is where it appears that your own interests are benefiting as a result of project decisions. For example, suppose you are part owner with your brother-in-law in a real estate firm. One of the requirements of your project is to locate and lease a building. You should not choose this real estate company as the firm to find the building needed for the project because there's not only a conflict of interest but a potential for personal gain as well.

    When in doubt, avoid even the appearance of impropriety.

Project managers should strive to maintain a level of professionalism that depicts honesty and integrity. Continuing education in your industry and project management techniques should also always be high on your personal to-do list. Respect your company's data and property, lead by example, and always report truthfully and honestly.

Chapter 2 includes an overview of Excel and other Office 2007 products. We'll incorporate their features into the following chapters and walk you through constructing processes and templates using these products.

Chapter 2

Establishing Excel and Office 2007 SharePoint Server Fundamentals

In this chapter, we'll examine some of the features and benefits of Microsoft Excel 2007 and Microsoft Office SharePoint Server (MOSS) 2007 in managing the mounds of project documentation we create, collect, and distribute during the course of a project. We'll give you some setup tips and walk you through how to create a document repository at the end of this chapter.

Like Chapter 1, this chapter is meant to establish the foundation for using Excel 2007 and other Office 2007 products in the coming chapters. The remainder of this book will blend the fundamentals we've established here and in Chapter 1 as we get hands on into creating and publishing a project and tracking its progress.

Using Excel and SharePoint to Manage Projects

Generally speaking, very few projects are successfully started and concluded with the efforts of only one person. If you think about it, even something as simple as building a doghouse might require at least two people at certain points in the project. No doubt about it, regardless of the project, people are the primary ingredient for success.

Technology has helped us to create the documentation, drawings, and plans we need to build better projects. Amy can sit at her word processor generating beautifully crafted planning documents. John can develop the project's schedule on his computer and then print it out and bring it to meetings to share with others. Office automation software has helped us become better project managers, keeping tighter track of our projects.

But one ingredient is missing: the link between people and technology. We have a very difficult time sharing documents. Oh sure, as authors, one of us can work on a chapter for the book and then send it to the other for review, revision, and addition. We turn Track Changes on in order to monitor each other's changes. We add something, send it back for review, and then send it onward to our editors for even more wordsmithery.

Can you see the problem with this scenario? We have to constantly send the document elsewhere for someone to revise. The document goes to the person instead of the person coming to the document. This sets up a less than ideal situation in which the following occurs:

- Time is wasted.
- Errors are introduced.
- Current status is in question.
- Changes are made and we don't know who made them.
- Restricting input and access to the document is difficult.
- There may be more than one "live" document—how do we know which changes are current, best, and authorized?

What we need is a way to centralize the management of the documents. This centralization serves as a collaboration point where all parties have access to the project documents and the ability to review, update, or modify depending on the roles and responsibilities they've been assigned.

It is with this goal in mind that Microsoft (long ago) began working on the concept of team-oriented collaboration software that we call a *portal*. SharePoint Products and Technologies (www.microsoft.com/sharepoint) is the result of this ongoing effort. SharePoint Portal Server (SPS) is a portal server product in its second version that helps organizations centralize, organize, and keep track of a variety of documentation sources and allows for nontechnical "authors" to place content on the portal. SharePoint technologies bring about the core collaboration elements within SPS, integrating them into Microsoft Office.

SharePoint was Microsoft's first iteration of document collaboration technology. SharePoint now has a new name—Office SharePoint Server 2007 (MOSS). And, in the Office 2007 products, you may see the menus reference it as Office Server. From here on we'll call it MOSS.

MOSS is built on SharePoint technologies but offers more efficient ways of sharing data than its predecessor and is now fully integrated with all Office products.

Finally, we should note that SPS in particular provides the ability to create different lists and document libraries. So you can have a list that points to very specific data and can be viewed by a limited group of people. And you can create product-specific document libraries (Excel, for example) that will contain documents available for review by—you guessed it—a limited group of people. The latest and greatest version of SharePoint Portal Server is going to be rebranded as Microsoft Office SharePoint Server (MOSS). The name is a reflection of the

What Is a Portal?

Perhaps you've heard the word *portal* before and don't really understand its context. Basically, portal software allows you to create a website that has added intelligence. For starters, there is usually some sort of authentication mechanism associated with a portal—login name and password. The portal needs to know who you are in order for you to use it. You might have experienced such a portal with MySpace, My Yahoo!, My AOL, and other Internet-based portal implementations.

Also, portals allow programmers and administrators to add small pieces of code, typically called portlets (but in SharePoint's case, Web Parts) that perform some service. For example, on My Yahoo!, you might subscribe to a stock ticker service and get your favorite daily cartoons and your local weather forecast. All of these are portlets, and others are available for you to add to the portal.

Additionally, portals support the notion of "subscribing" to document content. For example, suppose you are an avid reader of the science section of your favorite Internet portal and you want to know when there is content posted pertaining to global warming. You simply subscribe to that section of the portal, giving it key words to look for, and the magic begins.

Some portals also provide collaborative, interactive capabilities. You can jump on an online conference with others, sharing documents, and in some cases, even videoconference with one another.

These are the basic elements of portals: authentication, portlets, subscriptions, and collaboration. There is one other important element that some portals bring to the table: document authorization chaining—something we call *workflow*. The idea is that you have an important document that needs to be signed off by several different people. You create your document, you set up a forwarding chain, and the portal takes care of the rest—sending the document to each member of the chain for review and approval (or denial). Email is used to notify reviewers that they have a document to review, and you are notified when there is a denial. You can also view the progress your document makes as it traverses the chain.

In short, when you think of portals, think of documents. Rather than reading some static HTML content on a regular web page, you have the ability to leverage Internet technologies to add documents to the portal and even provide an automated review and approval mechanism.

SPS engine's tight integration with Microsoft Office. For several years now, you have been able to use Office products to directly interact with an SPS portal (or WSS installation), provided, of course you had the permission to do so (remember authentication). There are no other portal implementations that have this kind of office automation software to portal capability, singling SPS out as the collaboration software of choice when document storage, collaboration, and safekeeping are considered.

Let's sum up the three instances of SPS you might encounter in your work:

SPS 2003—a full portal product

WSS—a free downloadable SharePoint service that is installed on a Windows Server 2003 (W2K3) server by your local server administrator

MOSS—SPS 2007 rebranded as Microsoft Office SharePoint Server and, again, installed on a W2K3 server

One last SPS point you should keep in mind before we move on: SPS has at its core address a primary portal site. We use the word *site* to denote a primary location point that you navigate to with your browser. Suppose your portal's name was ACME, for example. You would likely simply key in `http://ACME` to go to the portal site page. Underneath that page will be a variety of *subsites*. In an SPS implementation, it would not be strange, for example, to have a subsite called SALES, another called MARKETING, and so on. And, within each subsite, you can have even more subsites. So, in the case of SALES, you might have a subsite called CONTACTS and another called NEW PRODUCTS, each of which contains a document library that contains documents germane to that section of the site, a list, or even a link to another list, that contains documents germane to that section of the site.

As a general rule of thumb, the administrators responsible for setting up the portal implement the initial site (perhaps with the help of graphic designers and the web team for a streamlined content fit) and create the subsites. But at that juncture, they defer the administration of your subsites to you. You are responsible for managing the content in your subsites and for creating and populating subsites within them.

In addition to SPS, remember that Microsoft has taken the underlying collaboration engine and bundled it into Windows Server 2003, calling it Windows SharePoint Services (WSS). Currently in its second version, soon to be in its third, WSS is an inexpensive way for those who want collaboration and sharing without going to the effort of deploying an enterprise-class product like SPS.

There are a couple of terms that we will be using in the book that we should explain before we go any further:

- When we say, "Office Server," what we're talking about is SharePoint technology running on a server in the form of what is called Office Server in order to host a collaborative document repository and portal environment. Office Server allows us to manage authorized users and provide a centralized location for our project documents.

- When we say, "workflow," we're talking about the notion of one person creating a document and then going through the act of publishing it to Office Server. At this point, it is available for others to review and make modifications, but only those who have permissions to do so. Documents that are published can be checked out, worked on, and checked back in. Version numbers are kept so that rollbacks of previous versions can be affected in the event there's a need to move back to an earlier version. In this way, tight collaborative control can be maintained over the contents of the document and who is eligible to be reading or modifying them.

SharePoint Costs

We should talk about the cost of the SharePoint product while we're at it. Like other portal products, there is a fairly steep price of admission—though SPS is by far one of the least expensive products available. With SPS 2003 and MOSS, you will pay for a server license for each server that will be running the product. (SPS can load-balance across servers and can also have a separate server instance running strictly for the purpose of indexing document content. Note that the indexing capability is not available in WSS, nor is the subscription feature.)

Additionally, you'll be paying for a client access license (CAL) for each user that uses the portal. An honor system is used for the CALs; SPS doesn't check for a valid license. In our experience, Microsoft SPS CALs are among the pricier end-user licenses you'll have to purchase for the organization. The price depends on the level of volume license agreement (Enterprise, Select, or other) that you have with Microsoft, but it would not be unreasonable to expect a CAL of $50 or more for each user on the system.

WSS has no server license cost associated with it (as long as you're properly licensed for Windows Server 2003), so you save the several thousand skins. However, the CALs are still required. WSS conforms to Windows Server 2003 licensing. If you're properly licensed for Windows Server, then you should be properly licensed for WSS.

The good news is that SPS is an enterprise-class piece of software. This means that it may already be in use, which means your friendly neighborhood CIO has already paid for the server licenses and probably the CALs. However, it is important to consider costs when you're mulling over the possibility of using portal collaboration software for your project management needs.

The latest iteration of SharePoint Technologies is found in Microsoft Office 2007 and includes two separate elements: MOSS and Office. The basic idea unfolds this way:

- MOSS is installed on a Windows Server 2003 computer that has gone through the code updates necessary to support it (Service Pack 1, .NET Framework 2.0, and .NET 3.0).
- The Office Client (Office 2007) is installed on every client computer that will be used in the collaborative environment. (Note that Office 2007 is natively equipped for use with the MOSS—that is, any user running Office 2007 has this capability. The notion of who can publish to MOSS is controlled via permissions on the server).
- Documents are created and checked into MOSS through a "check-in" process built into Office.

- Version numbering, revision monitoring, and tightly knit collaboration controls are thus introduced.

- Office 2007 programs such as Word and Excel have collaboration tools built into them for easy publishing, retrieval of published documents, tracking, and other collaboration elements.

 NOTE There are several Office products one could construe as an "Office server" product. Not to cloud the water, but you should be aware that there is an Office Groove Server product, for example, among other Office server products. When we refer to Office Server in this book, we're talking about MOSS, not the other products.

In this book, our primary focus is twofold: to introduce you to high-quality project management principles and to show you how to manage your entire project using Excel 2007. Keep in mind that it is within MOSS that our Excel work will be stored and shared with others during the project. Also note that the very same menu items are available with WSS as well. We are choosing to illustrate MOSS to you as the flagship product Microsoft has designed to go along with Office 2007. Our overarching goal, then, is to show you how to perform effective project management by using state-of-the-art collaboration tools.

How Excel 2007 and MOSS Support Project Management Processes

Take a look at Figure 2.1 This might be your first glimpse at the "new" Excel. You'll undoubtedly notice that the toolbar has gone through a remodel and the icons are more logically grouped. Activities akin to one another are segmented within a single icon group containing items pertinent to the activity you'd like to perform. For example, the Format section contains the spreadsheet formatting activities you will most likely want to perform. Microsoft calls this feature a *ribbon*. Collectively, all of these sections make up the Excel ribbon.

Excel has been written to take advantage of Windows Vista, the highly awaited next generation of Windows (see www.microsoft.com/windowsvista). Many new features reflect Microsoft's continued research into the art of developing carefully crafted interfaces. Microsoft and others like to call people like you and me *knowledge workers*. Microsoft developers continually pursue the refinement and enhancement of their product interfaces in order to enhance knowledge-worker capabilities. Because each Office program has so many features and choices built into it, Microsoft developers felt compelled to work on making the products easier to use and to make not-so-obvious choices available to users.

FIGURE 2.1   Excel toolbar

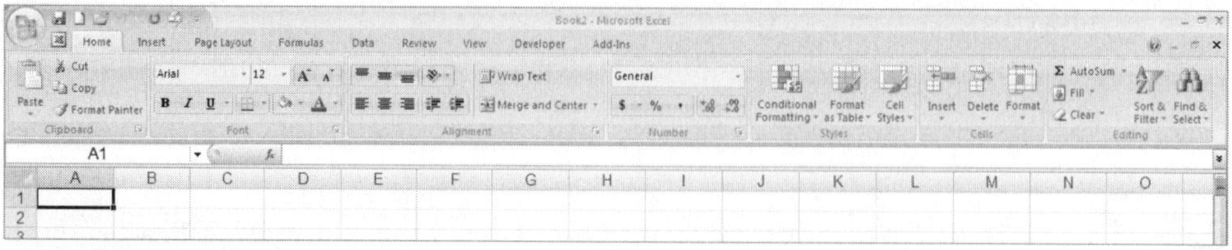

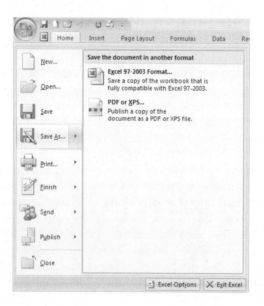

It is evident that users will have to go through no small amount of adjustment to get used to the ribbons. Microsoft has bundled into Office short videos that will help users understand the new interface.

In Figures 2.2, 2.3, and 2.4, you'll see that we've clicked the Office button (the round button with the Windows flag on it in the upper-left-hand side of the screen) to show you the submenus underneath Save As, Publish, and Finish. Notice that within each submenu, there are collaboration elements available to you.

FIGURE 2.2   Excel Save As menu

In Figure 1.3, notice at the top of the window that the file is saved in Compatibility Mode, meaning that it is backward compatible with Excel XP or Excel 2003—i.e., it is a binary file given an `.xls` extension. All Office 2007 files are saved in XML format and would thus normally not be readable by earlier versions. However, by using Save As to save the document in the older Excel formats, you make it available for others who don't have Office 2007. Microsoft has created a compatibility program that Office XP or Office 2003 users can install to make Office 2007 programs natively compatible.

Some of the new features in the Publish menu allow you to create a new document workspace and to formally publish the document to MOSS. Note that "Publish" is highlighted in yellow and its context menu appears in the right-hand pane.

The Finish submenus, as shown in Figure 2.4, give you the ability to inspect a document for private information, restrict permissions to the document to the list of users you select, add a digital signature, and perhaps the most important feature, mark the document as final (Mark as Final). Recall that the collaboration process involves various people checking out, working on, and then checking documents back in. Once finalized and complete, the document is said to be published to the Office Server. It is at this point that you would want a read-only copy of the document to be available. This is especially germane in the project management scope document, project budget, and project schedule documents. For example, once all the scope items are agreed upon and signed-off, it is important that no unauthorized changes be made to the document.

We'll look at each of these features more closely in the coming chapters.

FIGURE 2.3   Excel Publish menu

FIGURE 2.4   Excel Finish menu

Excel Is a One-Stop Environment For Project Documents

Excel 2007's new features (and those retained from previous versions) are a natural fit for project managers and provide a one-stop environment in which you can not only create (or link to) the project documents, you can also create and add the schedule, charts, and other elements. Excel goes well beyond the traditional ideas of what a spreadsheet is. We'll be exploring the following features of Excel as we progress on our project journey:

- Creating custom forms
- Developing a database
- Creating macros and developing module programming using Visual Basic for Applications (VBA)
- Establishing robust statistical and mathematical formulas that can be used to calculate and display project information

SharePoint Services

With or without SharePoint Services, Excel lends itself to project management techniques. SharePoint brings the ability to centralize the storage of your documents and provides a way to track who has edited what and when.

One of the new Office 2007 features is the notion of Office Live (see www.officelive .microsoft.com), a website that allows users to post such elements as Outlook free and busy times, retrieve templates, and discover other information about Office. While our focus in this book is on the benefits of Excel and project management, we will also explore some of Share-Point's features in terms of document publishing and sharing.

> Microsoft developers envision Office offering more than just internal collaborative benefits. They have recently acquired Groove, a company that has developed software that allows teams separated in diverse geographic locations to collaborate using the Internet. See www.microsoft.com/office/groove/default.mspx for more information.

Office 2007

Office 2007, of course, isn't just Excel. It also includes Word, Access, InfoPath, Outlook, PowerPoint, and Publisher—all of the tools you've become accustomed to over the years. All of them include the new stylized look that Excel 2007 bears.

There are actually six versions of Office 2007 available to customers. The most interesting is the Office 2007 Enterprise edition, which includes all of the Office elements mentioned plus some new, interesting elements:

Groove As mentioned in the note earlier, this feature allows disparate teams to collaborate using Groove Server and the Internet.

InfoPath InfoPath is a program that allows you to build electronic forms using Office technologies.

Integrated Enterprise Content Management (ECM) ECM involves centralizing and protecting the documents that an organization uses in its day-to-day business. For example, in a city government, disparate documents such as public works repair tickets, city court dockets, airport environmental action statements, and auditor spreadsheets, among others, can all be held in a centralized location, indexed, and managed by ECM administrators. Microsoft's ECM implementation includes MOSS 2007 and indexing and workflow capabilities as well as a variety of methods readers can use to access content. Some hardware companies have joined in the universal ECM efforts and have created disk arrays that allow administrators to place documents using policies that govern retrieval, erasure, and editing.

Communicator Essentially, Communicator is instant messaging (IM) on steroids. The idea is that you can instantly tell when someone you need to collaborate with is available for a chat conversation and you can integrate your telephone into the communicator using online directories.

SharePoint Designer SharePoint Designer (SD) is a website and portal design tool that will be used for people to create SharePoint sites. It will replace Microsoft FrontPage, which at one time may have been used by some to create SharePoint sites. FrontPage is being turned into a robust suite of three products (see the sidebar "What's Happening to FrontPage?"). SD is a tool geared toward professional web designers who need to design SharePoint sites. SD will include a workflow designer that will allow you to model human and process workflows within SharePoint.

What's Happening to FrontPage?

Microsoft FrontPage has gone through a significant genesis! In fact, it has grown into three different products all branded under the "Expression" suite nomenclature:

- Microsoft Expression Web Designer—The tool used to create the actual web pages (see www.microsoft.com/products/expression/en/web_designer/default.mspx)

- Microsoft Expression Interactive Designer—Used for creating 3D interactive, multimedia-centric environments (see www.microsoft.com/products/expression/en/interactive_designer/default.mspx)

- Microsoft Expression Graphic Designer—Used for creating graphic visual effects (see www.microsoft.com/products/expression/en/graphic_designer/default.mspx)

For those who are familiar with FrontPage, themes are permanently going away. You must use Cascading Style Sheets (CSS) instead. For a link to several CSS online tutorials, as well as blogs on the new Expression suite of products, see www.by-expression.com.

Excel 2007 and Office SharePoint Server 2007

Together, Excel and Office Server help you leverage the collaborative elements of your documents, which you could not natively accomplish simply by using Excel. That being said, if your office is like many project offices, where the staff is marginal and documents are easily shared, Office Server may be overkill for your needs—you can use the built-in capabilities of Office alongside peer-to-peer Windows networking or Windows server networking to accomplish your goals. In this book, our main area of interest will be in leveraging Excel for your project management needs. We simply want you to be aware that Office Server allows you to centralize and incorporate all of your project documents.

One thing Microsoft has done well is give you plenty of choices you can make about your computing needs. For example, maybe a SharePoint portal product is overkill for your simple project management office (PMO) needs. All you *really* need to do is create some documents in Excel and Word and let others pull them up for modification and saving with another name. No problem. Office tools will allow you to collaborate as far as you need to go in this simple environment.

Or maybe you need a bit more heft and you believe that a portal implementation will do the trick but you don't want to go through the brain damage of working with your server administrator to install WSS or MOSS and bring up a shared document library. No problem. Office Live will work for you.

Perhaps you're one of those aggressive types that wants to build out a full collaborative, workflow-centric PMO, with live, automatically updating documents. Then WSS or MOSS is your choice. If you already have a SharePoint portal up and running, getting things going will be easier for you.

In the next section ("Creating a Document Repository"), we'll assume some basic MOSS setup elements have been accomplished. Please note that the setup of these things may actually consist of a project itself! If you're a project manager, this may mean that you'll have to confer with your server administrator buddies to get this work done. We assume the following:

- Someone has installed MOSS on a computer running Windows Server 2003 (W2K3) and run the updates mentioned in the section titled "Using MS Excel 2007 and Office Share-Point Server 2007 to Manage Projects in a Workflow Environment" earlier in this chapter. We would recommend running MOSS on a dedicated computer, *not* on a server running other applications. While this server does not need to be a W2K3 domain controller (DC), it does need to be a member of the domain in order to retrieve the list of users in Active Directory (AD).

- Whoever is responsible for name resolution must assure that users are able to open their browser, key in the name of the MOSS site, and hit it by name. In other words, if the MOSS primary site is named PMServer, users must be able to open their browser and key in **http://PMServer** to successfully hit it. Note that all users will utilize their browser to navigate through the site but may use other Office products in reviewing various documents.

 Your server administrator may choose to assign a different *port* number (apart from the default port 80) to the site for added security purposes. Suppose port 8080 is assigned to the site. Users would then have to be aware that they'd navigate to the site using this address instead: http://PMHome:8080.

- Users have been created within MOSS. Note that the user list comes from AD. Simply by creating the users, you must choose what category of user each person will be.

- You will need Home Owner permissions to the MOSS site to correctly manage it. Otherwise you'll have to have a methodology set up in which you can request that various users be added.

It's fairly easy to set up users. From the main MOSS portal page, click Site Actions ➤Site Settings ➤People and Groups. In the resulting People and Groups: Home Members page, click New ➤ Add Users. In this form, you can select the user or group you'd like to add and apply the appropriate permissions (see Figure 2.5). Finally, note that you can add this person to a group that you have previously set up.

Note that there are (currently) seven different classes of user permissions:

Full control   These are the "owners" of the site.

Design   Those with design permissions are able to handle lists and document libraries from an editing perspective as well as manage website pages.

Contribute   People with contribute permissions can edit items in lists as well as documents, and they can view web pages.

Read   Readers are those with permission to read the content on a website but not edit any of it.

Approve   People with approve permissions can edit as well as approve pages, items in lists, and documents that will post to the site.

Manage Hierarchy   Hierarchy permissions allow people to create sites as well as edit the pages, items in lists, and documents on sites.

Restricted Read   Readers with this permission can only read *current* documents on the site, not historical versions. They can't view the list of user rights.

Three Basic Groups of Users

You can assign a new user one of seven different permissions, or you can simply assign them to one of three basic MOSS groups:

- Home Owners have full permission to the site—use sparingly!

- Home Members are able to contribute documents to the site. You may hear these people referred to as *authors*.

- Home Visitors are the ones who can read the documents but cannot add new ones or edit and delete existing documents. These people are called *readers*.

 If a user is not added to the list of users within MOSS, they *cannot* access the content at all, *regardless* of whether they have a valid domain logon account.

When assigning users to the site, you can simply select one of the predefined user types or assign custom permissions to a user.

Many organizations may already have an existing WSS, SPS, or MOSS structure. If this is the case with your organization, you have a true portal structure in which various departments are carved out into subsites. It is quite possible that your administrator will want to create a subsite for you as well. Suppose, for example, that your primary site is called ACME and users access it through `http://ACME`. Your administrator creates a subsite for you called PMHome. Users will access this subsite via `http://ACME/PMHome`. Permissions are managed the same way and user access can be easily restricted to only those with a need to access documents from your subsite. The only difference is that ACME is considered to be a portal site, with many subsites hanging below it. You can also create subsites within your subsite. You may, for example, create a subsite for each project you undertake. Or you may opt to create subsites for different document types that your PMO is involved with. These are just some options—the choices and creativity you have are fairly boundless.

FIGURE 2.5 Creating a new user

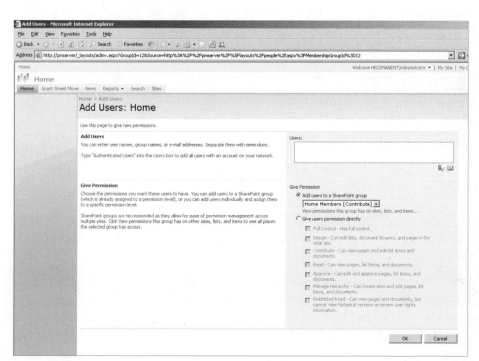

Creating a Document Repository

One of the beautiful features of MOSS is its ability to segment various classes of documents into isolated sections, called *sites* (called *workspaces* in previous SPS versions). By setting up different sites for your projects, you are able to isolate users to specific sections of MOSS and keep them away from others.

For example, suppose that you have two concurrent projects running: Project A, which involves people from Marketing and Sales, and Project B, which engages Engineering and Procurement. You can set up two separate sites, one for each project, and effectively separate the documentation as well as keep user classes separate from one another. This is huge, primarily because it cuts down the confusion level among stakeholders *and* project managers.

Creating a new site is quite easy. From the main MOSS page, click Site Actions ➢ Create Site (see Figure 2.6). Once the site is created and users are assigned to it, they simply navigate to it using `http://primary_site_name/new_site_name`. For example, suppose your primary site name is PMServer and your new site is GSM (short for Grant Street Move—this name coincides with the case study we will begin using very shortly and continue using throughout the remainder of the book). Users working on the project simply use their browser to navigate to `http://PMServer/GSM`. Remember that if they did not have permissions to a different site, the New Telephony System (NTS for navigation purposes) site for example, they could not navigate to `http://PMServer/NTS`. This is an incredibly effective tool for project managers to use in selectively isolating their project work.

FIGURE 2.6 Creating a new site

Notice in Figure 2.7 that within this new Grant St. Move site there are three document libraries automatically created by MOSS in a section called *Document Libraries*:

Documents To contain the documents you create for the site

Images For storing images you upload especially for this site

Pages To house the web pages you create for the site

Note that there are also other containers included in the new site as well, including Picture Library, Lists, Discussion Boards, Surveys, Sites and Workspaces, and the Recycle Bin.

While these are the only containers in which you can create new libraries or lists, you are not limited to creating new types of libraries or lists within any one site. For example, if you want another document library section called Project Spreadsheets, you can click the Create button shown in Figure 2.7 to pull up a new Create page, shown in Figure 2.8. Select Document Library, give it a name and description, choose navigation options, and select the type of documents it will store, as shown in Figure 2.9, and you're ready to go.

FIGURE 2.7   Viewing all site content

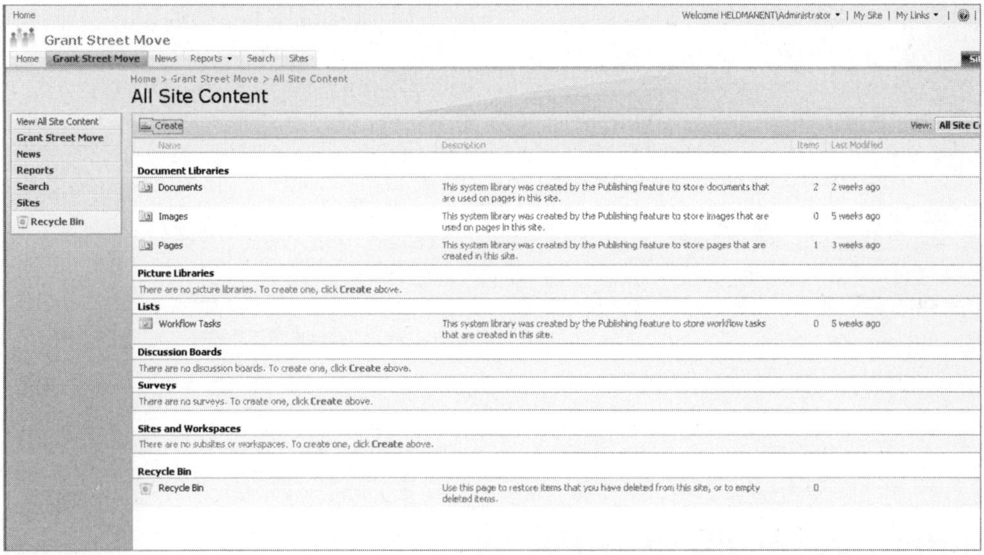

FIGURE 2.8   Creating new library or list types within a site container

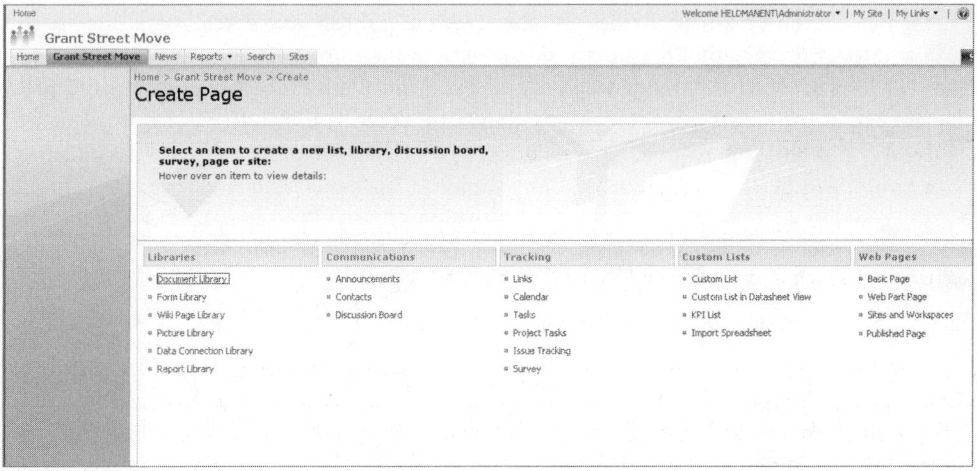

FIGURE 2.9   Creating a new document library

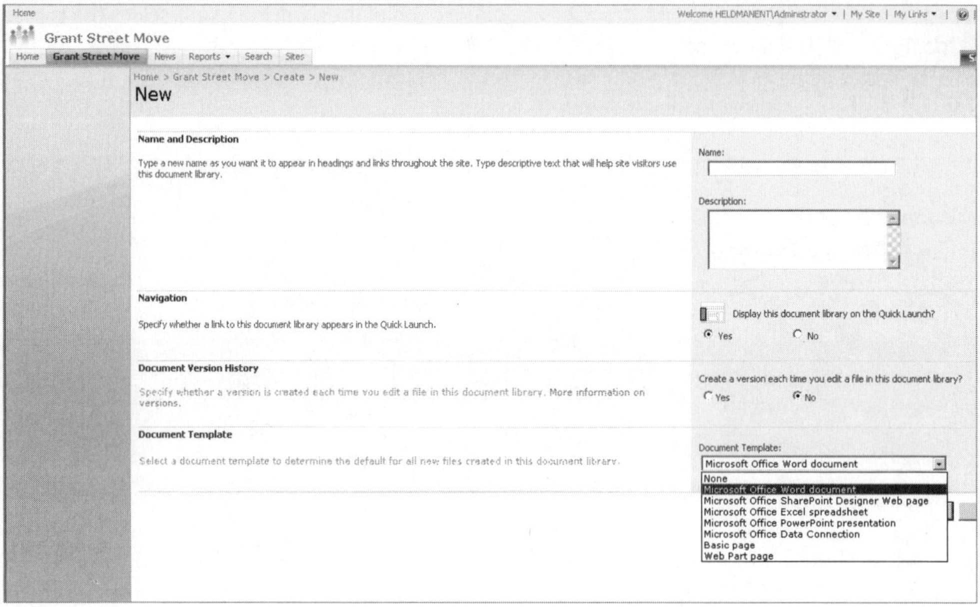

Setting Up MOSS Page Forms

As a project manager, you may or may not be an expert in Microsoft Office. After all, it is a *vast* product and you've been busy with other things! We've said our primary focus in this book is on Excel 2007, so we'll use Excel exclusively for publishing to MOSS.

Excel Calculation Services provides you the ability to publish your Excel work directly to MOSS and for readers to pull up the document right in their browser. However, you should be aware that your arsenal extends well beyond Excel. InfoPath 2007, for example, is a program you can use to create custom forms that you can directly publish to MOSS or use to set up a database connection.

> It is well worth your while to investigate the power of InfoPath as a part of your project management toolkit.

Which Template to Choose?

MOSS comes with the choice of the following templates:

- Team Site

- Blank Site

- Wiki Site

- Document Workspace

- Blog

- Records Repository

- News Home Template

- Publishing and Team Collaboration Site

- Publishing Site

In the case of Figure 2.7, we chose the Publishing and Team Collaboration Site template because it added the Documents, Images, and Pages containers listed earlier, whereas the more straightforward Team Site template would not. However, this is personal preference, strictly depending on the features you'd like to add to your site.

Note the new Wiki Site template. The idea behind this kind of site is to place a controlled area or areas in which different people can add or update information relative to a given topic—similar to a well-known wiki site, www.wikipedia.com.

The other template names should be self-explanatory.

Access 2007 is an Office product and a relational database management system (RDBMS) that brings tremendous database technologies right to your door. Microsoft has offered Access for over a decade—it is well adopted and understood throughout the world and a natural choice for those interested in progressive MOSS development activities. Access 2007 has changed dramatically from its younger brothers, so if you're accustomed to the "old" Access, be prepared for some interface surprises.

Excel functions quite nicely as a non-relational database system for those "one-stop-shopping" types not interested in learning about the heft and magnitude of Access.

Form design and publishing in the MOSS environment means that you select the logical program for the need. For example, suppose you're creating a list of projects that you've completed and you want the ability to add more to this list in the future. This kind of elementary list doesn't necessarily require the functionality that Access brings, so Excel is the likely choice.

People get in trouble when they pick the *wrong* tool for a particular function. For example, Word has some basic table calculation functionality built into it, but it's *not* Excel and isn't intended for the tasks you'd normally accomplish in a spreadsheet.

Embedded MOSS Form Links

When an authorized user navigates to a MOSS site, they are presented with links that will navigate them to other sections of the site or that open up documents to view. This is one of the best parts of MOSS—so much built-in technology brought to your fingertips with so little effort.

With any portal system, there is a concept called *portlets*. Essentially, a portlet is a piece of code that is written in HTML, DHTML, XML, JavaScript, or another web language and attached to the portal to bring some special functionality with it. In MOSS terms, we call the portlets *Web Parts*. There are numerous Web Parts that ship with MOSS and bring a variety of unique functions with them. To see the available Web Parts, simply click Site Actions ➢ Edit Page as we've done with the PMServer/GSM site page. You will be taken into design mode and will be able to add Web Parts as needed. Note that the site surface is broken out into left and right sections (Figure 2.10).

Finally, while looking at Figure 2.10, notice that we have gone ahead and modified the Summary Links Web Part to point to certain sections of our site for easier navigation purposes. By clicking the icon next to Document Templates in this Web Part and selecting Edit from the ensuing context menu, you get a Web Part dialog in which to edit this section of the Web Part, as shown in Figure 2.11. You can see in the Link URL box that we have created a link to an item, have named it Documents, and are pointing to the URL /GSM/Documents (simply a subfolder in the GSM website).

Web Designers Versus Project Managers

You should note in the figure above that we are currently viewing our site in web design mode—that is, we are editing fairly constant elements of the site, namely the web page(s) that users hit. Typically, these elements are managed by web design people—folks responsible for structure, with permissions like design and manage hierarchy. In rare cases, you may have a project manager playing a design role, but we see that only as a short-term thing. Once the system rolls into production, it is the web design people who will actually maintain the so-called "look and feel" of the site.

On the other hand, web design folks are not the ones who'll actually place content on the site. Those people are business users who are adding stuff to lists, libraries, and so forth. There are two kinds of people managing content: contributors and approvers. *If* the document library has approval turned on (*Document Library Name* ➤ Settings ➤ Versioning Settings), then a contributor can add documents, but they aren't visible until approved by someone with approver permissions. Permissions are set within Site Actions ➤ Site Settings ➤ People and Groups.

FIGURE 2.10   Adding a Web Part

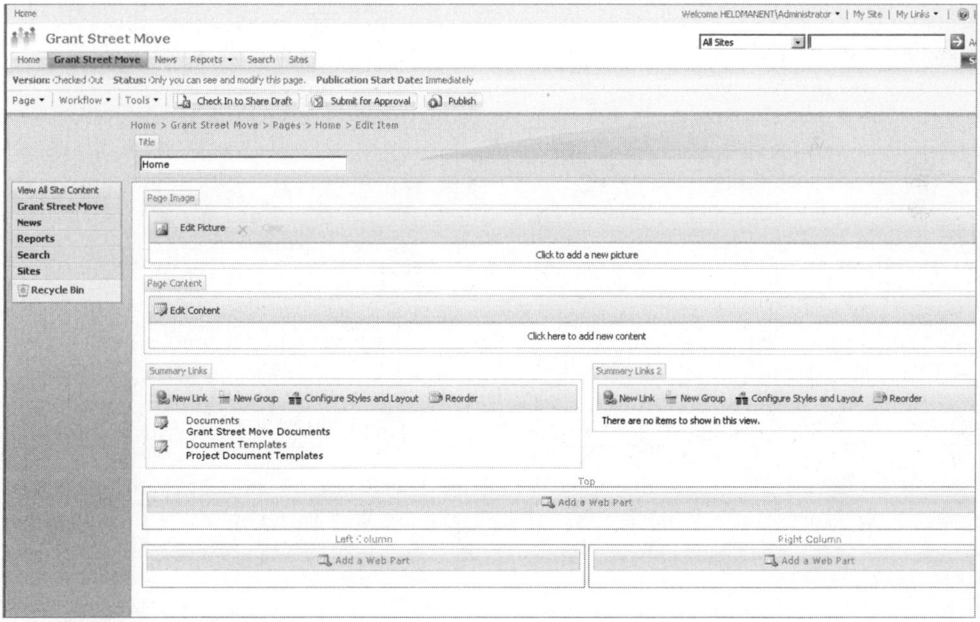

FIGURE 2.11 Editing a Web Part item

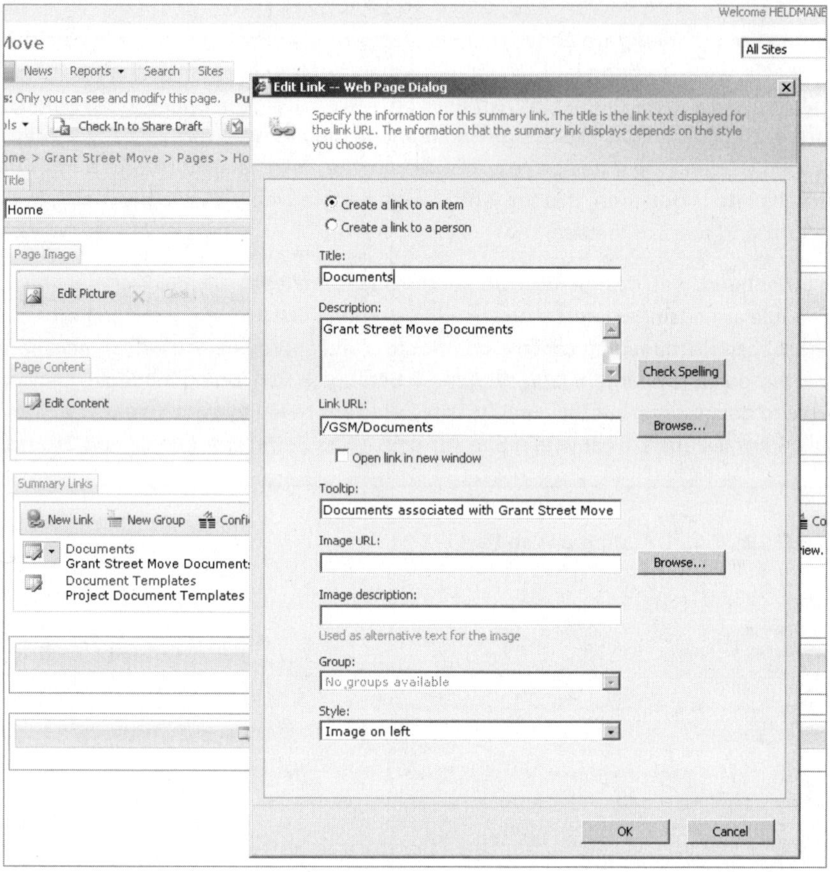

Other Web Part dialogs work similarly, though they might require different information elements to make them functional. Web Part items are movable. You can click and drag a Web Part item to a different Web Part if you so desire. To add new content to a Web Part, simply click the Add a Web Part button to pull up an Add Web Parts dialog box (Figure 2.12). Select as many as you like, and then click OK.

Note the "Click…" section within some Web Parts. The "Click…" verbiage changes depending on the Web Part section. For example, in the Page Image Web Part, you "Click to add a new picture," whereas in the Page Content Web Part, you "Click here to add new content." Clicking these elements brings up a context-specific dialog.

Once a Web Part has been added, the page needs to be checked in, approved, and published. The act of publishing it simultaneously approves and publishes, though you need to be a Home Owner (that is, have full control permissions) to accomplish this.

FIGURE 2.12   Searching for a Web Part to Add

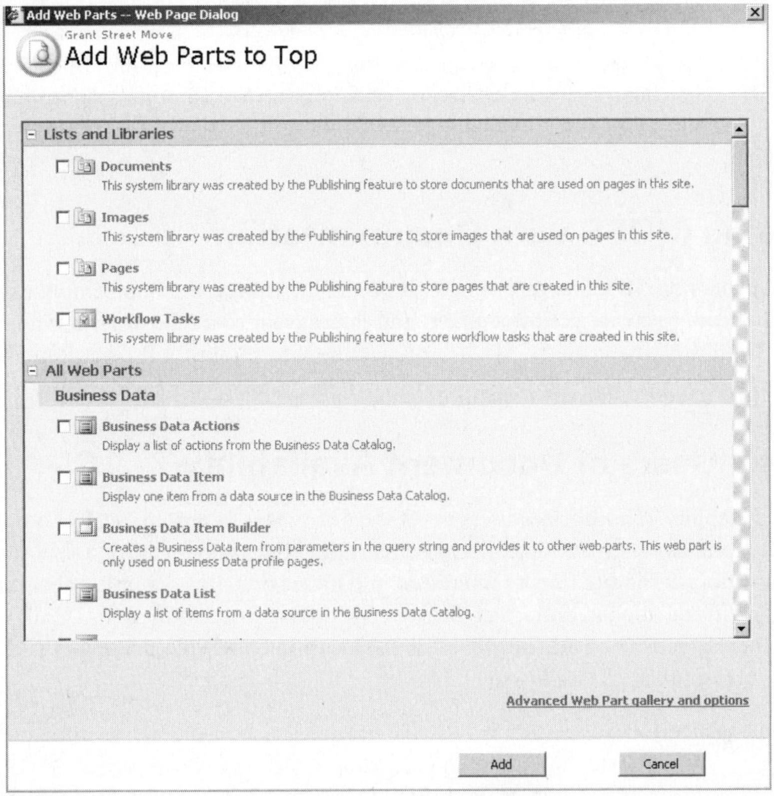

You can also modify a Web Part while in design mode. Simply click the arrow button on its header and select Modify Web Part. The drop-downs are easy to understand and navigate. Even nontechnical types can make changes to the site. Remember that changes to a Web Part require republishing the page before users will see the changes.

> **NOTE** Web Parts aren't the only things you can add to MOSS. Lists are another important element of the collaboration environment and MOSS brings many different list choices to you as well. Simply click View All Site Content ➢ Create ➢ Custom Lists. Important lists include such interesting elements as KPI Lists that allow you to track important goals, for example.

If you have a software development department, programmers can develop custom Web Parts for you. There is a Web Part software development kit (SDK) available from Microsoft for this.

Certain Web Parts allow users to connect to their email and calendar right from within the site. Outlook Web Access (OWA) has been a staple of Exchange Server (Microsoft's email server software) for many years. This technology has been available as a Web Part for use on MOSS portals since SharePoint's inception and is available to MOSS as well.

Populating MOSS with Documentation

Placing documents on MOSS is very simple. If you're an author, you can simply use your favorite Office tool to create your document and then save it to a repository on the server. In Chapter 3, "Initiating the Project," we'll show you how to publish a Project Request document to the server.

Notifying Users of Document Availability

Aside from the ability of authorized users to set their browsers to automatically connect to the site at startup, one of the great things MOSS offers is a subscription feature. Users simply navigate to the section of the site they're interested in (Documents, for example), click the drop-down for a specific document, and select the Alert Me option to be notified (by email) whenever a new document is published and approved at the location or when a document is changed, approved, and re-published (see Figure 2.13).

The Alert Me feature requires a Simple Mail Transfer Protocol (SMTP) linkage to an email server to work. Setting this up is beyond the scope of this text. See your friendly system administrator.

Users are not notified when a document is simply uploaded (that is, approved) to the site. All documents must undergo a publishing process before they are made visible to the users.

You probably noticed another interesting element in Figure 2.13—the ability to get Really Simple Syndication (RSS) feeds from the MOSS. How is this possible? Well, here's another great feature of Office 2007—every document you create in native Office 2007 format is an Extensible Markup Language (XML) document that is completely eligible for and compliant with RSS feeds. If users have an RSS reader (one of which is Outlook 2007), they may appreciate obtaining RSS feeds instead of email notifications. However, if the site is "noisy," that is, there's lots of documents and updates are being posted frequently, RSS may get a bit chatty. Figure 2.14 shows what the Grant Street Move/Documents folder's contents looks like within an RSS feed.

FIGURE 2.13 Setting up Alert Me

Home
Grant Street Move
Home Grant Street Move News Reports Search Sites
Home > Grant Street Move > Documents
Documents
View All Site Content
Grant Street Move
News
Reports
Search
Sites
Recycle Bin
This system library was created by the Publishing feature to store documents that are
New Upload Actions Settings
Type Name
CPUs
Project Request
Edit in Datasheet
Bulk edit items using a datasheet format.
Open with Windows Explorer
Drag and drop files into this library
Connect to Outlook
Synchronize items and make them available offline.
Export to Spreadsheet
Analyze items with a spreadsheet application.
View RSS Feed
Syndicate items with an RSS reader.
Alert Me
Receive e-mail notifications when items change.

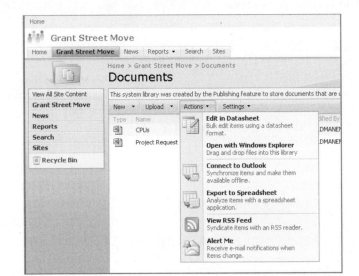

FIGURE 2.14 Viewing the contents of the Grant Street Move/Documents folder in an RSS feed

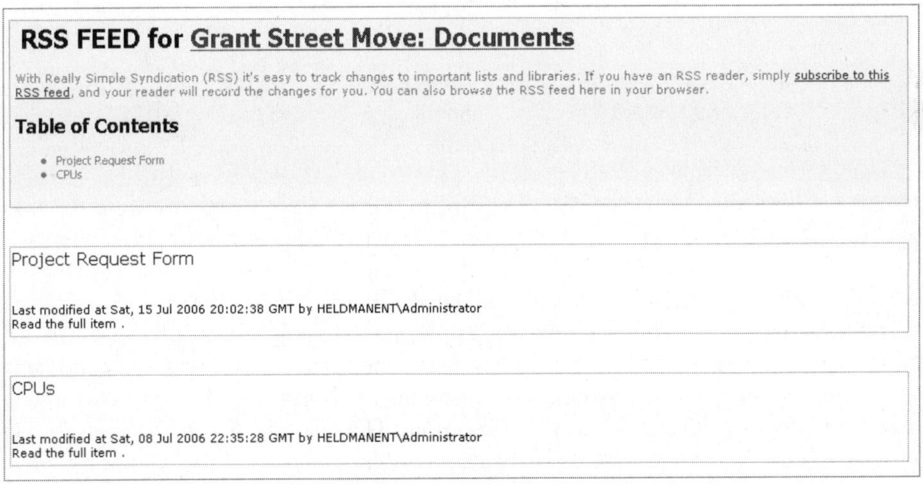

RSS FEED for Grant Street Move: Documents
With Really Simple Syndication (RSS) it's easy to track changes to important lists and libraries. If you have an RSS reader, simply subscribe to this RSS feed, and your reader will record the changes for you. You can also browse the RSS feed here in your browser.
Table of Contents
Project Request Form
CPUs
Project Request Form
Last modified at Sat, 15 Jul 2006 20:02:38 GMT by HELDMANENT\Administrator
Read the full item .
CPUs
Last modified at Sat, 08 Jul 2006 22:35:28 GMT by HELDMANENT\Administrator
Read the full item .

Click an item within the Table of Contents section to view the document's page (Figure 2.15) for more information and to edit the document itself.

The document called CPUs is included in a discussion in Appendix A.

In Chapter 3, we'll go into more depth with regard to project management using Excel, and in particular, we'll examine online project requests and the project charter.

FIGURE 2.15   Viewing document information via RSS page redirection

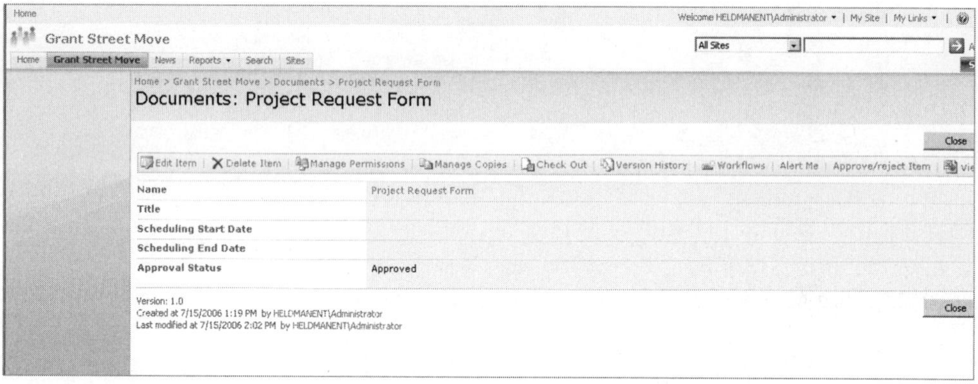

Home	Welcome HELDMANENT\Administrator ▼ | My Site | My Links ▼ | ⑦
𝕚𝕚𝕚 Grant Street Move	All Sites ▼ ⎵ ⮕ A
Home **Grant Street Move** News Reports ▼ Search Sites	

Home > Grant Street Move > Documents > Project Request Form
Documents: Project Request Form

Close

🗐 Edit Item   ✕ Delete Item   🗐 Manage Permissions   🗐 Manage Copies   🗐 Check Out   🗐 Version History   ▦ Workflows   Alert Me   Approve/reject Item   🗐 Vie

Name	Project Request Form
Title	
Scheduling Start Date	
Scheduling End Date	
Approval Status	Approved

Version: 1.0
Created at 7/15/2006 1:19 PM by HELDMANENT\Administrator
Last modified at 7/15/2006 2:02 PM by HELDMANENT\Administrator   Close

Chapter

3

Initiating the Project

Now that you understand the foundation of project management and its various processes and you have a high-level overview of the capabilities of Excel and SharePoint 2007, we're ready to kick off the process by initiating a project.

In this chapter, we'll start by outlining how to go about setting up a project initiation process with forms and templates. We'll also discuss the important role a project sponsor and other key stakeholders play in the project. Next we'll examine the project charter, its key elements, and the importance this document plays in the future of the project.

Let's get started with setting up a project initiation process.

Establishing a Project Initiation Process

Projects come about for many reasons. Examples include marketing demands, business needs, customer requirements, and legal requirements. Whatever the reason, once you and your team have established some success at delivering projects, the requests will start pouring in. You'll end up with more projects than you can work on (if you aren't already in this situation). You'll find yourself asking how you know which projects are worth pursuing, how many are waiting in the queue, and which one has the highest priority. Before this has a chance to get out of hand, it's a good idea to establish a project initiation request process. A project request process will allow you to take care of the following tasks:

- Determine the business justification for the project
- Establish a high-level cost estimate for the project
- Ensure that the project has management backing (a project sponsor)
- Make a go/no-go decision regarding the project
- Determine the project's priority among other projects
- Review the current and proposed project list at a glance

To adequately capture all of this information, the following elements will be created or determined when establishing the project request process:

- Project request form
- Project request tracking database
- Project selection criteria

We'll take a look at each of these in the following sections.

Components of the Initiating Process

In Chapter 1, we looked at a high-level overview of the components of the project management processes. Figure 3.1 shows a snapshot of the Initiating process.

FIGURE 3.1   Initiating process overview

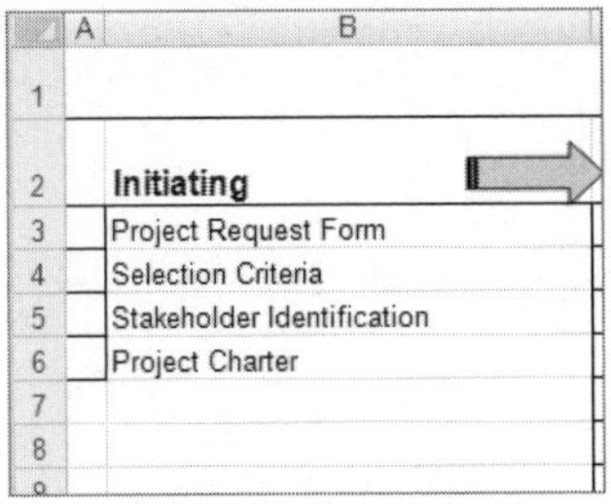

	A	B
1		
2	**Initiating**	
3	Project Request Form	
4	Selection Criteria	
5	Stakeholder Identification	
6	Project Charter	
7		
8		

As you can see, we have four action items we'll perform by the completion of this process:

- Submit project request form.
- Use selection criteria to determine if the project is a go or no-go.
- Identify stakeholders.
- Write and publish the project charter.

Remember that each process has outputs that become inputs to the next set of processes. For example, the project charter will become an input to the Planning processes, so it's important to make these documents as clear, complete, and accurate as you can given the information you have at the time. You can also come back and repeat a process when new information is discovered. For example, in the early phases of the Planning processes for this project, you may uncover information that will require an update to the project charter.

We'll cover each of these topics in detail in this chapter. Next, let's talk about the elements in a project request form and create a template using Excel.

The Elements of a Project Request Form

We've been in organizations where stakeholders whined like squeaky hinges when we implemented a project request process. They explained to us that they liked going directly to the programmer and asking for what they wanted. Sure, sometimes they used lunch or game tickets as a bribe to push their projects ahead of others, but they didn't see a thing wrong with this approach. That's exactly what we did see wrong with the process. Programmers shouldn't decide department priorities and stakeholders should learn to take turns like they did on the grade school playground.

> The not-so-good news is that you can expect a little push back when you implement a project initiation request process. The good news is that after everyone uses it, they'll wonder why they hadn't done it before.

The project request form provides a way to gather a few essential pieces of information. Figure 3.2 is a sample project request template.

FIGURE 3.2   Project request form

	A	B
1		**Project Request Form**
2	Tracking number	
3	Date	
4	Project Title	
5	Requestor	
6	Phone	
7	email	
8	Dept	
9	Sponsor	
10	Phone	
11	email	
12	Dept	
13	Description	
14	Business Justification	
15	Impact if project is not implemented	
16	Known dependencies	
17	Requested completion date	
18	Budget or Approximate Cost	
19		This Section To Be Completed By Reviewer
20	Date reviewed	
21	Name of reviewer	
22	Disposition	
23	Priority	
24	Comments	

Let's take a closer look at each of the elements in this template.

Tracking Number   The tracking number is used to create a unique identifier for the project. You'll use this number in the project request database as well. In Chapter 1, we talked about organizing files and data by using consistent and unique names. The same principle applies here. You could document your projects with the date first followed by a three-digit sequential number—for example, 011108-100. Or perhaps start with a sequential number and a short name: 100-New Product Launch.

Date   This is the date the request is written.

Project Title   The requestor should provide a title that adequately describes the project. The title should be brief.

Requestor   The requestor section captures the name of the person requesting the project and their contact information.

Sponsor   The sponsor section captures the name of the project sponsor and their contact information. This is not always the same as the project requestor. Project sponsors are usually managers in the organization who have the ability to authorize funding and resources for the project. We'll talk more about project sponsors in the section "Identifying Stakeholders" later in this chapter.

Description   This section should describe the "what" it is the project will accomplish once it's completed. High-level goals and objectives can be outlined here along with the description of the problem the organization is trying to solve (or the opportunity it is trying to take advantage of) by implementing this project.

Business Justification   The business justification section tells the reviewer why the project should be undertaken, what the benefits to the organization are if the project is successful, and alternative options for implementing the project. We'll discuss business justification in more detail in the next section.

Impact If Project Is Not Implemented   This section goes hand in hand with the business justification section. It describes what the impact will be if the organization does not implement the project.

Known Dependencies   Dependencies may include other projects that must be completed prior to beginning this project, infrastructure updates, vendor selection, waiting for a new boss to come on board, and so on. For example, perhaps your new web project can't be started until the infrastructure project is completed. You'd list the infrastructure project in this section along with its project tracking number.

Requested Completion Date   The requested completion date is noted here. If there is a critical completion date or a mandatory completion date, those should be documented as well.

Budget or Approximate Cost   Often projects are undertaken with a certain budget already in mind. For example, our stakeholder may have $100,000 to spend by the end of the fiscal year and she decides to implement a new software product that will increase order processing times. That doesn't mean the project can or should be completed within that budget. As more information is discovered and deliverables and requirements become clear, the budget will be firmed up. Assumptions about budgets or available funds should be noted in this section.

In the section to be completed by the reviewer, the Date Reviewed and Name of Reviewer sections are self-evident. The other sections are as follows:

Disposition   The final decision regarding the project is documented here. *Approved*, *canceled*, and *postponed* are typical descriptors.

Priority   If the project is approved, the priority is documented here. The priority will come from the project tracking database and the decision of the reviewer or the review committee about where the project falls on the list.

Comments   Comments provide a place to add notes regarding any of the areas on the form. If the project is not approved, the reasons should be noted in this section. Perhaps there wasn't sufficient information to make a decision or the timing is off. If it's a timing issue, for example, the request could be resubmitted at a later date.

Next we'll take a closer look at documenting business justification for the project.

Establishing the Business Justification

Business justification in its simplest form states the reason the organization should perform the project. It also usually includes a discussion of the benefits to the organization, the alternatives available, and a financial analysis to determine the project's investment value. In reality, a business justification could be its own document, particularly for large projects or those that carry a substantial amount of risk to the organization. If that's the case, make a note on the initiation form that the business case is attached. For small to medium projects (the day-to-day type of work), the benefits—including savings, cost reductions, revenue opportunities, and so on—can be listed on the initiation form itself.

Business justification is somewhat like the analysis we all do when making a major purchase. For example, say you're in the market for a new car. You know you want a convertible and you have a firm price in mind. You can't go over $35,000. Your next step is to determine which car manufacturers make convertibles within your price range (in project terms, you're exploring the alternatives). From there you determine the features you want and negotiate a final price (in project terms, you're determining the benefits of the features). You may also investigate financing alternatives and determine which interest rate and payment fits your budget. If your biggest concern is the total amount you'll pay for the car, interest included, you'll want the lowest interest rate you can find. If your biggest concern is monthly payments, you'll want a low interest rate but you'll probably be more interested in stretching the payments out over a longer time period to lower the monthly payment. A business justification examines similar factors.

Business Justification Elements

There are no hard and fast rules for documenting business justification. Typically, you're attempting to determine tangible results of performing or not performing the project. *Tangible* means measurable, as in cost savings, increased production or capacity, increased revenues, increased market share, and so on. You will have to work with your stakeholders to determine what is important to them.

The following list will give you some idea of the types of tangible elements you could research to help establish the benefits of the project. Not all these elements must be documented for every project; however, the more complex the project or the more risk it poses to the organization, the more elements you'll want to include:

- Savings
- Cost reduction
- Revenue opportunities and projections
- Market share
- Customer satisfaction
- Cash flow analysis

Cash flow analysis is documented as part of the business justification for the project and it's used to help reviewers or selection committees choose which project to implement. We'll look at several cash flow analysis techniques in the section "Project Selection Criteria" later in this chapter.

In addition to measurable benefits, you should include intangible benefits in the justification as well as other costs to the organization that should be taken into consideration. The following list includes a few examples:

- Transition costs
- Maintenance costs
- Changes in business processes
- Personnel changes
- Recurring benefits

Other Business Justification Considerations

Along with benefits and a cash flow analysis, a business justification should consider alternative solutions or methods for implementing the benefits of the project. For example, there are thousands of vendors with millions of products that promise to do x, y, and z and they all come with a price. So is the $2 million off-the-shelf solution the best way to go or is the alternative of partial off-the-shelf, partial in-house development a better alternative? This is the type of question a business justification should explore. Each alternative should include some of the tangible and intangible elements listed in the previous section.

The business justification may be written by the project sponsor or the project manager; it depends on the culture of the organization. Regardless of who writes the justification, at the conclusion of the project the sponsor is the one responsible for the success of the project's investment. The project manager is responsible for the successful planning, execution, and implementation of the project. In other words, the project manager is responsible for executing and delivering a successful project, but the project sponsor is responsible for the financial success or return on investment of the final product (or result) of the project.

Wrap up the business justification with a conclusion and a recommendation. Explain why you're recommending the alternative you picked and emphasize why it's the best option for the organization based on the facts outlined in the justification. If the justification is well prepared and documented, it will speak for itself—but tell them again which alternative is best anyway.

Creating the Project Request Form using Excel

Now let's go through some easy steps to create the Project Request Form document and put it online for others to see. Modify as you like—this document and all the forms you'll see throughout the remainder of the book are available at the book's download page.

If you're starting from scratch, open Excel and create the document using the fields you see in Figure 3.2 as your guide. Once you're done, you'll want to save the document off to SharePoint. But in this case, you don't want to save the entire spreadsheet; you just want to save a *range* of cells. The reason for this is to minimize the amount of content shared on SharePoint.

Highlight all the cells in the form, right-click anywhere within the range, and select Name a Range from the submenu as shown in Figure 3.3.

Figure 3.4 shows the New Name dialog box.

FIGURE 3.3   Naming a range

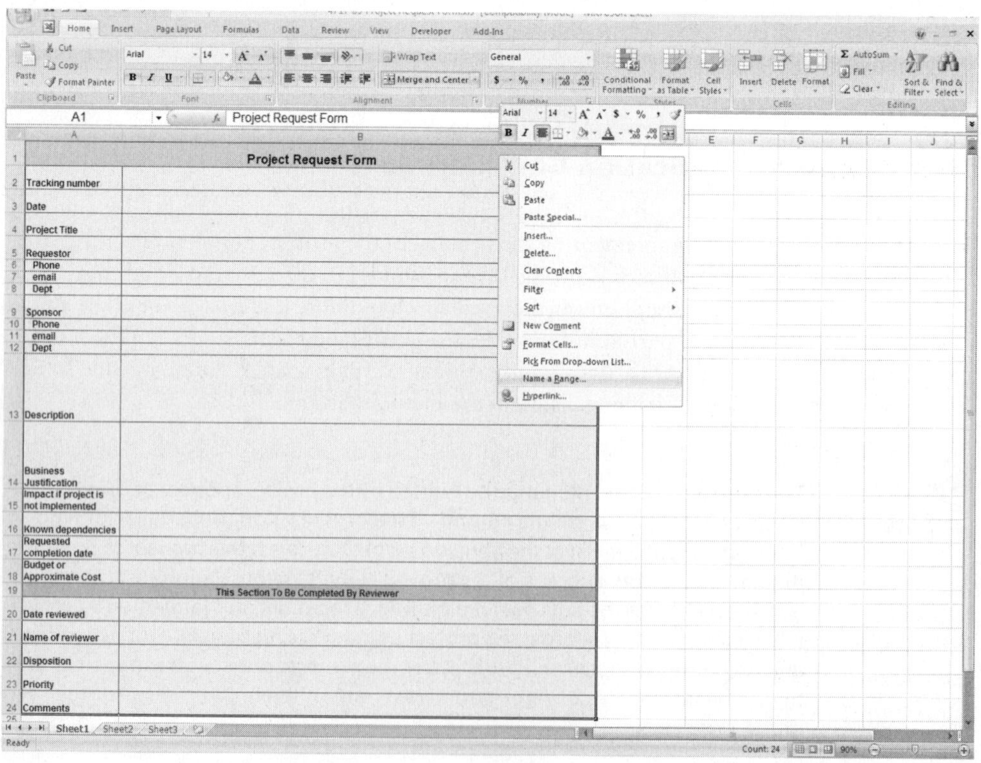

FIGURE 3.4   New Name dialog box

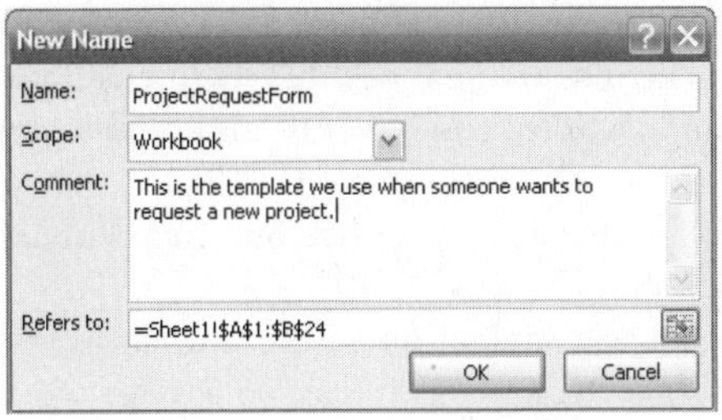

Figure 3.4 shows the name we've given the range of cells, ProjectRequestForm. Note that no spaces or special characters are allowed in the name field. The Scope drop-down box gives you four options in a new workbook: Workbook, Sheet 1, Sheet 2, or Sheet 3. (If you have more than three sheets in the workbook, all the sheets will show up here). Tell Excel how you want this range to apply by choosing one of the selections. The Workbook selection allows all range names to appear in the Go To dialog box. For example, if you bring up the Go To box (use the F5 key), all the range names you've assigned within the workbook scope will appear from any sheet within the workbook. If you assign the range name scope to only Sheet 1, when you are on Sheet 2 or Sheet 3 and press the F5 key, you will not see the range name you entered for Sheet 1.

In the Comment field, you can add notes about the range, and the Refers To field displays the range of cells the name applies to. In this case, the range of cells is Sheet 1 cells A1 through B24. The $ means the cells are absolute. In other words, the cell references will not change but will always be column A cell 1 through column B cell 24.

Next you'll want to publish your work. There are numerous ways to save a document in Excel, but in our case, we want to publish it to the SharePoint (or MOSS) site so others can use it.

Publishing the Project Request Form

In the case of our project request form, other people will use the document to fill in the information regarding their new project and then save it back to the Documents repository for you and your fellow project managers to read and authorize. In the publishing process, documents that are opened are said to be *checked out*.

Each SharePoint user is assigned into a group that has a specific role. Users may be given a *Home Member* role, allowing them to contribute content to the site, a *Home Visitor* role that allows only the ability to read the pages on the site, or *Home Owner*, a role that allows full control over the site. Roles determine whether you have the ability to author (that is write) a new document or modify an existing one or the ability to read only. Owners and Members can author and modify, Visitors can only read. For example, Members would have the ability to change the Project Request Form document itself. That's something we probably don't want everyone to be able to do. Visitors are required to view the document in read-only mode. If they want a copy of it, they must save it locally. This preserves the integrity of the original document.

Most everyone, besides you, who has access to the Project Request Form document should likely be assigned the Member role.

When a document is checked out by an Owner, modified, and then checked back in, SharePoint tracks the previous version numbers. The nice thing about this feature is if an author publishes a document update that they shouldn't have, you have the ability to revert backwards to a previous version.

To publish to the MOSS server in Excel, simply click the Office Button ➢ Publish ➢ Document Management Server, as shown in Figure 3.5.

When you publish, you're presented with a basic navigation pane, quite similar to the type you've become accustomed to in previous Office versions. Navigate to My Network Places and find the name of your MOSS server. In our case, we navigate to the MOSS server named PMServer and are prompted to key in our credentials, as shown in Figure 3.6.

Next, navigate down till you find the workspace in which you want to publish the document. In our case, we've created a subsite (more on that in a later chapter) named GSM (for Grant St. Move, we'll introduce this project later in this chapter) with a Documents folder, as shown in Figure 3.7. We will publish to the Documents folder and give the file its final name of Project Request Form.xlsb. The .xlsb extension means we're saving in a binary format. This is for security reasons—we're protecting the document so it is not openly readable by individuals who've happened to somehow hack into our site (a difficult thing to do). Because Excel and all other Office 2007 documents use an open XML file type and XML is eminently readable with a lot of different editors, using a binary form of the Excel sheet makes good security sense.

FIGURE 3.5   Publishing to the MOSS server, step 1

FIGURE 3.6   Publishing to the MOSS server, step 2

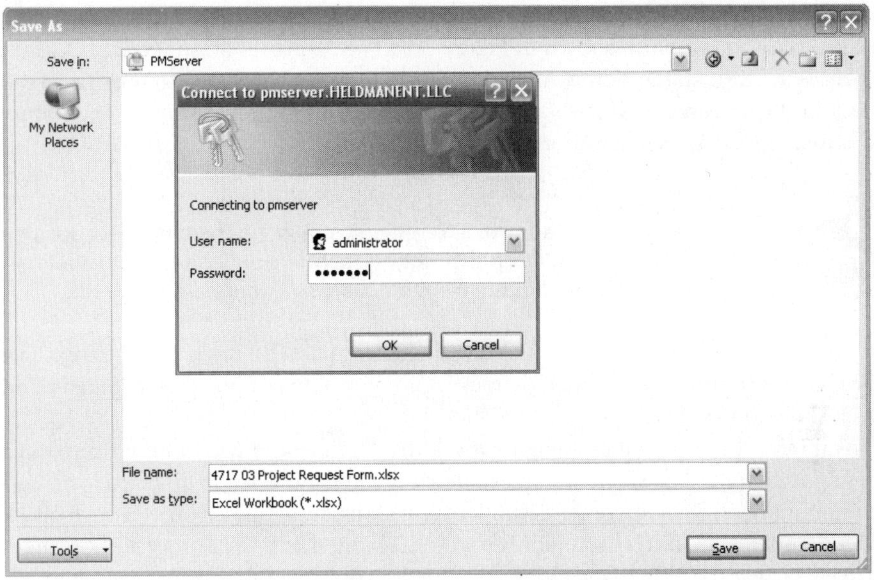

FIGURE 3.7   Navigating to the MOSS workspace for publishing

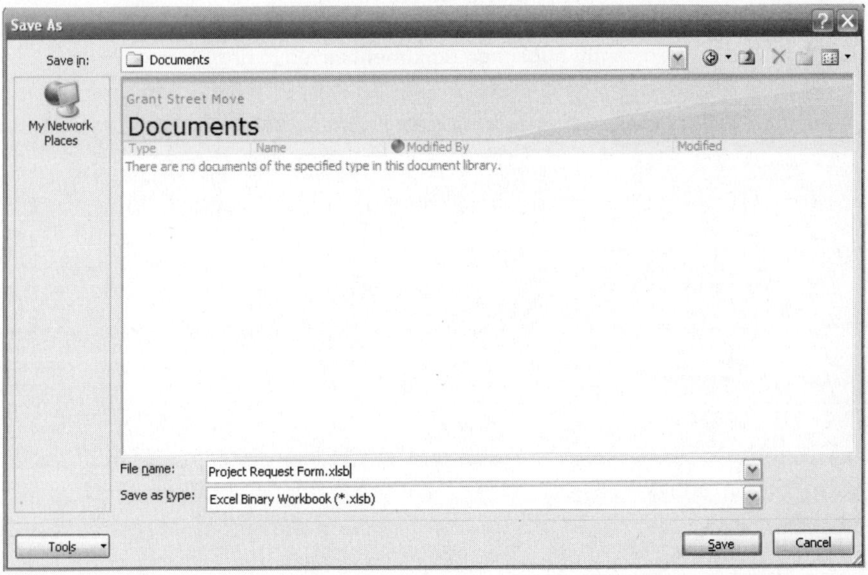

When we click Save, the name of the document will appear under the `http://PMServer/GSM/Documents` location.

Just because we've published the document does not mean it is available for users. Look at the Project Request Form shown in Figure 3.8. The Approval Status column shows this document is in Draft status. Someone with Owner or Member privileges must go to the site and check in the document. Note that as mentioned in Chapter 2, versioning and approval must be turned on for a document library to use these features.

> Users are alerted with a New! indicator when there is a new document in the folder. This isn't terribly handy if there are only one or two documents, such as with our folder, but tremendously so if there are hundreds.

To check in a document, you click the document name to bring up a context menu and select Check In from the list, as shown in Figure 3.9. You're immediately taken to a Check In page, shown in Figure 3.10.

You must decide if you're going to check the document in with a minor revision number (opting to continue keeping it in draft mode) or if you'll publish it in finalized form with a major revision number. The difference is subtle, yet very meaningful. If you decide to check the document in with a minor revision number, you're saying that you or other authors may yet want to make changes to it. In that case, the document won't be available for reading by Visitors. As a matter of fact, the document won't even show up in the Documents list in their browsers. Not until you publish the document in finalized format with a major revision number will it be visible to Visitors. Minor revision numbers increment on the right side of the decimal point (0.1, 0.2, 0.3...); major numbers on the left side (1.0, 2.0...).

FIGURE 3.8   A recently published document saved in draft form

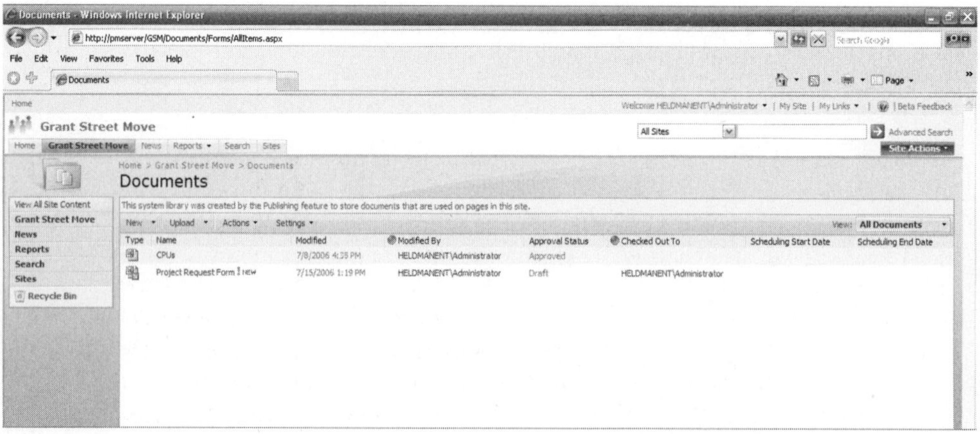

FIGURE 3.9   Selecting the Check In selection from the MOSS document context menu

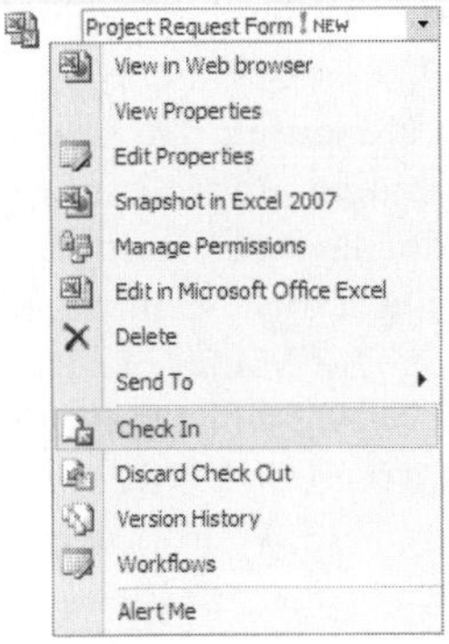

FIGURE 3.10   Check In page

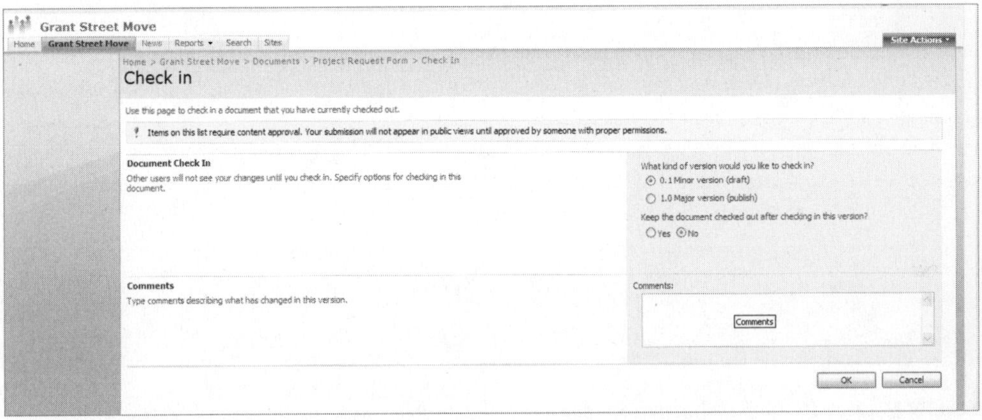

On the other hand, if you (and any other Members or Owners with a vested interest in the document) are done with it, you can opt to save it with a major revision number, thus finalizing and publishing the document for reading by others.

To clarify, suppose you work on the document and save it with a minor revision number. You're now at version 0.1. A Member pulls up the document and adds some things to it, again saving it with a minor version number. Now the version number is at 0.2. Once you decide to publish the document in finalized format, it takes on a major revision number. If the same Member and Owner check out a finalized document, adding updates one after the other and not finalizing it, the document will take on minor version numbers again—1.1, 1.2, and so on.

Simply checking in a document does not publish it! It must also be approved. Going back to our original `PMServer/GSM/Documents` folder (Figure 3.8) and clicking the Project Request Form item brings up a new context menu because the document is now checked in. Select the Approve/Reject option as shown in the list in Figure 3.11.

Clicking this takes you to an Approve/Reject page, shown in Figure 3.12.

The status of a checked-in but not approved document is pending. As an Owner managing the site, you have the ability to turn down publication of the document by rejecting it, or you can approve it for publication or continue to leave it in pending status. Members have this right as well. Only the document's creator and those with the right of Manage Lists (or higher) will be able to see the document sitting out there. Visitors will not. We will, of course, approve the document so others can see it. Click the Approve button and then click OK. The document will show up in the author's list as approved, as shown in Figure 3.13. Visitors will not see the approved notation.

FIGURE 3.11   Document options

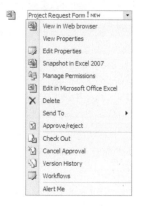

FIGURE 3.12   The Approve/Reject page

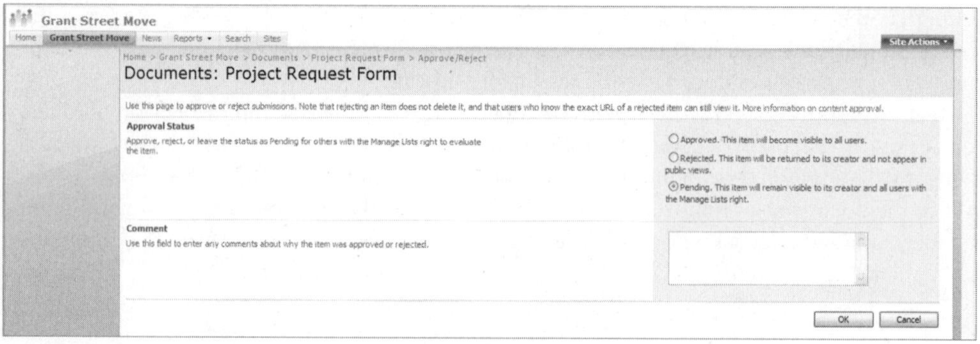

FIGURE 3.13   The approved document

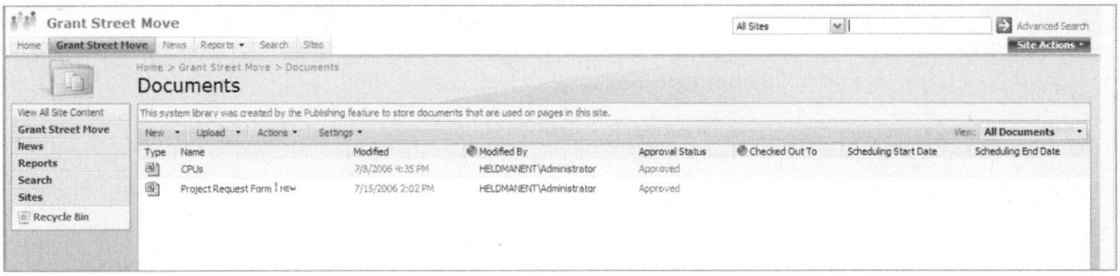

This process illustrates the SharePoint notion of workflow. The idea is that many different knowledge workers have some interaction with corporate documents. Some create a document, while others take a peek at it to see what they think and make recommendations. Others use the document for day-to-day work. The built-in check-in/check-out/approve workflow functionality that SharePoint provides allows people to do exactly that while keeping track of document version information.

When users (regardless of whether they're Visitors, Members, or Owners) open their browser and navigate to the `http://PMServer/GSM/Documents` folder, they are presented with a list of available documents. Owners and Members will see all documents, whether checked out or not. Visitors will see only those that have been checked in. When a Member selects a document they are given the option to simply read it in read-only status or check it out and edit it. The pop-up is shown in Figure 3.14.

When a Visitor views the Documents folder, the document context menu changes to what's shown in Figure 3.15. Visitors only have the option of viewing the contents in a browser or taking a snapshot of the data in Excel. They can save a local copy, but they don't have the ability to update the document on SharePoint.

If a Visitor uses the View in Web Browser option, Excel Web Services renders the document in a web page and gives them two options for manipulating the document, both via launching Excel, as shown in Figure 3.16.

FIGURE 3.14   Pop-up menu that appears when members open a document

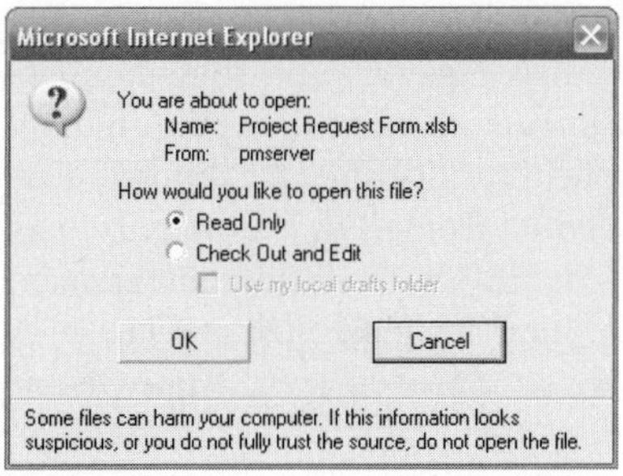

FIGURE 3.15   Visitor document context menu

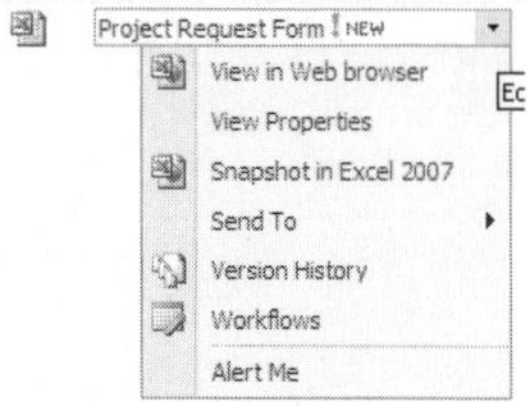

FIGURE 3.16   View in Web Browser option

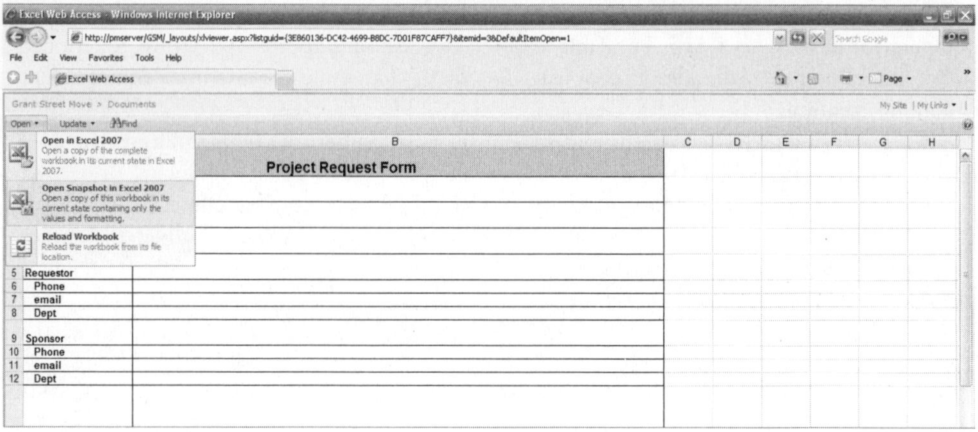

Open Snapshot in Excel varies somewhat from simply loading the document into Excel. Only the formulas and formatting are brought over, not other elements such as consolidation, for example. (We'll talk more about consolidation in the appendix.)

If the user chooses Open in Excel 2007, the document loads itself into their local instance of Excel 2007, as shown in Figure 3.17.

The user is able to fully manipulate this document in any way they like, but they can only save it locally. Members and Owners who select this option are able to manipulate the document and then save it to SharePoint with a new document name or republish it.

If a user assigned the Member or Owner role clicks the document, a different context menu appears, providing numerous menu options to choose from. (For example, Figures 3.9 and 3.11 show the context menu in different stages—Figure 3.9 shows the context menu when the document needs to be checked in, the Check In option is highlighted, and Figure 3.11 shows it when the document has been checked in but is not approved as the Approve/reject option is now available.)

FIGURE 3.17   Snapshot in Excel

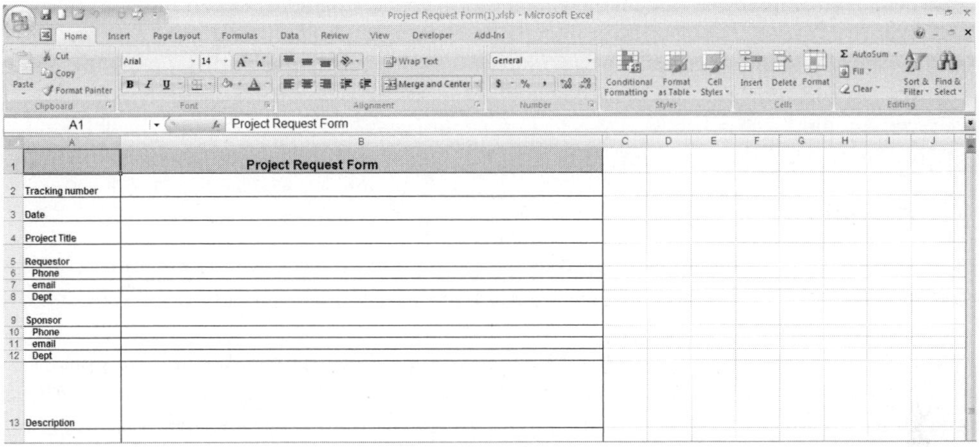

All of these workflow-centric elements allow Owners, Members, and Visitors to collaborate together toward complete and well-formulated documents all without leaving the comfort of their desks. And it started by opening Excel to create a simple form.

Project Selection Criteria

As we mentioned earlier, you'll likely find yourself in a situation in which there are more projects to work on than there are resources. This means there should be a mechanism in place for determining which projects should be worked on and in what order. In some organizations, one person (like a manager or executive) decides, and in others, a whole committee decides.

In either case, you'll want to acquaint yourself with the decision makers and with the organization itself. Begin by understanding what kind of information is relevant to them. What metrics are they looking for? How do they use them in decision making? For example, maybe all projects with payback periods of less than two years are considered a go. What are some of the intangible benefits your decision makers consistently look for? If improved customer satisfaction scores on the annual survey are important to them, you'll want to make certain you've outlined how the project will achieve that.

It would also be a good idea to become familiar with your organization's strategic plan. You may have projects that show immediate benefit but are not in alignment with the strategic goals of the organization. That's an automatic no-go decision.

Your decision makers will likely want to see some financial analysis to judge the value of the investment that will be made in the project. Financial analysis provides a relatively quick and easy method for determining if the project is likely to produce a reasonable return on investment and can carry a lot of weight in the decision-making process.

Remember that financial analysis is usually included as part of the business justification for the project. The reviewer or selection committee also reviews financial analysis to determine which projects to perform.

The most common cash flow analysis techniques are cost-benefit analysis, payback period, cash flow, and internal rate of return. We'll take a look at each one in the following sections.

Cost-Benefit Analysis

Cost-benefit analysis is a straightforward technique. Here you'll measure the cost of producing the product of the project against its expected benefits. If the benefits outweigh the costs, it's a positive indicator.

Don't forget to include all costs when performing a cost-benefit analysis—for example, the cost of implementing the project, ongoing support, maintenance, staffing, fixing problems that weren't resolved during the project, and so on. This method uses the full cost of the project and its ongoing operations after it's released to the organization, not just cost of the project, to produce final end result.

Payback Period

Payback period is the amount of time it takes to pay back the project's initial investment. Total project costs are compared to the revenue generated and the length of time it takes revenues to equal the project costs. When two or more projects of similar size and complexity are being compared, generally the project with the shortest payback period is chosen. There isn't a hard and fast formula for this technique. If project costs equal $100,000, for example, and expected revenues are $25,000 per quarter, the payback period is one year.

Discounted Cash Flows

If we told you we'd give you $1,000 today or $1,000 two years from today, which one would you take? The $1,000 today is worth more than $1,000 two years from now because you have the opportunity to invest the money now and make a return on it over the coming years. If, for example, you invested the $1,000 at 6 percent interest for two years, in today's dollars that investment equals $1,123.60.

The discounted cash flow technique compares the value of the future cash flows to today's dollars. In other words, it does the opposite of what we just explained. If you knew your project would return a total of $1,123.60 two years from now, (known as the future value or FV) the discounted cash flow technique tells you its value today. The answer, of course, is $1,000.

In order to calculate discounted cash flows, you need to know the value of the investment in today's dollars, otherwise known as present value. Present value is calculated as follows:

$$PV = FV \div (1 + i)^n$$

In English, this formula is saying the present value equals the future value of the investment divided by 1 plus the interest rate raised to the number of periods we're investing for.

You don't like math? No need to fear. Excel has the present value formula, along with a host of other financial functions, built in. Figure 3.18 shows the Function Library group under the Formulas tab and Figure 3.19 shows a partial list of the financial functions available.

Now back to our PV formula. Choose PV (for present value) from the functions list. You'll see a pop-up appear like the one in Figure 3.20.

FIGURE 3.18   Financial functions in the function library

FIGURE 3.19   Financial functions list

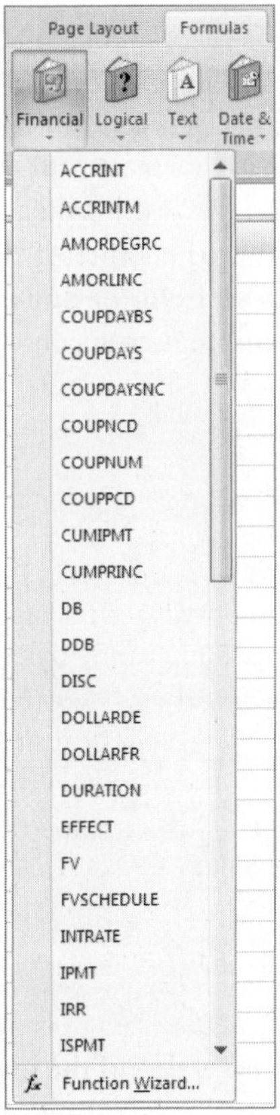

FIGURE 3.20 PV pop-up

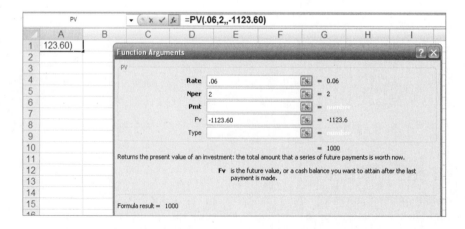

This pop-up box allows you to put in the various elements of the PV formula. First, you'll see that Excel asks for the interest rate per period. You can enter 6% or .06, assuming that interest is compounded annually. If the interest rate were compounded quarterly, you'd divide the interest rate by 4 and enter the result here. The next line is Nper, or number of periods. We're investing for two years. The payment amount is 0 because we're not making payments on this investment—we want to know what the value of this lump sum is in today's dollars. The next field is the FV, or future value, field. In our example, $-1123.60 is the future value of the investment. If you don't calculate future value as a negative number, your end result will be negative. Figure 3.21 shows the PV pop-up with our values entered into the correct fields.

FIGURE 3.21 PV formula

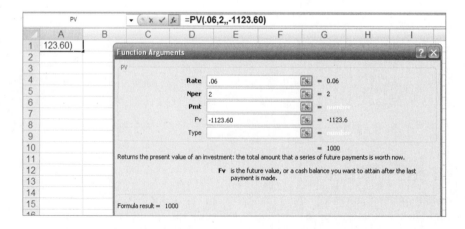

Each of the inputs in the pop-up box could be entered as a cell reference as well. For example, if we had .06 in cell C1, we could enter +C1 in the Rate field.

The pop-up box shows the result of our PV formula, which is 1,000 in this case. In the formula bar as well as cell A1, you can see the PV formula with the rate, number of periods, a second comma (which represents the payment field, 0 in our example), and the future value. As soon as you click the OK button, $1,000 (our result) will appear in cell A1.

If you don't want to go through the menus to get the PV function, you could type **=PV(** in cell A1. A tip box will come up that prompts you for the formula elements in the correct order. Figure 3.22 illustrates.

If you're uncertain what values you should plug into the formula, type **PV** in the Excel help box and choose the PV topic. Each value is explained with some detail.

If you're like us and get frustrated because the help box sometimes disappears behind your spreadsheet when you're trying to follow the step-by-step directions, copy and paste the help box information right into the spreadsheet temporarily and then delete it once you've entered the formula.

Now let's say your selection committee has three projects to choose from. Project A is expected to make $130,000 in two years, Project B is expected to make $140,000 in three years, and Project C is expected to make $148,000 in five years. Based on discounted cash flows alone and assuming the interest rate is 8 percent, which project should they choose? Project A has the highest return. Figure 3.23 shows the formulas and their results.

FIGURE 3.22   Present value formula

FIGURE 3.23   Project comparison with discounted cash flows

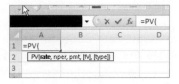

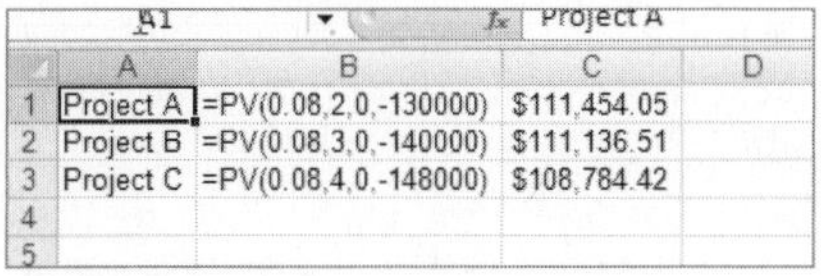

Net Present Value

Calculating net present value (NPV) is similar to the discounted cash flow technique in that you determine the future monies received in today's dollars. The difference is that with NPV, you'll apply the discounted cash flow technique to each period in which the inflows are expected rather than to one lump sum. The total present value of the cash flows is then deducted from the initial investment to determine NPV. The general rule of thumb is if NPV is greater than zero, accept the project. If it's less than zero, reject the project.

Project A has three years of expected inflows: year 1 is $150,000, year 2 is $195,000, and year 3 is $225,000. Our total initial investment is $550,000 and we'll assume an 8 percent interest rate. Using our formula, we'll calculate the present value of each year's expected inflows and subtract that total from the initial investment. Figure 3.24 shows the calculations and result.

FIGURE 3.24   Net present value calculation

	A	B	C	D	E	F	G
1	Net Present Value Calculation						
2							
3	Initial Investment =		$550,000				
4							
5	Project A	Inflows	Periods	Interest	PV	NPV Formula	NPV Result
6	Year 1	$150,000	1	0.08	$138,889	=$550,000-$484,682	$65,318
7	Year 2	$195,000	2	0.08	$167,181		
8	Year 3	$225,000	3	0.08	$178,612		
9							
10	Total PV				$484,682		
11							

Present value is calculated the same way it was calculated in the preceding section. The present value calculation in cell E11 is simply a sum of cells E7 through E9. The NPV formula is shown along with its result. (Alternatively, you can use the NPV formula built in to Excel.) And since our end result is positive, we should accept the project.

You can use this spreadsheet as a template for NPV calculations. Simply change the fields and add additional rows if needed by copying the formulas from the previous rows.

Internal Rate of Return

Internal rate of return (IRR) is the discount rate when the present value of the cash inflows equals the original investment. Without the use of a calculator or Excel, the calculation is a series of hit-or-miss guesses until you get the correct result. Figure 3.25 shows two projects and their resulting IRR. (IRR can be chosen from the financial functions listing as well.)

FIGURE 3.25 · IRR calculation

	A	B	C	D
1	IRR Calculation			
2				
3	Project A	Cash Flows	IRR Formula	IRR
4	Initial Investment	-550,000	=IRR(B4:B7)	2%
5	Year 1	150,000		
6	Year 2	195,000		
7	Year 3	225,000		
8				
9				
10	Project B			
11	Initial Investment	-500,000	=IRR(B11:B14)	6%
12	Year 1	150,000		
13	Year 2	195,000		
14	Year 3	225,000		
15				

There a few things to keep in mind when performing this calculation. First, the initial investment (cell B4, for example) should be a negative number. The expected cash inflows shown in cells B5 through B7 for Project A are shown as positive. However, you may have years where cash inflows are negative; if so, show them as negative. The IRR formula will not work without at least one positive and one negative number. And if you think about it, if all your cash inflows are negative, why would you consider doing the project anyway? Make certain your outflows and inflows are arranged in the order in which they'll occur because the IRR calculation will assume this order. In Project A, for example, Excel is calculating from cell B4 through cell B7.

When deciding among alternative projects, generally the project with the highest IRR value should be chosen. In this example, Project B is the best choice.

Now that we've discussed all the elements of the project request form and selection criteria, let's collect all that information in a database.

Creating a Project Request Tracking Log

The project request tracking log allows you to track the projects your department or organization is working on or has completed along with information you may want to know or research before beginning a new project. The tracking log is particularly useful for project managers who are responsible for overseeing multiple projects. It's also useful for the selection committee to help determine new project priorities or to reshuffle the priority of existing projects.

The tracking log should contain the following fields:

- Priority Number
- Tracking Number
- Date
- Project Title
- Sponsor
- Budget
- Disposition
- Comments
- Project Manager
- Project Status

Most of these are found on the project request form with the exception of the project manager and project status fields.

Alternatively, you could create a tracking database using the same fields. It makes sense to create a database when your list grows to more than a couple dozen projects. The beauty of a database is that you can query on almost any of these fields. If, for example, your management team wants to know how many project requests have been submitted by a certain sponsor or how many projects a particular project manager is managing, you can query on those fields and easily report on them.

We'll discuss creating databases in more detail in Chapter 6, "Assessing and Tracking Risk."

Identifying Stakeholders

We've mentioned stakeholders several times. If you aren't already familiar with the term, you've probably gathered by now that these are people that have an interest in your project. The definition of a stakeholder is anyone who has something to gain or lose from the project. As you can imagine, this can include a lengthy list of people, depending on the project.

Typically, stakeholders are people (or organizations) from inside and outside the organization, including functional managers, suppliers, project teams, contractors, and so on. You'll want to identify every group or person that is a stakeholder on the project before getting too deep into the planning processes. It's a good idea to understand the needs of each of your stakeholders and their goals and concerns for the project because you may successfully complete a project and meet its goals, but if the stakeholders aren't satisfied, well, nobody's happy.

 While you want to make certain to identify and include all stakeholders on your project, you should limit the day-to-day involvement or decision making issues to the key stakeholders on the project. Once you get more than 10 or 11 participants, things can get messy. The diagram showing the lines of communication in Chapter 1 (Figure 1.2) illustrates this point.

All projects should have at least two key stakeholders: the project sponsor and the project manager. We'll look at these and other key stakeholders in the following sections.

The Role of the Project Sponsor

The project sponsor is usually a manager or executive in the organization who has the authority to assign resources to the project. Resources in this case include both money and people. They may initiate the project or someone from within their department may initiate a project on their behalf.

The project sponsor should be easy to recognize. They are the driving force behind the project. Sponsors rally support from other managers and executives and convince them to support the project. They are actively engaged with the project issues and serve as a final decision maker. The project sponsor has the final say on whether the project has satisfactorily met the goal it set out to accomplish.

The project sponsor and the project manager share equal responsibility in ensuring a successful project outcome. It's the project manager's responsibility to get the project completed on time and within budget, but it's the sponsor's responsibility to remove the obstacles in the way of the project team and make timely decisions to help keep the schedule on track. The project manager and the project sponsor are partners in the truest sense of the word. Be aware: You may do everything right with regard to the project management principles on the project, but if the sponsor is not engaged, is not making timely decisions, and is not supporting the team or providing adequate resources, the project may not succeed. We believe an active, engaged sponsor is one of the critical elements of a successful project.

Keep your sponsor informed. As your partner in the project, they shouldn't be blindsided by problems or issues they haven't heard about from you first.

You sponsor is your best advocate. Go out of your way to forge a meaningful, professional relationship with your sponsor. Be forthcoming with all project issues and win the trust of the sponsor from the beginning. That way, when the project hiccups occur (and you can be certain they will), the sponsor will have enough experience with you to know that you're telling the truth, that you're giving them all the information you have, and that you have best intentions for the project at heart.

Key Stakeholders

Key stakeholders will likely vary from project to project unless you work in a small organization. Even then, your external customer (a key stakeholder, of course) will likely be different for each project. Typically, most projects have a few folks that are essential to the project:

- Project sponsor
- Project manager
- Project team
- Managers from other departments
- Accounting and or procurement personnel
- External customer
- Vendors and suppliers

These folks can be identified by asking a few questions. Who will the final product of the project be delivered to? Which department will assume ongoing responsibility for support of the project once it's completed? Which departments may be impacted? Will workflow processes change as a result of this project? If so, which departments are impacted by the change? Are contractors or suppliers involved? Are there any external dependencies (regulations, laws, best practices, and so on) the team should be aware of?

Questions like these will help you identify those stakeholders that likely have a significant role in the project. And each of these stakeholders will have different responsibilities, depending on the role they have. Again you'll want to understand their individual goals and concerns for the project. As you get further into the planning processes and begin to document the scope and requirements of the project, these stakeholder goals and issues should be taken into consideration. Forge relationships with these folks as well because you'll want as many stakeholders supporting the project as you can get.

Key stakeholders may come and go. For example, you may have a contractor or supplier that's critical to the project but perhaps they only have one deliverable. In this case, they aren't key throughout the duration of the project but sometime before and during the timeframe in which their deliverable is expected.

As the project manager, you are also a key stakeholder. Your number one responsibility for the project is communication. You must keep the sponsor and the stakeholders informed of project progress and issues. You'll also use those negotiating and conflict resolution skills we talked about in Chapter 1. But you can't communicate if you don't know who your stakeholders are. As with most project information, you should document stakeholders and their needs. We'll look at that next.

Documenting Key Stakeholders

Identifying and documenting key stakeholders is one of your first roles as a project manager. Later in the project we'll also be identifying project team members and capturing the same type of information as we're documenting for the stakeholders. Figure 3.26 shows a sample portion of a contact file.

FIGURE 3.26   Contact list

A1	▼	*f* Title							
A	B	D	F	G	H	I	J	L	M
Title	FirstName	LastName	Company	Department	JobTitle	BusinessStreet	BusinessStreet2	BusinessCity	BusinessState

You aren't able to see all of the columns in the figure because of the size of this spreadsheet. We used the Outlook Contacts schema for the column names you see in Figure 3.26, so make certain to enter your column names as shown. For example, there's no space between *First* and *Name*. Better yet, download this from the book's download page and fill it in. You'll notice we've kept the entire schema intact and have simply hidden the columns that we don't want to use in this particular list. Highlight all the column headers and then right-click and choose Unhide to see all the columns.

> This workbook probably looks a lot like contact information to you. It is—and there's no need to have to re-enter everything in Outlook Contacts. We'll show you how to create this spreadsheet in Outlook Contacts format in Chapter 5, "Planning and Acquiring Resources," so that you can import the pertinent fields into Outlook.

When capturing stakeholder information, be certain to fill in at least the following fields:

- Title
- FirstName
- LastName
- Company
- Department
- BusinessPhone
- EmailAddress
- Categories

In the Categories column, use the word *Stakeholder*. Later when we add team members, we'll use *Team Members* here. You can quickly sort by the stakeholders category if needed. First—and very important—select all the data in your spreadsheet. Press Ctrl+A to do this quickly (Excel knows to exclude the first row because it includes column headers). Then select the Sort option from the Data menu. You'll be asked what you want to sort by. Select Categories (which should be column BC) and then by your next most important criteria. That might be last name or company. You might also want to include address information in the list if your stakeholders are not all located in your building or if you have stakeholders external to the organization.

You may want to create a contact database instead of a list. That way, you could include fields to capture information like roles and responsibilities on the project, special needs and concerns, and so on. The choice is yours.

Defining Project Goals and Creating the Project Charter

The first official document you'll produce for the project will likely be the project charter. The project charter formally authorizes the project to begin. It describes the goal of the project and provides a high-level overview of the product or service that will be produced as a result. Some of the elements already outlined in the project request form should be further developed and included in the project charter.

Before we describe the elements of a project charter and go about creating a form, let's first look at a few goal setting principles.

Principles of Goal Setting

When you look up the definition of *goal* at `www.dictionary.com`, you'll see several references to sports, such as the finish line, the area where you hope to place a ball or puck, a score, and so on. If you think about goals in this perspective, you can see that there's a definite end result. For example, the small, round, white ball makes it into the not-much-bigger hole in the ground hopefully a few points under par. You know the goal's been reached because it's easily measured. In order to meet that goal, you probably devised a plan of action and used a particular club and a certain stance, for example, all of which is also determinable.

Project goals are similar. They define how you know when you cross the finish line. The goal should clearly state what it is the project hopes to accomplish and how you'll know you've accomplished it. There are probably hundreds of books that discuss goals and goal setting. Most of them agree on a few basic principles. The following information is included in effective goal statements:

- Clear descriptions of the desired outcome
- Realistic and attainable outcomes
- Measurable criteria to assess if the goal was accomplished
- A time frame or time limit by which the goal will be reached

Goals aren't much more than wishes if you don't write them down. When they're written, stakeholders are less likely to try to change the goal months into the project. It's funny how memories change over time. Writing down the goal keeps everyone focused and helps prevent fuzzy memories. You'll record the goal in the project charter document. We'll look at all the elements of a project charter next.

Project Charter Elements

Project charters authorize the project to begin. As we stated earlier, they describe the project and some of the reasons for undertaking it. The charter should give us enough information to begin the planning processes.

Figure 3.27 shows a typical project charter template. We'll take a look at each of the elements of the charter in detail. You can also make this an online form by following the steps outlined in the section "Publishing the Project Request Form" earlier in this chapter.

We're going to kick off a project now that we'll follow throughout the remainder of the book. The following list includes a description of the type of information each field should contain and then the information specific to the project. Our project is called the Grant St. Move project and involves moving 1,500 people from disparate locations to a new location in downtown Denver, Colorado.

FIGURE 3.27   Project charter form

	A	B
1		**Project Charter**
2	Project Number	
3	Date	
4	Project Title	
5	Project Goal	
6	Business Justification	
7	Project or Product Description	
8	Deliverables or High-Level Requirements	
9	Budget	
10	Schedule Milestones	
11	Project Manager	
12	Other Departments	

Project goal   The project goal should be one to a few sentences that describe the overall goal of the project. It should include a time frame, should be specific and realistic, and should be measurable.

The overall goal of the Grant St. Move project is to have all employees moved by October 6 with no loss of productivity and no downtime. There will be no phone, electric, or network outages. All cubicles, conference rooms, and office space will be set up and available for immediate occupancy upon arrival. Employees will move in phases based on their location.

Keep in mind that *measurable* doesn't necessarily mean a quantifiable number. In the case of our project, the measure is all employees are moved by the final date without interruption to their work. Also note we will be examining the Grant St. Move project primarily from an information technology (IT) perspective.

Business need or justification   We talked about the business justification earlier in this chapter. This section of the project charter contains the reasons for undertaking the project and what the organization stands to gain from it.

The business justification for the Grant St. Move project is primarily twofold. The first benefit is that all employees will be located in the same building. This will eliminate trips across town and lost productivity. The feasibility study conducted for this project showed a savings of $325,000 a year in productivity because drive time for meetings at different locations will be eliminated.

The second benefit is savings on lease, utility, and building maintenance fees. Currently the organization leases three buildings. Consolidating everyone into one building results in savings estimated at $1.5 million over the next three years.

Project description (or product description)   This section describes the project itself, or what it is you hope to produce at the end of the project. If the end result of your project is a product of some sort, describe the product here in as much detail as you know at this point.

The Grant St. Move project involves moving 1,500 employees from three different locations. The Main St. location has 750 employees. This location includes the most employees. The Elk St. location holds 500 employees and the Park St. location has 250. Park St. employees will move first followed by Elk St. and then Main St. All moves will occur on a weekend to minimize downtime.

High-level deliverables or requirements   Deliverables are measurable outcomes or results that must be produced to consider the project complete. They should be specific and verifiable. If our project involved setting up a conference for our customers, the deliverables might include securing a location for the conference, renting audio visual equipment, booking conference speakers, and determining food choices.

Requirements are characteristics of the deliverables. For example, a requirement of the secure location deliverable might be that the location is close to the airport or has a certain number of rooms available to accommodate the anticipated number of attendees. We'll talk more about requirements in Chapter 4.

The Grant St. Move project might include the following deliverables:

- Document organizational needs
- Document IT needs
- Prepare the Grant St. facility
- Prepare each location for move

Budget   The budget information can come from the project request form. Or perhaps by this point in the project the budget has been officially set and approved. Record the budget and any approval information here.

The approximate budget for the Grant St. Move project is $3.5 million, including the physical move, IT data center setup and new purchases, IT professional services, office build-outs, cubicle purchases and construction, office furniture purchases, and professional services.

Schedule milestones   Schedule milestones may include initial due dates for the deliverables listed earlier. These dates will be further defined during the planning processes.

The Grant St. Move milestone dates are as follows:

- Document organizational needs by May 1
- Document IT needs by May 1
- Prepare the Grant St. facility by Sep 30
- Prepare each location for the move not known at this time

Project manager   The project manager is named in the project charter. It's a good idea to also include the level of authority the project manager has, including elements like decision levels and hiring and firing capability. For example, the project manager may have the authority to approve all budget changes with less than a five percent impact to the overall budget. All budget decisions above this threshold require a change request and approval by stakeholders.

The project manager for the Grant St. Move project is Kim Heldman.

Involvement of other departments   Note any involvement needed from other departments in this section. If you know the types or level of involvement needed, detail that here as well. For example, perhaps your information technology department is needed at one point in the project to burn in a new server and install software. Outline their involvement here.

The Grant St. Move project will require involvement from the IT department, the procurement department, and the customer service department. IT is responsible for moving all IT equipment, preparing the new location (for example, pulling cable), and installing all IT equipment at the new location.

Once the charter is complete, you'll want to publish it in draft form for a period of time and allow the stakeholders to read it and comment on it. Follow the steps in the section titled "Publishing the Project Request Form" and allow your stakeholders to view it. Once you've reviewed the comments and made any reasonable changes needed, the next step is getting formal approval for the charter and signoff. We'll look at that next.

Obtaining Approval

After publishing the final version of the project charter you'll want the project sponsor and key stakeholders to approve it. This signifies they agree with the purpose of the project and hopefully ensures their commitment to it. We'll walk through the steps for creating an approval process with MOSS in Chapter 4, "Determining Project Requirements."

The approved charter should then be posted on the SharePoint site designated for the project. Train your users at the beginning of the project to set themselves up for automatic alerts when new documents are posted. That way, you don't have to bother with broadcast emails to let everyone know documents have been published.

Keep in mind that not all stakeholders will set up automatic alerts. For important documents such as the project charter, it might not hurt to also send an email to let stakeholders know they should go out to the MOSS site and read the project charter.

In the next chapter, we'll look at defining the deliverables and requirements for our building move project. These, along with the overall project goal, will serve as our foundation for defining project success.

Chapter
4

Determining Project Requirements

Now that we're armed with our approved project charter and have created our document repository, we're ready to dig further and uncover the deliverables and requirements of the project. That means we've successfully completed the Initiating processes and are beginning the Planning processes.

In this chapter, we'll examine the project scope statement and what elements should be included in this important document. We'll look at some popular techniques for fleshing out the requirements of the project and documenting them. We'll also take a look at the components of a solid communication plan. All of these documents will be created in Excel and posted to the project site on SharePoint. Last but not least, we'll also create some reporting templates to capture project progress. We'll look at both status reports for individual team members and status reporting for stakeholders. We'll use the Grant St. Move project to help us with these tasks, so let's get started.

Creating the Project Scope Statement

The project scope statement is the first document we'll create in the Planning process. Figure 4.1 shows the Planning portion of the project process overview we talked about in Chapter 3.

FIGURE 4.1   Planning tasks

Project Proce
Planning
Project Scope Statement
Communications Plan
Status Reports
Action Item Database
Issue Log
Team Roles and Responsibilities
Procurement Plan
Vendor List
Risk Identification Form
Risk Register
Risk Response Plans
Quality Management Plan
Activity List
Work Breakdown Structure
Activity Estimator
Project Schedule
Project Budget
Change Control Request Form
Change Control Database

We'll talk about the project scope statement, communication plan, status report, action item database, and issue log in this chapter.

The purpose of the project scope statement is to document the goals and deliverables of the project along with constraints, assumptions, acceptance criteria, and other key elements. Once approved, the project scope statement becomes the baseline for future project decisions. We said in Chapter 3 that project goals are the "what" it is the project is trying to accomplish. The project scope statement more completely answers the question, What are we trying to accomplish? It's here the project goal is further broken down into deliverable components and then more detailed planning can take place.

The scope statement is the foundation for the remaining planning documents and becomes your road map for success. It establishes the common understanding among stakeholders and team members as to the purpose of the project. It details the criteria you and the stakeholders will use to determine if the project met its goal and was successful. It's important to spend the time to discover and document all the deliverables of the project. The deliverables will help you later in the Planning process to determine resource estimates, time estimates, cost estimates, and activities and to develop a project schedule.

> The project scope statement, schedule, and budget are three of the most important documents you'll create for the project. Make certain to spend the time to make these documents as sound and accurate as you can. We'll look at schedules and budgets in Chapter 8, "Constructing the Project Schedule and Budget."

Once project scope is determined and agreed upon, you'll want all the key stakeholders to sign off indicating their approval. That way, as changes come about, and they inevitably will, the approved scope statement can be used as the baseline for making change decisions. And of course, you don't want stakeholders making changes at their whim as the project progresses or else the scope will quickly spiral out of control, defeating all the hard work you went through to create the scope document in the first place. Once the scope document is approved, no changes should be allowed without going through the change control process. We'll discuss proper change control procedures in Chapter 9, "Establishing Change Control Processes."

The scope statement also becomes a way to manage stakeholder expectations throughout the project. Since it clearly defines what the project will accomplish and what it won't, there's less chance for the stakeholders to say, "That's not what I wanted," when the final deliverables are produced. That isn't to say that won't happen, but you can help keep your stakeholders and team members grounded on the goal and deliverables of the project by referring to the scope statement throughout the project. This isn't as hard as you think because as we progress with building the project planning documents, we'll refer back to the scope statement (and the requirements document), which is another opportunity to remind everyone what you're trying to accomplish.

> A statement of work (SOW) can also serve as a project scope statement. An SOW is often used when contracting with vendors to perform project work. A SOW typically contains the same type of information as a project scope statement.

We'll look at the elements of a solid project scope statement next.

Essential Elements of the Project Scope Statement

The essential elements of any project scope statement are the project goals, deliverables, assumptions, and constraints. (These are the same elements for a SOW). The scope statement isn't limited to these elements, however. The following list shows the primary components of a well-documented scope statement, including those elements already mentioned:

- Project goal
- Project description
- Comprehensive list of deliverables
- Acceptance criteria
- List of exclusions from scope
- High-level time and cost estimates
- Schedule milestones
- Assumptions
- Constraints
- Critical success factors

Figure 4.2 shows a project scope statement template with these elements. You'll also want to record the project number and name and the project manager's name.

The complexity and size of the project will determine how much information you may include in the scope statement. For small projects, it's possible to include other elements, which we'll discuss in later chapters. For example, you can include roles and responsibilities, detailed schedule and cost estimates, organizational charts, stakeholder needs, and the communication plan, which we'll cover in the last section of this chapter.

The project goal and project description can be taken from the project charter. The idea here is to give the reader a high-level refresher on what the project is about. As you'll recall from Chapter 3, our Grant St. Move project concerns moving employees from disparate locations to the Grant St. building by October 6 with minimum disruptions to work. We'll take a look at deliverables in the next section and then examine the remaining elements of the scope statement following a discussion on creating a requirements document in Excel.

Determining Deliverables and Acceptance Criteria

The first step in documenting our project scope is determining the deliverables needed to make up the end product or service of the project. Before we document some of the deliverables for our Grant St. Move project, let's look at how we go about identifying what the deliverables are. We have two favorite methods, brainstorming and sticky-backed notes. Let's look at each.

FIGURE 4.2   Project scope statement

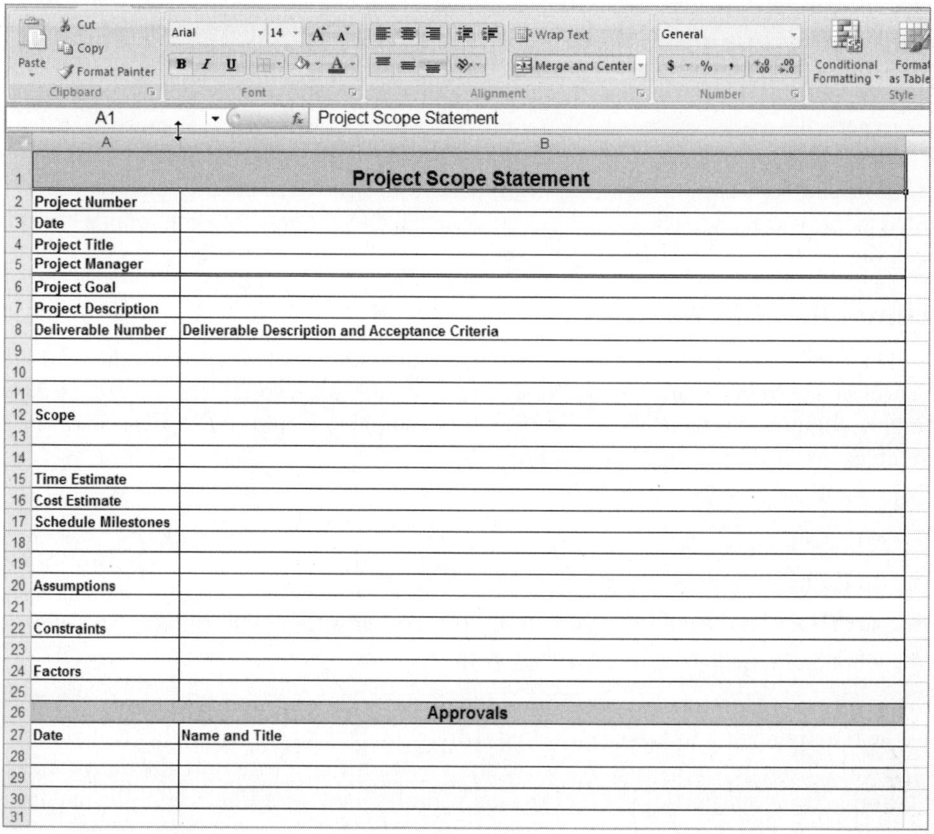

Brainstorming

Brainstorming sessions are facilitated by the project manager. The idea here is to allow the free-flow exchange of ideas with no judgments on whether an idea is good or bad. Get all of your key stakeholders in a room and have an assistant attend the meeting to take notes and record the list of deliverables as ideas are flowing. Have your assistant open up an Excel spreadsheet and use a projector to display the spreadsheet onto a whiteboard so the meeting attendees can see what's being recorded as you go. At this point, only two or three columns are needed. Column A should have a sequential set of numbers that will serve as identifiers for the deliverables and Column B will hold the deliverables. If the deliverables aren't self-explanatory, you could enter a few words of explanation in Column C. Remember, no idea is a bad idea.

Sticky-backed Notes

Another favorite method for generating ideas is the sticky-backed note method. Come to the meeting with a stack of sticky-backed notes and a pen or marker for each participant. Ask each participant this question: If you could have only one deliverable at the end of this project, what would it be? Obviously, a project with only one deliverable probably isn't realistic. But the idea is to get your participants to think about the absolute most important, must-have deliverable out of this project. Collect the notes and stick them to a whiteboard or have an assistant record them in Excel. Eliminate the duplicates and read them all to the group so they aren't repeated in the next round. Then ask the question again and continue holding rounds like this until all the deliverables have been discovered.

Documenting Deliverables

Deliverables are products, services, or results that must be completed in order to fulfill the goals of the project. Deliverables, like goals, should be measurable and verifiable. When all the deliverables are completed satisfactorily, the project is complete. Here is a list of a few of the deliverables for the Grant St. Move project:

- Perform physical move
- Prepare building security
- Set up Grant St. IT data center
- Prepare Grant St. offices and conference rooms for network connections
- Install phone system (Voice over IP, or VoIP)

This is a partial list of deliverables, but already our minds are jumping ahead thinking about the requirements and tasks associated with them. Don't get too far ahead of yourself and allow that to happen just yet. At this stage, we want to capture only the deliverables. You'll notice from our partial list that the deliverables look a lot like accomplishments. You can imagine that there are a lot of individual tasks that make up each of these deliverables. And as you're documenting the deliverables, you may find your team moving into the requirements realm. For example, someone may say, "We need to install and test the card-reader system for building security and make sure each employee has a card before they report to work. The card-reader system needs power and cable runs." There are two ways to look at this. Installing the card-reader system could be a deliverable of its own. Or in this case, the Prepare Building Security deliverable may have subdeliverables under this heading, one of which is Install the Card Reader System. A requirement of the installation is that power and cable is run to each of the readers. If you're working on a large project with deliverables and subdeliverables, we recommend working on the first level of deliverables first. Capture ideas as they come up regarding subdeliverables and requirements, but keep the team focused on the primary deliverables. Then working with one deliverable at a time, break these down into subdeliverables and eventually requirements. (We'll look at requirements in the next section).

There may already be several resources available to you to help with deliverables and requirements definitions. First, check with your project management office if your organization has one. Then check industry standards. For example, if you work in the information technology field, you might refer to the *Guide to the Software Engineering Body of Knowledge* for IEEE software standards recommendations.

Acceptance Criteria

Acceptance criteria defines how you know the deliverable has been completed satisfactorily. If you've documented deliverables that are measurable or verifiable, acceptance criteria should be relatively easy to define. For example, the Prepare Building Security deliverable acceptance criteria might be something like this: Card-reader systems will be installed, tested, and functioning at least three days prior to the Park St. employees move date. All alarm systems will be tested and functioning at least two weeks prior to the Park St. employees move date.

The final project should also have defined acceptance criteria. If your project goals are well defined, they can be used to formulate the acceptance criteria. The Grant St. Move project's acceptance criteria might read something like this: All employees were relocated to the Grant St. building by Oct 6. All employees were able to report to work the day after their move date and have immediate network and phone access. No more than one hour of downtime was experienced by any employee due to office preparation and network connectivity problems.

Documenting Requirements

If you're checking up on us, you noticed that requirements weren't on the list of elements included in the scope statement. Requirements may or may not be included in the scope statement depending on the complexity of the project. Typically, requirements, even for a small project, turn into a lengthy list. Most project managers record requirements in a separate document, but there's no rule that says you can't create a section within the scope statement to contain them.

Requirements describe the characteristics of the deliverable. If we're designing a rubber ball, for example, a requirement might be that the ball is red, the ball will bounce a minimum of 3 feet when bounced from a hard surface, and so on. Requirements usually contain a "must have" or "must be" statement. For example, the Set Up the Grant St. Data Center deliverable mentioned earlier may have requirements like the following:

- Data center location must be on the second floor for flood prevention.
- Data center must have both production and test areas.

- Data center backbone wiring must be fiber optic.
- Router and switchgear must be kept separate (in the data center) from servers.
- Switchgear must be installed in intermediate data facility closets on every floor.

You can use the brainstorming and sticky-backed note methods to determine the requirements as well. When documenting requirements, make certain to number each one for easy identification and tracking, and keep the requirements associated with their deliverable. Figure 4.3 shows a sample portion of the requirements for the Office Network Connections deliverable of the Grant St. Move project.

FIGURE 4.3 Requirements document

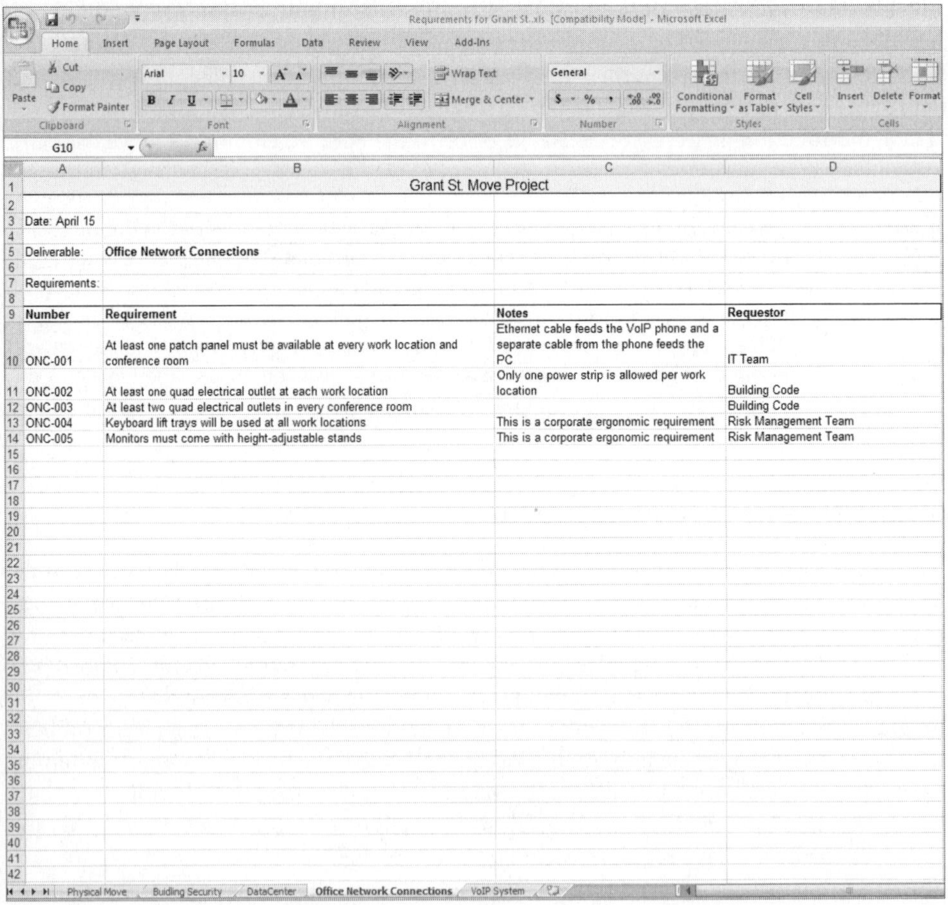
Grant St. Move Project

Date: April 15

Deliverable: **Office Network Connections**

Requirements:

Number	Requirement	Notes	Requestor
ONC-001	At least one patch panel must be available at every work location and conference room	Ethernet cable feeds the VoIP phone and a separate cable from the phone feeds the PC	IT Team
ONC-002	At least one quad electrical outlet at each work location	Only one power strip is allowed per work location	Building Code
ONC-003	At least two quad electrical outlets in every conference room		Building Code
ONC-004	Keyboard lift trays will be used at all work locations	This is a corporate ergonomic requirement	Risk Management Team
ONC-005	Monitors must come with height-adjustable stands	This is a corporate ergonomic requirement	Risk Management Team

Requirements should be as clear and precise as possible. Incomplete or unclear requirements lead to confusion once the work of the project begins. Confusion leads to change orders, lots of change orders, and the next thing you know you have a project with the dreaded scope creep disease. Scope creep occurs usually under two conditions: the first is poor scope and requirements definition, and the second is uncontrolled change. Make certain you capture all the requirements and they're documented as clearly as possible. As we mentioned earlier, we'll deal with change in a later chapter.

Creating the Requirements Table

You can create an Excel workbook that contains both the deliverables and requirements. If your project does not have too many deliverables, consider creating a sheet for each deliverable. At the bottom of Figure 4.3, you can see we have five tabs with the names of the deliverables we listed earlier. To create a new tab, right-click on any of the existing tabs, choose Insert, and then choose Worksheet. To rename a tab, right-click and choose Rename. You can drag the tabs into any order you'd like. Excel has no limit on the number of sheets you can create, other than your system's memory.

Following the deliverable name in Figure 4.3 are columns for the requirement number, the requirement description, notes, and the requestor. The requestor is important to capture because once you get into the work of the project, if questions come up or changes are needed for a particular requirement, you may need to clarify with the original requestor. Also, make certain your numbers are unique. Don't assign 001 as the first requirement number for both the Office Network Connections and VoIP System deliverables. Later when you're in team meetings and discussing specific deliverables, you won't know if 001 means the Office Network Connections deliverable or not. We've used the first letter of each word in the name of the deliverable to number our requirements. You could alternatively number each deliverable and use that number as the prefix for the requirement number. For example, Office Computing Needs might be deliverable number 003. The first requirement in this deliverable could be numbered 003-001, the next 003-002, and so on.

When you've typed in a few requirement numbers (such as ONC-001, ONC-002, and ONC-003 as shown in Figure 4.3 cells A10 through A12), Excel makes it easy for you to replicate them quickly so you can avoid all the typing. First, highlight cells A10 through A12. You'll notice that the range is outlined with heavy dark lines and there is a very small square box in the bottom-right corner of the last cell. Hover over that square until your mouse pointer turns into a black plus sign. Click and drag downward in column A. Excel will automatically fill in the series as you drag.

Now we're going to take this same spreadsheet and turn it into a table. Table formatting in Excel 2007 is even easier than before and provides you with a quick way to create professional-looking output. (Note that Tables as described later replaces the Excel 2003 List menu item.) Notice in Figure 4.3 that we've created a title row labeled Grant St. Move Project (row 1). Several rows below this (row 9), there is a header row that contains the names of the columns: Number, Requirement, and so on. It's important to differentiate between a title row and a header row. A title row is simply the title of what the worksheet contains. A header row contains a title for each column that will be a part of the table. In this case, row 9 is the header row for our table.

Formatting the table for a more professional look is easy. Start by highlighting the header row and all data rows beneath, as shown in Figure 4.4. If you're not done creating requirements, you can also highlight blank rows, adding the formatting to them before they contain data.

Next, with the Home tab highlighted, choose Format as Table from the Styles group. You'll see a variety of table formatting choices, as shown in Figure 4.5.

Select a formatting style—we chose Table Format Medium 12. You'll be presented with a display that shows the row area you selected for applying the new table format, as shown in Figure 4.6.

In this example, the table area begins at A9 and extends to D20. Note that the My Table Has Headers check box is checked. That tells Excel that the first row of the selection (in this case, row 9) is the header row. One of the reasons this is important is that when you're performing a sort on the data, you want the header titles isolated and don't want them sorted into the data. In other words, the word *Requirement* from cell B9 stays in cell B9 rather than getting sorted with all the requirements.

FIGURE 4.4   Highlighted rows

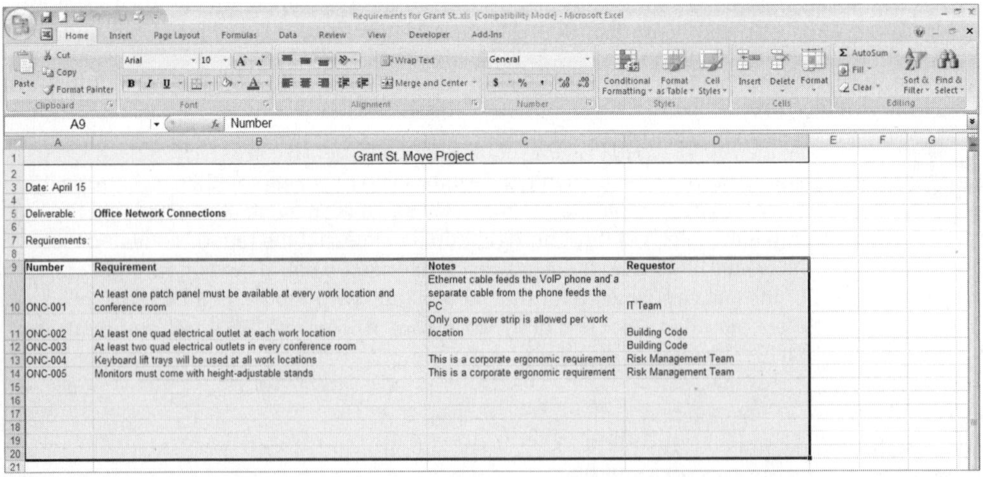

FIGURE 4.5   Formatting options

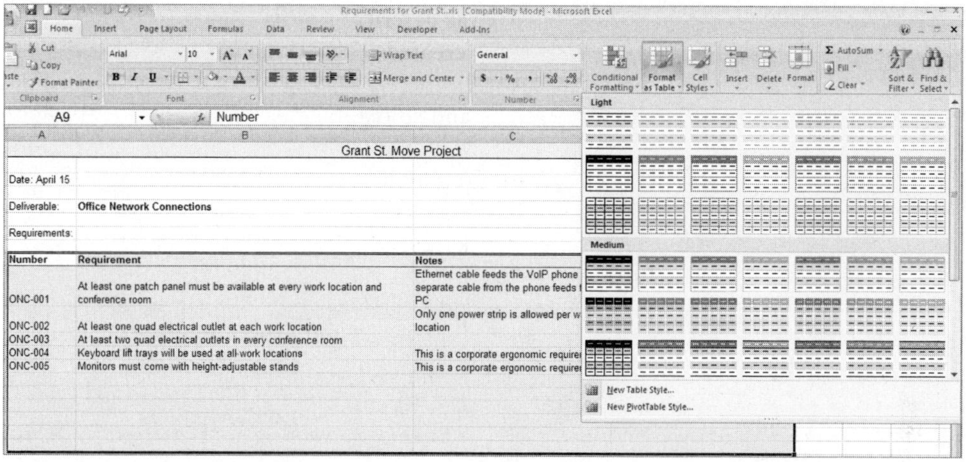

FIGURE 4.6   Formatting area

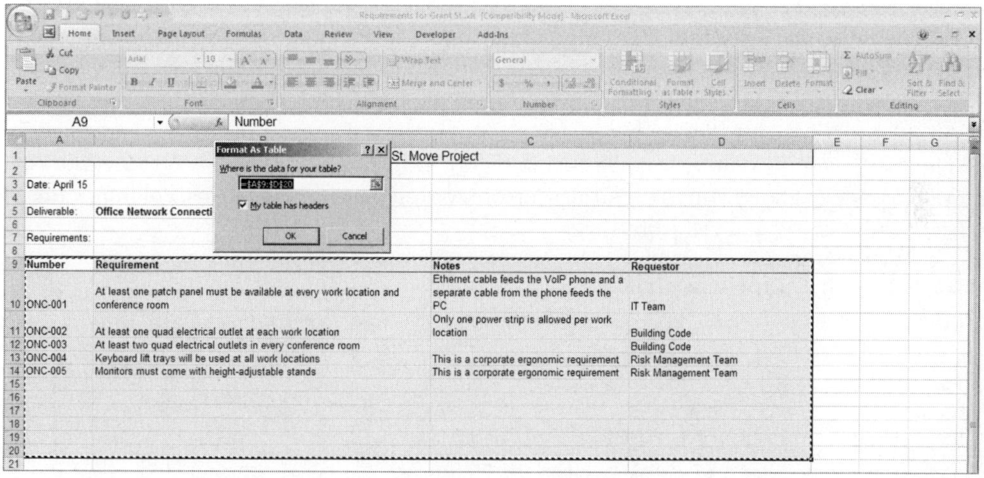

Clicking OK creates the table format shown in Figure 4.7.

Notice in Figure 4.7 that the formatted row numbers are marked by a different color than the rest of the rows. There is a new menu tab floating over the ribbon called Design and the table format we selected is the primary focus of the ribbon. You have the option of choosing another style before moving on from here.

FIGURE 4.7 Formatted table

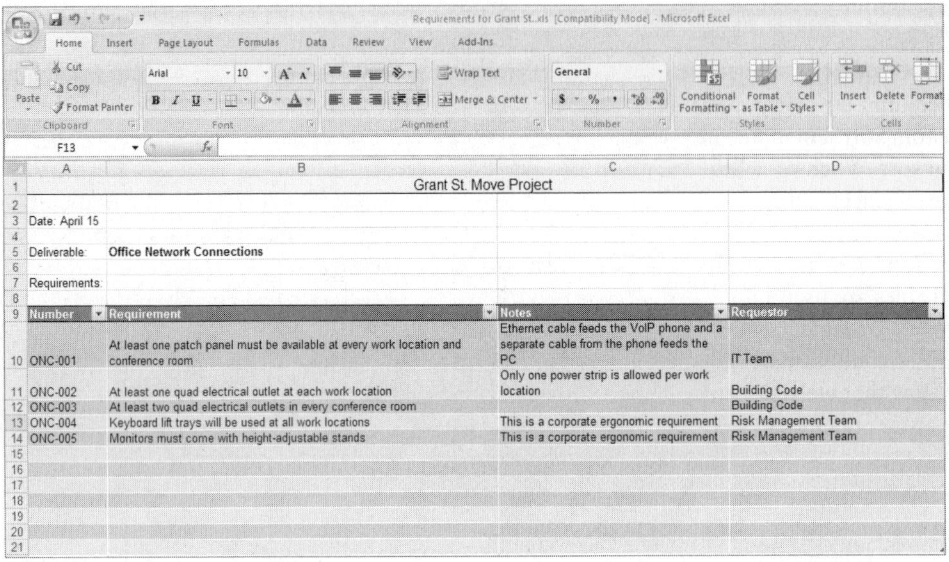

In Figure 4.8, you'll see that a drop-down button has been added next to each column header. Clicking this button brings up various sorting and filtering options.

Sorting allows you to display *all* of the records in the table. Filtering allows you to exclude specific records so you can concentrate on records of interest. For example, if you want to sort the Number column (column A as selected in Figure 4.8), you can sort from A to Z, Z to A, or by color, which allows you to perform a custom sort on the following fields: column, value, cell color, font color, and cell icon.

FIGURE 4.8 Drop-down buttons

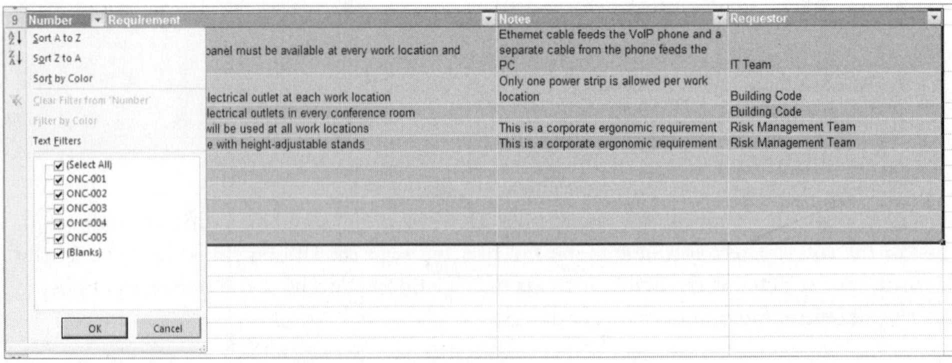

Filtering allows you to exclude rows if you choose. If you want to exclude all blank rows, uncheck the (Blanks) check box. (Blanks) by default is always checked, and if blank rows are included in the filter criteria, they will sort to the bottom when an A to Z sort is chosen and they'll sort to the top when Z to A is chosen.

If you want to sort on two columns—for example, Number (in column A) and Requestor (in column D)—click the drop-down button in column A and choose Sort by Color and then Custom Sort. Fill in the drop-down boxes presented in the sort dialog box with the criteria for your sort. When you click the Sort By drop-down button in the Column column, all of the field name headers will appear in a list. Choose Number (see Figure 4.9). Then click the Add button on the toolbar to add the Requestor header into the sort. You may also choose criteria for further sorting in the Sort On and Order columns (see Figure 4.10).

Tables are useful in any situation in which you want the ability to quickly sort data, and Excel 2007 makes it very easy to create them. Several of the templates we'll talk about in this chapter could also be created using the table format.

Now that we've recorded our requirements, we'll take a look at the remaining elements of the scope statement.

FIGURE 4.9   Custom sort

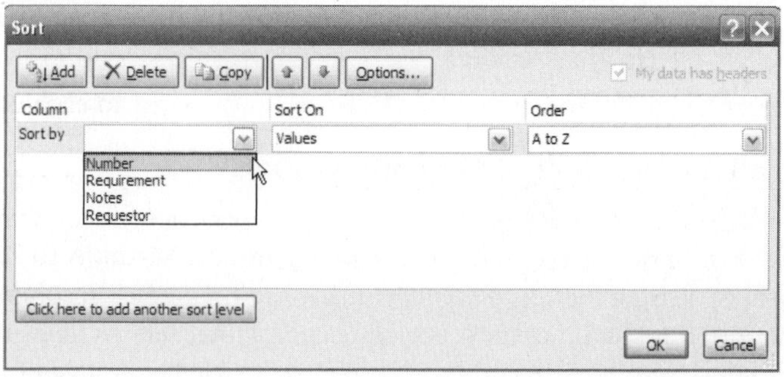

FIGURE 4.10   Custom sort add

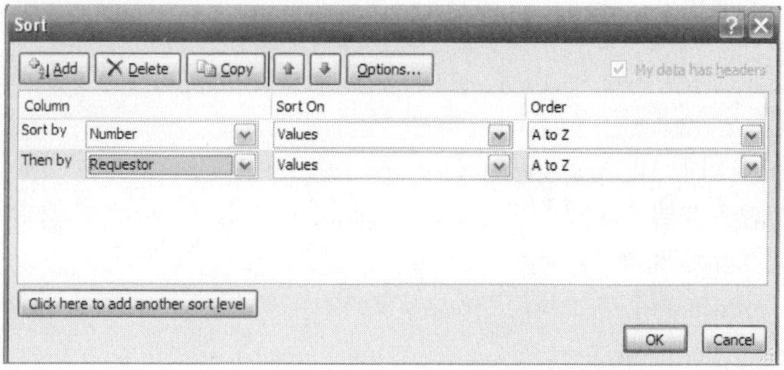

Remaining Scope Statement Elements

The scope statement describes the work of the project in the form of goals and deliverables. It may sound odd, but the scope statement should also state what's not going to be accomplished on the project. The exclusions from scope section in the scope statement is where you'll document this information. For example, the Grant St. Move project may have exclusions from scope such as leasing activities and vacated building cleanup. Since our project concerns only the physical move and facilities preparation, these activities must occur outside of it.

The reason you want to document exclusions is to avoid confusion and misunderstanding. Imagine if the Park St. director came looking for you to make changes to the cleanup schedule for the old building. If you've documented and communicated this exclusion from scope ahead of time, it will be easier to remind this stakeholder that the cleanup activity belongs to another project. Exclusions from scope are especially important when you're working on a project that has multiple phases. Each phase in the project may have its own scope statement or addendum to the overall project scope statement. For example, suppose you're installing a new system. The first phase of the project includes installing basic functionality only. Once the system has been tested and running in production for three months without major problems, another set of more complex functionality will be installed. If you neglect to exclude the complex functionality from the scope of the first phase of this project, stakeholders may assume they're getting everything at the end of the first phase. Likewise, if you have multiple projects that are dependent on each other, make certain to exclude the scope of the subsequent (or preceding) projects in the current scope statement.

High-Level Estimates and Schedule Milestones

We talked about high-level estimates in the project charter document in Chapter 3. The same idea holds here. You may or may not have more information about time estimates and cost estimates at the time you're writing the scope statement. If you don't, copy the information from the project charter into this section of the scope statement. However, it's likely that after you've taken the time to flesh out the deliverables, you'll have a little better idea of time and cost estimates.

Schedule milestones are probably more apparent at this point in the project as well. Again, you've taken the time to discover the deliverables and perhaps the requirements of the project and may have a better idea of the milestone dates. Milestone dates for the Grant St. Move project are as follows:

- Perform physical move for Park St. on Sept 14–15, Elk St. on Sept 21–22, and Main St. on Sept 29–30

- Prepare building security. Alarm system tested and functioning by Sept 1; card readers installed and functioning by Sept 13

- Set up Grant St. IT data center by Sept 7

- Prepare Grant St. offices and conference rooms for network connections by Sept 14

- Install phone system (VoIP) by Sept 12

Documenting Assumptions and Constraints

The next two sections of the scope statement deal with assumptions and constraints. Assumptions are anything believed to be true. Constraints are anything that dictate or restrict the actions of the project team. Both assumptions and constraints should be documented. Don't take anything for granted when writing the scope statement. If you find yourself saying, "Everyone knows *that*," you've just stated an assumption. Everyone might know it, but chances are everyone doesn't. And the one person that doesn't is the one who'll cause you grief later on in the project.

 Don't assume stakeholders know the assumptions. Write them down.

Leasing activities are excluded from the scope of the Grant St. Move project. But if the leasing activity isn't completed or isn't completed on time, it will delay our move. Therefore, one of our assumptions is that the lease activity will be completed on time.

Project constraints usually involve scope, budgets, and dates. In fact, these are called the triple constraints, and most projects are subject to them. Scope is usually the constraint that succumbs to the axe because most projects have limited budgets and limited time frames. So in order to perform the project within the time frame and dollar amount allotted, something has to give and that something is usually scope.

Oct 6 is a constraint on the Grant St. Move project, as is the project budget of $3.5 million.

Make certain to identify all of the assumptions and constraints regarding the project. We'll reference these later during risk planning for the project.

Identifying Critical Success Factors

Critical success factors are those elements of the project that positively must be completed (and completed accurately) for the project to be considered a success. We typically think of critical success factors as key deliverables. In the Grant St. Move project, we couldn't consider the project a success if the network was not functioning prior to the Park St. employees move. Therefore, the Set Up the Grant St. Data Center deliverable is a critical success factor.

Deliverables are usually the first thing to spring to mind when talking about critical success factors, but they can also be requirements, actions, management decisions, and so on. For example, another critical success factor we always identify for every project is an active, engaged project sponsor.

Discuss critical success factors with your team and stakeholders. Ask them what one or two deliverables or actions must be completed in order for them to consider the project a success. Again, we'll come back and look at these when we get to risk planning. If setting up the data center is a critical success factor, it's likely we'll need to identify the risks associated with completing this deliverable and devise a plan in case things go wrong.

Obtaining Buy-in and Approval

The project scope statement is another document you want the project sponsor and key stakeholders to review and approve. This is your road map for the remainder of the project. Future project decisions will be weighed against the information outlined here. It's also a way to keep expectations and sanity levels in check. If anyone has objections to the project scope and what should or should not be included, now's the time to voice them. Once you have approval, you'll want to publish the document to SharePoint. And it wouldn't hurt to occasionally review the scope statement in status meetings once the work of the project starts. That way, you can help avoid the "Oh I thought it *was* going to have that feature" remark.

> **NOTE**
> Once you've published the scope statement, be ready to answer the ever-present questions on the lips of sponsors everywhere: "Can we do it for less cost than that?" followed by "Can we do it faster?" *Cheaper—faster* is the mantra of executives everywhere. They're taught to say this on their first day of grad school and aren't awarded their master's degree until they can say it without consciously thinking about it. Remember that cheaper and faster means fewer features (scope). Be prepared for these questions with alternatives. For example, consider moving some deliverables to phase two of the project or cutting some of the requirements where possible.

See Exercise 4.1 below for a sample of creating a form using InfoPath to create a Status Report form.

EXERCISE 4.1

Using InfoPath to Create a Form

InfoPath is an electronic forms creation tool. If you've worked with Microsoft Access to create data entry forms, you'll be somewhat comfortable with InfoPath. However, when working with InfoPath forms, be aware that you're not creating a stand-alone form. You'll likely want to link the form to a data source. In the following screen, you can see that we started with an InfoPath document that comes with the Forms library. Why build new when there are examples included that you can modify for your own use? We picked the form Sample—Status Report for our modification purposes.

There are two views to InfoPath: Filling out a form and designing a form. We'll do our work while in design mode. Note the icon in the upper northwest corner of the screen, just below the File menu. Like Microsoft Access, this icon allows you to toggle between design and edit modes.

Note that the objects are placed into the form from a Control pane on the right, *and* they are table based. That is, you need to understand the notion of tables, adding and inserting rows, and so forth, in order to fully comprehend what's going on in InfoPath for MOSS. (We'll talk more about tables in the section "Reporting and Tracking Project Progress" later in this chapter.)

To modify the form, double-click to obtain an object's properties. This allows you to rename the object and perform other functions. The following screen shows where you'd double-click if you want to edit the Project Description text object.

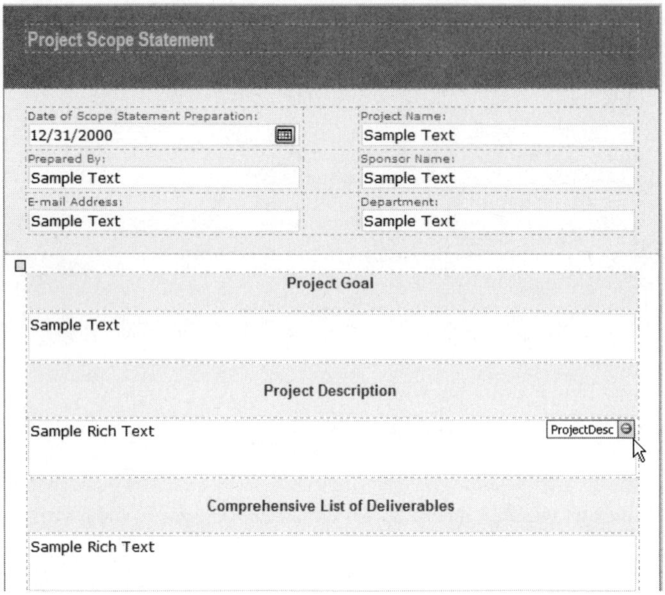

When you want to add new objects, you must add rows first and then select the control you want to include from the Controls pane. Once the form is done, you can use the InfoPath Publishing Wizard to publish it, as shown here.

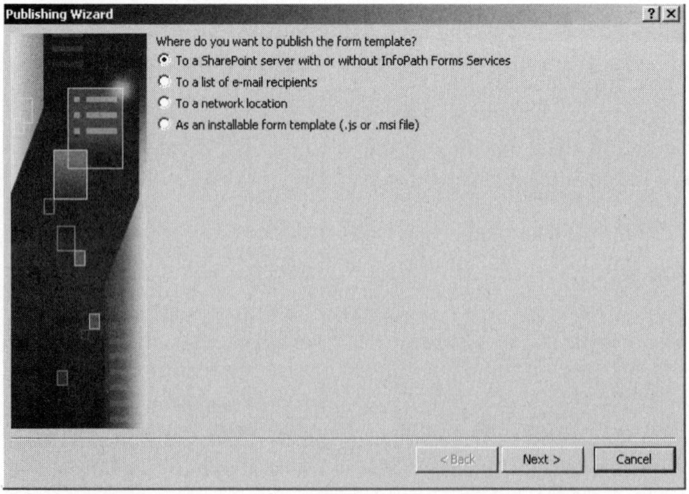

EXERCISE 4.1 *(continued)*

Tell InfoPath where to publish by pointing the publish operation to a site and folder, such as `http://0xyserver/PMSite`.

Once the form is placed on the site, authors can select the document they want from the list, in this case the Project Scope Statement form, and fill in the form.

 Data entered into InfoPath forms is stored in XML files. By default, XML is designed to query and extract data from a database. Since InfoPath 2007 is an XML-based forms generator linked to a data source, it can help organizations that use XML and its complementary standards to query and extract data.

Creating the Communication Plan

We've already been involved with our stakeholders and asked for approval of several project documents. The who, what, and when on the receiving end of this communication and all future project information should be documented in the communication plan. This plan describes the people and organizations who should receive the information, what kind of information they should receive, and when they should receive it.

This is a simple, straightforward plan that records when communication is going to occur and who the interactions should be with.

The recipients of information may include stakeholders, team members, the management team, and others outside of the project that may have interest, like vendors, the public, government entities, and so on. The following list includes some of the types of information you'll publish and distribute:

- Scope statement
- Status reports
- Public information and updates
- Request for proposals
- Contracts
- Risk response plan
- Quality metrics
- Project schedule
- Budget
- Performance measurements
- Change notices
- Lessons learned

When you first develop the communication plan, you may know who you're distributing to and what but not when. Come back and fill in the when after you've completed the Planning processes or note the when "as published." Change notices are a good example of using "as published" because they aren't predictable, so it isn't possible to determine a publish date. Status reports, on the other hand, should be frequent and regular. For example, status reports may be published every Friday.

Figure 4.11 shows a communication plan template.

FIGURE 4.11   Communication plan template

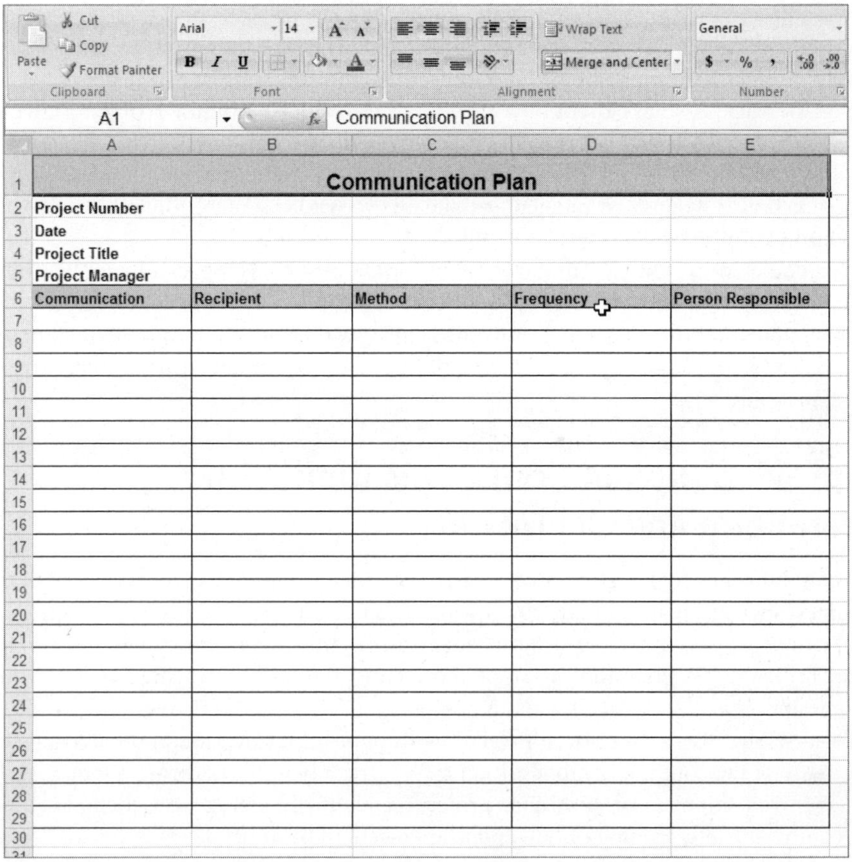

Determining Communication Needs

It may seem obvious that the project sponsor and stakeholders need to communicate about the status of the project. What might not seem so obvious is what they want to know and how they want to see the information. For example, many executives like information arranged as overviews, bullet items, and dashboards. A dashboard is simply a high-level review of the project that highlights issues and gives an overall status or rating for the project. (We'll talk more about these in the section "Reporting and Tracking Project Progress" later in this chapter.) However, don't assume that's all they want to see. Ask the sponsor and your key stakeholders what their particular hot buttons are. Find out what issues they want to know about immediately. Budget issues may be of high interest to one stakeholder while vendor delays may impact another. Also ask them how they want to be alerted that a problem is occurring or about to occur. This may not take the form of the documents noted in the section "Creating the Communication Plan." The sponsor and stakeholders may want an email or phone call or personal visit when their particular issue hits the radar screen. Make a note of that in the communication plan.

You could create a section in the communication plan called Special Issues that outlines the issues your sponsor and key stakeholders want to know about immediately. List the issues by category and note who wants to be informed and how they want to receive that communication.

Next we'll look at an improved feature of MOSS for communication among team members and stakeholders.

Improving Project Communication with SharePoint and the MOSS

The communication plan should be created early in the Planning process. As with the other documents we've created so far, you'll want to publish this to the project site on SharePoint. Unlike the scope statement or project request form, this document should not be an online form. Typically, the communication plan is created once and is updated as new information becomes known.

Because SharePoint is a portal product with built-in notification and messaging capabilities, many of the communications efforts a PM typically initiates through manual efforts can be automated. For example, notifying project members of a change to a document involves the PM composing and sending out an email or voicemail or notifying each person, perhaps at a meeting. But thanks to SharePoint's subscription services capability, members can be notified by email when a document is altered without any other intervention by the PM.

While this book is predominantly oriented toward using Excel as a project management tool, it is to the project manager's benefit to dig into the meat of SharePoint and its interaction with Office products to create a robust project management environment. Excel in and of itself is certainly a fine tool for project management purposes. When bundled with an office-automation-software-centric portal product (such as Office 2007 teaming with SharePoint), you have the ability to drastically cut your workload and automate processes.

Since we're on the topic of communication, let's briefly look at one of the new features of MOSS called Groove client. The Groove client feature in Office 2007 is designed to allow you to communicate with someone else on your project team (that is, someone else who is also connected to the Office server) via instant messaging (IM) technology.

Office Server natively supports the Groove client with its own internal directory structure, or optionally you can use an Internet-based Groove directory. In either case, you should be aware that the Groove client isn't for use in the way we think about traditional IM clients. The Groove client has more to do with the "quick phone call" notion: "Hi Bob, how ya doin', got a question about the task you listed here in the work breakdown structure."

Why not just use email? That's actually the beauty of Groove. Most people working at their computer don't seem to be as likely to routinely check their email (and respond back) as they are to answer a phone call or—you guessed it—an IM. Got a quick question? Shoot it off in Groove. It's easy and fast to answer. Need more detail? Send an email or telephone the person.

Figure 4.12 shows the Groove Client up and running with two people, some guy named Bill Heldman and another one who chooses to give only the name Test.

FIGURE 4.12   Groove Client

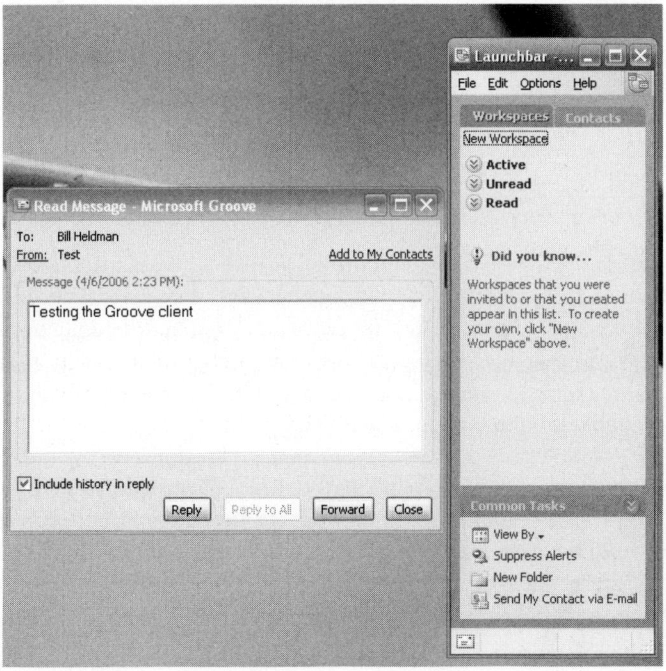

Reporting and Tracking Project Progress

In Chapter 1, we discussed the process groups the project progresses through starting with the Initiating processes and progressing through to Closing. Status reporting kicks into high gear during the Executing processes because that's when the work of the project begins. However, having said that, we begin status reporting shortly after the Planning processes have started. Project management activities are an important part of the project and it's a good practice to get your stakeholders involved as early in the project as possible. That means setting up status meetings and getting them in the habit of attending. You can begin even at this stage of the project by reporting on the progress of the scope statement, when you anticipate approval, when you anticipate having a project schedule for them to review, and so on.

Status Reporting

Project managers are responsible for reporting the status of the project. We can't stress enough how important it is to be honest and accurate in your reporting. Nothing will ruin your integrity quicker than reporting that the project is on schedule and on budget when it's not. We have witnessed project managers who chose to report what they thought the project sponsor wanted to hear (that is, on time and on budget) rather than report on the issues that were delaying the schedule. Not only was this a bad career move for the project manager, it put the project sponsor in a bad light with their peers.

Unfortunately, we've seen the reverse of this situation as well. The project sponsor either required the project manager to report all was well or changed the status report to reflect a good status. If you find yourself in this situation, it's probably time to look for a new job.

Status reports can range from summary level detail to highly detailed. You'll need to find out from your sponsor and stakeholders what level of detail they're looking for in the status report. You might find you'll have to create two or three status reports for different audiences. For example, the stakeholders and team members involved in the day-to-day activities of the project will likely want more detail than the project sponsor.

Some projects have steering committees in addition to the sponsor and key stakeholders. Steering committees may be made up of key stakeholders who are outside the organization but are impacted by the results of the project. (They usually have key stakeholders from within the organization as well.) This may include customers, citizens, other organizations or entities, beneficiaries of the project results, and so on. These people probably don't work within the organization but have a strong interest in the outcome of the project. For example, the state may be responsible for registering and licensing motor vehicles. Instead of performing this work itself, it turns to the county and local government agencies to assist. Therefore, if we have a project that involves modifying the motor vehicle system that the counties use, it's likely we'll have a steering committee made up of county representatives to help make decisions regarding the project. Steering committees are not generally involved in the day-to-day work of the project and will have their own requirements regarding status. Find out what those requirements are.

We'll look at templates for three types of status reports in the next section: team member status reports to the project manager, status reports for the stakeholders, and executive team or steering committee status reports.

Creating Reporting Templates with MS Excel

The project manager is the one responsible for reporting project status, and that status is the culmination of the progress the project team has made to date. There are two ways to gather this information: formally and informally. We recommend using both methods.

The informal method can be the most valuable. If you've established a high level of trust and good working relationships with your team (and we'll talk more about that in Chapter 5, "Planning and Acquiring Resources"), they'll feel comfortable alerting you to issues as soon as they arise. You can't truthfully report status if you're team members aren't comfortable telling you about problems, so encourage them to be honest and don't punish them for telling the truth.

Informal methods are just as they sound. Walk around during the day and ask your team members how things are going. Engage them in conversation about the project. Watch their body language and listen to what they're saying. Ask stakeholders (and members of their departments) what they're hearing. Hang around the water cooler or the kitchen and listen up when project conversations occur.

In addition to conversation, you should require a formal project status report from your team members. The status report shown in Figure 4.13 shows the types of information you might want to collect. This doesn't have to be pages and pages in length. The idea is to understand what activities they've worked on during the reporting period, the progress on those activities, and the work they expect to begin or complete in the next reporting period.

FIGURE 4.13 Team member status report

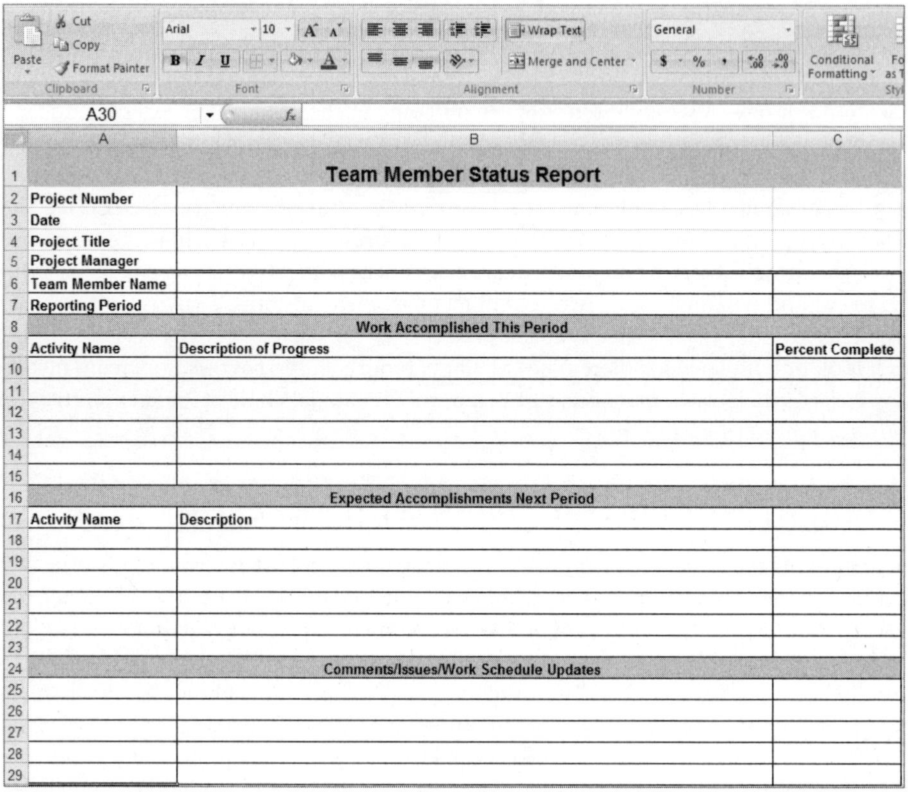

Team member status reports work well as online forms. Set up a notification for yourself on the project site so that you'll know when the reports have been posted.

The stakeholder status report is the report you'll use to conduct the project progress meetings. This is the most widely distributed status report. This form looks a lot like the team member status report, but you've distilled the information, so to speak, so that the activities associated with key deliverables in which the stakeholders have a particular interest are reported. Issues that may need decisions from the stakeholders are reported here as well. Figure 4.14 shows a project status report template.

FIGURE 4.14 Project status report

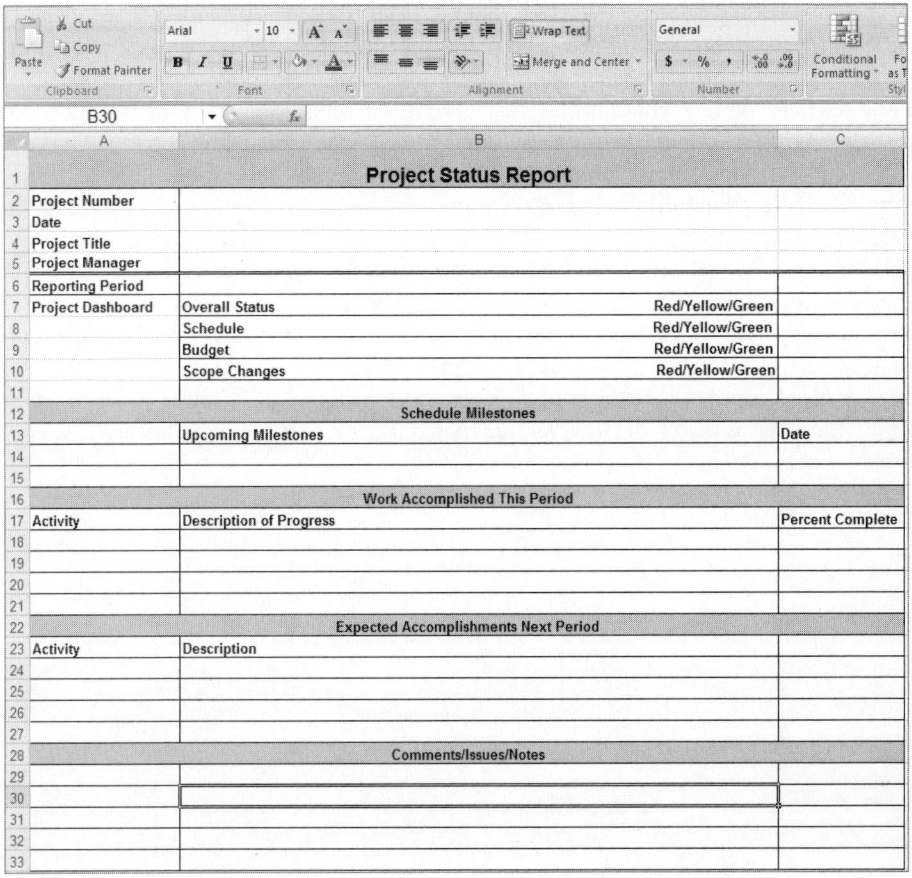

	A	B	C
1	**Project Status Report**		
2	Project Number		
3	Date		
4	Project Title		
5	Project Manager		
6	Reporting Period		
7	Project Dashboard	Overall Status Red/Yellow/Green	
8		Schedule Red/Yellow/Green	
9		Budget Red/Yellow/Green	
10		Scope Changes Red/Yellow/Green	
11			
12	**Schedule Milestones**		
13		Upcoming Milestones	Date
14			
15			
16	**Work Accomplished This Period**		
17	Activity	Description of Progress	Percent Complete
18			
19			
20			
21			
22	**Expected Accomplishments Next Period**		
23	Activity	Description	
24			
25			
26			
27			
28	**Comments/Issues/Notes**		
29			
30			
31			
32			
33			

NOTE

As the project manager, you'll want to understand your level of authority on the project. This should be established as early in the project as possible. Work with the project sponsor (and key stakeholders if necessary) to understand what level of control you have over the project and at what point they want to be involved in decision making. For example, you may have the authority to hire and fire team members, but the sponsor may want to review the issues surrounding a team member that isn't performing as expected. Or the stakeholders may want to review purchases greater than certain threshold amounts. Understand your level of authority before beginning the work of the project and know when to escalate issues appropriately.

The project manager of the Grant St. Move project, as with most projects, will report on the progress of the key deliverables identified in the scope statement. Obviously, you'll report on the deliverables that the team is working on or about to begin as well as provide a schedule update.

The final status report, shown in Figure 4.15, is a condensed version of the project status report in Figure 4.14.

In both of these figures, you'll notice a dashboard reference indicating the overall project status. Dashboards are popular with executives. They provide an at-a-glance view of progress. In this example, the dashboard is represented by a green-yellow-red rating.

Green means everything is on track and there are no major issues. A yellow rating indicates that there are slight delays in project progress and likely some issues that need resolution. Yellow is in an indicator that corrective actions may be necessary to get the project back on track. Depending on the action needed, the stakeholders and or sponsor may need to make decisions or be involved in updating the project plan. Red status indicates trouble. The project has significant delays or overruns, corrective action is needed to get the project back on track, and there are major issues that need resolved. This is where the honest reporting comes into play. It's a lot easier to report a project in yellow status than red. However, red may be the more accurate indicator.

FIGURE 4.15 Executive status report

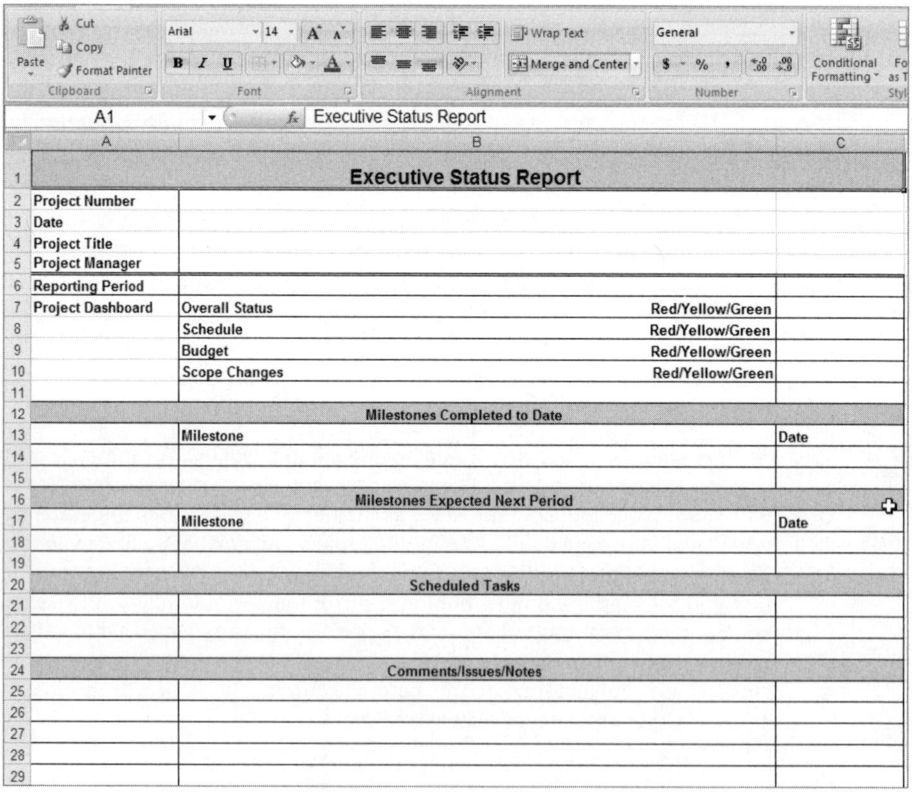

	A	B		C
1	**Executive Status Report**			
2	Project Number			
3	Date			
4	Project Title			
5	Project Manager			
6	Reporting Period			
7	Project Dashboard	Overall Status	Red/Yellow/Green	
8		Schedule	Red/Yellow/Green	
9		Budget	Red/Yellow/Green	
10		Scope Changes	Red/Yellow/Green	
11				
12	Milestones Completed to Date			
13		Milestone		Date
14				
15				
16	Milestones Expected Next Period			
17		Milestone		Date
18				
19				
20	Scheduled Tasks			
21				
22				
23				
24	Comments/Issues/Notes			
25				
26				
27				
28				
29				

You should publish both the status report and executive status report on SharePoint. Be aware that executives may or may not want to go to the project site to retrieve their status reports. They may want the report emailed to them instead. (They can be picky that way.) If that's the case, note this in the communication plan.

Two other documents go hand in hand with the project status report. They are the action item log and the issues log. We'll look at both of these next.

Action Item Log

During the course of your project status meetings, you'll likely have questions or issues come up that need action and some type of follow-up. You could write those questions on scrap pieces of paper, but you won't be able to track them very efficiently that way. It's a much better idea to record them in an action item log.

Action items are items that need resolved or researched. For example, during a status meeting for the Grant St. Move project, a stakeholder wants to know if the card readers are able to record the time employees enter certain areas of the building. This isn't a project activity, but the question is important to this stakeholder because they're responsible for securing archived records that contain sensitive company data. The stakeholder's department performs audits of the room these records are stored in and who accessed the room. If the new card-reader system doesn't have this capability, this stakeholder will have to research other options and it could potentially impact the project depending on the results of the research.

This information will be recorded on the action item log along with a number, date, owner or responsible party, resolution status, and resolution date. Figure 4.16 shows an action item template.

We use three status indicators for action items: active, resolved, and canceled. Once the action item is resolved or canceled, we like to carry them for one more reporting period and then retire them so they don't appear on future reports. You don't want to lose the data, however. Create a new sheet in the workbook called Closed. Once the data has expired, move those rows from the Active sheet to the Closed sheet. To do that, set the action item log up as a table as we explained in the section Documenting Requirements earlier in this chapter. Then perform a sort by the resolution date and action item number. Sort resolution date using the A to Z option. Cut the rows that have old information and paste them into a new sheet titled Closed.

We'll refer to both the action item log and issues log at the end of the project when we're gathering lessons learned information. There could be action items or issues that came up during the course of the project that will help us better plan our next project.

FIGURE 4.16   Action item log

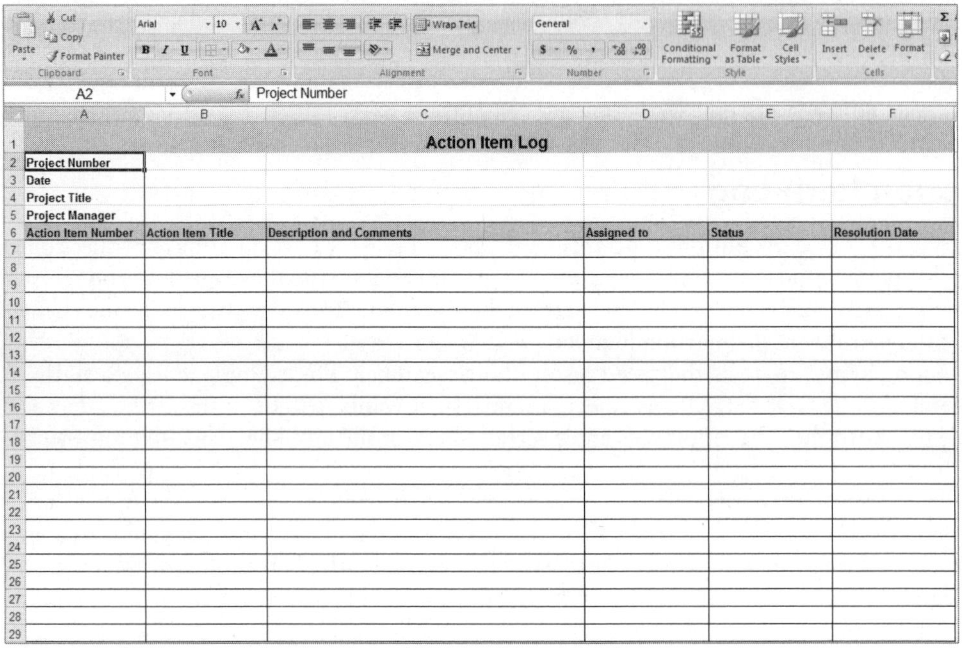

Exercise 4.2 walks you through the steps to create a custom list in SharePoint. Conveniently, we can use our Action Item List as an entry point in learning about SharePoint custom lists.

EXERCISE 4.2

The Action Item List as a Custom List in SharePoint

The action item log (Excel sheet) can be published as a SharePoint list. Here's how:

1.   Click the Office button (the Windows Flag button) and choose Publish ➢ Document Management Server.

2.   A navigation pane comes up allowing you to browse to the document management server. In our case, we chose PMServer and then GSM (for Grant St. Move) and then Document Library—a total of three levels of browsing choices.

EXERCISE 4.2 *(continued)*

3. Next, selected the kind of file you're saving (Excel 2007 worksheet) and give it a name as shown here.

You're then notified that the document is saved but not checked in. This means users will not be able to see it until you check it in and publish it.

4. Click Office Button and choose Server Tasks ➤ Check In. (Server Tasks only shows up in the menu list when a document has been saved and is ready for check-in.)

EXERCISE 4.2 *(continued)*

You have the option of simply checking the document in but not publishing it, which gives the document a minor version number and saves it in draft form. Or you can simultaneously check it in and publish it, which gives it a major version number. Choose the Major Version radio button.

Remember that documents checked in but not published can only be read by those with Owner privileges. Those with read-only privileges will not be able to see the document.

5. Next, highlight the Action Item Log range, right-click, and select Name a Range. A New Name window appears, as shown in the figure below.

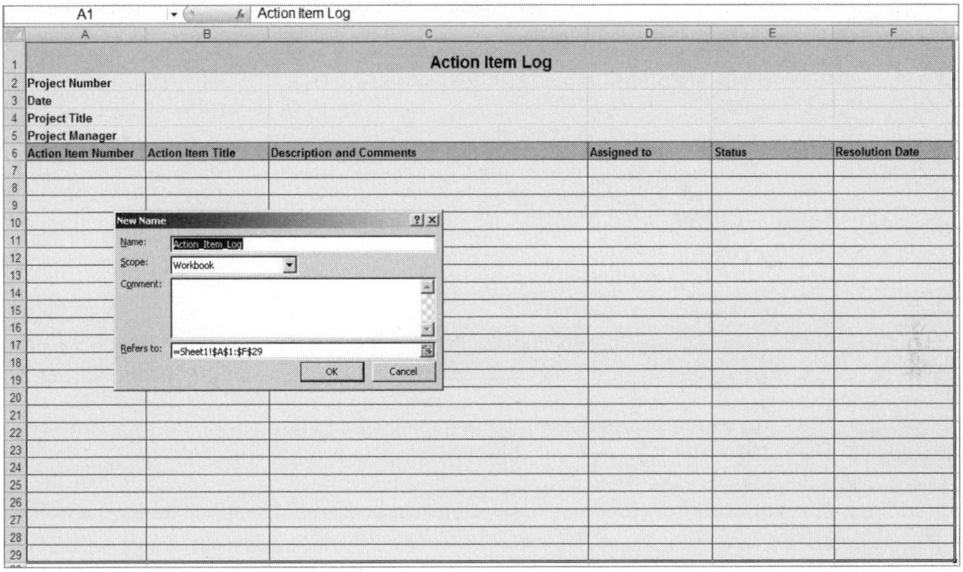

6. While you still have the named range selected, click Format as Table and select a table style. (We chose Medium 12 again.)

7. With the Table Tools subgroup highlighted, select Export ➢ Export to List.

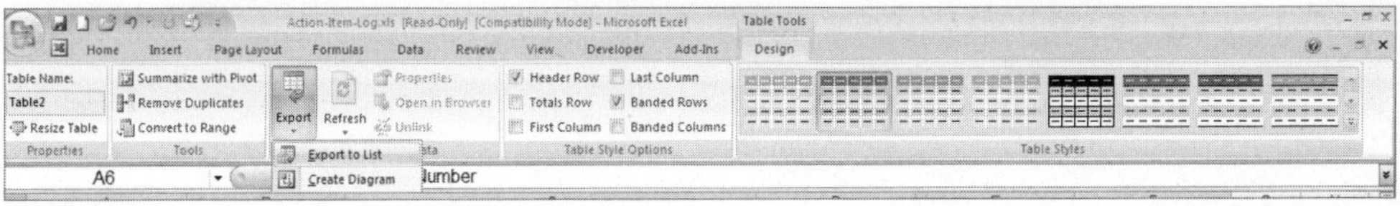

8. An Export Table to SharePoint List wizard box appears, as shown in the graphic below. Key in the URL of the SharePoint server and give the list a meaningful name and a description.

(Remember that we previously created the list destination folder within the SharePoint server.)

You are prompted with the type of cell (text, number, and so on) that will be saved, as shown here.

9. Click Finish and the list is published.

Users can navigate to http://*Server_name*/*Site_name*/Lists to view the published list. In our case the URL is http://PMServer/GSM/Lists. The Action Item Log list is shown here.

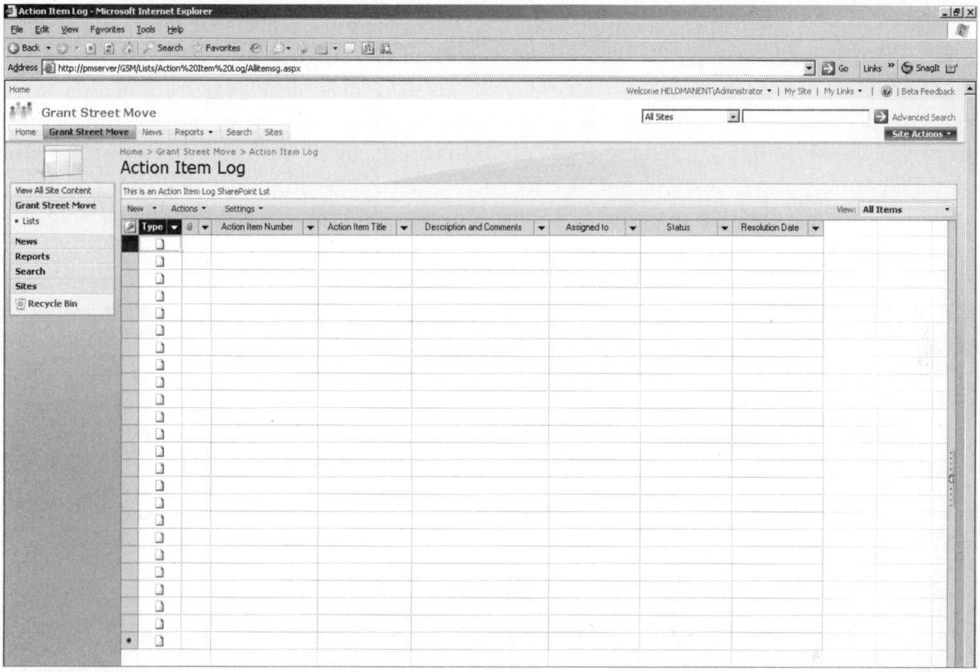

The great part about a list, as opposed to a published spreadsheet, is that the list can be edited either by using Excel or by simply browsing to the SharePoint site and editing the list within a browser, as shown in the preceding screen. Additionally, each item in a list can be subscribed to so that users can receive a notification when any element of the list changes.

Issues Log

Issues are similar to action items but are usually more complex in nature. They may require management intervention or decisions, whereas action items typically do not.

An issue has surfaced on the Grant St. Move project. The Main St. director has three employees with disabilities that prevent them from being able to pack and unpack their workplace belongings. These three employees have special accommodation needs for their work areas as well. The accommodation needs were recorded as requirements under the facility build-out deliverable, but no one thought about the assistance the employees would need with packing and setting up their new work areas. We can hear you asking, "Shouldn't this have been discovered when we talked about requirements or in some other planning phase of the project?" The answer is yes, it should have, but no project planning process is perfect. Chances are good you'll discover issues that will not surface until after the work of the project begins. There are as many reasons for this as there are issues that may arise. This doesn't mean you can skimp on the Planning processes and figure you'll catch whatever requirements or needs you didn't document as an issue. You should work as diligently as you can to uncover all the requirements in the Planning processes. One of the questions you can ask when discussing requirements is, Is there anything else or any other need associated with this requirement? If that question were posed when the accommodation needs requirement was being discussed, it might have triggered someone to recall the need for assistance with packing as well.

Figure 4.17 shows an issue item log. It contains similar information as the action item log. You could publish this log as a SharePoint list as well by following the directions in Exercise 4.2.

FIGURE 4.17   Issues log

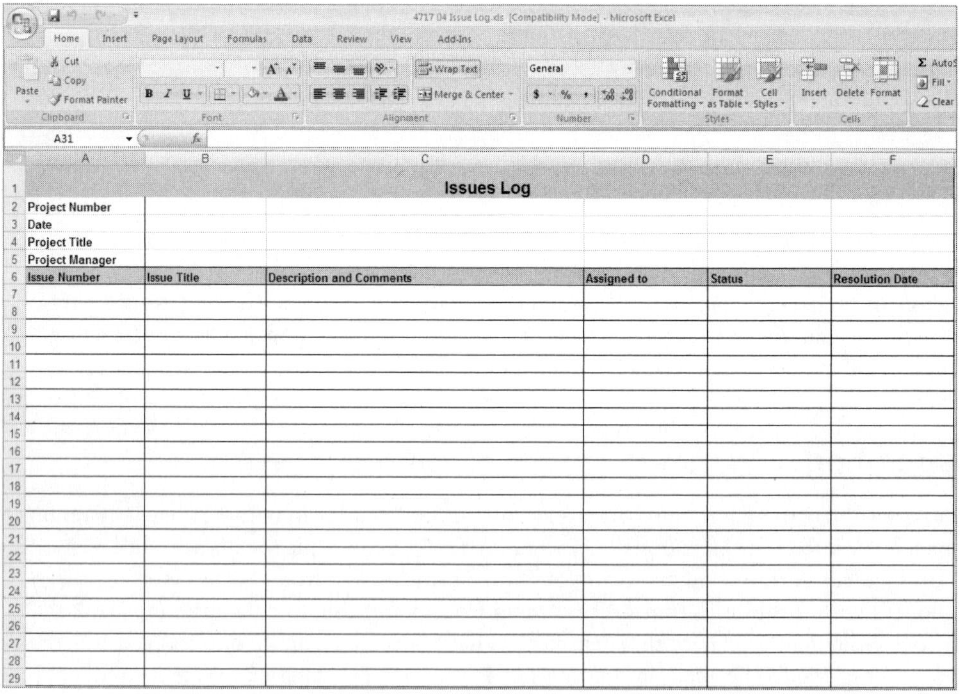

Issues often occur in information technology projects. For example, a business desires to automate a process or replace an antiquated system with a newer system. End users are so ingrained with their current processes that they often take them for granted. They may not consciously think about how a document is processed behind the scenes because "the computer does it." This may call for a new or modified business process to account for the "new" way of doing business. That means the manager of the business unit must devise a new process or business rule or policy and this issue becomes an entry on the issue log.

For large projects, you might consider creating both the action item log and the issue item log in database format. We'll describe how to create databases in Excel in Chapter 6, "Assessing and Tracking Risk."

We're well on our way to completing the project Planning processes. As we stated earlier, the scope statement (and requirements if it's a separate document) is one of the most important documents you'll create for project planning purposes. The scope statement will help you define activities and develop estimates and a project schedule later in the Planning process. Before we get to those activities, we'll talk about acquiring resources—both team members and materials needed to perform the work of the project—in the next chapter.

Chapter

5

Planning and Acquiring Resources

We'll take a slight detour in this chapter from deliverables and requirements and talk about the project team, the skills they need for the project, and their roles and responsibilities on the project. Now that we understand the deliverables and the requirements of the project, we're starting to get an idea of the types of skills we'll need to perform the work to complete them. The resources we need may or may not exist within the organization, so the sooner we start looking at resources, the better.

We'll also look at the procurement process and begin to plan for resources from a materials and equipment perspective. In the case of the Grant St. Move project, we'll be hiring a moving company to perform the office moves. We'll also be hiring a contracting company to pull all the cables through the building for the information technology piece of this project. If we wait too long into the Planning processes before we begin procurement, we could potentially delay the project schedule. Let's start off by identifying the human resources needed for the project.

Establishing the Project Team

The most important part of any project in our experience is building the project team. You can have the best project planning documents, a realistic schedule, and a more than adequate budget, but if you don't have a skilled, cohesive project team to carry out the work of the project, the perfect schedule and budget won't do you much good.

Efficient, productive teams are the result of careful selection involving evaluation of skills, ability, and personality traits among other things. Before we go into detail on these items, let's first consider where team members come from along with your organization's policies on recruiting them.

Team Member Recruitment

Planning for team members on an upcoming project almost always starts within our own departments. Who has the skills? Who has worked on projects similar to this in the past? and Who is available? are the typical initial questions we ask ourselves. When thinking about team members, keep in mind that you'll likely need people from other departments or potentially experts or others from outside the organization to assist with project tasks as well. And when you're working with other departments, you'll have to coordinate with the managers of those departments for their employees' time. That means you'll need those negotiation skills we talked about in Chapter 1.

Your company may have organizational policies that dictate how employees are transferred or loaned to a project. Job descriptions may need to be updated (or created). The employee may report to you for the course of the project or they may report to their departmental manager, depending on the policy.

Recruitment policies are another consideration, especially if you need to hire some of the resources for the project. Some organizations have arduous recruitment policies that can prolong the process by weeks if not months due to the mounds of paperwork and approvals needed to make it happen (do we sound like we're talking from experience?). Make it a point to get to know your human resources contact early in the project so they'll be familiar with your project and know the types of skills and experience you'll need to recruit.

There are other elements to consider when building the project team as well. This list includes some of the more obvious ones:

- Skills

- Knowledge

- Availability

- Experience

We'll talk about identifying skills and experience in the section "Performing a Skills Assessment" later in this chapter. An assessment allows you to determine and document the types of skills available in the organization and those you'll have to recruit. Skills and experience are two of the key elements of the recruitment process whether team members come from within the organization or not. For example, if you need team members who understand Internet telephony concepts, an expert in tax law probably won't fill the bill.

 Availability is usually one of the first things we consider when choosing potential team members. But repeat after us: Availability is not a skill set. Just because an employee is available does not mean they're suited for the work of the project or that they'll "fit" with the project team. Give other factors more weight than availability when picking team members.

Here are some of the not-so-obvious elements you'll want to consider when choosing team members:

- Personality fit with the other team members

- Ability to work well with others

- Ability to learn new things

- Ability to adapt to change

In some ways, the intangible, or not-so-obvious, elements may be just as important if not more important than skills and knowledge and experience. If you have team members with superstar skills in their knowledge area but they're absolute bears to work with, you might be setting yourself up for more tasks than you have time for. We call these types of people high-maintenance team members because they require a lot of intervention and mediation between themselves and other team members or stakeholders. Who serves as the mediator? Do we have to answer that?

Stages of Team Development

High-performance teams are those that function in the most efficient and productive ways possible. They possess a synergy that other teams don't possess. A high-performing work team has the following characteristics:

- High levels of trust for each other and for the project manager
- Enthusiastic commitment to the project
- Creative problem solving
- Enhanced communication
- High levels of job satisfaction
- Shared accountability and rewards
- Joint decision making

One of the most important characteristics of high-performance teams is the level of trust among the team members and their level of trust for you as the project manager. Honesty and openness with your team members will go a long way toward establishing a level of trust that helps teams perform at their best.

Another element of trust involves creating a safe environment for team members to report project issues. If your team members know they can bring issues and concerns to you without being unduly reprimanded or reproached, you and the project will benefit. You'll know about risks before they occur and your team members will continue to keep you informed because they know you won't shoot the messenger.

Enthusiastic commitment to the project is probably the second biggest contributor to developing effective teams. Commitment comes about because of belief in a common goal and belief in that goal comes about through communication. It's difficult for the team to be committed to a common goal if they're unclear what the goal is. As the project manager, it's your job to keep your team focused on the project goal and to clarify when it's not clearly understood.

Teams don't typically start out as high-performance teams. It takes time working together to get there. Dr. Bruce Tuckman discovered that teams progress through four common stages of development: forming, storming, norming, and performing. Making certain new team members "fit" with the other personalities on the team will help the team reach the highest performing stage sooner. We'll look at the characteristics of each of these stages next.

Forming   Forming is the first stage of team development. This occurs when team members are introduced to each other and begin working together. Team members are reserved in this stage and wonder what's expected of them, what role they have on the project, and if they'll be able to successfully complete their assignments. The project manager should make the goals of the project clear in this stage and should also make sure each team member knows what's expected of them. Teams quickly progress from here into the storming stage.

Storming   Storming is just as it sounds. This is the stage in team development where people are more comfortable with each other and will challenge one another for position and status within the team. Flair-ups occur and conflicts over tasks and processes arise. Team members begin asking who will perform which task, what processes should be used, and how the work will get completed. While our tendency as the project manager may be to jump in and solve their problems for them, at this stage it isn't wise to do so. Questions and conflict actually help clarify the goals of the project for everyone on the team. And as long as the team is working through the issues and agreeing upon resolutions on their own, it's good to let them continue to work it out without intervention. They'll progress to the next stage, norming, all the sooner.

Sometimes teams don't progress out of the storming stage. This is a risk to the project and is an indicator that the project manager should step in and take action. Consider replacing team members who are contentious without cause and those who aren't adding value but simply stirring up conflict.

Norming   Norming is the stage where the team settles in and performs the work of the project. Team members know their place on the team and what their own role is, and they're comfortable working with each other. Conflicts subside in this stage and team members tackle the problems and issues surrounding the project rather than each other.

In this stage, you will want to do some intervention to keep the team from slipping back into the storming stage. Team meetings are one way to keep the team focused, monitor participation, and create an environment for sharing information and asking questions. Hold one-on-one conversations with your team members as well.

The norming stage produces functioning, efficient teams. Your team members will likely be productive and focused on the project goals. This is a good stage for them to operate from, and most teams that make it through storming end up functioning at this stage. But it's in the next stage of development, called performing, that the teams turn into high-performance teams.

Performing   The performing stage is where teams function in the most productive and effective ways possible—they are high-performing teams in every sense. They support one another, they monitor themselves, and they achieve great things in this stage. Teams that operate in the performing stage are almost unstoppable.

Not all teams make it to this stage. We've been fortunate enough a time or two in our careers to manage teams that function at this stage and it's an awesome experience. But this stage can't be forced. It happens because team members have high levels of trust and high levels of mutual respect for one another and for you as the project manager and because they're wholly dedicated to the goals of the project. They've accepted the project as their personal responsibility and hold themselves accountable for doing the job well.

It's rare to have teams that reach the performing stage—this occurs a handful of times in a career. It's much more likely teams will progress to the norming stage of development. They'll produce great results and work efficiently, but the synergy that occurs at the performing stage is missing. You can help keep your team in the norming stage and help them potentially get to the performing stage by communicating effectively—this tops the project manager's list of things to do. Communicating includes passing information to your team and soliciting feedback and input from them (and acting on it). Resolving conflict effectively and knowing when to resolve conflict will also keep the team functioning efficiently. And we've said this before but it's worth repeating: be a truth teller—always be honest with your team and tell them everything you can without jeopardizing confidences.

Performing a Skills Assessment

Before you can perform a skills assessment, you should know the deliverables of the project. We documented those in the project scope statement in Chapter 3. It doesn't hurt to know the tasks associated with the deliverables as well. We'll talk about breaking down the deliverables into tasks and assigning individual resources to specific tasks in Chapter 8, "Constructing the Project Schedule and Budget." Sometimes, though, you don't have the luxury of waiting until you document the tasks. If you have a lengthy recruitment process (or procurement process), you'll need to identify resources and start the processes to get them on board sooner rather than later.

If you're an experienced project manager, you may be able to use the deliverables to identify the types of resources needed fairly easily. Whether you're experienced or not, you should dig out the documentation from prior projects that are similar in scope to this one. The skills assessment and roles and responsibilities for the completed project may coincide nicely with your current project and keep you from starting from scratch.

If you don't have prior documentation or if you're working with deliverables you're not familiar with, it's time to interview some experts. For example, if you need to know the types of skills it takes to set up the data center in our Grant St. Move project, ask the folks who do that kind of work.

As is often the case with small to medium projects, you'll likely know who most of the team members are early on in the project. They're probably the same people you worked with the last time you worked on a project similar to this one. If that's the case, you can pull out the skills assessment you performed for the last project (you did one, right?) and update it with additional training folks have taken or with new team members.

Skills assessments are designed to record the types of skills, training, education, and special talents team members have so that you can begin to plan task assignments and acquire resources from other departments and from outside the organization. Figure 5.1 is a skills assessment template.

The skills and training column should list the special skills and training programs employees have attended. For example, if we're looking at a network administrator as the first entry, this person may have skills such as Microsoft Exchange administration, MOSS administration, telephony, firewall, and so on. We would list each entry on its own line and then record the number of years experience the person has with this type of technology. The Education/Certification column is where you can note if the person holds certifications— such as Microsoft Certified Systems Engineer (MCSE) or Project Management Professional PMP)—and what type of degree or special education they've had. In Chapter 8, we'll use the skills assessment and a few of the other documents we'll create in this chapter to assign team members to specific tasks.

Table 5.1 shows a sample portion of a skills assessment for our Grant St. Move Project team.

FIGURE 5.1   Skills assessment template

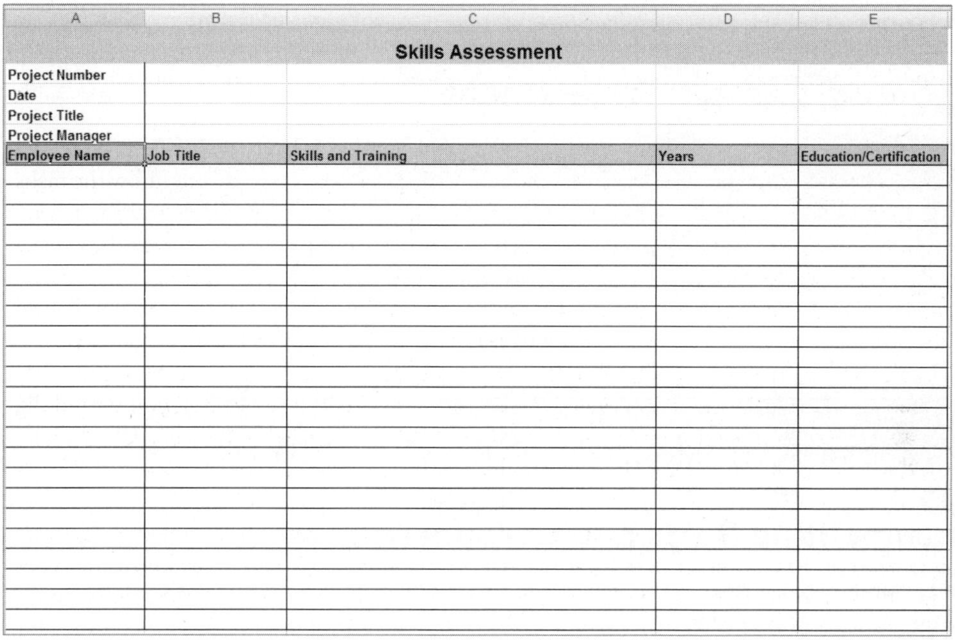

	A	B	C	D	E
			Skills Assessment		
Project Number					
Date					
Project Title					
Project Manager					
Employee Name	Job Title	Skills and Training		Years	Education/Certification

TABLE 5.1   Skills Inventory

Employee	Job Title	Skills/Training	Years	Education
Steve Green	Senior Network Administrator	Degree		BS in computer science
		Exchange administration	10	MCSE certification
		Networking skills (router, switches)	8	Working on certification
		Security administration	8	Training classes
		Disaster recovery planning	5	
		Database administration	5	
		VoIP	3	Training classes

TABLE 5.1   Skills Inventory *(continued)*

Employee	Job Title	Skills/Training	Years	Education
Aimee Owens	Network Administrator	Degree		BS in computer science
		Exchange administration	4	Working toward MCSE certification
		Active Directory administration	4	
		Disaster recovery planning	2	

Next we'll document the roles and responsibilities of the project team.

Documenting Roles and Responsibilities

Most projects need a team of people to accomplish the work. There're usually also a host of others who are intently interested in the outcome of the project and its impact on their individual organization as well. At a minimum, there will most likely be a project sponsor, stakeholders, the project manager, and one or more team members. Let's look at a high-level description of the responsibility of each of these categories of people.

Project sponsor   An executive in the organization who oversees the project. Advises the project manager, resolves issues, serves as a tie breaker or final decision maker, serves on the steering committee, champions the project to other executives and the organization.

Remember that the project sponsor is the one who has the authority to make decisions, assign team members to the project, allocate budget and other resources, and officially authorize the project to begin. In return, the project manager should strive to keep the sponsor informed of key issues. The project sponsor should be the first, not the last, to hear about project conflicts or problems. The sponsor has a vested interest in the project and will work with you to help resolve the problems if you've kept them informed and escalated issues appropriately.

Stakeholders   May serve as advisor to the project manager. Assists in the development of the project plans. Provides input regarding project decisions, serves as a business expert. Key stakeholders approve the project plans and recommend corrective actions.

Project manager   Manages the project, creates project plans, measures and monitors project performance, recommends corrective action, manages the project team, and reports status.

Team members   Complete the work of the project.

Another method for depicting responsibility is called a RACI chart. The RACI chart shows at a glance who is accountable for what. The letters in the acronym are designations shown in the chart:

R = Responsible for performing the work

A = Accountable, the person or group who is responsible for approving or signing off on the work

C = Consult, someone who has input into the work or decisions

I = Inform, someone who must be informed of decisions

An example RACI chart is shown in Figure 5.2.

You can use a RACI chart for deliverables, tasks, or milestones. As you can see in Figure 5.2, we've listed some of the requirements for the data center deliverable and assigned our network administrator, Steve, and his assistant, Aimee, as accountable for the tasks. Even though vendors will perform most of these tasks, Steve and Aimee will be the ones responsible for overseeing the work. Alternatively, you could construct this chart to have the names of the team members and stakeholders across the columns and put the R-A-C-I designations on the lines where appropriate.

FIGURE 5.2   RACI chart

Description or Task	Responsible	Accountable	Consult	Inform
RACI Chart				
Project Number				
Date				
Project Title				
Project Manager				
Description or Task	Responsible	Accountable	Consult	Inform
Datacenter will be on 2nd floor for flood prevention	Jenni-Facility Committee	Steve Green		
Datacenter will be completely wired & ready for servers & switchgear	Vendor	Steve Green		
Datacenter will have a fire protection system	Vendor	Aimee Owens	Facility Committee	Building Inspector
Datacenter will have air conditioning system	Vendor	Aimee Owens	Facility Committee	Building Inspector
Datacenter will have power conditioning equipment	Vendor	Steve Green		Building Inspector

While each of these examples is a good high-level description, you don't want to leave it at that. You'll also want to document the specific roles and responsibilities of each of these members on the project. You could create a spreadsheet with the names of the team members in the first column, the description of their responsibility in the second, and other information that could be useful, such as when they're needed on the project (are they needed full time on the project or only during certain phases), training needs, the department or organization they work in, level of authority, special considerations, and so on. Figure 5.3 shows an example template.

You could combine the information captured in the skills inventory chart we talked about earlier in this chapter with the roles and responsibilities document. Alternatively, you could identify the types of skills needed and indicate whether this person has what's needed or will require training to attain the skills. As you've probably determined, there are several ways to document this information. Use the format that will work for you and modify the columns to include (or exclude) information depending on the complexity of the project. Don't forget to post this document to the project management site on SharePoint.

FIGURE 5.3   Roles and responsibility chart

A	B	C	D	E	F	G
Roles and Responsibilities Chart						
Project Number						
Date						
Project Title						
Project Manager						
Employee Name	Responsibility	Phases Needed	Skills and Training	Training Needs	Authority	Organization

Creating a Project Organizational Chart

A project organizational chart is much like an ordinary organizational chart, starting with the biggest boss in the top box and progressing down through the departments. In the case of the project organizational chart, the project sponsor is in the top box followed by the project manager, team members, and so on. One of the primary reasons for creating a project organizational chart is to outline the levels of authority and the escalation path for project issues.

The project organizational chart is most useful for medium to large projects where there could be multiple assistant project managers who are responsible for subprojects or individual deliverables and report to the senior project manager. Figure 5.4 depicts a sample project organization chart.

Organizational charts are easy to create in Excel. Navigate to the Insert tab on the ribbon, and in the Illustrations section, click the SmartArt button. The Choose a SmartArt Graphic window appears (Figure 5.5).

FIGURE 5.4   Project organizational chart

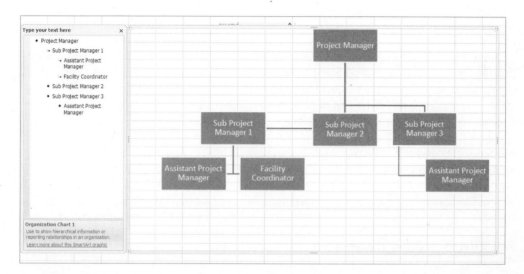

FIGURE 5.5   Choose a SmartArt Graphic window

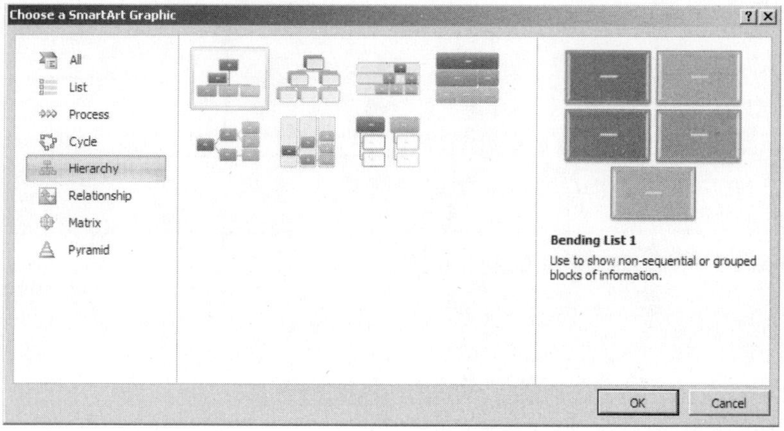

Highlight the Hierarchy selection on the left-hand pane of the window, then choose the Organizational Chart 1 selection in the middle pane (upper left in the list of choices), then click OK. A blank org chart appears (Figure 5.6).

Looking at Figure 5.6, you can see that the left-hand section of the org chart is an outline-based tool that allows you to key in the titles you want for your chart. Click the text button and start typing. Pressing Enter gives you a new line at the same level you're currently working on. Pressing Enter and then Tab causes a sublevel to appear. (Pressing Ctrl+Tab takes you back one level.) Figure 5.4 (shown earlier) is our completed org chart.

You can highlight any of the org chart objects in the right-hand pane and move them anywhere you like. SmartArt will keep track of the links for you. Use the corner and side handles to resize any graphic. You can also rotate a particular graphic by grabbing the yellow rotation handle. Highlight several objects by holding down the Ctrl key and clicking those you want. Close the left-hand "Type your text here" pane when done. Finally, note the drag-bars on each side of the org chart window itself. It's easy to move the org chart around and resize it as needed.

Note that in order to facilitate org charts in Office 2007, you must first check to make sure that the Organization Chart Add-in for Microsoft Office Programs is installed. By default it is not. Close all Office programs (including Outlook). Open Control Panel and then Add or Remove Programs. Find Microsoft Office Professional 2007, highlight it, and click Change. The Change Your Installation of Microsoft Office window comes up. Click Add or Remove Features and click Continue. Click the plus sign next to Microsoft Office PowerPoint to find the Organization Chart Add-in for Microsoft Office Programs. (The org chart add-in has been associated with PowerPoint for many years, though it's available for other Office programs.) Click the drop-down and select Run from My Computer, as shown in Figure 5.7. Click Continue.

Our team members' roles and responsibilities are documented and posted to the MOSS. Now how do we go about motivating this newly formed team? We'll look at that next.

FIGURE 5.6   Org chart template

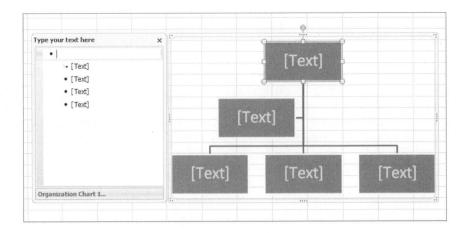

FIGURE 5.7   Setting up Office to include the Organization Chart add-in

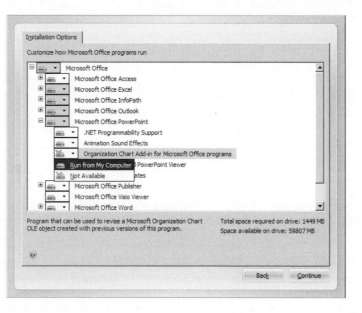

Motivating Teams

One of the most important roles the project manager is responsible for is building and motivating the project team. It's important to encourage and recognize efforts well done and to prevent or correct actions that are unproductive and ineffective. Motivation is the reason we do the things we do. For example, most everyone likes their coworkers and managers to appreciate the contributions they make. Appreciation and recognition are motivators. So are many other things, such as time off, bonuses, stock options, awards, and game or concert tickets. Correction or negative consequences are also motivators, although not ones we want to use often and only in those cases that call for it.

Motivation encourages people to work more efficiently and produce better results. Highly motivated teams will achieve the norming or performing stage of team development quickly. One of the keys to motivation is communication, that is, clearly outlining the goals of the project and making certain each team member understands what's expected of them. It's also a good idea to ensure that team members have an understanding of project management principles, how to report issues or problems, organizational policies that may impact them or the project, and proper escalation paths and techniques.

Types of Motivation

There are two types of motivators: extrinsic and intrinsic. Extrinsic motivators are external to the individual, like bonuses, time off, and the other examples mentioned earlier. They are usually material in nature. Extrinsic motivators encourage people to perform tasks in order to receive benefits they perceive have value.

Intrinsic motivators are internal to the individual and have no material value. For example, some people take great pride in their work. They are driven to succeed for the joy of accomplishing the goal. Others may work hard because they require the best performance out of themselves. Others will perform for the benefit of the team's accomplishment. The reasons the individual performs comes from within.

Most people are motivated by both extrinsic and intrinsic factors. Most of us go to work every day because we receive a paycheck at the end of the month. Moreover, most of us do a good job at work because we want to make valuable contributions to the team or the organization—if we're rewarded for those contributions in addition to our paychecks, all the better. We'll look at some ways to reward and recognize team members in the next section.

There are many theories on motivation and team behavior. In fact, there are countless books devoted to the topic and it's beyond the scope of this book to go into much depth. If motivation, rewards, and recognition are subjects you're not familiar with, we encourage you to do some reading or take some classes on these topics. Your team will thank you for it, and your projects may be more productive and successful as a result.

Rewards and Recognition

Rewards and recognition are powerful motivators. They are also relatively easy ways to engage team members in high levels of performance. The first thing you should do is determine if your organization has policies regarding rewards. You will likely find that monetary awards are limited to certain amounts or can be given only in certain increments. Nonmonetary awards may also have limits. If your policies dictate certain amounts—for example, no more than $50 per employee per project (don't laugh, our organization's limits are less than this)—you'll have to work within that amount. Don't make the mistake of thinking this amount is too small, particularly for an extraordinary effort on an important project. It isn't so much the amount that matters to your team members—it's the fact that you took the time to recognize their effort.

Every new project has the potential for success or failure. Even when, as a project manager you're working with the same team members you worked with on a similar project that was successfully completed, the current project still has the potential to fail. Make certain your team members understand the goals of the project and spend some time devising ways to reward and recognize them accordingly.

Rewarding Performance

Rewards and recognition should be in proportion to the achievement and they should be realistic. For example, promising all-expenses-paid ski vacations for the successful completion of a small project with minimal impact to the organization probably isn't in keeping with the level of effort expended, nor is it realistic—not to mention you'd never get approval to offer a reward like this for a small project. The point is, if you promise rewards that aren't realistic or that the team knows you can't produce, they're meaningless and won't work to motivate the team. In fact, they're likely to have just the opposite effect.

Linking rewards to performance is one of the most effective ways to use extrinsic motivators to increase the team's productivity. Let's say your project is constrained by budget. Most projects are, but budget happens to be of particular importance to this project. Designating rewards for meeting or beating the budget would be very effective in this case. For example, in our Grant St. Move project, the original design required miles of Ethernet cable run from the data center to the network closets on each floor as well as to each desktop and conference room. The team designed an architecture using wireless access points, thereby reducing the amount of Ethernet cable originally required. This redesign dramatically reduced the cost of cable (and the contractor costs to run the cable), even taking into account the expense of installing the wireless access points. In this case, the performance of the team resulted in an overall reduction of $100,000 in expenses. There are any number of rewards that would be appropriate in this case, depending on company policy and culture. You could award monetary bonuses to the team members who came up with the new design and recommendation, you could cater in lunch, you might consider purchasing jackets or shirts for the team with the company logo, and so on. The ski vacation mentioned earlier would still be overkill—make certain to match the level of effort with the reward.

Another important consideration is not over- or underusing rewards and recognition because they'll either lose value in the eyes of your team members or your team members will go out of their way to do only the tasks or perform only the behaviors you consistently reward. Use different types of rewards also. If the team sees that every time you recognize someone for a job well done you give them a restaurant gift certificate, it will lose meaning and effectiveness.

How do you remember which team members got which rewards and what exactly were they given? Good question. Track rewards in a spreadsheet so you don't use the same one over and over and so the same person isn't consistently rewarded when others are not. You might want to record the date, the team member's name, the reward type, and the amount (or equivalent). Figure 5.8 shows a reward tracking template.

If you have a large team and are tracking all employees in one spreadsheet, consider turning this into a table. That way, you can sort on employee name (or other criteria) and view related information quickly.

FIGURE 5.8   Reward tracking template

	A	B	C	D	E
	Reward Log				
	Project Number				
	Date				
	Project Title				
	Project Manager				
	Date	Employee Name	Reward Given	Amount	Reason

Recognizing Team Members

Recognizing team members goes hand in hand with rewards. That is, by rewarding a team member, you are in fact recognizing them as well. However, you can recognize team members without giving a reward. For example, mentioning the effort or achievement of a team member in a status meeting is one form of recognition.

Having team members recognize each other is another powerful motivator. You could set up a nomination system where employees explain in an email (or use a recognition form of some sort) the type of help they received from someone else or the accomplishment their fellow team member achieved. Announce these at the team or status meetings, or better yet, have the employee that wrote the nomination read it at the meeting.

Recognition is as important as rewards. In organizations where monetary rewards are not permitted, recognition may be the only form of acknowledgment you can give to a team member who has performed above and beyond. A fun way to recognize performance is by designating an object (a statue, a stuffed animal, a trophy, for example) as the Star Performer award. When a team member is nominated, they keep the statue or object in a prominent place in their cube until such time as the next team member recognition is announced. Then the statue is passed to the new employee. Here are some other ideas for nonmonetary awards:

- Email congratulations with a copy to the team
- Paid time-off certificates
- Leave-early or come-late-to-work passes
- Handwritten thank-you notes
- Framed certificates of achievement

You should keep a few things in mind when recognizing team members—with or without monetary rewards attached. Consider the preferences and cultural differences of the individual (or team), especially when you're working with teams in different geographic locations. Some people do not like to be recognized in front of a group and would prefer the project manager to approach them one on one. Some cultures believe it's appropriate to only recognize teams and not individuals. Make certain you understand your team members' preferences and any cultural influences that dictate how they should be recognized.

Adding Team Members to MOSS

Now that we know who our team members are, we're ready to add them to MOSS. Not all team members need access to everything. Office Server gives you the ability to keep unauthorized users from viewing your project documents. You also have the ability to customize permissions for users, should you have the need.

You will recall that there are three basic categories of users:

Home Owners   Home Owners have full control over the site. Assign these rights sparingly.

Home Members   People who can view pages and edit list items and documents.

Home Visitors   People who can view pages, list items, and documents.

As we said, not everyone on your project needs to have full access to the MOSS site and full rights to the documents on it. Think about the kinds of rights various individuals require to do their work and don't give out more rights than they need.

You can easily create groups in MOSS, making it simpler to give users the rights they need, once added to a group. This also provides you the ability to at-a-glance understand who is able to do what.

Adding users to MOSS is a two-part proposition, potentially three if you want to add users into MOSS groups.

First, ascertain what kind of user structure you have at your workplace. Most likely you'll have a Windows Active Directory (AD) user structure, though it's possible you have a peer-to-peer (P2P) workgroup environment in which there is a W2K3 server—one that has not been made into a domain controller running AD.

If you don't know how your users and groups are created and managed, or what tool is used to manage them, take some time to meet with your system administrators and find out. You don't need to be a guru in the area of AD—it is an extremely technical and difficult subject—but you should understand what a directory structure is and why your company uses the one it does. For example, you should know what the corporate naming protocol is for new users and who creates them.

MOSS assumes that you'll be pointing to usernames in AD, although we had good luck creating usernames in a stand-alone Windows Server 2003 (W2K3) server installation as well. We'll show you how in the sidebar at the end of this section.

Assuming you know the usernames you'll be adding, here's how to add users to your MOSS installation. Start by bringing up the home MOSS site. In our case, we navigate to `http://PMServer` (PMServer is the NetBIOS name of our W2K3 server), and then click Site Actions ➢ Site Settings ➢ People and Groups (see Figure 5.9).

This action brings up a page called People and Groups: Home Members (see Figure 5.10). Next, click New ≻ Add Users to bring up the main user addition page (Figure 5.11). In the Users field, key in the name of the user you want to add or use the Browse button. Note that Home Members (Contribute) is, by default, the permissions choice presented upon going into the New Users screen. You may, of course, adjust the permissions level to your liking for the user account you are creating.

Select the permission group you'd like the user to be in. We've selected Add Users to a SharePoint Group, as shown in Figure 5.12. The drop-down box becomes active when you choose this selection and you can give the user full control or read or contribute rights. Or you can click the Give Users Permission Directly radio button and select the check boxes that apply to the permissions you want to assign. (Figure 5.11 shows both of the radio button selections.)

FIGURE 5.9 Site Actions menu

FIGURE 5.10 People and Groups page

Once the user is created, their account will show up in People and Groups: Home Members (see Figure 5.13).

At this point, you can edit the user information by clicking their name to bring up the User Information screen, shown in Figure 5.14. Alternatively, when your user logs onto the site, they can update their own information.

FIGURE 5.11   Add Users window

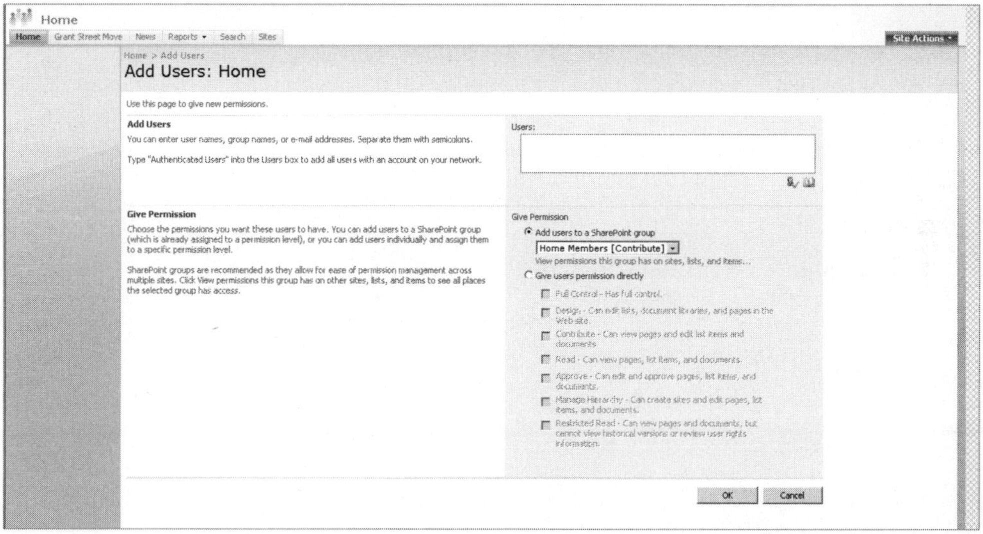

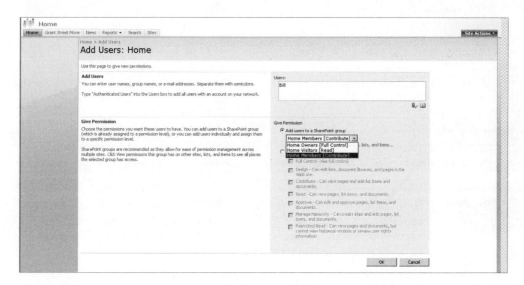

FIGURE 5.12   Giving permissions

FIGURE 5.13   Home Members

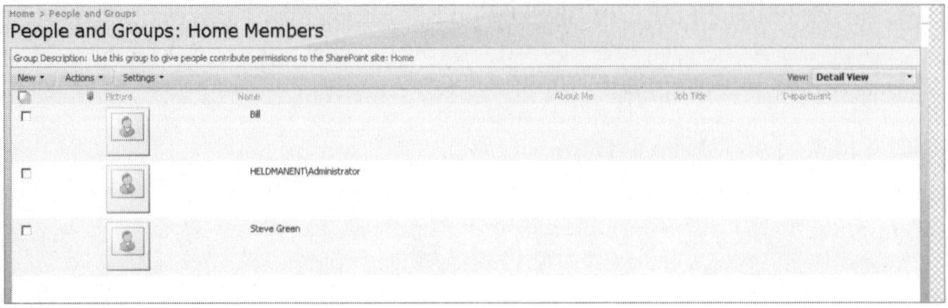

Home > People and Groups
People and Groups: Home Members

Group Description: Use this group to give people contribute permissions to the SharePoint site: Home

New ▾   Actions ▾   Settings ▾   View: **Detail View**   ▾

		Picture		Name	About Me	Job Title	Department
☐				Bill			
☐				HELDMANENT\Administrator			
☐				Steve Green			

FIGURE 5.14   Editing user information

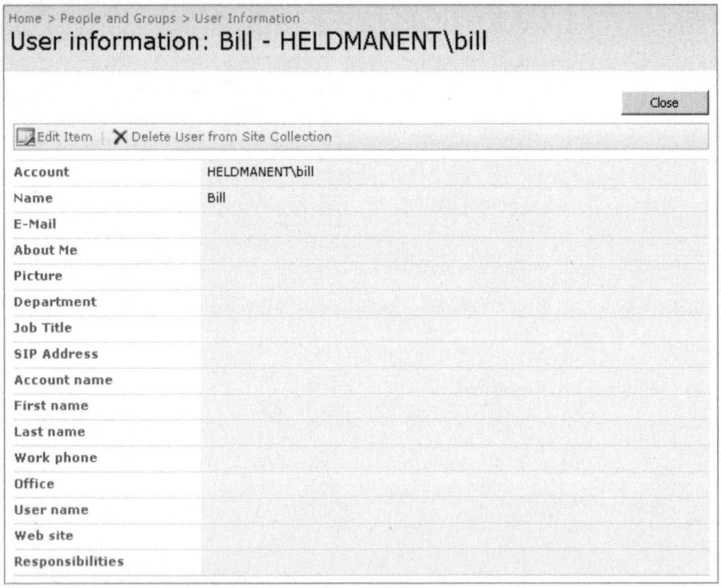

Home > People and Groups > User Information
User information: Bill - HELDMANENT\bill

Close

📝 Edit Item | ✖ Delete User from Site Collection

Account	HELDMANENT\bill
Name	Bill
E-Mail	
About Me	
Picture	
Department	
Job Title	
SIP Address	
Account name	
First name	
Last name	
Work phone	
Office	
User name	
Web site	
Responsibilities	

You have the ability to add a picture to the user's information if you'd like, thus putting a face with a name.

You can make it a matter of policy to decide if users should fill in their own information (provided it was not already filled in as a result of being imported from AD) and if pictures are required.

In an AD environment, a single sign-on (SSO) process can be initiated in MOSS, allowing pass-through authentication into the site. MOSS server must be a member of the domain and able to contact a domain controller. When setting up SSO in MOSS, consult with your administrators.

Last we'll point out that MOSS has the ability to import AD information into your site through a profile importation process. If there is user information in AD you'd like to capture, you can configure a profile import to run within Office Server. This profile will cause Office Server to crawl Active Directory (determine the information contained therein) and write the attributes into MOSS database. This AD information is used in conjunction with what little information is already contained in the database. The profile import can be scheduled and is one way to comply with in-place AD infrastructure management policies.

If this sounds complicated, it is. It is beyond the scope of this book to go into detail about this topic, and we recommend consulting your network administrator and Microsoft blogs, newsgroups, and websites to get more complete details.

MOSS and Windows Server 2003 (W2K3)

In a workgroup setting where the server is stand-alone and not a domain controller in an AD environment, users will have to first log onto the network as they normally do and then log onto the project management site. The credentials (username and password) they'll utilize to access the site are identical to the network logon, but they have to do it twice. So do you need to set up a full-blown AD environment to support MOSS and its features?

There are two possible answers to this question. The first is this: Adding AD to a server running W2K3 isn't very difficult, doesn't take up that much extra space or processing power, and is easily accomplished in just a few steps. But perhaps you might have outsourced the initial installation of your server and you don't want to pay to have it upgraded. Or maybe the server is a member of a workgroup that's been functioning fine and you don't want to disrupt something that's working well. And maybe you've already installed MOSS and don't want to go through the installation process again.

The second possible answer: No worries. You can create user accounts in the W2K3 server's local account database and users can log onto MOSS site just fine. Here's how:

1. On the W2K3 server, right-click My Computer and select Manage.

2. Expand the Local Users and Groups selection.

3. Click Users.

4. Right-click in the Users pane and select New User.

5. Fill in the detail information for your new user account.

6. Repeat as needed to add as many accounts as required.

When users navigate to your MOSS site, they simply key in the name of the server, a back-slash, and their username, along with their password, as in the following example:

Username: PMSErver\Bill

Password: *Bill's password*

Contact List Update

Fortunately for us, Microsoft Outlook and Excel play nicely together in the sandbox. We started a contact list in Chapter 3. Now that we have our new team member information, we can add that to the list and easily import this data into Outlook Contacts. Figure 5.15 is the contact list we started in Chapter 3.

The first row is the Contacts row header. (We exported a contacts list from Outlook in an Excel format so that we could determine the exact column header names that Outlook expects to see.) As we noted in Chapter 3, it's important that you do not change any of the column header names or the import will not work. We've also hidden some columns—such as column C (Middle Name)—but this won't affect the import. When Outlook imports the contact list, it will check the columns under each header name for data and put the data it finds into a new contact profile. Make certain to add contacts one after the other in the spreadsheet without leaving blank rows in between. And one more note—if you add Grant St. Move in the category column for each of your stakeholders and team members, once you've imported the information into Outlook Contacts, you can perform a selection in Outlook on the category called Grant St. Move to find all contacts associated with the project.

Let's say that we want to import the contact information for Steve Green, our senior network administrator, and Aimee Owen, his assistant, into our contact list. We just key in the information we know under each of the column header names starting with Title, FirstName, LastName, and so on.

FIGURE 5.15   Contact list

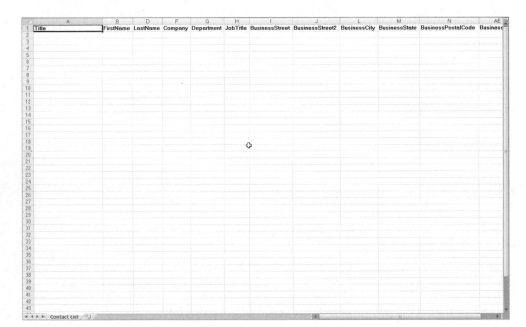

Next we go to Outlook and click File ➤ Import and Export... and choose Import from Another Program or File, as shown in Figure 5.16.

Click Next and select Microsoft Excel as the file source program, as shown in Figure 5.17.

Click Next again and browse to find the contacts list you want to import. Note the options to allow duplicates to be allowed, replaced, or discarded (Figure 5.18).

FIGURE 5.16   Importing a file

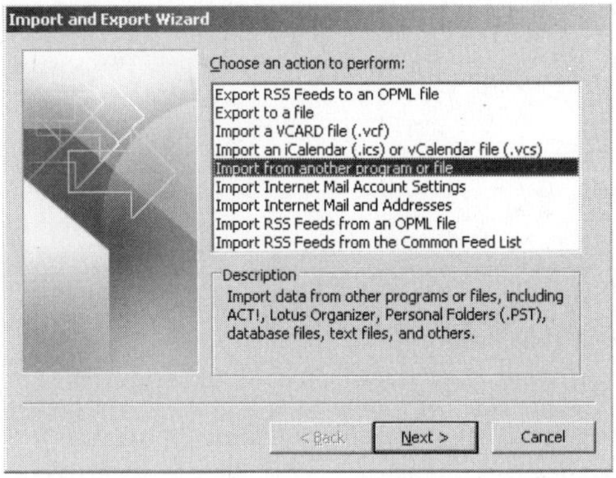

FIGURE 5.17   Choosing Microsoft Excel as the file source program

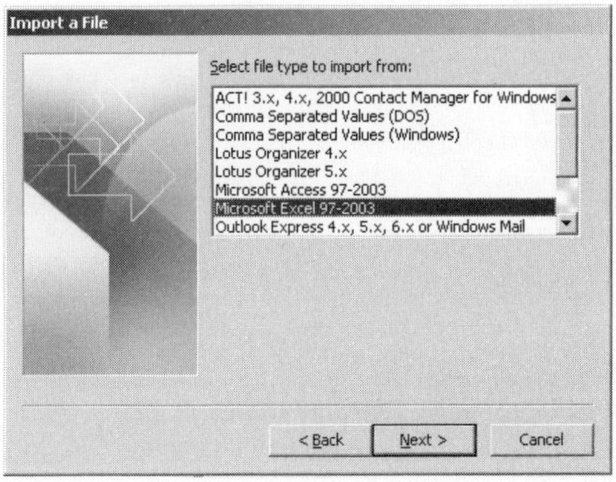

Select the destination folder in which to place your new contacts. Of course you'll probably opt for the Contacts folder, as shown in Figure 5.19.

Click OK and Finish. Provided you've properly prepared your import file, the import process will place new contacts into your Contacts folder.

Now that our team members have been added to the contacts list and safely imported into Outlook Contacts, we'll look at the supplies and materials we may need for the project.

FIGURE 5.18   Choosing the file to import

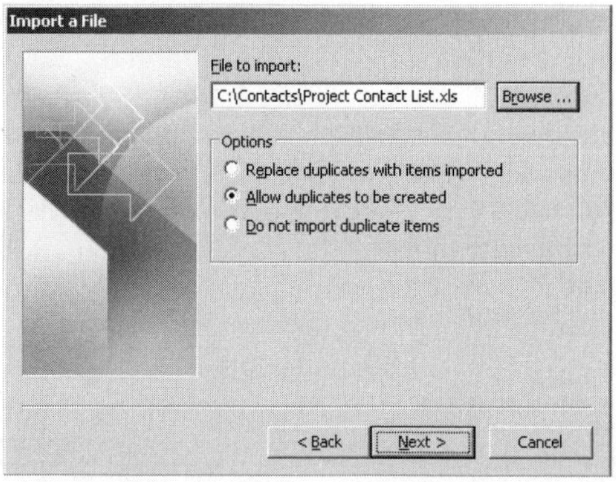

FIGURE 5.19   Choosing a destination folder

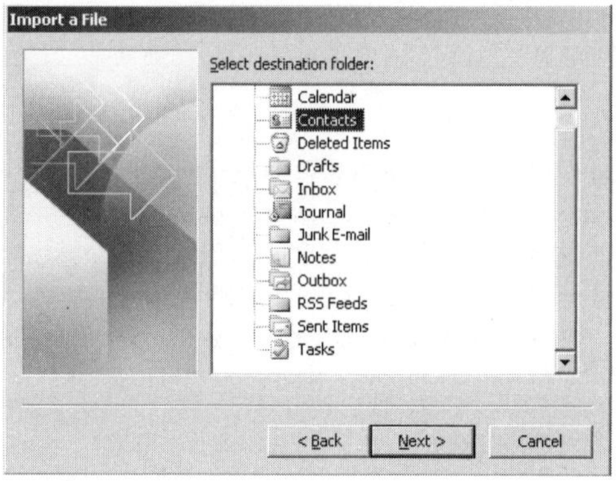

Procuring Materials, Supplies, and Equipment

All projects require human resources to complete the tasks. Most all projects also require materials or supplies or equipment of some type. One of the prerequisites for determining material needs is the project scope statement and requirements document. Understanding the requirements for each of the deliverables will help you determine what types of materials you may need for the project. For example, one of the requirements for the Grant St. Move office connections deliverable is at least one quad electrical outlet to be installed at each work location. We also know we need servers for the data center. These are obvious examples of materials or equipment needed for the project. It's a relatively simple matter to document these items in a materials list, which we'll do next.

Defining the materials and supplies needed for the project, along with identifying the human resources needed, will help you determine cost estimates for the project. We'll look at cost estimates in Chapter 9, "Creating the Project Budget and Determining Performance Measures."

Creating a Materials List

There's no rocket science behind a materials list. It's fairly straightforward. For example, when determining the number of quad outlets we need, we multiply the number of workstations by the number of outlets and add in the additional ones for conference rooms, common areas, kitchens, the data center and closets, and so on.

You should begin to capture the essential information for materials as soon as you know it. You guessed it—we're going to create a spreadsheet form to capture this information. Figure 5.20 shows an example.

You can see some of the obvious information captured in the example, like the description of the equipment, quantity needed, and cost. We've also tied the equipment to the requirement in the Requirement Number column. Remember those requirements numbers we devised in Chapter 4? You might recall that ONC-002 was the number assigned to the quad outlets for the office network connections deliverable. When you tie the materials list to the requirements, you can easily track the project budget and know exactly what was spent for each deliverable by summing up all of the materials for all of the requirements for each deliverable.

FIGURE 5.20   Materials list

A	B	C	D	E	F
Materials List					
Project Number					
Date					
Project Title					
Project Manager					
Description of Equipment	Quantity	Cost	Total	Date Required	Requirement Number
			0		
			0		
			0		
			0		
SubTotal for Requirement Number:			0		
			0		
			0		
			0		
SubTotal for Requirement Number:			0		
Total			0		

We've also included a formula to automatically calculate amounts in the Total column (this is quantity times cost). You should include sum calculations as the last row of each group of requirements (those that belong to the same deliverable), and the last row is a total sum of all costs on the materials list.

> You could begin compiling your materials list after you have the requirements document completed. If your organization has a lengthy procurement period for high-dollar items, you'll want to order them as soon as possible so that you don't impact the project schedule. It's also a good idea to come back and finalize the materials list after you've identified the project tasks. You may find the act of identifying tasks brings up new requirements not recorded early on in the project, and those new requirements may need supplies and materials. We'll talk about documenting tasks in Chapter 8, "Constructing the Project Schedule and Budget."

Not all materials are easily purchased off the shelf. Sometimes you'll need to determine whether you should make or buy the materials or services needed; oddly enough, this is called make-or-buy analysis.

Make-or-Buy Analysis

Make-or-buy analysis involves determining whether the goods or services needed for the project should be purchased or developed within the organization. The make-or-buy question could be asked for individual requirements, deliverables, or the project as a whole. In our Grant St. Move project, the question is fairly easily answered for the physical move itself. The organization is not equipped and doesn't have the resources needed to physically move all the assets from one location to another. They aren't planning on going into this line of work anytime soon either, so the buy decision is fairly easy to make.

> Typically, make-or-buy decisions for the project as a whole are made at the Initiating stage.

There are several things to consider when determining whether to produce the product or service needed or whether to buy it. Cost is one of the most significant factors. So is time. And sometimes, cost and time together will determine the answer to this question. For example, if we stick with our original design at Grant St. for a moment, our team could pull the cabling to all work locations and conference rooms. But our team is not experienced at this task and it could be completed much more quickly and efficiently by a vendor who does this regularly. Additionally, if the terminations are not crimped correctly, there could be reduced bandwidth (which means lots of complaints going to the help desk). Does it make sense to spend the additional time to train our staff on proper techniques and add time to the project to account for the team's inexperience at this task? The answer is—it depends. And that's an example of the type of questions you need to ask when performing make-or-buy analysis. If you can add additional time to the project and reduce costs by training a few of your own staff to perform this function, it could be the right thing to do. If time is a constraint on the project, it may well be worth the cost to hire a vendor to perform this task.

When considering costs in make-or-buy analysis, don't forget to include all the costs to produce the product, like materials, goods, facilities, salaries, and indirect costs. Indirect costs include such things as management costs, training costs, administrative overhead, ongoing maintenance, and so on. Don't overlook other factors like skills and ability of the team, capacity issues, availability, and priority of projects or assignments when performing this analysis.

The goal of this process is to decide if it's more cost effective and efficient to make or buy the goods and services needed for the project. Remember the old saying that time is money— even if there are not tangible costs associated with a make decision, there is a time cost. Your resources will be working on producing this product rather than working on another deliverable of the project.

Soliciting Bids and Proposals

Once you have your materials list in hand and know which services you need to buy, you're ready to prepare proposals for potential vendors to bid on. Some purchases are small enough you can simply prepare a purchase order for the goods and you're done. In the case of movers for the Grant St. Move project, we'll want at least a few different moving companies to bid on the project so that we get the most service at the best price. In order to do that, we'll need to prepare a request for proposals (RFP) or request for bids (RFB).

 When writing the RFP, describe the business requirements you're trying to fulfill and avoid spelling out detailed technical specifications aside from the absolute essentials. You may find that responses from vendors include more than you anticipated and they'll come up with some creative strategies for meeting the requirements you didn't think about.

Some organizations have procurement departments that will handle the RFP process for you. However, you'll still need to prepare the requirements and a statement of work that outlines what you want the vendor to bid on. The project manager should also have a solid understanding of the procurement and contracting process within their organization. It's beyond the scope of this book to go into all the details of contracting and what constitutes a solid RFP document. Make certain you're familiar with your organizational policy for requesting bids and preparing contracts. And remember that you aren't off the hook just because you have a procurement department to handle this for you. The contract manager will look to you to provide them with information regarding the work and the vendor's performance once they start.

Selecting a Winner

Even if you do have a procurement department to handle bids and contracting, you will most probably be involved in the vendor selection process. After all, you're the one who'll have to work with the vendor and oversee their performance and determine if they deliver what they said they would.

There are many ways to select vendors. Your organization may have a prequalified list of vendors that you can choose from to do the work. If you don't have experience working with a particular vendor, it's important to check their references. You want to know if they have experience working on other projects of similar size and scope and if they have the specified qualifications and skills to perform the work. It's also important to know if their employees interacted with the organization's team members in a friendly and professional manner. In the case of reviewing bids and proposals, you might use additional, detailed methods of selection, such as a screening system or weighted scoring model. We'll look at both next.

Screening Systems

Screening systems have predetermined criteria that are used to evaluate the proposals. If the response does not meet the predetermined criteria, they are eliminated. For example, one of the screening criteria we could use for the cabling contractor in the Grant St. Move project is that they have experience working with fiber-optic cable. If the potential vendor's proposal doesn't mention this fact, they do not progress to the next stage of procurement.

Screening criteria is determined at the time the RFP is prepared. The project manager and other selection committee members work together to determine appropriate measurements for selection.

Procurement processes may involve a few steps for smaller purchases or several for larger ones. Typical procurement steps include advertising an RFP, accepting responses, vendor presentations, interviews, question period and opportunity to amend the RFP, vendor selection, and contract.

Screening systems are often used in combination with weighted scoring models, which we'll look at next.

Weighted Scoring Model

Weighted scoring models are an objective way to score vendor responses to RFPs. It assures that the selection committee members are all using the same criteria to evaluate the responses.

As with the screening system, the criteria for the weighted scoring model is determined about the same time the RFP is completed. Sometimes, the scoring model may be included in the RFP so vendors know what they'll be judged on.

Several criteria are outlined for the model, and each is assigned a weight depending on its importance—the higher the importance, the higher the weight. Assigning weights of one to five (five being the most important) is common. Each selection committee member is given a copy of the RFP response and they rate each of the criteria in the weighted scoring model according to how well the vendor can meet the requirement. The score assigned is based on individual judgment and interpretation. If there are a sufficient number of reviewers—we recommend at least three to five—the final scores will more accurately reflect the vendor's ability than if there's only one reviewer. After everyone has scored the RFP responses, their weighted scores should be averaged together for an overall, final score.

If we were weighting criteria for moving companies for our Grant St. Move project bid, they might look something like what's shown in Figure 5.21. (This is only a sample portion of the criteria we'd use.)

As you can see in this example, our most important criteria are experience with corporate moves and certified to move computer equipment. The weight for each factor is multiplied by the rating given by the reviewer and then all the scores are totaled to come up with a final score. You can see that Vendor B scored the highest.

This is easy to set up in an Excel spreadsheet like the one we set up (Figure 5.21). Multiply Vendor Score for each vendor by the weight to determine Vendor Weighted Score. Use sums to total all the scores in this column.

FIGURE 5.21   Weighted scoring model

A	B	C	D	E	F
Weighted Scoring Model					
Project Number					
Date					
Project Title					
Project Manager					
Criteria	Weight	Vendor A Score	Vendor A Weighted Score	Vendor B Score	Vendor B Weighted Score
Bonded and insured	3	5	15	5	15
Certified to move computer equipment	5	2	10	4	20
Ability to move at least 250 offices at once	4	4	16	4	16
Experience with corporate moves	5	3	15	5	25
Total Weighted Score			56		76

Managing Vendors

Once you've selected a vendor, you'll have to manage them. Or did you think you could just turn the project (or deliverable) over to them and ask them to phone you when they're finished? Unfortunately, we've seen project managers do this, and often the project suffers for it. Vendors have a vested interest in their own company. Does that mean they won't work hard for you or deliver on time or produce outstanding work? Of course not. We've had the pleasure of working with some outstanding vendors over the course of our careers. But never forget that vendors have taken on the work to make money for their company, to establish experience in a particular industry, to establish experience with this type of project. That means you'll have to work closely with them to develop a work plan, monitor the quality and quantity of their work, and assure that they meet deliverable due dates.

You'll also work as the liaison between the vendor and your organization (or assign someone you trust and who has experience to this task) to ensure that the vendor gets what they need from your team members in order to meet their deliverables. It's difficult and unfair to hold vendors accountable for incomplete deliverables that require involvement or information from your organization before they can complete the work. Be sure you've documented the roles and responsibilities of team members and other departments within your organization and include the interaction expected of them and the vendor.

Here is a list of some of the questions and factors the project manager should focus on when managing vendor relationships. This isn't an exhaustive list by any means, and several of these items could be detailed in the RFP or contract statement of work. The moral of the story is that the project manager, that's you, will have to make certain the vendor performs as expected.

- What project management processes will the vendor use? Review their process and work through modifications if needed to meet your requirements.

- How often will the vendor report on progress and in what format? How will progress be measured?

- Do the vendor's employees have the skills, experience, and education required to complete the tasks? Sometimes the answer to this question won't become evident until the work begins. Don't hesitate to require that the vendor replace someone who's obviously struggling with inexperience.

- Have acceptance criteria been documented for the deliverables (and for the project if needed)? These are typically spelled out in the contract or statement of work. Acceptance of the deliverables and determining if they meet the acceptance criteria will be up to the project manager.

- Is long-term maintenance of the deliverable required upon completion? If so, how will turnover or knowledge transfer occur? Will the vendor perform maintenance for a period of time or will the organization be responsible for this?

- Are there security and or privacy requirements that should be adhered to? Is the vendor working with personal or financial data, for example?

- Have you informed the vendor that all contract provisions apply to the vendor's subcontractors as well?

- What provisions have been detailed in the contract to require that the vendor correct problems, to rectify late delivery, or to terminate their work?

Depending on the requirements of the project, you may need to document an escalation path and have contact information for after hours support. Record the after hours support numbers in your contact list and don't forget to add your vendors' contact information to the contact list we started in Chapter 3. Follow the same steps we outlined in the section "Adding Team Members to MOSS" earlier in this chapter to add vendor information.

Chapter 6

Assessing and Tracking Risk

We are well on our way to completing the project planning documents for our project. In this chapter, we'll turn our attention to risks and the creation of risk response plans.

Risk is apparent in almost everything we undertake. As far as our project is concerned, we want to know as much as we can about the threats and opportunities that may appear during the project so that we can minimize negative impacts or take full advantage of positive ones and increase the potential for a successful outcome.

We'll examine identifying risks, performing risk assessments, documenting risks in a risk register, creating plans to minimize their impacts, tracking the risks and responses, and more. Let's get started.

Identifying Risks

Each of us takes risks on a daily basis. We don't know about where you live, but in our city just getting to work every morning is a risk. Between the red light runners, rapid lane changers, and road rage warriors, it's a wonder we don't all drive tanks to assure that we get there safely. Speaking of driving, have you ever seen those dream catchers some drivers have hanging from their windshields? Imagine that's your project instead and think of it as an inherent risk catcher. Risk by definition is uncertainty, and it's not possible to have a project without having risk.

Our job as project managers, then, is to identify the type of threats or opportunities that may creep up on us before they happen. The key word here is, of course, *before*. It's much better if you're prepared ahead of time and know what could happen and how to deal with it when it does. If you simply wait for something to happen—they will, we promise.

We'll take a look at some identification techniques in the next section.

Identification Techniques

There are many ways you might go about identifying risks, ranging from brainstorming sessions to detailed industry-specific checklists. We'll outline some of the more popular techniques in this section. The most important thing about identifying risks is that you do—just the act of thinking about and writing down what could potentially happen will give you a head start toward a successful project.

Although we tend to think of risks in a negative light, not all risks are bad or pose painful consequences to the project. Some risks are opportunities in disguise. Going through the exercise of identifying risks may reveal some alternative ways of performing the project work or provide opportunities for the organization you hadn't thought of before.

Historical Information

The first place to start with risk identification is reviewing historical documentation. Past projects of similar size and scope are a great starting place because the risks that occurred (and those the team thought might occur) have been recorded along with the success or weaknesses of the response plans. Use this documentation as your starting point for the remaining techniques we'll talk about.

Brainstorming

We talked about brainstorming in Chapter 4. The same principle applies here. In the case of risk identification, you could start first with the historical documentation and have the facilitator read through the list of risks that occurred on the past project. Then the group can yea or nay the risks for inclusion on this project. Remember, the ground rules are that no idea is a bad idea. Everyone has equal opportunity to express ideas, and the beauty of this technique is that one person's idea may produce another idea from someone else that leads to another and so on.

Have a facilitator record the risks and begin grouping them into similar categories. You might have an assistant bring a laptop to the meeting and start recording these in an Excel spreadsheet right away. (We'll talk about documenting all this information a little later in this chapter.)

Nominal Group Technique

The nominal group technique is almost identical to the sticky-backed note technique we talked about in Chapter 4. The question to ask regarding risk is, What is the absolute worst thing that could happen during the project? Again, have a facilitator gather the sticky-backed notes and put them on a whiteboard according to logical groupings. When you're done with the negative impacts, ask this question to uncover the opportunities: What events could occur on the project or as a result of the project that may produce opportunities?

Assumptions Analysis

We recorded our assumptions in the project scope statement back in Chapter 4. You'll recall that assumptions are things we believe to be true. The further along you are in the project planning process, the more information you're going to know and uncover. That means you should take another look at your assumptions and make certain the reasoning still holds true for each of them. When you wrote the project scope statement, you may have assumed that a particular vendor you trust and have experience working with would be available to assist on this project. Ask the team some questions: Is the assumption still true? What if after working on the project the assumption proves to be false? What are the impacts to the project if this vendor isn't available when needed and we need to make some other arrangements? Is their participation critical to the project's success?

Go through each assumption and ask similar questions. There are two you should always ask: Is the assumption still true? and What impact is there to the project if the assumption turns out to be false?

Interviews

Interviews are question-and-answer sessions with subject matter experts, stakeholders, team members, customers, and anyone else who might help you identify risks. Their experience on past projects will help bring to light issues you could face on this project. Show them your list of assumptions, the project deliverables, and some of the key requirements of those deliverables to get them thinking about what could happen.

Industry Checklists

Don't forget to do some research into your own industry, including associations or special groups supporting your industry, for information they may have about common project risks. For example, the construction industry has been at project management for a very long time and there are university courses devoted to risk management for their projects. Check to see what's available for your industry.

 Don't forget that these techniques can be used to perform requirements gathering and analysis as well.

Take care with any of these techniques that you're bringing to light the root cause of the risk and not just the symptom. Sneezing, itchy and watery eyes, and a sore throat are all symptoms. The cause could be allergies, a cold, an infection, and so on. We'd treat an infection with antibiotics, but they'd have no effect on allergies. So the cause is what we're after—understanding what's at the root of risk—so that we can develop effective response plans.

Common Project Risks

Risks come in all flavors: chocolate, vanilla, and strawberry and every other flavor you can imagine. Some risks will be obvious and stand right out, others you may know about but not have a good understanding of their impact, and there are risks you don't know about. Obviously, you can't identify the risks you don't know about because, by definition, you don't know what they are.

Risks not only come in all flavors, they can occur both inside the organization and outside the organization. Internal risks come about due to the nature of the project itself, management decisions or changes, organizational issues, budget issues, and resource issues. External risks come about for many reasons as well, such as weather, legal issues, market issues, timing, social concerns, environmental issues, and changes in vendors' organizations. Look both internally and externally for obvious common risk events that may occur.

Project constraints are another thing to examine for common project risks. Constraints aren't risks in and of themselves, but they may lead to risk events. For example, we've worked on countless projects with restricted budgets. Oddly enough, many of those projects suffered from further budget cuts once they began. We started out with a constraint (a restricted budget) and then additional cuts were taken (a risk event). Take care to look at time-related constraints as well. If the project must be completed by a specific date, what would the loss of key personnel or the unavailability of a vendor or critical piece of hardware do to the project?

Dig out your planning documents as well to uncover risks. Is the scope statement well defined? If not, there are probably risks associated with it. It's a good idea to reexamine risks after you've completed the project task list and schedule. Working through the schedule and assigning resources may highlight some potential risks you didn't think about earlier in the planning process. Also, reexamine risks when change requests are submitted. Changes to scope, time, or budget may bring new risks to the surface.

A rule of thumb for risk identification is to review risks at every status meeting, ask if there are risks that could occur that haven't been identified, review the impact of change requests as they pertain to generating risks, and review any changes to scope, schedule, or budget for risks.

The following list includes some of risks we've identified for the Grant St. Move project:

- Power conditioning units (they assure that precise voltage and amperage are delivered to the computer servers in the data center) are not sized correctly.

- Computers are not installed at each workstation by each scheduled move date.

- Telecommunications company can't provide the circuits needed to the building by the due date.

- Building security system is not functioning at move-in date.

- Moving company is not available as scheduled.

We'll add these risks to the risk register later in this chapter.

Risk identification is not a one-time event. This is something that should happen continually on the project. Devote a few minutes at each status meeting to discuss potential risk events and those that have or look like they are going to occur.

Creating a Risk Checklist

In this section, we'll collect all the risks we talked about in the previous section (and throw in some new ones) into a risk checklist (see Figure 6.1). This checklist is a template that you can use to help you get started identifying risks for the project. We encourage you to modify and add to this list for your particular industry and organization. It will make risk identification on future projects much more efficient.

FIGURE 6.1   Risk checklist

	A	B	C	D	E	F
	A6	▾	ƒx	Risk Number		
1			Risk Checklist			
2	Project Number					
3	Date					
4	Project Title					
5	Project Manager					
6	Risk Number	Risk Category	Risk Name	Risk Score	Response Plan Y/N	Responsible Party
7						
8						
9						
10						
11						
12						

The checklist, as you can see, shows for each risk the type, characteristic (or its impact on the project), category, and a place to check off that you've examined it. Categories help you put risks into common, logical groupings. We recommend that you define the categories of risk before you begin the risk identification process. You can modify these categories and add another one or two when you've finished the initial identification exercise, but it's easier to begin grouping risks into categories as you start identifying them than it is to go back through the list and do it later. At the end of the project when you're looking back over the things that went well and not so well, you'll find that some categories of risk are more prevalent on the project than others. This will help on future projects because you may find, for example, that the team wasn't as successful identifying external risks as they were finding project management risks. You might use the following risk categories:

- Project management
- Personnel
- Financial
- Organizational
- External
- Internal
- Scope
- Schedule

- Budget
- Technical
- Quality

The next step is to document the risks. You could do this in a two-step process. That is, first perform risk identification with your team, record all the risks in a spreadsheet, and assign categories to them. The next step involves performing risk assessments and looking at the potential impact risks may have on the project. This information should also be recorded along with the risks in what's known as the risk register. We'll talk about documentation and the risk register in a later section of this chapter.

Performing Risk Assessment

Risk assessment involves analyzing each risk you've identified to determine what probability the risk has of occurring and what impact it will have if it does occur. The end goal of risk assessment is to determine which risks need response plans. For example, say we've identified the CEO's resignation as a risk on the Grant St. Move project. Our team has determined that at this point there would be little impact if this risk occurred because the new lease has been signed at the Grant St. building and notice to terminate leases has been given for all the current locations. In other words, the move is on no matter whether a new CEO takes over or not. The new CEO may decide the move isn't a good idea, but it would be so costly to reverse these decisions at this point that it wouldn't be feasible to cancel the project. Therefore, no response plan for this risk is needed. It doesn't mean the risk can't occur; it just means the team has made a conscious choice to not prepare a plan for this event.

After analyzing each risk on the list, we'll decide which ones need plans based on their risk score. Before we get into the analysis techniques, we need to understand the risk tolerance levels of our organization. We'll look at that next.

Risk Tolerance

Risk, like other project planning processes, concerns balance. You want to find that point at which you and the stakeholders are comfortable taking a risk based on the benefits you can potentially gain. In a nutshell, you're balancing the action of taking a risk against avoiding its consequences or impact.

Organizations have risk tolerances just as individuals do. You'll have to determine the risk tolerance levels of the stakeholders, management team, customers, and others involved on the project. Keep in mind that risk tolerances will vary among different groups of stakeholders, so find out if they're risk takers or risk avoiders. You might also want to know if risk tolerances are higher for different categories of risk; for example, the stakeholders may be more tolerant of schedule risk than financial risk. Use interviewing techniques, ask previous team members or other project managers who've worked with some of the people involved on this project, and don't forget to review past project information to discover what the tolerance levels are.

Determining Tolerance Levels

Let's look at an example of risk tolerance that involves very simple, everyday activities.

Most all of us bathe frequently (we hope so anyway). The risk exists that you may step on a bar of soap when you're in the shower or bath, slip, and potentially injure yourself. Do you let this risk keep you from taking a shower regularly? Of course not—if you do, you need to be reading books on topics other than project management!

Your tolerance for this risk is extremely high, and you're willing to take on the possibility of the consequences occurring to reap the benefits (and your coworkers thank you for that). Now let's say you cross a busy intersection on the way to your work building every morning. This intersection is notorious for car-pedestrian accidents. How likely are you to cross against the light in this intersection to be at work a minute or so earlier than you would if you waited for the walk signal? Well, if you could answer, we're guessing 80 percent of you would wait for the light. The other 20 percent might do an extra good job of surveying the traffic and make a dash for it. Those 20-percenters, and you know who you are, have a higher risk tolerance than the wait-for-the-light group in this situation.

Risk Probability and Impact

There are several ways you can determine probability and impact. We'll look at two of them in this section: risk probability and impact charts and a probability and impact matrix. First, let's look at the definitions of *probability* and *impact* so we're all on the same page.

Probability is the likelihood a risk event will occur. For example, when you throw a coin into the air, you have a 50 percent chance of it coming up heads and a 50 percent change of it coming up tails. Determining probability for risks isn't necessarily this easy. Typically, you'll use experts to "guess" at the probability for the risks you've identified on the project. Granted, the guess is an educated one based on their past experiences with other similar projects, so it's still better than a coin toss.

Choose the subject matter experts and stakeholders you'll use for this exercise wisely. You want experts who have varied backgrounds and experiences so that you don't get caught up in the "group think" problem. If all your experts have information technology backgrounds, for example, risks associated with budgets or marketing may not end up with the right levels of probability associated with their occurrence.

Impact is the amount of pain a negative risk event may cause or the amount of gain a positive one may have. Impact is usually dependent on the risk and is a little more definitive than probability. If we wanted to determine the impact of losing a key resource on our Grant St. project for example, we could approximate the amount of time the schedule would be delayed while we searched for someone else with those skills (and then give them time to get up to speed on the project). We could also approximate the cost associated with delaying orders, extending vendor contracts due to the delay, and so on.

Risk Probability and Impact Charts

Probability and impact may be expressed as either a number or a value. Numbers are always expressed as percentages that range from 0.0 (meaning there's no probability of a risk event occurring) to 1.0 (meaning there's a 100 percent chance of the risk occurring). Values are usually measured by a high-medium-low scale or some variation.

Figure 6.2 is a risk probability and impact chart template. We've designated a risk score column that combines the probability and impact scores for a total. We'll plug in some example data shortly.

We've used values (high, medium, and low) in our risk probability and impact chart. These are applicable for small to medium projects and even large projects where there are a minimum number of risks. Figure 6.3 shows the risks we identified for the Grant St. Move project with values assigned to each. (This isn't a full list of risks of course).

FIGURE 6.2   Probability and impact chart

	A	B	C	D	E
	A20		f_x		
1		**Probability and Impact Chart**			
2	Project Number				
3	Date				
4	Project Title				
5	Project Manager				
6	Risk Number	Risk Name	Probability High-Med-Low	Impact High-Med-Low	Risk Score
7					
8					
9					
10					
11					
12					

FIGURE 6.3   Probability and impact chart for Grant St. move

	A	B	C	D	E
1		**Probability and Impact Chart for Grant St. Move**			
2	Project Number				
3	Date				
4	Project Title				
5	Project Manager				
6	Risk Number	Risk Name	Probability High-Med-Low	Impact High-Med-Low	Risk Score
7		Power conditioning units not sized correctly	Low	High	Low/High
8		Computers not installed at workstations on time	Low	High	Low/High
9		Telecomm cannot provide circuits on time	High	High	High/High
10		Building security system not ready on due date	Low	Low	Low/Low
11		Moving company not available as scheduled	Medium	High	Medium/High
12		Scope statement does not detail all requirements	Medium	Medium	Medium/Medium
13		Key IT personnel not available	Medium	Medium	Medium/Medium
14		Management turnover--move is canceled	Low	Low	Low/Low
15		Scope statement is not approved by stakeholders	Low	Low	Low/Low
16		Company is bought out while planning the move	Low	Medium	Low/Medium
17		Employees not packed by moving day	Low	Medium	Low/Medium

Let's walk through the first risk, "the power conditioning units are not sized correctly." The probability for this risk based on our expert's opinion is low. The impact, however, is high. The team's reasoning is that if this risk were to occur, server performance would be erratic at best, meaning users could not send email, access software programs needed to perform their jobs, or access the Internet. That would mean our project would not meet its goal of "…no loss of productivity and no downtime." The risk score is a combination of the probability and impact scores, so this risk is low/high.

> You can use brainstorming techniques, the nominal group technique, or interviews to determine the risk probability and impact values for each risk. For example, ask your group this question to determine impact: If this risk event occurred, what's the worst possible impact it could have on the project, to the customer, to the organization, and so on? Does that make it a high, medium, or low impact risk?

Risk Impact Scales

Next we want to devise a probability and impact matrix (PI matrix), which is much like the probability and impact chart in that you determine both the probability and impact that a risk event might occur and assign the risk an overall score. Typically, numbers are used for the values for a PI matrix. Since we only have low, medium, and high values so far, we need to create a risk impact scale as our first step.

It seems to be much easier for teams to assign a "medium" impact to a risk than to assign a percentage, and with the risk impact scale, they still can. The twist here is that we'll assign numbers to the values so that we can then plug those numbers into the PI matrix. The impact scale goes one step further and describes a range of possible impacts or consequences to help better determine what score should be assigned for the impact. Time and cost are almost always included as an impact. Your team will have to define other criteria for the scales depending on the nature of your project. For the Grant St. Move project, we added Productivity—downtime for computer or phones—as a criteria. Figure 6.4 shows an impact scale.

Looking at the scale, the team told us that the impact of the power conditioning units not being sized correctly would affect productivity. They've determined that the impact of this risk is high, so it receives an impact score of 0.7. Now we'll determine probability.

FIGURE 6.4   Risk impact scale

	A	B	C	D	E	F
1			**Risk Impact Scale**			
2	Project Number					
3	Date					
4	Project Title					
5	Project Manager					
6	Criteria for Risk Events	Low-Low	Low	Medium	High	High-High
7	Score	0.05	0.1	0.04	0.7	0.9
8	Time	No significant impact	Less than 5% increase	5–10% increase	11–15% increase	More than 15% increase
9	Cost	No significant impact	Less than 2% increase	2–5% increase	5–8% increase	More than 8% increase
10	Productivity (computer or phone outages)	No significant impact	Outages less than 1 hour	1 hour–2 hour outage	2 hour–4 hour outage	More than 4 hour outage
11						

If you want to stick with the low-low to high-high values for probability as well, you could devise probability scales like the one we did for impact. For example, a low-low probability for the productivity criteria may have a 0.05 score. We find that the team doesn't seem to have as much trouble assigning a percentage for the probability of a risk event as it does assigning a percentage to its impact.

Probability for the power conditioning units sizing risk is low, so we've assigned it a 0.2 chance of occurring. Probability is multiplied by impact (0.2 × 0.7) to come up with the final risk score, in this case 0.14. Now we'll go to the PI matrix to determine if this risk needs a response plan.

To determine the total risk score quickly and easily, you might want to use the spreadsheet we developed in the section "Risk Probability and Impact Charts" (shown in Figure 6.2) and modify it to include a formula in the Risk Score column that multiplies probability by impact.

Probability and Impact Matrix

The PI matrix has a series of possible risk scores based on the values we assigned to both probability and impact. To complicate matters, we're now going to assign high-medium-low values to ranges of these numbers. The organization or project team will have to decide what the range values should be based on their risk tolerance levels. Perhaps only risks that fall into the high range on the PI matrix need response plans. Figure 6.5 shows a PI matrix.

FIGURE 6.5   Probability and impact matrix

	A	B	C	D	E	F
1				PI Matrix		
2	Project Number					
3	Date					
4	Project Title					
5	Project Manager					
6	Probability	Impact Scores				
7		0.05	0.1	0.4	0.7	0.9
8	0.8	0.04	0.08	0.32	0.56	0.72
9	0.6	0.03	0.06	0.24	0.42	0.54
10	0.4	0.02	0.04	0.16	0.28	0.36
11	0.2	0.01	0.02	0.08	0.14	0.18
12	0.1	0.005	0.01	0.04	0.07	0.09
13						
14	PI Matrix Legend					
15	Low = no formatting	0 - 0.09				
16	Medium = italics	0.1 - 0.32				
17	High = bold	0.33 - 1.0				

The legend at the bottom of the PI matrix tells us that all scores from 0 to 0.09 have a low ranking (there is no formatting on these numbers in the chart). Scores of 0.1 to 0.32 are medium ranking (these are formatted in italic), and scores of 0.33 to 1.0 are high (these scores are formatted in bold). Our organization has determined that any risk score that falls into the medium or high rank on the PI matrix needs a risk response plan. In this case, the power conditioning units risk needs a response plan.

You could use colors to create the high-medium-low values for the PI matrix to make it easier to see. If you're limited to black and white for printing purposes, use formatting to designate the values as we've done here.

All of you experienced Excel users probably caught on right away, but for those of you new to Excel, notice that in Figure 6.6 we've highlighted the formula in cell C9.

FIGURE 6.6   Excel formula

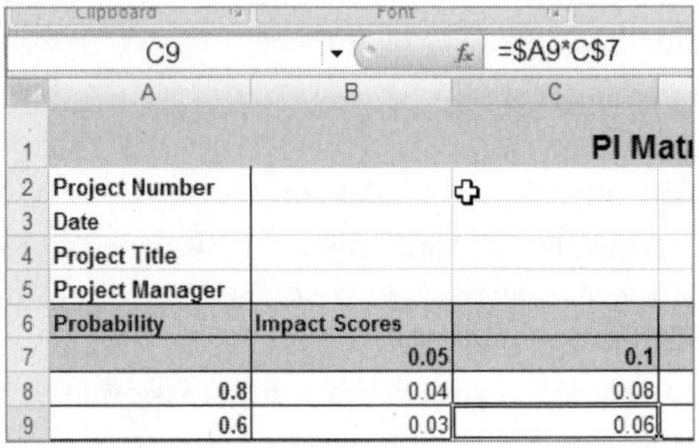

C9		f_x	=$A9*C$7
	A	B	C
1			**PI Mat**
2	Project Number		✛
3	Date		
4	Project Title		
5	Project Manager		
6	Probability	Impact Scores	
7		0.05	0.1
8	0.8	0.04	0.08
9	0.6	0.03	0.06

The formula contains dollar signs, which indicate "absolute." In Excel terms this means don't change the reference of the column or row immediately following the dollar sign. So in the case of $A, we're telling Excel to always reference column A (this column has the probability scores). The $7 means always reference row 7 (this row has the impact scores). That way, as you copy the formula across the spreadsheet, Excel knows to always reference both the probability values (column A) and the impact scores (row 7) when populating the remaining cells with the formula.

Before we talk about devising risk response plans, we want to document all the information we've just discovered. Let's do that next.

Documenting the Risk Register

The risk register is the place to document the risks you've identified so far and their scores. Figure 6.7 is a sample risk register template. We'll be adding to this a little later in this chapter, but we'll cover the information shown here first.

FIGURE 6.7 Risk register template

Risk Register					
Project Number					
Date					
Project Title					
Project Manager					
Risk Number	Risk Category	Risk Name	Risk Score	Response Plan Y/N	Responsible Party

The risk number is a unique identifier for each risk. As you brainstorm the initial list of risks, record them in the Risk Name column. Then come back and categorize them and assign each a risk number once you've finished with the identification process. If you have a long list of risks for a large project, using numbers is an easy way to keep track of all of them.

We talked about categories in the section "Creating a Risk Checklist" earlier in this chapter. The risk name is a short name or description of the risk, and the risk score is the total score you calculated using either values or numbers. The Response Plan Y/N column is a place to note whether the risk needs a response plan. The Responsible Party column notes the person responsible for monitoring the risk and developing and or implementing the risk response plan (and tracking its effectiveness). Each risk should have an assigned owner. If there are several risks that require response plans, it isn't possible for one person to track them all and know when or how to implement their response plans.

You might be thinking that the risk register has much the same information as the probability and impact chart—you're correct. If you're working on a small project, you could easily begin recording risks straight away in the risk register and skip the probability and impact chart altogether. However, if you find you have a large list of risks, you'll want to break this process out into a couple of steps—the first simply being identifying them and analyzing them for probability and impact. You may find that many risks fall into the low-low or low-medium ranking and won't require response plans or further attention, so there's not a big need to track them further. Risks that will require response plans or further checking as the project progresses should be transferred to the risk register and assigned owners to monitor them.

You can easily create the risk register in table format and use Excel's pivot table feature to report on the information. We'll look at that next along with an example risk register for the Grant St. Move project.

Creating a Risk Register with MS Excel

Excel's strength is built on tables. Tables are used within databases, but Excel is not a database management system. Let's take a brief look at what databases are and when you'd use them.

Databases are a way to collect information in a logical way, and they allow you to quickly pick and choose what pieces of information you want to report on. You can filter data, perform calculations, generate reports, and so on. Tables and databases are closely related, but they don't do the same thing.

Databases are made up of tables. We talked about tables and how to construct them in Chapter 4. Tables consist of rows and columns, which are analogous to fields and records in database terminology. The columns are the fields; that is, they contain individual pieces of information about the record. The record (or row) is the collection of all the information for one unit or element. For example, thinking back to our contact list (Figure 5.15 in Chapter 5), we had columns to hold title, first name, last name, and so on. One row of this table is considered a record, and it holds all the contact information (fields) we need to know about a particular person.

Individual tables created in enterprise-class database applications such as Microsoft SQL Server and Oracle can be interrelated using key fields to connect them. For example, we might use employee number to tie a contact list table to an employment record table. On a smaller scale, Microsoft Access allows for this interrelatedness as well. Excel, however, does not natively allow you to build relationships between tables. Excel is best suited for lists of data (particularly numeric data) that do not need to be related. In Excel, each worksheet in the workbook can be a table. You can have as many worksheets in your Excel 2007 workbook as there is system memory to contain them. With over 1 million rows and in excess of 65 thousand columns per worksheet, you certainly don't have many space considerations to be worried about if you're considering using Excel for single-table structures. If, however, you have a need to work with interrelated elements among multiple tables, you should consider a relational database management system (RDBMS) such as Access or SQL Server, as they are built for such tasks.

If you want to try your hand at database work, Microsoft has a free edition of SQL Server called SQL Server 2005 Express Edition. It's easy to use and easy to learn and will give you a basic introduction into RDBMSs. The good news is everything you learn in the Express Edition is transferable to SQL Server 2005.

Creating a Pivot Table

A pivot table allows you to manage a large array of data in a table. You can quickly burrow into the data, look at it from different angles, and easily change the view.

Figure 6.8 shows our risk register template populated with some risks for the Grant St. Move project.

This is a nice assemblage of data, but imagine what a list like this would look like if there were dozens of project team members and hundreds of risks listed here. It wouldn't be nearly as easy to read or to make sense of.

Using Excel 2007, let's turn this list into a table with row header designations that we can filter on. (Remember that you should not have any blank rows or blank columns separating the data.) You'll recall from Chapter 4 that you simply highlight the rows you want to include and then click on a table style you'd like to implement. Excel 2007 does the rest. A small portion of the table is shown in Figure 6.9.

 Rather than start with a set of data keyed into a spreadsheet (without table formatting applied), you can just as easily predefine a table format and then key in the data.

Now that the data is in a table format, we can set up a pivot table. With your cursor positioned in any cell of the table, click the Insert tab and select PivotTable ➢ PivotTable, as shown in Figure 6.10

FIGURE 6.8   Grant St. Move project risk register

Risk Number	Risk Category	Risk Name	Risk Score	Response Plan Y/N	Responsible Party
1	Technical	Power conditioning units not sized correctly	0.14	Y	Steve Green
2	Technical	Computers not installed at workstations on time	0.18	Y	Aimee Owens
3	Technical	Telecomm cannot provide circuits on time	0.56	Y	Steve Green
4	Technical	Building security system not ready on due date	0.02	N	Facility Coordinator
5	External	Moving company not available as scheduled	0.36	Y	Moving Coordinator
6	Scope	Scope statement does not detail all requirements	0.08	N	Project Manager
7	Personnel	Key IT personnel not available	0.24	Y	Project Manager/Dept Managers
8	Organizational	Management turnover--move is canceled	0.01	N	Project Manager
9	Scope	Scope statement is not approved by stakeholders	0.02	N	Project Manager
10	Organizational	Company is bought out while planning the move	0.14	Y	Project Manager/Dept Managers
11	Personnel	Employees not packed by moving day	0.06	N	Moving Coordinator

FIGURE 6.9   Table format

Risk Number	Risk Category	Risk Name	Risk Score	Response Plan Y/N	Responsible Party
1	Technical	Power conditioning units not sized correctly	0.14	Y	Steve Green
2	Technical	Computers not installed at workstations on time	0.18	Y	Aimee Owens
3	Technical	Telecomm cannot provide circuits on time	0.56	Y	Steve Green
4	Technical	Building security system not ready on due date	0.02	N	Facility Coordinator
5	External	Moving company not available as scheduled	0.36	Y	Moving Coordinator
6	Scope	Scope statement does not detail all requirements	0.08	N	Project Manager
7	Personnel	Key IT personnel not available	0.24	Y	Project Manager/Dept Managers
8	Organizational	Management turnover--move is canceled	0.01	N	Project Manager
9	Scope	Scope statement is not approved by stakeholders	0.02	N	Project Manager
10	Organizational	Company is bought out while planning the move	0.14	Y	Project Manager/Dept Managers
11	Personnel	Employees not packed by moving day	0.06	N	Moving Coordinator

You are given the option of what range of cells to select, including the ability to select an external range of data (from an external database like SQL Server, for example). Note in Figure 6.11 that we stick with the Table/Range setting (Table1), which is automatically chosen by default.

Clicking OK brings up the Pivot Table Field List pane, showing all of the field names and drop zones that we can use in the pivot table, as shown in Figure 6.12.

The fields in the Pivot Table Field List pane (shown on the right side of Figure 6.12) are the column header names taken from our table. The drop zones represent the various ways we can display the data. Think of the drop zones as a three-way palette. Let's say we want to know the count for each category of risk. In other words, how many external risks do we have? Start by dragging the Risk Category field as shown in Figure 6.13 to the Drop Row Fields Here zone (see Figure 6.12 for the location of this zone).

FIGURE 6.10   Summarize with Pivot

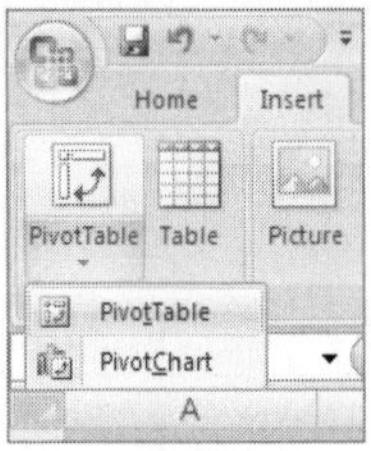

FIGURE 6.11   Table/Range setting

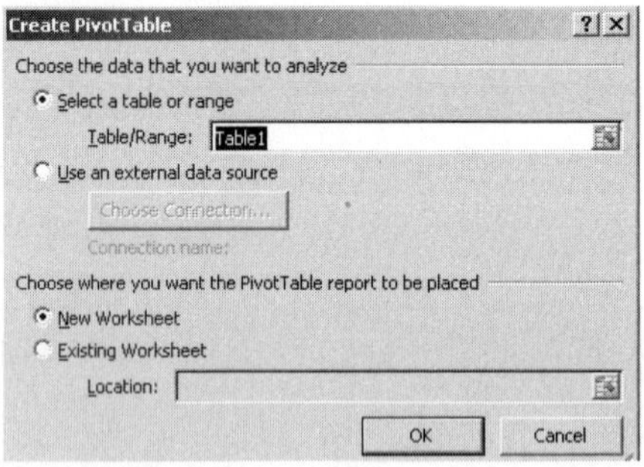

FIGURE 6.12   Pivot Table Field List pane

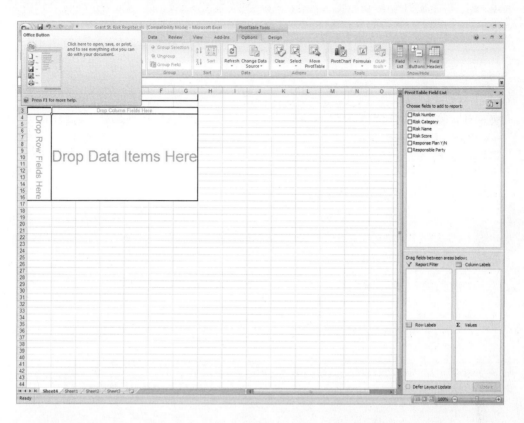

At the bottom right in Figure 6.13, you'll see that Risk Category has been added to the Row Labels area. Next, drag and drop Risk Name into the Drop Data Items Here zone as shown in Figure 6.14.

Excel has added Total to the header line because we're looking for the count of risk names by category. Now we can quickly see that the Personnel category, for example, has 2 risks, the Technical category has 4, and so on. The last row is a Grand Total row showing 11 risks total in all categories.

FIGURE 6.13 Risk Category in Rows zone

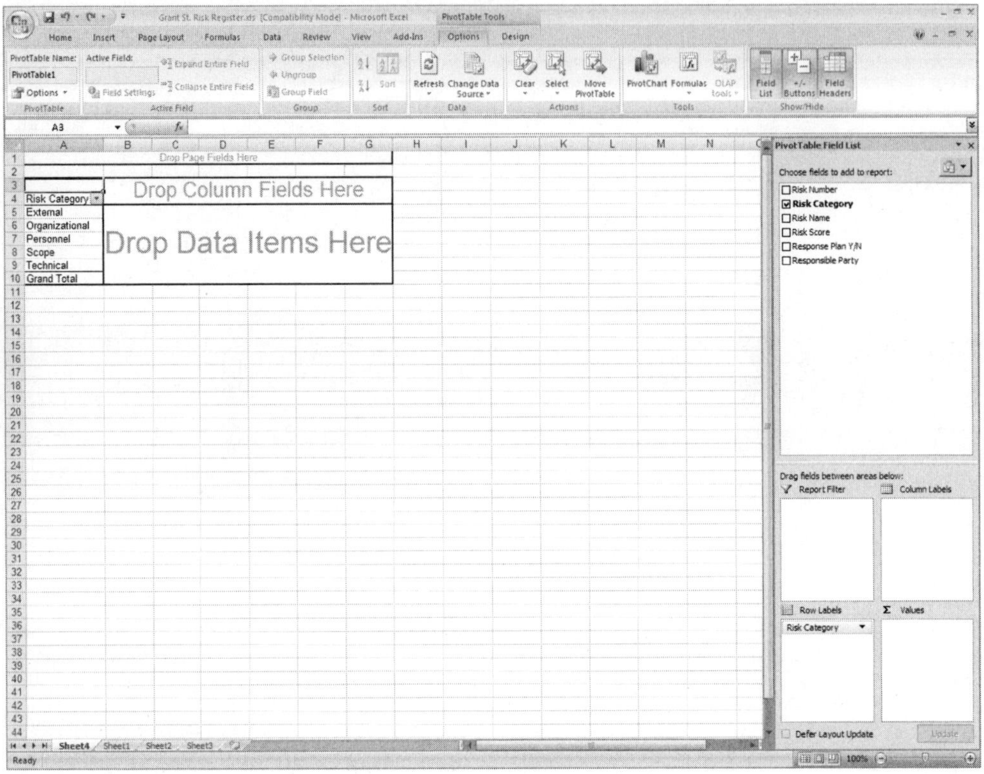

The bottom right of Figure 6.14 now shows Count of Risk Number in the Values area. There are dozens of ways to display, view, and count data in Excel pivot tables. Spend some time dropping data into the different zones to see the results and counts Excel will give you.

Filtering Data with Pivot Tables

As we mentioned earlier, any risk that has a score over 0.1 for our Grant St. Move project will require a risk response plan. An easy way to tell which risks qualify is to use our pivot table's capability. Building on the pivot table we created in the preceding section, drag and drop the Response Plan Y/N field into the Drop Column Fields Here zone. Now we can see which risks by category did not require a response plan. See Figure 6.15.

FIGURE 6.14 Risk Name in Data Items zone

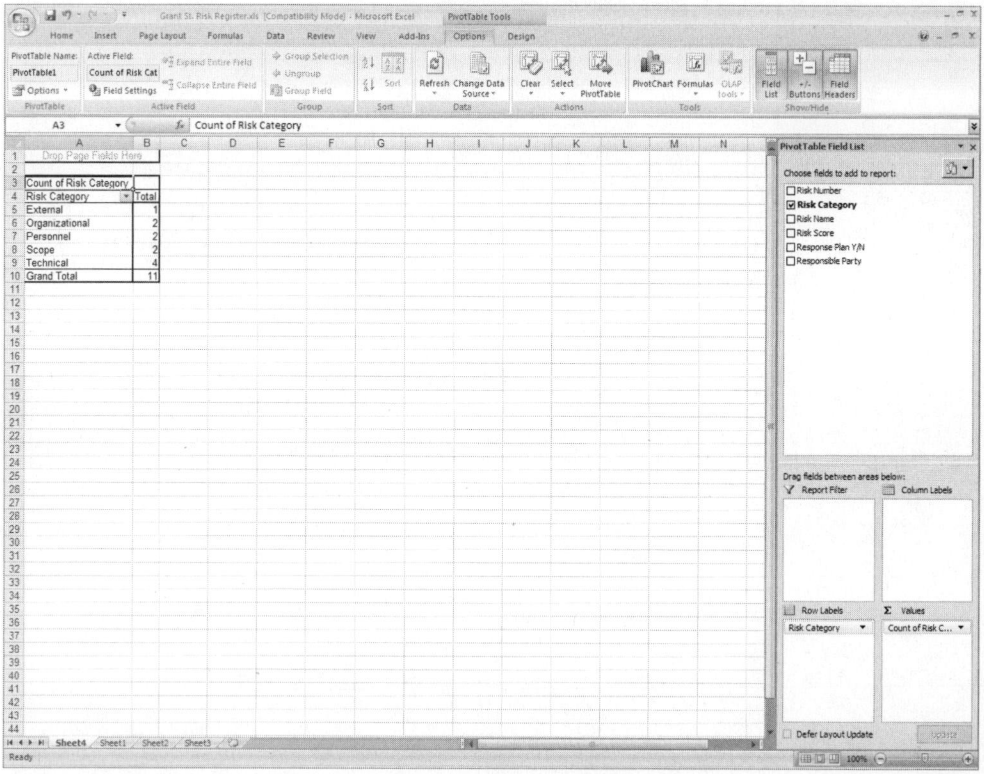

Now let's filter this data. We only want to see Yes responses. Notice the drop-down arrow next to the Response Plan Y/N column label (cell B3 in Figure 6.15). Click this arrow and uncheck N and leave the Y box checked, as we've done in Figure 6.16.

Figure 6.17 shows the results of our filtering. Now we see in each category only the risks that require response plans. The column header row shows Y; N has been filtered out. Also, the Response Plan Y/N column header has a filter icon in place of the drop-down arrow.

FIGURE 6.15 Response plan Y/N by Risk category

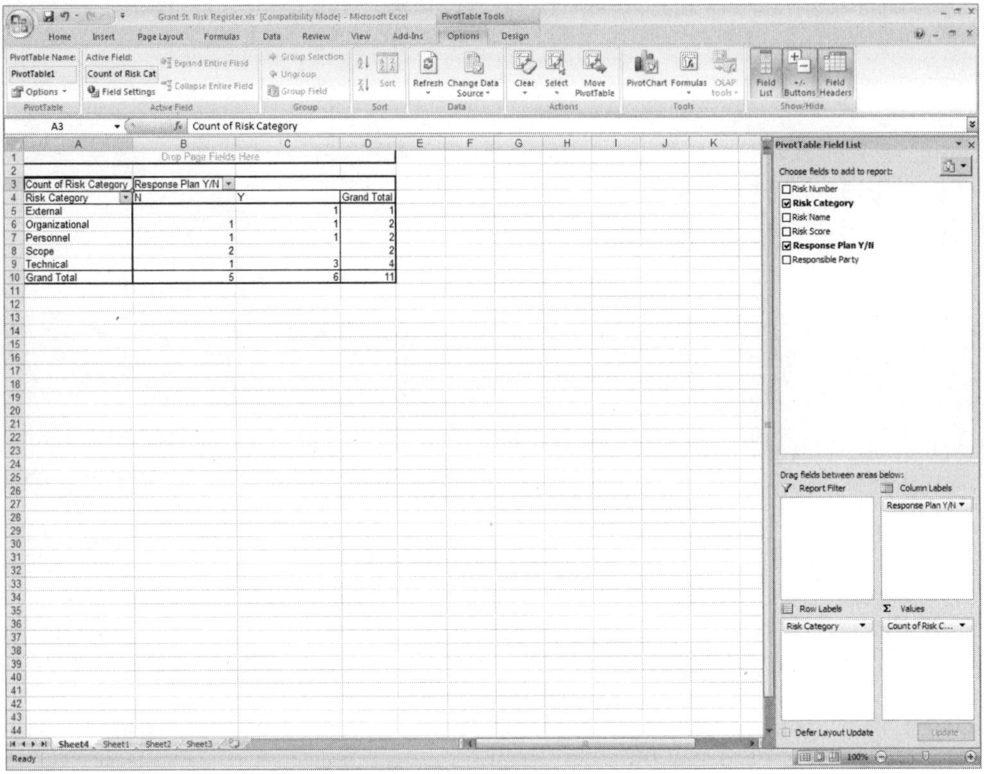

FIGURE 6.16 Filtering on Y

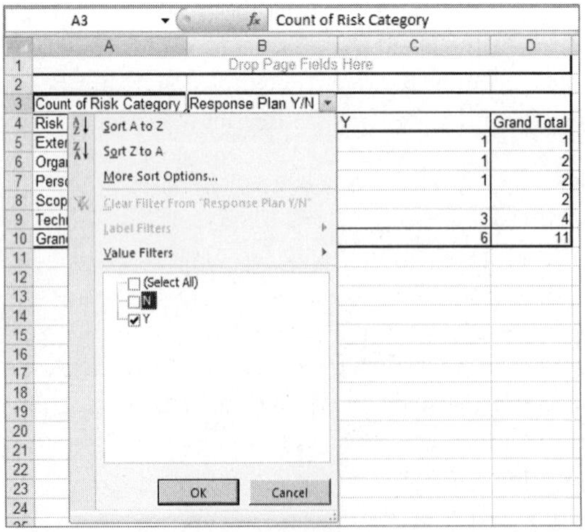

FIGURE 6.17 Response plans required

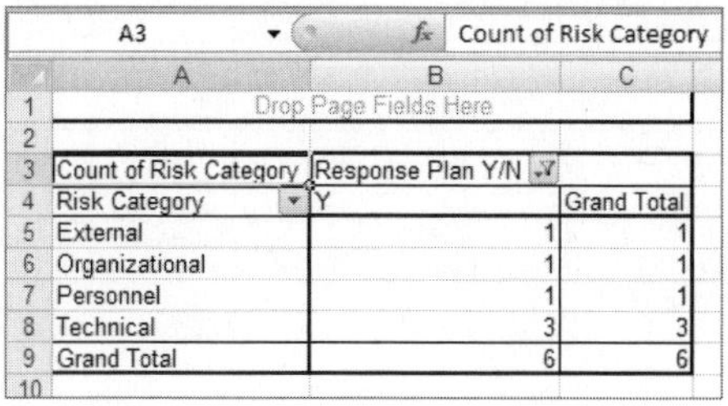

A3 | Count of Risk Category

Count of Risk Category	Response Plan Y/N	
Risk Category	Y	Grand Total
External	1	1
Organizational	1	1
Personnel	1	1
Technical	3	3
Grand Total	6	6

Formatting for Printing

To set the page formatting options for printing, click the Page Layout tab on the ribbon and modify accordingly. Note the Width and Height settings, shown in Figure 6.18.

By default, Width and Height settings are set to Automatic, meaning Excel determines the best layout for the print job. In order to get this pivot table report to print on one landscape sheet, we changed this setting to one page wide by one page high. Additionally, we set margins to Narrow. Setting headers and footers is quite similar to setting them in older versions of Excel.

Highlight all rows in the pivot table and click the Print Area button from the Page Layout group, then click Set Print Area. When you're ready to print, click the Office button in the upper-left corner of the window (round button with Windows flag) and select Print from the menu or, if you've added a printer icon to your Quick Access Toolbar, click it.

FIGURE 6.18 Page layout

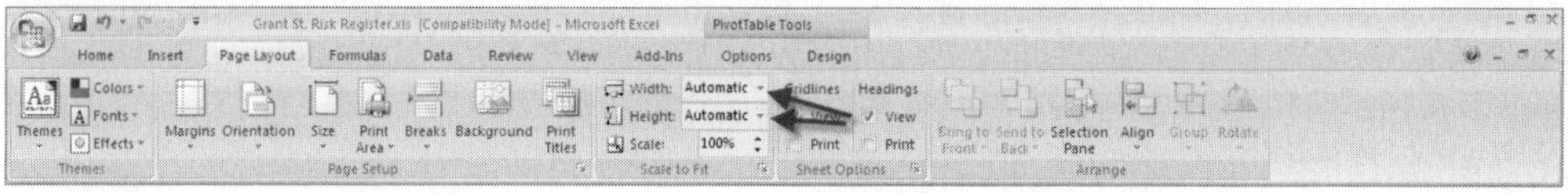

More Table Functionality

Excel has some other functionality that may come in handy when constructing tables.

Let's say we wanted to add a Priority column to the risk register table. Simply type the column name to the immediate right of the table as shown in Figure 6.19 and press the Enter key. Excel assumes that you want to add Priority as a new column.

Now let's take another example. Suppose you have a table with row headers called FY01 and FY02. Now you have data you want to enter into a new column that should be called FY03. There's no need to type the header because Excel is going to do that for us. Start typing the data in the first cell beneath the row header, as we've done in Figure 6.20. Excel assumes you're talking about FY03 and creates the appropriate row header.

FIGURE 6.19   Adding a column

Risk Number	Risk Category	Risk Name	Risk Score	Response Plan Y/N	Responsible Party	Priority
1	Technical	Power conditioning units not sized correctly	0.14	Y	Steve Green	
2	Technical	Computers not installed at workstations on time	0.18	Y	Aimee Owens	
3	Technical	Telecomm cannot provide circuits on time	0.56	Y	Steve Green	
4	Technical	Building security system not ready on due date	0.02	N	Facility Coordinator	
5	External	Moving company not available as scheduled	0.36	Y	Moving Coordinator	
6	Scope	Scope statement does not detail all requirements	0.08	N	Project Manager	
7	Personnel	Key IT personnel not available	0.24	Y	Project Manager/Dept Managers	
8	Organizational	Management turnover--move is canceled	0.01	N	Project Manager	
9	Scope	Scope statement is not approved by stakeholders	0.02	N	Project Manager	
10	Organizational	Company is bought out while planning the move	0.14	Y	Project Manager/Dept Managers	
11	Personnel	Employees not packed by moving day	0.06	N	Moving Coordinator	

FIGURE 6.20   Excel adds column header

FY01	FY02	FY03
123	143	116
132	126	
111	113	
114	150	
116	99	
117	109	
101	119	
131	126	
141	140	
120	114	
117	111	

Autocomplete is another great feature of Excel that has been around for a long time. The idea is that Excel remembers what you typed into a column and suggests recently typed entries based upon the letters that you start entering into a new cell. For example, the risk register has several risk category entries. Once we've typed **Technical** into a cell and go into another cell and press T, Excel gives us an autocomplete option and displays the word *Technical*. If we press the Enter key here, Excel will fill in the cell for us. If we want to enter the word *Time* instead, we'll have to type it out the first time. Once Excel sees the *Ti* combination in a cell, it will offer *Time* as an autocomplete option.

If you're entering information into a spreadsheet and have blank rows between your data, the autocomplete function won't work. So you can type **Technical** in A1, leave A2 blank, and type T in A3 and no autocomplete function comes up. However, if you've formatted your columns as a table, the auto-complete function *will* work for all the cells in the columns within the table, even if there are blank rows between data. This allows for tremendous efficiency when someone is keying in rows and rows of information because autocomplete helps decrease the time to enter the data while also reducing the possibility of keying mistakes.

Now that we have our risk register documented and have learned a few new tricks about Excel tables, let's look at creating response plans for risks that require them.

Responding to Risk Events

The project team or stakeholders should determine early in the project which risks need response plans. It makes sense that most risks with a high probability of occurring or causing a significant impact will need response plans. And in an earlier section we discussed how the PI matrix can help the team decide which risks need plans. But you aren't limited to medium or high risks on the PI matrix. Your organization may determine that in addition, all risks within a particular category, technical for example, need a response plan as well.

Some organizations determine the criteria for risk response plans ahead of time. The project management office is the likely place to find any risk policies your team should follow. If you don't have official policies, you and the key stakeholders should determine the criteria for deciding when to create a response plan early in the planning stage of the project.

Risk response plans are documented procedures for dealing with the risk event should it occur. The amount of detail required in a response plan is dependent on the severity of the risk or its impact. Some response plans may be a few sentences, while others could be a few pages (or more). Response plans should also list the owner's name (we listed them in the risk register as well) and a place for documenting whether the risk event occurred and the effectiveness of the response plan. This is great material to review prior to starting a new project. Figure 6.21 shows a risk response template.

FIGURE 6.21   Risk response template

A	B
	Risk Response Form
Project Number	
Date	
Project Title	
Project Manager	
Risk Number	
Risk Category	
Risk Name	
Risk Description	
Risk Score	
Response Stragegy	
Owner	
Did Risk Event Occur? If so, when?	
Outcome/Effectiveness of Plan	
Risk Number	
Risk Category	
Risk Name	
Risk Description	
Risk Score	
Response Stragegy	
Owner	
Did Risk Event Occur? If so, when?	
Outcome/Effectiveness of Plan	

You could track the risk responses together on one spreadsheet as we've shown on the template (there is room for two responses in this example), or you could track them individually on separate sheets within a risk response workbook, depending on how many responses you need to track.

Next we'll look at some specific techniques you can use for responding to risks.

Risk Response Techniques

There are many techniques for responding to risks, including accepting, transferring, avoiding, mitigating, contingency planning, and workarounds. Each one has its own advantages and uses. You'll typically choose one of these techniques for each risk, although having a contingency plan in addition to the risk response strategy isn't a bad idea for risks with high probability and significant impact. We'll look at each next.

Accepting

The acceptance strategy is just as it sounds. Rather than creating a response plan, the team determines to accept the consequences of the risk event should it occur. The reason you might choose this strategy for a risk with a high probability and high impact is because the consequences of the risk are favorable. It may also be that an adequate response cannot be planned for or determined. Don't let this be an opt-out excuse, however. The team should work diligently to determine a plan. The Grant St. Move team might want to consider accepting the risk "moving company not available as scheduled." They could choose the transfer strategy (we'll talk about that next), but technically speaking, if the moving company isn't available on a moving day for whatever reason, there isn't much that *can* be done short of employees loading up rental moving vans themselves. And that brings in a new set of risks and worker's compensation issues.

Transferring

Transferring risk involves assigning the risk and its consequences to a third party. Insurance is a classic example of risk transference. Many of us purchase insurance on our household goods in the event there is a fire, theft, or other disaster that destroys those items. If the worst happens, the insurance company reimburses us some portion of the value of those goods so we can go buy new stuff. The risk hasn't gone away, but someone else (or some other organization) is responsible for dealing with it should it occur.

There is usually a cost associated with this strategy, so make certain to take this into account when formulating the project budget. In fact, it's a good idea to take all risk strategies into consideration in the budget because many of them may require additional resources (outside of the plans of the normal project activities) to carry out.

It's possible for the Grant St. Move team to choose this strategy for the "moving company not available" risk, but realistically, the only thing they could probably recover is monetary damages. If the moving company isn't available on the move dates, no one is moving. This is why accepting and transferring are both acceptable strategies in this case.

The Grant St. Move team could also use this strategy for the "power conditioning units not sized correctly" risk. If they hired a third party to take on this task and made it clear in the work order that the third party is the one responsible for sizing these units correctly and then fixing any problems that arise or replacing units with larger ones if needed, the third party takes on the risk rather than the organization.

Avoiding

The avoiding strategy works by eliminating the cause of the risk or changing the project plan to protect the project from the consequences of the risk, thereby avoiding it. Again calling on the Grant St. Move project, we could use the avoidance strategy with the "scope statement does not detail all requirements" risk. We could avoid this risk by adequately documenting all the requirements and making certain we closely monitor and control changes to scope throughout the project. Some other actions you can take to avoid risks are improving communication, assigning additional resources to the project, refining project scope, and so on.

Mitigating

Mitigating a risk involves reducing the probability of its occurrence and reducing its impacts to an acceptable level. Taking action early on to mitigate a potential risk event is easier and less messy than cleaning up after the risk event has occurred. For example, performing adequate testing on the servers in the data center in the Grant St. Move project will help assure less (or zero) downtime. This strategy could be used with the "telecomm cannot provide circuits on time" risk by checking on availability and vendor time frames prior to signing the lease on the Grant St. building. This strategy could also be used with the "moving company not available as scheduled" risk by making certain you've chosen a reliable, experienced vendor and checking their references.

Contingency Planning

Contingency planning is a form of acceptance and involves developing alternatives to deal with the risk should it occur. Contingency planning often involves allowances or reserves. For example, you might set up a contingency reserve fund to deal with the "employees not packed by moving day" risk so that if employees are not packed on time, additional resources can be brought in to help with this task. Reserves are a portion of the budget specifically set aside to deal with risks. You may also have contingency allowances in the project schedule for additional time to deal with risks should they occur. Again, remember to account for contingency reserves when developing the project budget.

Workarounds

Workarounds are unplanned responses to unknown risks or they are responses to risks that were previously accepted. Remember that unknown risks are, well, unknown until they happen. A workaround comes into play as soon as you realize a risk has occurred.

As this book is being written, one of the authors (Kim) is working on a critical project in her organization. Two unknown risks occurred on the project. The vendor subject matter expert broke his wrist and was out of the office for a week. Fortunately, the accident occurred at a "good" time in the schedule, so we were able to rearrange some tasks and stay on track (thus employing a workaround). Believe it or not, six weeks later the same subject matter expert broke his leg (in two places)! This accident occurred at the worst possible time. A critical install was scheduled for the Monday after he broke his leg. You may argue that vendor unavailability is a risk we could have planned for, but having it occur twice on the same project at different times in the schedule isn't something most of us would think about. Our workaround the second time was an immediate phone call to the vendor. Fortunately, they had another subject matter expert they could supply in the place of our accident-prone resource and the critical installation occurred only a few days behind schedule rather than a few weeks.

When you document the technique you're going to use on the risk response template, you'll also want to detail the plan itself. So, if you're using the transfer technique, for example, you'll want to spell out who is taking on the risk, for what consideration, what exactly does that cover, how and when will the third party be notified if action is required, and so on. You can note the name of the strategy you're going to use in the risk register.

Documenting Risk Response Results

One of the responsibilities of the risk owner is to document the outcome of the risk and the effectiveness of the response plan. The risk response template is the perfect place to capture this information. It's important to note the effectiveness of your response plans because future projects will benefit from how you handled the risks on this project.

The following list includes some of the information you should document:

- When the risk occurred
- Which stage of the project management process the risk occurred (Planning, Executing, and so on)
- Risk impact and its severity, including financial impacts and time delays if appropriate
- Secondary risks that occurred as a result of this risk event
- How well the plan worked and what could have been done differently

Secondary risks are additional risks that come about as a result of the initial risk event occurring. For example, perhaps we're hiring contractors to wire the telecomm closets for Grant St. and our vendor suddenly becomes unavailable. After an initial search, we find that there are only two other vendors in our area that can do this task and they are both engaged on other projects for the next six weeks. The unavailability of other vendors is a secondary risk.

Updating the Risk Register

There's one more addition to the risk register you'll want to make. Once the work of the project has begun, add a column that indicates whether the risk event occurred and another one to note if the response plan was implemented. Figure 6.22 shows an updated example of the risk register with this information.

FIGURE 6.22   Updated risk register

A	B	C	D	E	F	G	H	I
				Risk Register				
Project Number								
Date								
Project Title								
Project Manager								
Risk Number	Risk Category	Risk Name	Risk Score	Response Plan Y/N	Responsible Party	Response Strategy	Did Risk Event Occur Y/N	Response Plan Implemented Y/N

The risk register becomes a quick, at-a-glance reference on future projects to determine the types of risks that occurred and which ones had response plans implemented. If you've designed this as a table or database, it's also easy to sort and report on risk information at the conclusion of the project.

Closing Out Risks

Much like the action item log and issues log we developed in Chapter 4, you'll want to create a closed section for the risk register. Once risk events occur, responses are implemented, and the risk impacts are dealt with, you'll want to close the risk out and move it into the closed section. This will keep the active portion of the risk register clean, so to speak. Remember that risk identification and monitoring are an ongoing process throughout the project. If you have a large list of risks, it's easier to scan through all of them at a status meeting than to stop and skip over those that are no longer a threat. One word of caution before you move those risks to the closed section—make certain they no longer pose a threat and they won't occur again. Who would think a subject matter expert would break both their wrist and their leg while working on the same project?

Chapter

7

Quality Management

Quality is an issue that affects all projects. In this chapter, we'll explore quality, the theories behind the cost of quality, and how to measure and report on quality. We'll also examine some charting techniques using Excel to plot our data.

We also thought this chapter would be a good place to talk about securing your project data. This isn't a quality issue per se, but if you haven't taken the proper security precautions to protect company resources, it could have a significant impact on the project and the organization.

Let's start off by taking a look at the quality plan.

Quality Management Plan

Quality is a distinguishing characteristic that determines if stakeholder expectations are met. That's a fine definition for the project as a whole. But you can also break that down into deliverables and individual components of the deliverables. Then quality becomes a measurement or characteristic that determines if the component is acceptable. For example, if our new project involves creating chocolate truffles and we advertise them as weighing 2 ounces each, any truffle weighing less than 2 ounces does not meet the quality standard. Those truffles are diverted and packaged under a different brand name.

Quality is affected by scope, time, and cost. In our chocolate truffle example, we could cut costs by buying cheaper cocoa powder. But when we do that, the quality of the truffle is impacted and our customers will likely notice. We could potentially produce them faster, but this may affect their taste, thereby affecting quality. The bottom line is this: If you're being asked to do something cheaper or faster, you will almost certainly impact the quality of the end result.

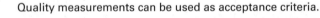

Quality measurements can be used as acceptance criteria.

The quality management plan details the specifications and criteria used to determine if the deliverable (or any element of the project) is complete and correct. The quality plan will of course depend on the type of project you're undertaking. A quality plan for a research project for a new pharmaceutical drug will look much different than one for a condominium building construction project. The most important element to capture in the quality plan is the specifications of the deliverables and how you know the specifications have been met. You should also consider the following elements when drafting your quality management plan:

Standards   Standards involve guidelines, rules, or characteristics that should be followed when producing the product of the project. Your organization may have its own standards established and your industry may also have standards that should be adhered to. Standards are not always required (as are regulations), but it's usually a good idea to follow them.

 The Project Management Institute (PMI) has worked hard to establish standards and guidelines for sound project management techniques. Its standards are great examples of industry standards.

Regulations   Regulations are mandatory and must be adhered to. Governments, institutions, and organizations have the ability to implement regulations. You or your organization could face fines, lawsuits, or stop work orders if you violate them.

Quality Policy   Quality policies are developed by the organization and usually published by the executive management team. They contain predetermined guidelines regarding quality standards for projects.

Make certain to check for any standards, regulations, or policies that apply to projects within your organization and either incorporate them into the quality management plan or reference them there.

Your project management plan itself could also encompass a quality management plan. You might want to note any standards or regulations needed for the plan itself. For example, your organization may require that Project Management Professional (PMP) certified project managers manage all projects with budgets greater than $5 million. Record any guidelines you'll use for creating the project planning documents in the quality management plan also. For example, you might require approval signatures from certain executive team members for the scope statement.

The quality assurance process should also be documented in the quality management plan. This process describes how the team will assure that quality standards and criteria are being met. The quality assurance process may be used by the project manager, vendors, or others responsible for overseeing it. Quality audits may also be part of the quality assurance process. They are performed to identify ineffective or inefficient processes on the project and make certain standards and regulations are being adhered to.

After you've completed the quality management plan, you'll want to post it to MOSS with your other project documents.

Cost of Quality

It costs you something to meet the quality standards of the project, most typically time and resources. Producing the product of the project to meet those standards is known as the cost of quality. Not producing the project to standards also costs you something in the form of rework (to get the product up to the standards), reduced confidence levels of the stakeholders, and potentially an unsuccessful project.

In the following sections, we'll take a brief look at the costs typically incurred when you're attempting to meet quality standards and the theories behind quality management. This will give you a background for understanding the measurements used in tracking and verifying quality, which we'll cover later in this chapter.

 Quality should be built into the product, not inspected in after the fact. The quality management plan details how that will happen.

Costs Associated with Cost of Quality

The cost to produce the product according to the quality standards should include all the work necessary whether the work was planned or unplanned. There are three costs typically associated with cost of quality including: prevention costs, appraisal costs, and failure costs.

Prevention costs   Prevention costs are the costs of keeping defects out of the hands of the customers and satisfying customer requirements by meeting quality standards. Prevention costs are usually incurred early in the project and include the cost of quality planning, training, design review, and so on. Prevention costs associated with the project plan may include the time and expense it takes to research, write, and review the plan, particularly if you must comply with regulations or legal requirements to carry out your project. Those regulations must be researched and incorporated into the correct place in the project plan (for example, are they noted in the budget or the quality plan or the human resources plan?).

Appraisal costs   Appraisal costs are the costs associated with examining the product and making certain it meets the standards. Inspections and testing are typical types of appraisal costs. As your project management plan nears completion, you'll have quality costs associated with reviewing the project plan and verifying that any standards that you established or are required to adhere to are met. For example, you'll have to verify that the project manager you're hiring for the $5 million project is actually certified.

Failure costs   Failure costs are also known as the cost of poor quality. From this you can probably conjecture that these costs are incurred when the product doesn't meet quality standards. There are two types of failure costs: internal and external. Internal failure costs occur when customer requirements are not met while the product is still in the control of the organization. External failure costs occur once the product reaches the customer and it doesn't meet their requirements. Typically, failure costs associated with poor quality for a project relate to a poor job of project management and particularly the project planning processes.

Cost of Quality Theories

There are three key pioneers in the field of quality management. These men have each made significant impacts in the area of quality management and their theories have been put into practice worldwide. We'll take a brief look at each next.

W. Edwards Deming   Deming proposed that the cost of quality is a management problem, not an employee problem. He theorized that employees have little control over quality. Deming is also considered by many to be a major contributor to the Total Quality Management (TQM) theory, which states that the process is the problem, not the people. TQM says that quality must be managed into the process and that quality improvement should be a continuous process throughout the project, not just a one-time event.

Joseph M. Juran   Joseph Juran proposed the fitness for use theory. Fitness for use reflects the expectations of the stakeholders and customers regarding quality and assures that the product meets or exceeds their expectations.

Philip B. Crosby   Philip Crosby is noted for the zero defects practice. Zero defects means exactly that—perform the process right the first time so there are no mistakes. He proposed that quality processes must be performed early on in the project and that prevention is the key. He believed it's cheaper to ensure quality is being met up front than to perform rework to repair the product later in the process.

Determining Quality Metrics

Quality metrics are measurements used to determine how and if quality standards are met. The metrics are actual measurements, not yes or no responses. Remember that in Chapter 3 we said deliverables needed to be verifiable and a yes or no response could suffice. That's not so for quality metrics. In order to determine that quality standards are met, measurements must be taken. That also means you need to define what the measurements look like.

In the following sections, we'll look at some common methods for determining and measuring quality metrics. Many of the methods we'll discuss use graphs and charts to display the data. We'll also show you how to create these graphs in Excel as we discuss each method.

Benchmarking

Benchmarking compares previous similar activities to the current project activity to establish a standard to measure performance against. For example, if you're considering purchasing equipment for a manufacturing process, the existing equipment could be the benchmark. Perhaps your existing equipment produces a minimum of 300 parts per day. The new equipment must have this capacity at a minimum. Therefore, 300 parts per day becomes the benchmark.

If you're undertaking a new project that has processes that are similar to those of a previous project, you can use the processes in the previous project for your benchmark. For example, let's say you're constructing a new commercial building. This building is similar in size to a project you worked on two years ago. You could use benchmarks for the construction process (the time it takes to pour the foundation, construct the frame, and so on) as well as developing the project plan. If it took three months to develop the project plan and obtain approvals on the previous project, you could use that as a benchmark for this project.

Cost-Benefit Analysis

We talked about cost-benefit analysis in Chapter 3 in terms of determining whether the project is worth undertaking—that is, do the benefits of the project outweigh the cost of producing the product or service of the project? In quality terms, cost benefit considers the cost of producing the product according to quality standards versus the benefit gained. Those benefits might be as follows:

- Increased stakeholder satisfaction

- Lower costs

- Higher productivity

- Less rework

Most of the time, the benefits gained far outweigh the costs. It's easier to build according to quality standards the first time than it is to fix problems after the fact (think of Philip Crosby's zero defects theory from earlier in this chapter.

Affinity Diagrams

Affinity diagrams take the brainstorming technique one step further than a hodgepodge of ideas. After random suggestions have been identified, affinity diagrams chart them into similar groupings or categories. If you're using sticky-backed notes, this can be accomplished easily. As the suggestions are offered, post the notes on the wall or whiteboard until no more are forthcoming. Then group the ideas according to similarity. What you end up with is a chart that resembles an organizational chart only it isn't necessarily hierarchal in nature. The main idea occupies the top box or note, and from there a header row of notes is established that describes categories of ideas. The brainstormed notes are then arranged under each category. You can use the same format and instructions we gave in Chapter 5 for constructing an organization chart to create an affinity diagram.

This technique is most appropriately used for determining quality standards and quality requirements. You can also use this technique for requirements gathering and risk identification.

Pareto Charts

You've probably heard of Pareto—Vilfredo Pareto discovered the 80/20 rule. He came across this theory by analyzing the land ownership statistics in Italy and found that 80 percent of the land was owned by 20 percent of the population. From there, the 80/20 rule was found applicable to many disciplines across all industries.

Pareto theorized that a small number of causes (20 percent) created the majority of the problems (80 percent). A Pareto chart captures this information in the form of a histogram. Histograms are bar charts that display the distribution of variables over time. In terms of quality, the variables are rank-ordered by factors such as defect rates, costs, delays, and so on. Pareto believed it was more efficient and beneficial to spend time fixing the issues that caused the most problems.

Suppose our project concerns developing a new manufacturing process. One of the things we'll want to know is the rate of defects in this new process. We can create a Pareto chart to display this information. The first step is collecting the data. Figure 7.1 is an example of quality metrics regarding defect rates. We use the formula =+B2/$B$7*100 to attain the percentage figures in column C row 2, =+B3$B$7*100 in column C row 3, and so on to generate our percentages. The idea is that we're taking the value in the Defect Frequency column, dividing it into the total defects, and multiplying that figure by 100 to attain the percentage. Column C is formatted to reflect a percentage value. In column D, we start out in row 2 with the formula =+C2 and then begin to increment the succeeding rows by adding the previous row's value. For example, in column D row 3, we have the formula =+D2+C3. We are taking the current row's value and adding it to the contents of the previous row. We will go like this until the final row adds up to 100.

The data in this chart has been rank-ordered by defect frequency. Part E has the highest number of defects and Part B has the lowest. The percentage of defects is shown in column C, and column D shows the cumulative percentage of the defects. In this example, it's easy to see that we should spend the majority of our time working on fixing the problems with part number E and C since they're causing 80 percent of our problems. Figure 7.2 shows this same information in Pareto chart form.

We'll use two steps to build this chart. First, highlight the data in cells A2 through B6, and while holding down the Ctrl key, also highlight cells D2 through D6. Then choose the Insert tab, choose Column from the Charts group, and then the 2-D column, as shown in Figure 7.3. The chart is shown in Figure 7.5 if you want to peak ahead at the results of this selection.

You'll notice that the last option on the Column list in Figure 7.3 is All Chart Types. This option is available no matter which chart type you choose. If you click this option, all chart types (Column, Line, Pie, and so on) are displayed. See Figure 7.4.

FIGURE 7.1   Defect frequency rates

	A	B	C	D
1	Part Number	Defect Frequency	Percent of Defects	Cumulative Percent
2	E	112	44.44%	44.44%
3	C	84	33.33%	77.78%
4	A	31	12.30%	90.08%
5	D	18	7.14%	97.22%
6	B	7	2.78%	100.00%
7	Total		252	

FIGURE 7.2   Pareto chart

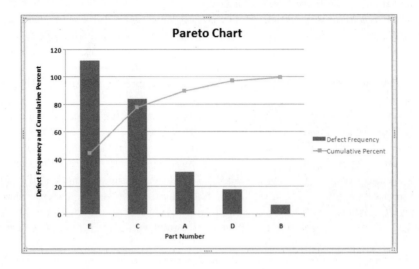

FIGURE 7.3   Inserting the Column chart

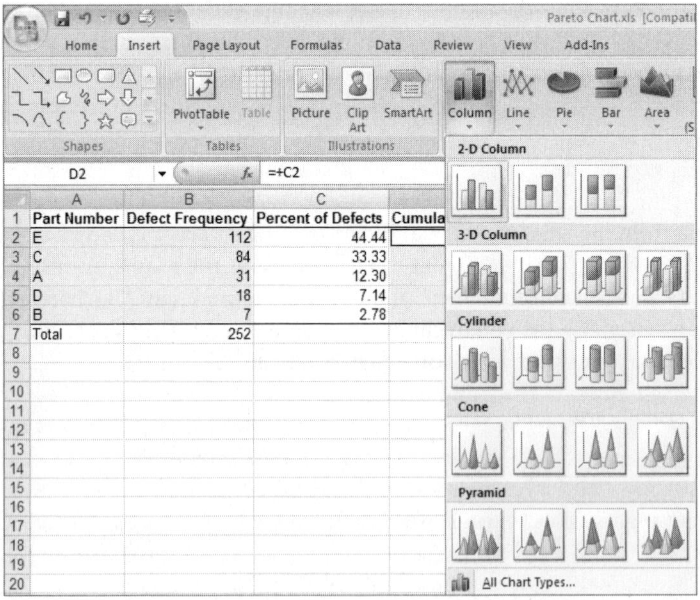

FIGURE 7.4   All of the chart types displayed

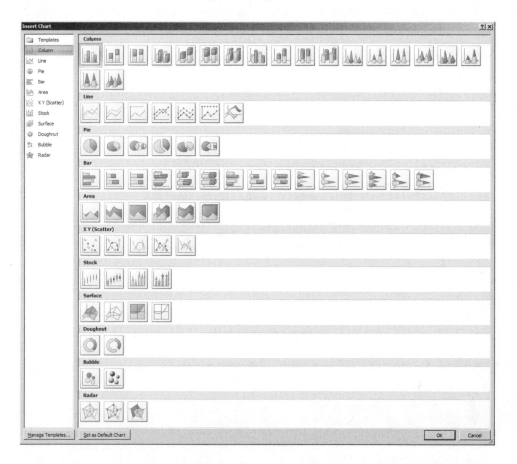

Once the chart is created, several new menu options become available, including Design, Layout, and Format. Design allows you to change the color and design of the lines or bars. Use the scroll bar to view the options and click on a few to see what they look like. The Layout tab gives you the ability to name the chart and the axes, add legends, and so on. We'll do that shortly. First, we need to add a secondary vertical axis to display the cumulative percentage information in line format. Click the bars in the chart that represent Series2 data (or in our case, the cumulative percent), and then right-click to bring up the context menu shown in Figure 7.5.

Now choose the Change Series Chart Type option. You will see a selection available just as in Figure 7.4. What we want to do is change the cumulative percent data from a bar display to a line display. Choose the Line with Markers chart (note that a help dialog will display as you hover over each chart type, giving you its name) and click OK. Figure 7.6 shows the Series2 cumulative percent data changed from a bar to a line display.

FIGURE 7.5 Changing the series chart type

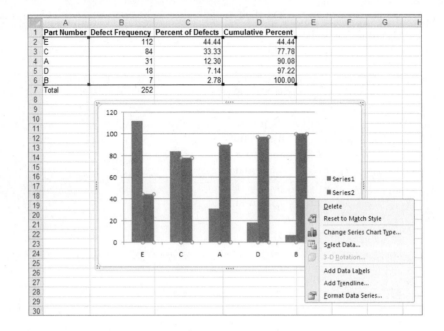

FIGURE 7.6 Line with markers – changing Series 2 to a Line chart

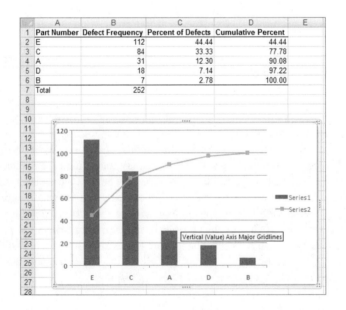

The chart is now properly formatted. Next let's name the chart and the vertical and horizontal axis.

Click on the chart so it's active. On the Layout tab, choose Chart Title from the Labels group, as shown in Figure 7.7.

> You can see from Figure 7.7 that you have a lot of layout options. You can modify the plot area, change an axis, create text, and so on.

When you click Chart Title, you're presented with three options: None, Centered Overlay Title, and Above Chart. Centered Overlay puts the title in the chart without resizing it. Above Chart does resize the chart (it shrinks it to make the title fit). We'll use Above Chart for our example and resize the chart to accommodate the title by grabbing one of the chart's corners (sometimes called handlebars) and pulling it out a little. Once you click the selection, Excel places a box above the chart, as shown in Figure 7.8.

FIGURE 7.7   The Chart Title option

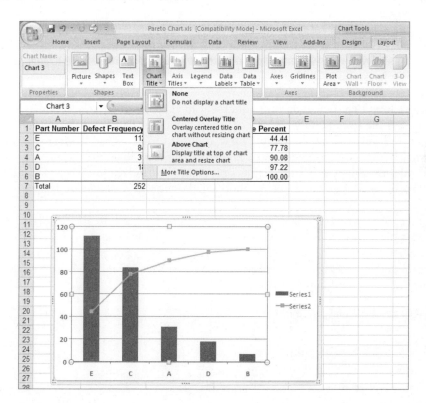

FIGURE 7.8   Naming the chart

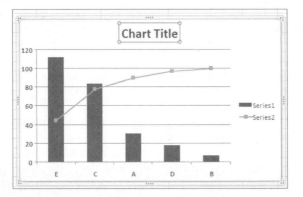

Click inside the box and type the name of the chart. Axis titles work the same way. Make certain the chart is highlighted and on the Layout tab, choose Axis Titles and select the axis you want to name. For the horizontal axis, you have two options: None, or Title Below Axis. For the vertical axis, you have several options: None, Rotated Title, Vertical Title, and Horizontal Title. There's a sample picture of the way the title will appear beside each option.

The Format ribbon allows you to format the appearance of the text, add fill, change the format of the outlines, and so on. For example, we changed the text fill in our chart title and axis titles to make the font a darker color. Figure 7.9 shows the Format ribbon.

If you've forgotten to include your column headers in the original selection as we did, you'll see that the legend on the right of the chart names the data series Series1 and Series2 (see Figure 7.8). That isn't very helpful. We want Series1 to be instead Defect Frequency and Series2 to be Cumulative Percent. Here's how to fix that. Highlight the legend section where Series1 and Series2 appear. Then you can either right-click and choose Select Data or choose Select Data on the Design tab. Either method will present you with the Edit Data Source dialog box, shown in Figure 7.10.

Highlight Series1 and choose Edit. The Edit Series dialog box will appear (Figure 7.11).

The first entry in the Edit Series dialog box asks for the Series1 name. Click cell B1 and click OK and Series1 will change to Defect Frequency, as shown in Figure 7.12.

Perform the same steps to rename Series2 and you'll have a completed chart. (Refer back to Figure 7.2 to see the completed Pareto chart.)

FIGURE 7.9   The Format ribbon

FIGURE 7.10   The Edit Data Source dialog box

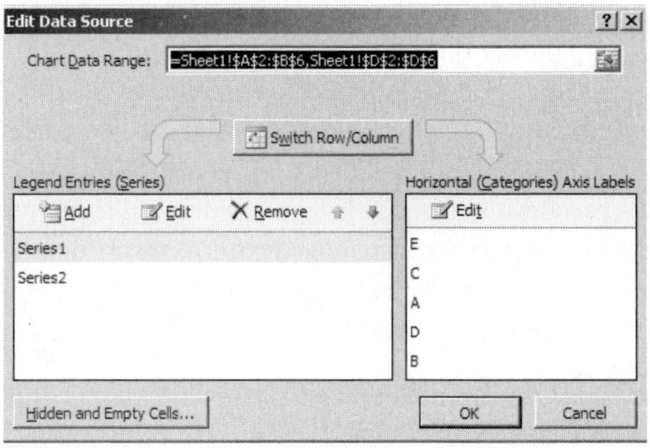

FIGURE 7.11   The Edit Series dialog box

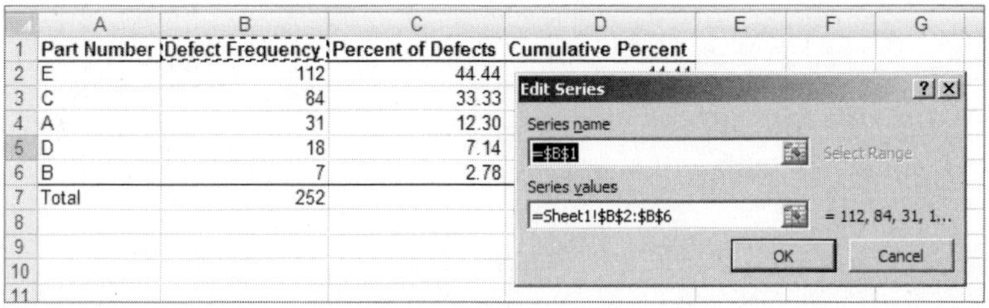

FIGURE 7.12   Renaming the legend entries

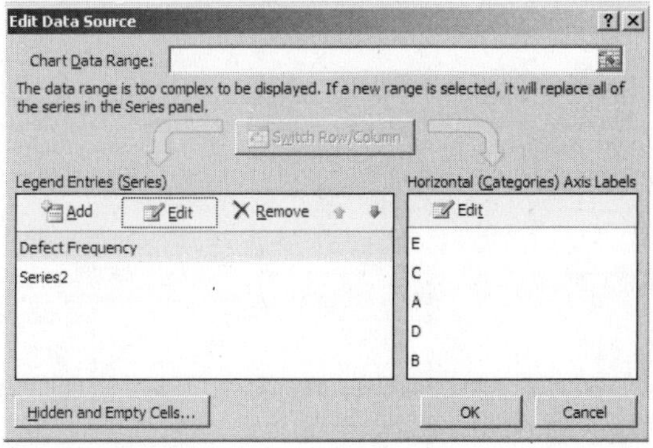

Scatter Diagram

Scatter diagrams are used to identify potential relationships between two variables. For example, when thinking about quality, perhaps you gather data that compares the length of time it takes to produce a component part with the number of defects found in those parts. Scatter diagrams plot this data, and using some interpretation, you determine whether there is a correlation between the two variables.

Figure 7.13 shows a scatter diagram comparing a sampling of production times with defect rates. In this example, it appears that longer production times result in fewer defects.

Excel has a built-in scatter diagram option. Start by highlighting cells B2 through C9. Click the Insert tab and choose the scatter chart option, as shown in Figure 7.14. A drop-down menu will appear. Choose the top-left chart.

FIGURE 7.13   Scatter diagram

FIGURE 7.14   Creating a scatter diagram

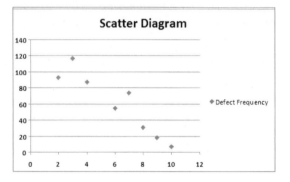

Name the chart and the horizontal and vertical axis as we did in the Pareto chart example.

If you'd like to print just the scatter diagram, click on the chart so it's highlighted. Click the Office button, choose Print, and then choose Quick Print (Figure 7.15). To play it safe, you could choose Print Preview first to make certain you're printing what you think you are. Alternatively, press Ctrl+P (for Print), and as long as the chart is highlighted, that's what will print.

FIGURE 7.15   Printing the chart

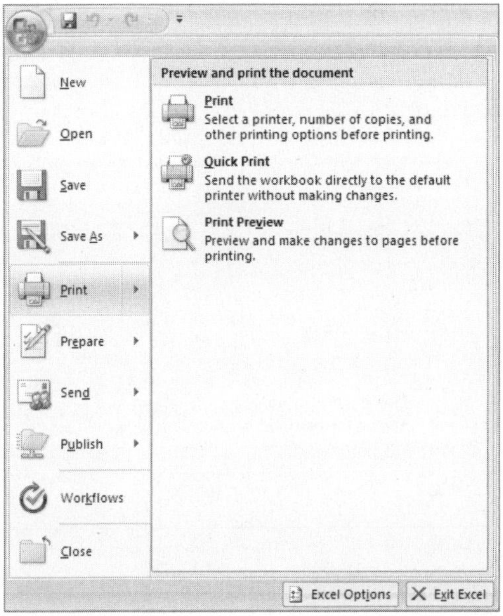

Flowcharts

Flowcharts are visual representations of the steps in a process. They are useful in terms of quality because plotting the process may help you spot bottlenecks that could be causing quality problems.

Flowcharts can be constructed in Excel, although the process is a bit cumbersome. If you have a very large flowchart to construct, we'd recommend using a software package designed for that purpose. If you're working with a simple flowchart, like the one shown in Figure 7.16, give Excel a try.

FIGURE 7.16 Flowchart example

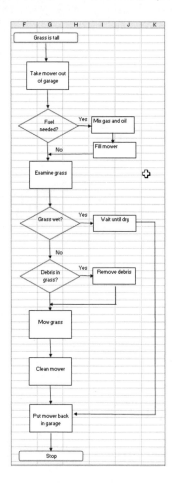

Small flowcharts can be created in Excel using the Shapes option. Shapes is a gallery in the Illustrations group within the Insert tab, as shown in Figure 7.17.

Click the arrow on the bottom of the Shapes button and a drop-down will appear with all the shapes that are available to you. Flowchart options are the seventh from the top, as shown in Figure 7.18.

FIGURE 7.17   Shapes

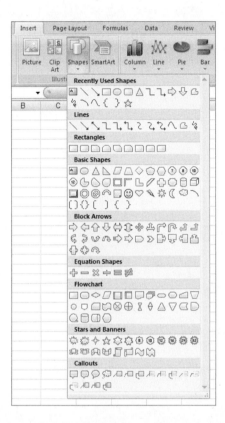

You can see that there are several shapes to choose from. Click the shape you want to add to the flowchart and place it on the worksheet. Once you've placed the shape on the worksheet, the Format ribbon is activated. This gives you the option to change the fill selection or format the figure. We've filled the "Grass is Tall" box with the last color in the Shape Fill drop-down in the under the Drawing Tools and Format tabs, as shown in Figure 7.19 (note that the figure is in black and white).

Click inside the shape, type the text desired, and continue to add shapes until the flowchart is complete. Connect the shapes using lines and arrows from the Lines selection in the Shapes group (see Figure 7.18).

FIGURE 7.18   Flowchart shapes

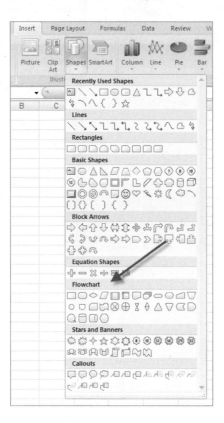

FIGURE 7.19   Assigning to a shape a fill color by using shape themes

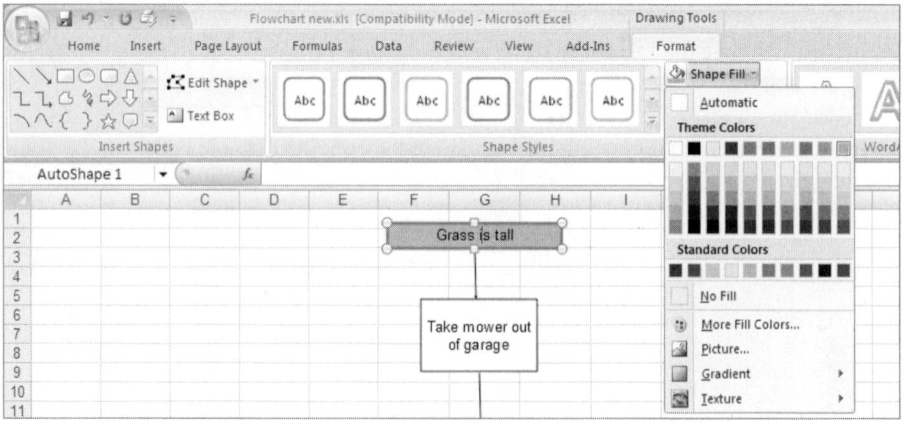

Control Chart

Control charts are a way to monitor variations from the quality standards. Variations that exceed the limits are said to be out of control, and those within the limits are said to be in control (if you want to peek ahead, you'll see that Figure 7.21 shows measurements that drop below the lower control limit line and above the upper control limit, which means this process is out of control). Quality management theories say you should adjust only processes that are out of control.

Data gathering occurs by taking samples at intervals during the process. The samples are measured and recorded in a spreadsheet much like the sample shown in Figure 7.20.

In this example, we've taken the mean of the sample measurements and, using standard deviation calculations, determined the upper and lower control limits for our process. It's beyond the scope of this book to go into the theory and formulas that make up the control chart. Let's instead concentrate on creating the chart itself. The control chart, based on the data gathered in Figure 7.20, is shown in Figure 7.21.

FIGURE 7.20   Sample control data measurements

	A	B	C	D	E	F	G	H	I	J
1	Date	Sample 1	Sample 2	Sample 3	Mean	Average of All Means	Standard Deviation	Average of Standard Deviation	Lower Control Limit	Upper Control Limit
2	5/1	0	4	5	3.00	2.48	2.65	1.30	1.17	3.65
3	5/2	3	1	3	2.33	2.48	1.15	1.30	1.17	3.65
4	5/3	4	2	3	3.00	2.48	1.00	1.30	1.17	3.65
5	5/4	5	3	0	2.67	2.48	2.52	1.30	1.17	3.65
6	5/5	0	1	1	0.67	2.48	0.58	1.30	1.17	3.65
7	5/6	2	3	1	2.00	2.48	1.00	1.30	1.17	3.65
8	5/7	5	4	3	4.00	2.48	1.00	1.30	1.17	3.65
9	5/8	2	3	5	3.33	2.48	1.53	1.30	1.17	3.65
10	5/9	3	3	4	3.33	2.48	0.58	1.30	1.17	3.65
11	5/10	4	4	3	3.67	2.48	0.58	1.30	1.17	3.65
12	5/11	0	2	4	2.00	2.48	2.00	1.30	1.17	3.65
13	5/12	3	0	1	1.33	2.48	1.53	1.30	1.17	3.65
14	5/13	2	1	3	2.00	2.48	1.00	1.30	1.17	3.65
15	5/14	2	0	2	1.33	2.48	1.15	1.30	1.17	3.65

FIGURE 7.21   Control chart

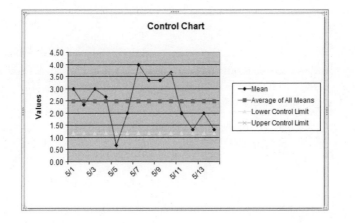

This is a simple line chart. Start by highlighting the data cells in columns A, E, F, I, and J (data cells are in rows 2 through 15 for each column). Remember to hold down the Ctrl key while selecting the columns because the data is not contiguous. Then select the Insert tab and choose Line, then 2D Line. We chose the Line with Markers chart format. If you want a different style, highlight the chart, choose the Design tab, and click the bottom arrow in the Chart Styles group to show all the line style options. Figure 7.22 shows the choices.

Name the chart, the horizontal and vertical axes, and the legend as we did previously.

FIGURE 7.22   Line chart design choices

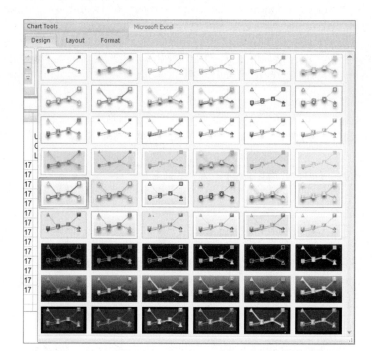

Inspection

Inspection is as it sounds—it's physically looking at, measuring, or testing the end result for conformance to quality standards. Inspections can occur at any point in the process and again at the end of the process. Decisions are made during inspection to accept or reject the work. Many of the techniques we've already discussed involve inspection.

Controlling Quality

Quality control concerns gathering data as we discussed earlier in this chapter and determining if the work complies with the quality standards as documented in the quality management plan. Quality control occurs from the moment work begins on the project (typically the Executing processes) throughout the remainder of the project. The purpose behind controlling quality is to identify the cause of variances in the processes and correct or remove them. It also makes certain the end result conforms to the product descriptions and requirements documented during the Planning processes.

When quality measurements are not in control, it often results in rework. This usually means the process has to be repeated (after it's been corrected). And it's likely the work already performed must be scrapped. Rework impacts the project schedule, it impacts team morale, and it may require after-hours work, which can lead to more errors or other negative impacts. Monitoring quality early and often can help alleviate rework if you're able to correct the process quickly.

Next we'll put a different twist on the topic of quality and look at it from the perspective of formatting and securing your project data and implementing security measures.

Security and Formatting Elements of MOSS

We talked about MOSS and its ability to house project planning documents throughout this book. Further, we talked about InfoPath and its integration into Microsoft Office. In this section, we'll talk about the security elements you should consider when working with a shared document repository and MOSS-capable Office programs.

To begin with, we must first point out the notion of shared libraries. Like a brick-and-mortar library that houses real books that are cataloged and housed in different sections, a click-and-mortar document repository houses documents of different types that are also cataloged and stored in meaningful locations. We call these repositories document libraries and they are easily created. While document libraries can contain a variety of Office file types (e.g., Word, Excel), it may be a good idea to separate document content into different libraries based upon functionality (not necessary, but it reduces confusion and complexity).

 It's important to note that each document library can only have one type of *document template*. When a user clicks the New button, that document template is utilized.

For example, we might want one document library allocated for Excel spreadsheets and another for Word documents. Here's how to get started.

On the home page of the MOSS server, click Site Actions ➢ View All Site Content. This brings up a screen similar to the one shown in Figure 7.23.

Next click the Create button near the top of the screen. This brings up a new page, similar to the one shown in Figure 7.24.

You can see that you have a myriad of creation types to choose from on this page. For example, you can opt to create libraries, web pages, contacts, and calendars. But for our current purpose, we're interested in creating a new document library. Under the Libraries tab, click the document library link. Figure 7.25 and 7.26 show examples of Excel and Word document libraries we've created and named. In the Document Template section, we chose the appropriate document type for our library. (Note that we could opt to create a form library if we had XML-based electronic forms, so-called "e-forms" created with InfoPath.)

FIGURE 7.23   The All Site Content screen

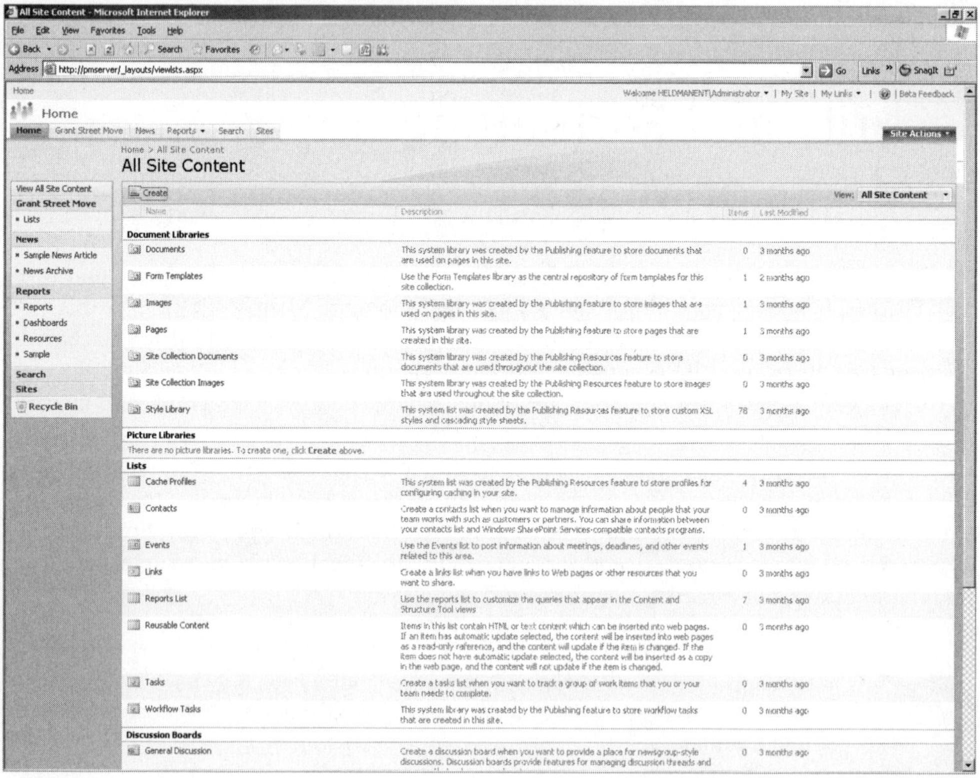

FIGURE 7.24   The Create Page screen

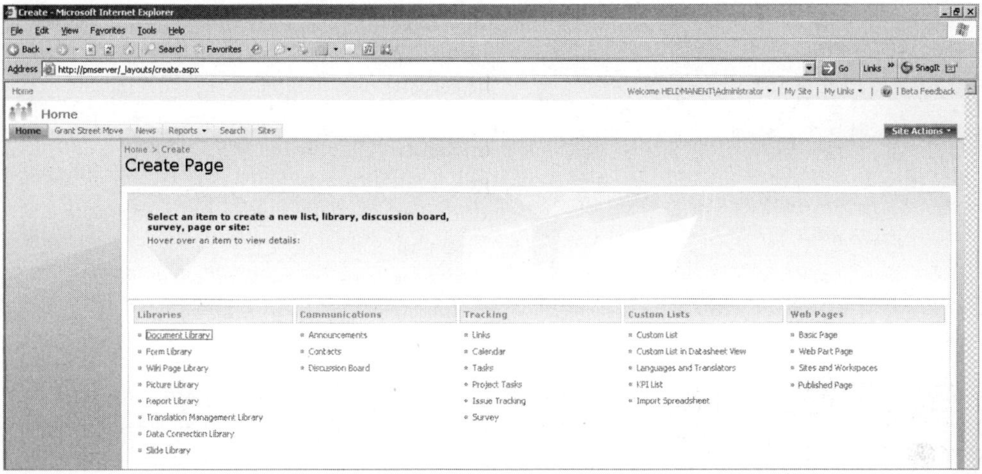

FIGURE 7.25   Excel document library

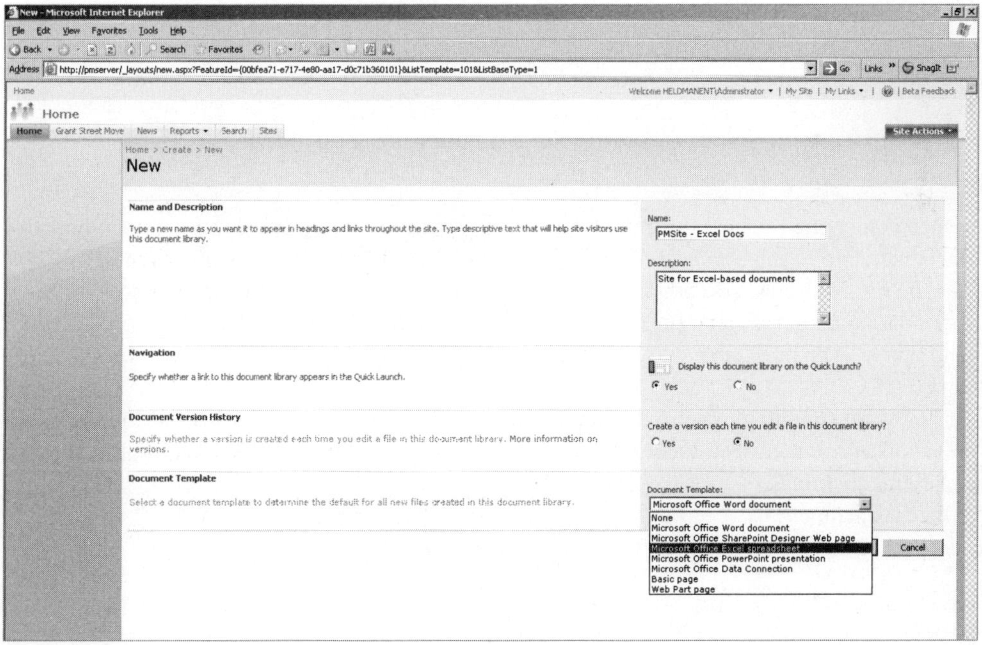

FIGURE 7.26   Word document library

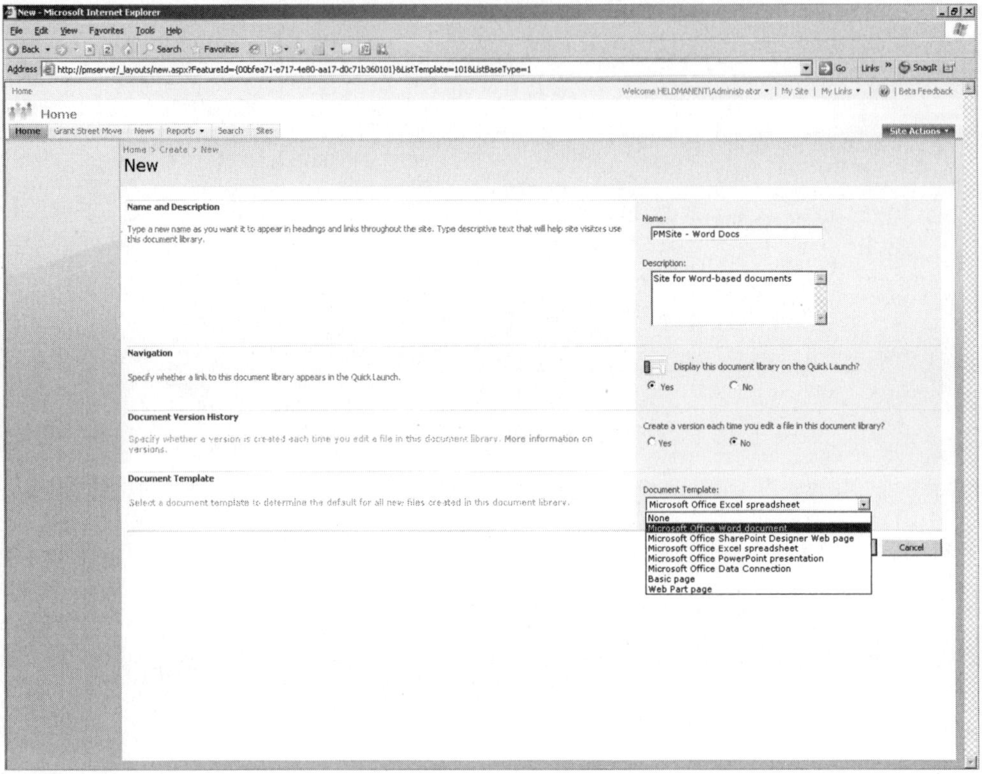

Once you create the new documents and you're ready to upload them to the document library, navigate to the library and then click the Upload button, as shown in Figure 7.27.

As the figure shows, you can upload a single document or multiple documents. You can also upload documents using the Publish feature in Word or Excel 2007. If you choose single document, you're presented with the option to browse to get your document, as shown in Figure 7.28.

If you want to upload several documents at once, you're presented with a selection screen similar to the one shown in Figure 7.29. Check the box next to each document you want to upload and click OK.

Once a document has been uploaded, it appears in the repository with a New! emblem, ready for readers to view it. Figure 7.30 shows an example.

FIGURE 7.27   Uploading documents to the library

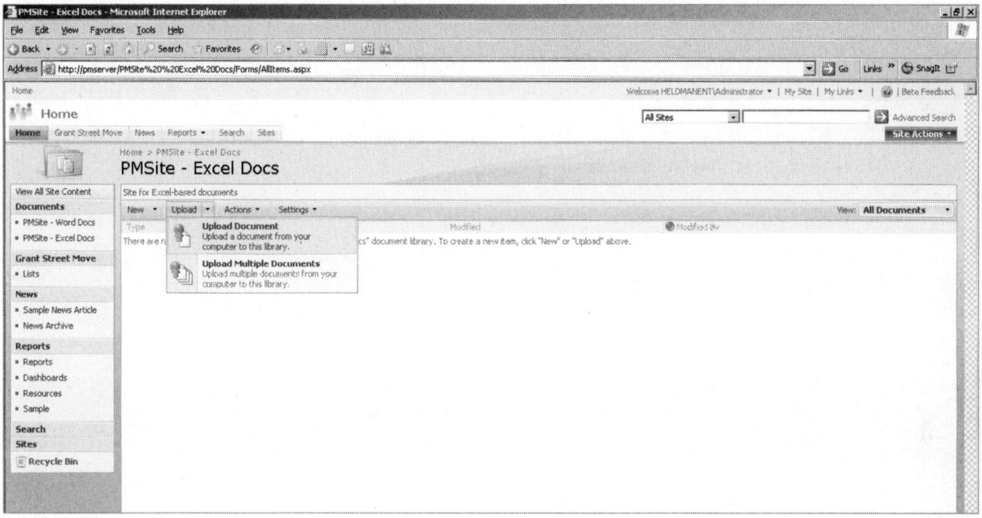

FIGURE 7.28   Uploading a single document

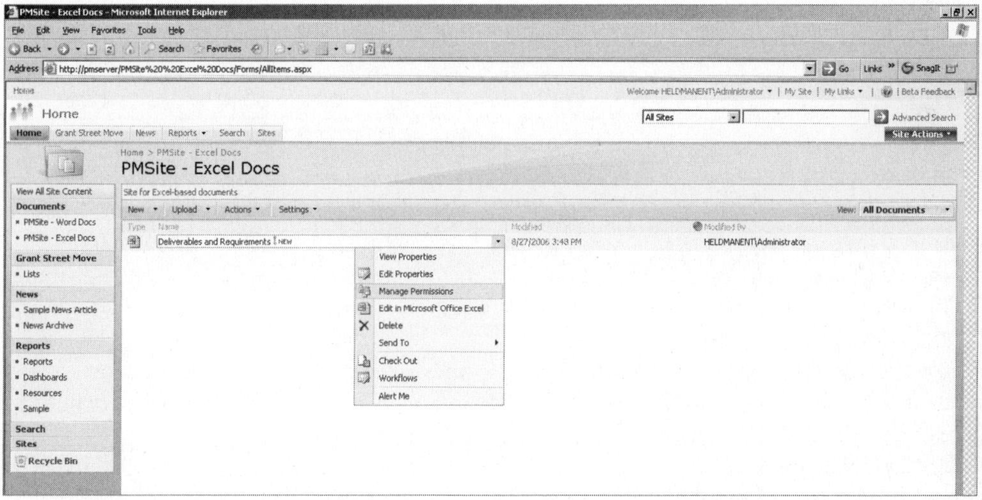

FIGURE 7.29 Uploading multiple documents

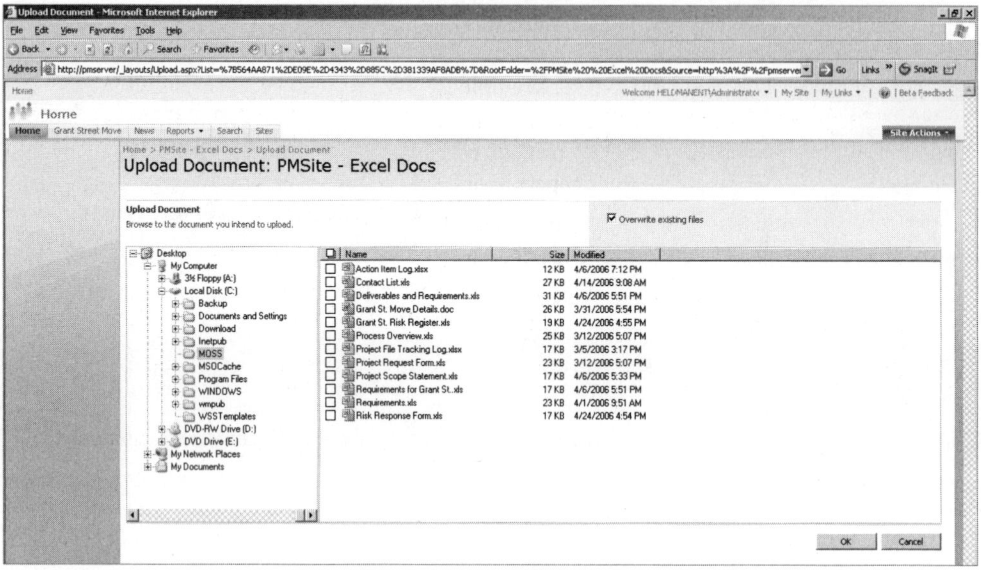

FIGURE 7.30 A new document in the Document Library

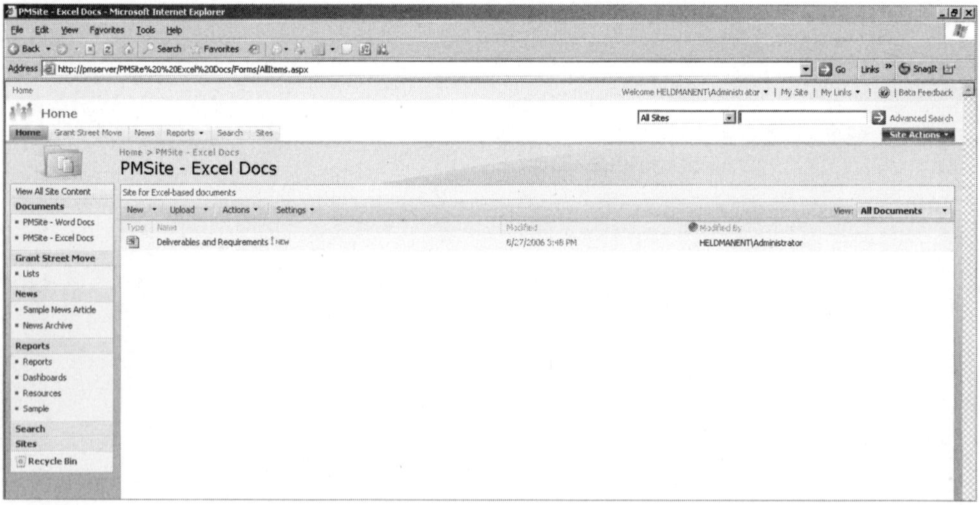

Highlight the document and a drop-down menu appears. Among the options in the list is the ability to manage permissions, as shown in Figure 7.31. (Note that "readers" will not have this setting to play with.) But permissions go substantially beyond this setting and we'll talk about that momentarily.

Most individuals have limited control. We uploaded this document while logged on as a user named HELDMANENT\Administrator —an account with full control rights. The Home Owners group has these rights as well. Everyone else has limited access with some special permissions. Let's take a look at the special permissions and their meanings:

- Approvers are users who have the ability to approve documents that are ready for check-in to the site. They can edit and approve pages as well as list items and documents.

- Contributors, of course, are those users authorized to contribute documents to the site. They can edit list items and documents.

- Designers are users responsible for site and form design. They can edit lists, document libraries, and pages within the sites.

- Hierarchy managers are able to create sites, edit pages, and list items and documents.

- A restricted reader *cannot* view historical versions, nor can they review user rights information.

- Finally, limited access means that users can view specific lists and document libraries, and they can list items, documents, and folders when given the appropriate permissions.

FIGURE 7.31   The Manage Permissions option

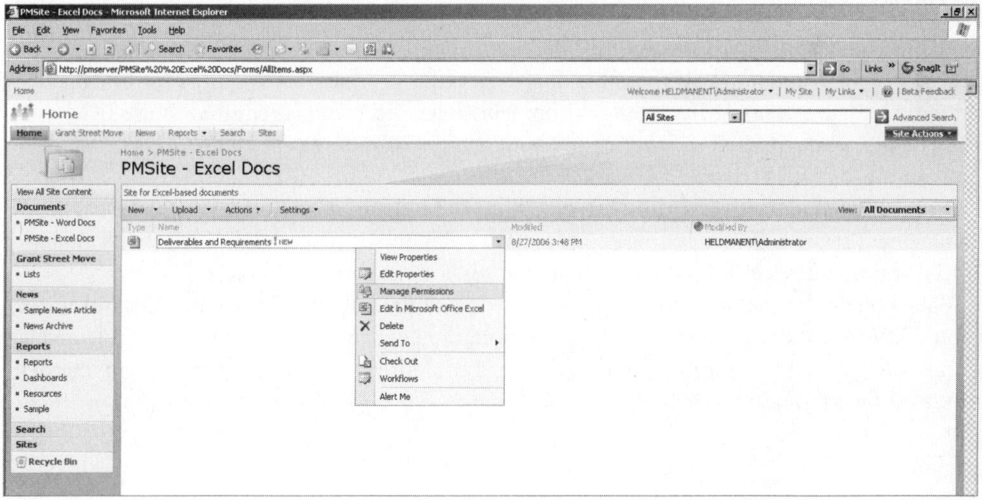

All of this means that you have detailed control over the things users can do to the site. If someone has limited access with appropriate permissions, they can pull up a document in your library, review it, and even add data to it, but they cannot make significant structural changes to it.

It is advisable for you and the others on your team to take some time to explore site permission options so you have a clear understanding of what users can and cannot do. Set up an experimental site where you have a workstation or two loaded with the Office software and Office Server. Then, log on with different user accounts and permissions and see what it feels like to be a user working with MOSS.

Make certain to work with your network administrators when exploring permissions and such in MOSS. Most MOSS implementations will have a security plan in place and you'll need to adhere to those policies. The plan will likely define security and permissions for MOSS and for the sites on the portal. Let your network administrator know what you want to do and they can brief you on the security plan and perhaps set up a test area for you to use to explore all the options.

Information Rights Management (IRM) and Office 2007

Thanks to all of the security shenanigans that have been going on in the last few years, Information Rights Management (IRM)—the ability to control who has what rights to view documents, even if they're posted on the Internet—has come to the fore. Microsoft has made a Rights Management Service information protection technology available for Windows Server 2003 (W2K3). With this tool, document creators can apply a persistent policy that stays with the document, whether it is utilized in-house or over the Internet. A client-side component is required along with the server service, and it may be possible that third-party products are required for documents that will be used in a non-Microsoft environment. Extra licensing is required to use IRM as well. For more information see `www.microsoft.com/windowsserver2003/technologies/rightsmgmt/default.mspx`.

Office 2007 ships with the ability to install an IRM client and interface with the Rights Management service. When getting ready to save a document, you simply click the Windows Office button and select Prepare ➢ Restrict Permission, as shown in Figure 7.32.

When you do this the first time, you're given some initial information about IRM and asked if you'd like to install the client. After installation, the next time you try to restrict document permissions, you'll see a notification that there is a trial Internet-based service you can interact with, as shown in Figure 7.33.

FIGURE 7.32   The Restrict Permission option

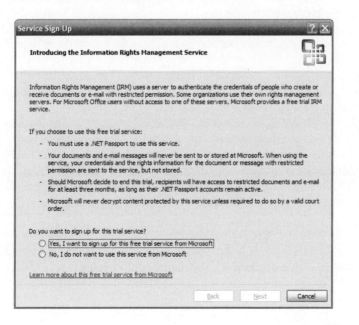

FIGURE 7.33   IRM notification

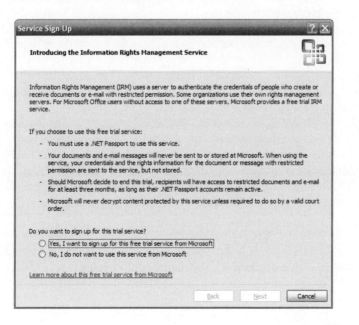

Digital Signatures

Finally, you have the option of saving an Office document with a digital signature. It's important to fully understand what is really happening with digital signature technology because enabling it will require infrastructure that is capable of handling the signatures.

There are three components involved in creating digital signatures:

- Hashing
- Key encryption
- Certificates

Two of these elements are contained within the document itself (key encryption and certificates).

Once a document has been created and a digital signature is applied, the data in the document is crunched down (hashed) into what is called a message digest. (At this point, we say the document has been hashed.) Then the document is encrypted with what is called a private key. The resulting document is a garbled message that cannot be read by someone illicitly accessing it. Should a hacker or malicious software try to change the document, the reader will be aware of it because when they try to open it, the resulting message digest will be different than the one to which the key was applied, thus rendering it a fake and unreadable.

Digital signatures use public key encryption technology inside a public key infrastructure (PKI). The idea is that there are two keys: public and private. Documents are saved with a private key. Users receiving or accessing a document obtain a public key. Together, the two keys can unlock the document. This and the message digest comprise the "digital signature" technology.

 For a fun, easy explanation of PKI, visit www.youdzone.com/signature.html. For the more academic version, check out http://en.wikipedia.org/wiki/Public-key_cryptography.

But the problem is that if a public key is freely available and a scurrilous individual gains access to a signed document even though they should not have rights to it, they can then open the document (because they have the public and private keys) and masquerade as though the document came from them—freely altering it at will and giving it to whomever they please. This is where certificate technology comes in.

Some of the security innovations Microsoft has developed in order to cope with hackers centers on the notion of using certificates to validate authority. Microsoft server software has long had the ability to create and manage digital certificates. The idea is that the public key is tied to a certificate validating that it came from the source it says it originated from. Someone receiving a digitally signed document that uses certificates knows for a surety that the document came from the person they believe it was supposed to come from and not someone posing as that person.

Microsoft's certificate authority (CA) is an important part of the security elements needed to make digital signatures actually work. It is quite possible your local server manager may have installed a CA on your local network, giving you the ability to fully implement digital signatures. Setting up a CA can be a complicated process, but it is the last full step in digital assurance.

An internal CA is generally fine for a corporate environment in which documents are being transmitted internally and not sent to others outside the company. However, when documents need to be accessed by non-company personnel—such as a contractor, for example—an internally generated certificate may not pass security muster. How can a contractor know for sure that you sent the document and that your certificate wasn't (easily) duplicated by someone outside your company?

Third-party certificate providers such as VeriSign can be used to set up certificates that validate the documents came from you. In an environment in which documents are digitally signed and sent out to others outside your organization, procuring a digital certificate provider may be a necessary step. Don't forget to include this expense in the project budget.

A user who wants to digitally sign a document simply clicks the Office button and selects Prepare ➤ Add a Digital Signature, as shown in Figure 7.34.

A warning dialog box similar to the one shown in Figure 7.35 appears notifying you that Microsoft cannot warrant a digital signature's legal enforcement due to the fact that evidentiary laws vary by jurisdiction.

FIGURE 7.34   Adding a digital signature

FIGURE 7.35   Microsoft Cannot Warrant dialog box

Microsoft Office Excel

Microsoft Office digital signatures combine the familiarity of a paper signing experience with the convenience of a digital format. While this feature provides users with the ability to verify a document's integrity, evidentiary laws may vary by jurisdiction. Microsoft thus cannot warrant a digital signature's legal enforceability. The third-party digital signature service providers available from the Office marketplace may offer other levels of digital signature assurance.

☐ Don't show this message again

[Signature Services from the Office Marketplace...]   [OK]

You are next presented with a Sign dialog box. You are told that you are about to add a digital signature to the Excel document, as shown in Figure 7.36.

Keying in a signing reason brings up a Signature Confirmation box, similar to the one shown in Figure 7.37.

Additionally, a Signatures pane shows up in the Excel document, notifying you that the document has been digitally signed, as shown in Figure 7.38.

At the end of the day, posting documents to MOSS probably will not require something as elaborate as digital signatures. There are so many permissions and security controls already built into the system that you simply don't need the heft and additional burden of the signatures. Sending documents outside, however, may well necessitate digital signatures. Thankfully, the Office 2007 suite is capable of working within all of these confines to help you get your work done in a secure way.

FIGURE 7.36   You Are About to Add a Digital Signature dialog box

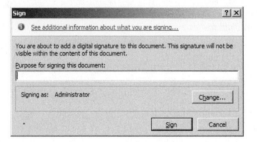

FIGURE 7.37   Signature Confirmation dialog box

FIGURE 7.38   The Signatures pane of an Excel document

Chapter 8

Constructing the Project Schedule and Budget

When you bring up the term *project plan*, nine out of ten people will say the project schedule *is* the project plan. All of you know that's wrong! The project schedule is one of the documents in the project plan—but it's not the project plan. We've discussed many other components of the project plan so far, including the project scope statement, the communications plan, roles and responsibilities, procurement plans, risk plans, and quality plans.

Now we're ready to get down to the individual components of the work of the project. We'll start this chapter by discussing the work breakdown structure. After that's completed, we'll discuss estimating techniques for scheduled tasks, sequencing tasks, determining the critical path, and finally constructing the project schedule.

Creating the Work Breakdown Structure (WBS)

A work breakdown structure (WBS) is a way to graphically display the work of the project. It typically shows all the deliverables of the project along with the individual components of work that it takes to complete them. The WBS organizes the work of the project into logical groupings and it's hierarchical in nature.

We'll need some documents we've already created to help us construct the work breakdown structure and the project schedule. The first one is the project scope statement. You'll recall that the scope statement lists the project deliverables. This will become the first level of the WBS. You may also want to review the requirements document (or the scope statement if you recorded the requirements there) to help with this exercise.

Constructing WBS Levels

The WBS looks much like an organization chart. For small to medium projects, the top box contains the name of the project and the next level of boxes show the deliverables. If you're working on a large project with many subprojects under it, the WBS still starts with the project name at the top, but the next level contains the name of the subprojects rather than the deliverables. The subproject managers are then responsible for creating the WBS for their individual subprojects. Figure 8.1 shows the first two levels of the WBS for the Grant St. Move project. (Keep in mind that this is only a partial list of the deliverables.)

FIGURE 8.1   Level 1 WBS for Grant St. Move

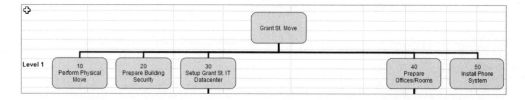

Each entry on the WBS should have a unique identifier. As you can see in Figure 8.1, Setup Grant St. IT Datacenter has a number 30 above it. This code, or identifier, is used for accounting purposes to track the work components. All the levels under this level will begin with 30. (You can get a sneak peek at this by looking ahead to Figure 8.2.) Team members should use these codes to record their time. Additionally, if materials and equipment are needed for the work, the WBS code can be used to track these expenses as well. This way, the project budget can be devised, tracked, and monitored by deliverable.

The idea with a WBS is that you start out at the highest level (in our case, the deliverables) and display more detail with each successive level of the WBS. Most shouldn't go deeper than five or six levels. Eventually, you get to the lowest level, called the work package level, where you can easily estimate, schedule, and assign the work package to an individual or an organization.

Work Package Level

The work package level is always the lowest level of the WBS, whether there are two levels or six levels. The idea is that the work package level is easily assigned to a group or an individual and the amount of time it will take to complete the work package can be easily estimated. The work package may include subprojects, milestones, summary tasks (which are groupings of similar tasks), and for small projects, the tasks themselves.

Figure 8.2 shows a partial view of our Grant St. Move project WBS decomposed several levels. We constructed the WBS like an organization chart. If you need a refresher on how to build the organization chart, refer to Chapter 5.

You may notice that our requirements for this project helped us define some of the tasks. For example, the requirement "at least one quad electrical outlet must be available at every work location" led to the inspect and test wiring and run wiring tasks.

The WBS for medium and large projects won't likely break down to the task level because the WBS would contain too many levels to be useful. Task level detail for medium to large projects (and small projects too) is broken down separately on a task list that can be constructed using an Excel spreadsheet and on the project schedule.

FIGURE 8.2   Partial WBS for Grant St. Move

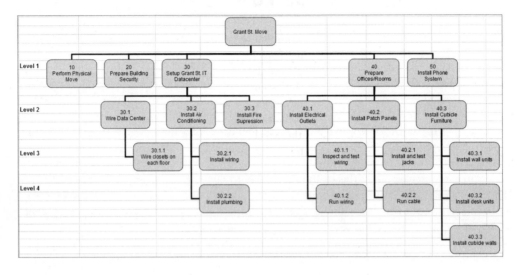

The WBS should display only the work of the project. If the work is not included in the WBS, it's not part of the project. Remember back in Chapter 4 that we talked about this same concept when constructing the scope statement. By including only the work of the project in the scope statement and the WBS, you'll go along way toward preventing scope creep.

Defining Resources for Work Packages

Once the WBS is constructed and the work packages are defined, the next step involves assigning resources to the work packages. The purpose is twofold. First, the person or organization that's assigned the work package is responsible for completing the work (correctly and accurately, of course). Second, we'll want to determine time and cost estimates for the work and the logical person to determine estimates is the person who will be completing the work. We'll cover how to determine time estimates in the next section, "Estimating Project Tasks."

In Chapter 5, we performed a skills assessment and documented those skills in the skills assessment template. In addition, we documented some high-level roles and responsibilities in the RACI chart. Both of these documents are useful in helping us determine who is assigned to each of the work packages by matching skills and responsibilities with the work.

Depending on your preference, you could note the name of the person or organization responsible for the work package in parentheses under the work package name on the WBS. Alternatively, you could create a worksheet that lists the work package and the person assigned to it in the next column. If your work package level contains summary tasks, for example, you could then use this spreadsheet to break down the work package level into individual tasks—the person assigned to the work package could do this for you. This is a helpful step when creating the project schedule because you can take the tasks from this worksheet and plug them right into the schedule.

Estimating Project Tasks

Now that we know the tasks needed to complete each deliverable, the next thing we need to do is estimate how long it will take to finish each task. We'll need this information to build the project schedule and to help determine a total duration estimate for the entire project.

There are several methods you can use for estimating tasks, and it's not uncommon to use two or more of these methods in combination. And some task estimates may be easily determined by your project team while others may take some analysis. We'll look at each of the estimating techniques next. Keep in mind that many of these techniques can be used to estimate costs as well. We'll look at costs and budgets in Chapter 9, "Establishing Change Control Processes."

Expert Judgment

Expert judgment is an estimating technique that relies on people who have hands-on experience performing similar tasks in the past. Since they have experience, they will likely have a good idea of the duration of a similar task. This is an effective technique for simple, repetitive, or well-known tasks. However, this technique is still after all a best guess. It's best to use this technique in combination with historical information on past projects of a similar nature and with the other techniques we'll discuss in the following sections.

Top-Down and Bottom-Up Estimating

Top-down estimating is a form of expert judgment. This technique is also known as analogous estimating. This technique compares current project tasks with similar tasks that have been completed on past projects. For example, if it took two weeks to run fiber cable in a building similar to the Grant St. project building, then it's likely it will take two weeks to run fiber cable in this building as well.

This technique can also be used to estimate the duration of the entire project. Think of the top-down technique as taking one long drink as opposed to little sips (which is what bottom-up estimating is like).

The opposite method, the bottom-up estimating technique, estimates each work component individually and rolls up the individual estimates into one. This is the method we'll use for the Grant St. Move project. After we've determined the estimates for all project activities, we'll add them together to come up with an overall duration for the entire project.

Parametric Estimating

The parametric estimating technique is a quantitatively based method that multiplies the work by the rate to determine the estimate. For example, in the Grant St. Move project, we've been told by the moving company that it takes three people 8 hours to load 10,000 pounds onto the truck and then unload it at the new location. The Main St. employees have approximately 30,000 pounds of boxes and furniture to move. Performing some simple math, we can see it will take two people 24 hours to move Main St. That doesn't fit with our goal of getting employees moved over the weekend with minimum downtime. That means we need to add more people to the moving crew. Nine movers can move all 30,000 pounds in 8 hours, or alternatively, six people could move them in 12 hours.

The concept of adding people to the moving crew and adjusting hours is known as resource leveling. We'll talk more about that in the section "Documenting the Project Schedule" later in this chapter.

Three-Point Estimates

Three-point estimates are determined by averaging three estimates—the most likely, optimistic, and pessimistic—to determine an overall mean estimate for the task. Three-point estimates are also known as PERT estimates—PERT stands for Program Evaluation Review Technique. This estimating technique is especially useful for tasks that the team has not performed before.

There is still some expert judgment happening even with three-point estimates. You should ask the person assigned to the task (and maybe an additional expert or two as well) to tell you how long they think the task will take if everything goes better than planned and there are no problems along the way. The next question is, How much time will it most likely take to complete the task? And the last question is, If the worst happens and everything that can go wrong does go wrong, how long will it take? Then, take those three numbers and plug them into the following formula:

three-point estimate = (optimistic + (4 × most likely) + pessimistic) ÷ 6

The most likely estimate is weighted four times more than the others because it represents the mean estimate.

Let's say our network administrator has given us these estimates for WBS deliverable 30.1, wire data center: optimistic = 70 hours, most likely = 80 hours, pessimistic = 120 hours. We could calculate this by hand but a spreadsheet is much handier. Figure 8.3 shows this WBS task with the three-point estimate calculation.

Cell F8 contains the formula for the three-point estimate, as shown in Figure 8.4.

FIGURE 8.3   Three-point estimate worksheet

	B	C	D	E	F	G	H	I	J	K	L	M
1				**Three-Point Estimates**								
2												
3												
4												
5												
6												
7	WBS Task Description	Optimistic Estimate	Most Likely Estimate	Pessimistic Estimate	Three-Point Estimate	Approximate STDEV	-1 STDEV 68% CF	+1 STDEV 68% CF	-2 STDEV 95% CF	+2 STDEV 95% CF	-3 STDEV 99% CF	+3 STDEV 99% CF
8	Wire data center	70	80	120	85.00	8.33	76.67	93.33	68.33	101.67	60.00	110.00

FIGURE 8.4   Three-point estimate formula

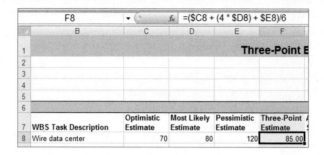

You can use this spreadsheet to list all of the tasks and record their estimates. It's a good idea to use the same unit of measure for all tasks; we used hours. If you begin mixing hours and days, for example, it will make it more difficult to keep all the estimate times straight. You can always convert all estimates back to a common unit (days, for example) when constructing the schedule.

Now let's say we want to know within a level of certainty how confident we are in this estimate. We can do this by using an approximation of the standard deviation calculation. We aren't performing a true standard deviation because we have only one estimate—we don't have a sample of data to work with. The formula for the approximated standard deviation is as follows:

STDEV = (pessimistic optimistic) ÷ 6

Figure 8.5 highlights cell G8, which contains this formula. Remember we're using the $ to make certain the formula references the correct columns when we copy the formula to succeeding rows.

Subtract this result from the three-point estimate to come up with the − 1 STDEV and add it to the three-point estimate to get the + 1 STDEV result.

FIGURE 8.5   STDEV formula

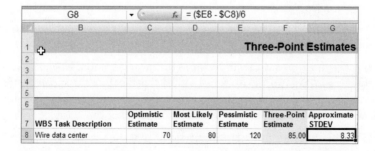

So, what does this number tell us? Generally, there's a 68 percent chance of the task being completed within plus or minus one standard deviation. Plus or minus two standard deviations gives us a roughly 95 percent chance of the task being completed within that time span. Therefore, we can say with a 68 percent confidence factor that the wire data center task will be completed within the time span of from 76.67 to 93.33 hours. If you want to up the ante, the 95 percent confidence rating says we'll finish in 68.33 to 101.67 hours. There's a wider spread of hours here but a greater chance we'll fall within this time span. A 99 percent confidence factor is calculated using plus or minus three standard deviations.

You don't have to complete the standard deviation portion of the worksheet; you could use the three-point estimate for your schedule. However, depending on the tasks and your team's familiarity with them, you might want to consider using the longest time estimate from the plus or minus one standard deviation calculation. The reason for this is to give the team a little breathing room in case the work isn't as clear-cut as they thought or it takes longer than anticipated. This added time is known as buffer time.

Use buffer time wisely when constructing the project schedule. Perhaps consider adding a percentage of buffer time to the deliverable rather than adding it to each task. Or, for highly complex tasks, you could use buffer times for both the task and the deliverable it's associated with.

If you get too carried away with buffer times, you'll end up with an extended project schedule that isn't realistic. If you consistently build schedules that aren't realistic and your team completes the project well ahead of the anticipated completion date, you'll be accused of padding the schedule. If you don't include any buffer time, you might have to adjust the schedule midway through the project to account for the increased time it takes to complete complicated tasks.

Sequencing Tasks

Out next step is to sequence the tasks we've documented in the proper order. Some tasks have dependencies—that is, they can't start or finish prior to another task starting or finishing. There are two types of tasks: successor and predecessor. As their names imply, successor tasks follow after another task and predecessor tasks are those that come before other tasks.

There are four relationships between predecessor and successor tasks that you should be aware of. We'll look at each next.

Finish-to-start (FS)   The finish-to-start relationship is the most common dependency. In this relationship, the predecessor task (or the *from* task) must finish before the successor task (or the *to* task). For example, in the Grant St. Move project, the moving boxes can't be moved until they're packed. Therefore, packing must finish before moving can start.

Start-to-Finish (SF)   The start-to-finish relationship states that the successor task must start before the predecessor task can finish. This relationship is seldom used.

Finish-to-Finish (FF)   Finish-to-finish says that the predecessor task must finish before the successor task finishes.

Start-to-Start (SS)   The start-to-start relationship says the predecessor task must start before the successor task can start.

Let's go back to our lawn mowing example for a moment. Remember we constructed a flowchart for mowing the lawn back in Chapter 7. If we assume our grass is tall and we need to mow, we'll convert some of the flowchart elements to tasks and line them up in the correct order. We'll get something that looks like Figure 8.6.

What you see in Figure 8.6 is known as a precedence diagram. This is the method most project management software programs use to sequence project tasks. You can clearly see the sequence of events. You have to get the mower first—Get Mower is a predecessor task. Then, if the mower needs fuel, you'll proceed to the Mix Gas and Oil task—this is a successor to the Get Mower task. Next is Fill Mower with Fuel, which is a successor task. If the mower doesn't need gas, you could start with the Check Grass for Debris task and then proceed to Mow Grass, Clean Mower, and Put Mower Away. The Mix Gas and Oil task and the Fill Mower with Fuel task have a dependency relationship to each other, but there's no relationship between those tasks and the Check Grass for Debris task. You could perform either of these tasks first; however, they all have to be completed before the Mow Grass task can begin.

This is another place where those sticky-backed notes come in handy. Write each task on a note and use a large whiteboard to arrange and rearrange them until you get them in the correct order. Then record the final outcome in the precedence diagram. And if you're working with a lot of tasks, it's a good idea to include task numbers in each box.

You could create a diagram like this in Excel using the drawing tools (as we did for the flowchart in Chapter 7). If you're working on a large project, you might consider using a project management software program such as Microsoft Project to help you with this.

 Another alternative you could consider is creating the diagram as described in this section and then importing it into Microsoft Visio. Visio can easily create Gantt charts and schedules. Then you could export the Visio diagrams in HTML format and upload them to SharePoint.

FIGURE 8.6   Precedence diagram

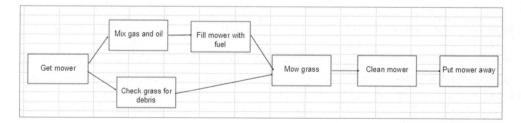

Determining the Critical Path

Creating the project schedule is our ultimate goal in this chapter. As you've seen, many of the steps in the project management process build on each other. We started with a definition of the deliverables, defined the requirements, determined the tasks, estimated their durations, and put them in the correct sequence. Next we need to determine the critical path. Critical path helps us determine the amount of schedule flexibility we have for each task. The critical path is the longest path on the project, and it comprises those tasks that do not have any flexibility, or float time. Float time is the amount of time you can delay the start of a task without delaying the end project date or the amount of time you can delay starting a task without impacting the start of a successor task.

We'll use the deliverable called Prepare Offices/Rooms to illustrate how to calculate critical path. In this example, you'll notice that we have some tasks that are finish-to-start and others that are start-to-start. For example, Install Jacks cannot start until Run Cable has finished. However, the desk units and wall units do not require that the walls be finished before they can start. In other words, as long as cubicle walls are up (the task is started), then desks and wall units can be installed (started). All walls don't have to be up prior to all desks being installed. Therefore, these tasks have a start-to-start relationship and we can begin the desk install prior to the cubicle walls completing.

Figure 8.7 shows how we calculated critical path for the Prepare Offices/Rooms deliverable.

FIGURE 8.7   Critical path

	A	B	C	D	E	F	G	H	I
1			Grant St. Move Critical Path						
2	Task #	Task Description	Dependency	Duration (in Days)	Early Start	Early Finish	Late Start	Late Finish	Float Time
3	40.2.2	Run cable		16	18-Aug	2-Sep	18-Aug	2-Sep	0
4	40.2.1	Install and test jacks	40.2.2	5	3-Sep	7-Sep	3-Sep	7-Sep	0
5	40.1.2	Run wiring		8	18-Aug	25-Aug	26-Aug	2-Sep	8
6	40.1.1	Inspect and test wiring	40.1.2	3	26-Aug	28-Aug	26-Aug	28-Aug	0
7	40.3.3	Install cubical walls	40.2.2, 40.1.2	12	3-Sep	14-Sep	3-Sep	14-Sep	0
8	40.3.2	Install desk units	40.3.3	7	4-Sep	10-Sep	8-Sep	14-Sep	4
9	40.3.1	Install wall units	40.3.3	7	4-Sep	10-Sep	8-Sep	14-Sep	4
10				36					

Calculating the Forward Pass

Let's walk through how we came up with the early start and early finish dates for this deliverable. This calculation is known as the forward pass. Note that we're ignoring weekends and holidays for this example, but you could easily include them by adding or subtracting the appropriate number of days where needed.

Start by putting Aug 18 in cell E3, which is the Early Start column. We determined this date by contacting the contractor we're going to use to run the cable and talking with our own team members about availability. We'll talk about resource availability later in this chapter.

In the Early Finish column in cell F3, add the duration of the task (cell D3) and subtract 1 to come up with the early finish date of Sep 2. Figure 8.8 shows the formula in cell F3.

FIGURE 8.8   Forward pass

f_x	=+E3+D3-1		

C	D	E	F
Grant St. Move Critical Path			
	Duration	Early	Early
Dependency	(in Days)	Start	Finish
	16	18-Aug	2-Sep

Excel will automatically perform this calculation for you and return a date provided you have the cells in column F formatted as dates. Copy this formula down the spreadsheet.

Calculating the Backward Pass

Next we'll calculate the backward pass. This is the opposite of the forward pass and helps us determine late start and late finish dates. The last task, Install Wall Units, can't finish any later than Sep 14. Since employees are due to move in Sep 15, the walls must be finished by Sep 14. This task is dependent on the Install Cubical Walls task starting, which means we couldn't finish installing wall units any later than Sep 14 (presuming the wall unit installers are working right behind the cubical wall installers).

Now in the Late Start column we'll perform a calculation that's opposite the one we performed earlier to determine the late start date. Figure 8.9 shows the formula in cell G9.

The Install Wall Units task can start as late as Sep 8 and still finish by the late finish date. When you get to the Run Wiring task, you'll see that this task can finish as late as Sep 2, which is one day before the Install Cubical Walls task can start (late start).

FIGURE 8.9   Backward pass

f_x	=+H9-D9+1		

C	D	E	F	G
Grant St. Move Critical Path				
	Duration	Early	Early	Late
Dependency	(in Days)	Start	Finish	Start
	16	18-Aug	2-Sep	18-Aug
40.2.2	5	3-Sep	7-Sep	3-Sep
	8	18-Aug	25-Aug	26-Aug
ng 40.1.2	3	26-Aug	28-Aug	26-Aug
40.2.2, 40.1.2	12	3-Sep	14-Sep	3-Sep
40.3.3	7	4-Sep	10-Sep	8-Sep
40.3.3	7	4-Sep	10-Sep	8-Sep

Calculating the Critical Path

The last column, Float Time, determines if there is any float time for the tasks. This is determined by subtracting the early start date from the late start date. Make certain to format this column as a number or you'll end up with a weird-looking date or an error in this column. We're looking for a number here. Figure 8.10 shows the formula in cell I5.

FIGURE 8.10   Float time

fx	=+G5-E5						
C	D	E	F	G	H	I	
Grant St. Move Critical Path							
Dependency	Duration (in Days)	Early Start	Early Finish	Late Start	Late Finish	Float Time	
	16	18-Aug	2-Sep	18-Aug	2-Sep	0	
40.2.2	5	3-Sep	7-Sep	3-Sep	7-Sep	0	
	8	18-Aug	25-Aug	26-Aug	2-Sep	8	

Three tasks have float time: Run Wiring, Install Desk Units, and Install Wall Units. All the other tasks have zero float time. Therefore, the critical path tasks for this project are Run Cable, Install and Test Jacks, Inspect and Test Wiring, and Install Cubical Walls. If you add up the duration of each of these tasks, you'll come up with a total duration of 36 days.

If the start or finish dates slip for these critical path tasks, they will impact the completion date of this deliverable. You can see that if the Run Cable task goes over its estimated time, the Install Cubical Walls task start date will be delayed because it's dependent on Run Cable task finishing. One task pushes the start date of another task, which extends the end date for the entire deliverable. If this deliverable is on the critical path for the project, the entire project will be delayed.

Crashing the Schedule

Once the work of the project begins, it's obvious you'll want to monitor the critical path tasks closely. If it looks as though you're going to run into trouble, there a couple of options you can use to help get the schedule back on track.

First, you could bring in more resources and try to complete the deliverable on time by adding these new people to the critical path tasks. This is known as crashing the schedule. Adding resources is usually the first thing we think of when schedules are running behind. However, more resources don't always help the problem. It might take longer to get those people up to speed, thereby taking valuable team time away from actually working on the task, than it would if the team kept working and finished the task themselves. There's an old saying that "Nine women can't have a baby in one month," which illustrates the dilemma of adding more people to a project—some tasks cannot be completed faster simply by adding more people.

Additional resources cost money. The project budget may or may not be able to support this added expense, so before using the crashing technique, make certain you have the budget for it.

 Crashing the schedule examines cost and schedule trade-offs. More resources is a good option when it works, but it isn't always possible.

Another crashing technique involves limiting or reducing the project requirements. If you can move some of the requirements to phase two, you may be able to complete the remaining requirements in the time allotted. You could also try arranging the tasks in a different order to gain schedule time. Depending on the number of critical path tasks, this technique is not always possible.

You could also do what's known as fast-tracking the schedule. You start two tasks at the same time that were originally scheduled to start at different times. The example we have developed for calculating critical path has already assumed that multiple tasks can start on the same day. However, in a full project schedule, there are likely places where you could start two independent tasks at the same time that weren't originally scheduled that way.

Time delays in critical path tasks will delay the completion of the project. If noncritical path tasks are delayed beyond their float time, they will also delay the finish date of the project. For example, if the Install Desk Units task in the Grant St. Move project slips by more than four days (or starts later than Sep 8), it will impact the completion date of this deliverable.

Before we construct the schedule, we'll look at resource availability. Our critical path tasks are the ones that must be completed on their scheduled start and finish dates, so we need to make certain we have the right resources available during those time frames. We'll look at that topic next.

Determining Resource Availability

Resource availability is the last, but not the least, step we need to consider before putting the schedule together.

We've already said we need Steve and Aimee—the IT resources—for the Grant St. Move project. Further, we know that the physical moves for the three locations will begin on September 15. That means Steve and Aimee (and the contractor assisting them) must have completed the cable runs and the closet wiring before the first employees arrive. We know the cable runs will take two weeks. This task will be performed by a contractor. The closet wiring will take a week with some additional help from the contractor. The cable has to be run before the closets can be wired. And, adding in some buffer time to account for unforeseen issues, the cable runs will have to begin by August 18.

After checking with both Steve and Aimee, we find that Steve has some minor surgery scheduled for August 23 with two additional days of recovery time. We could back up the start date by three days to August 15 to account for the time Steve is out. However, Steve and Aimee won't be able to start wiring the first closet until at least one floor of cable is run. Steve will return to work prior to beginning work on the closets, so a start date of August 18 is acceptable. Take note that this is a good time to develop a contingency plan for the possible risk event of Steve not coming back after surgery as planned. We sure wish him well, but lots of things can happen.

Juggling schedules is difficult to do when you have multiple project team members to account for. There a couple of ways you can manage this issue. First, you could create a spreadsheet with a list of all the resource names. Place the names of the months (or weeks if the duration of the project is short) in the column headers. Then note the dates that the resources are not available.

FIGURE 8.11 Excel calendar templates

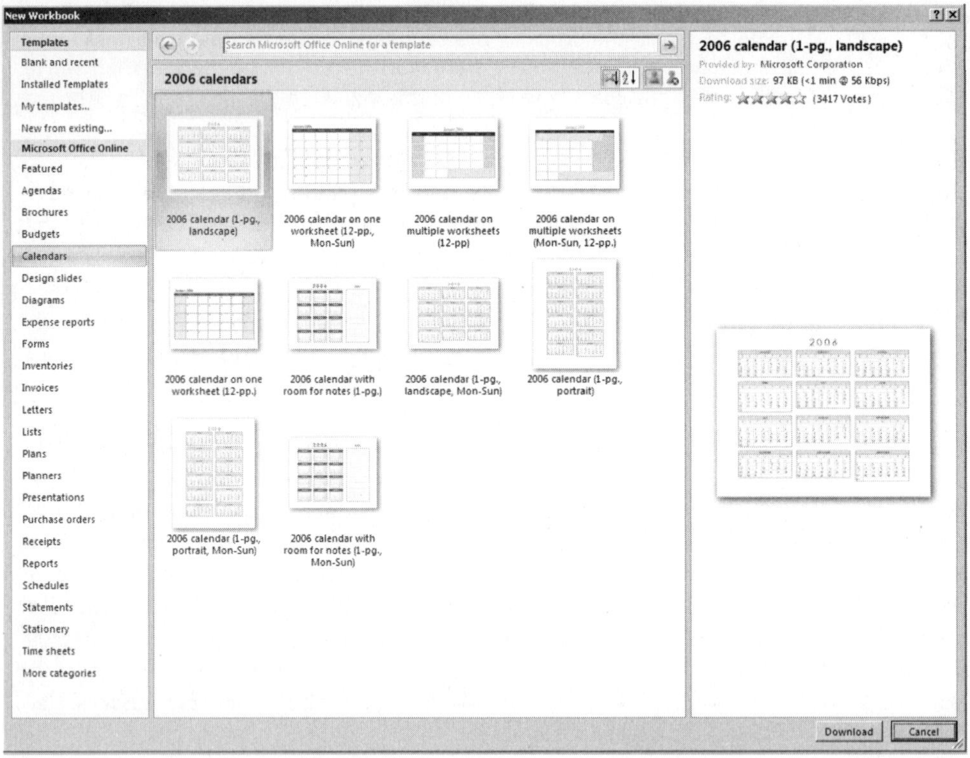

Alternatively, you could create a resource calendar. And that leads us to the perfect time to talk about the template options in Excel. Excel has a large variety of templates available for you to use. There's no sense in reinventing the wheel. Click the Office button and choose New. Then choose Calendars from the list on the left and you'll see calendar options similar to the one in Figure 8.11.

Choose the template you'd like to use and click the Download button on the bottom right of the screen.

The next time you use the calendar template option, you'll see a list similar to the one in Figure 8.12.

We choose 2007 Calendar Options from the list. After clicking on it, we're presented with another set of selections similar to those in Figure 8.13.

FIGURE 8.12   Calendar templates

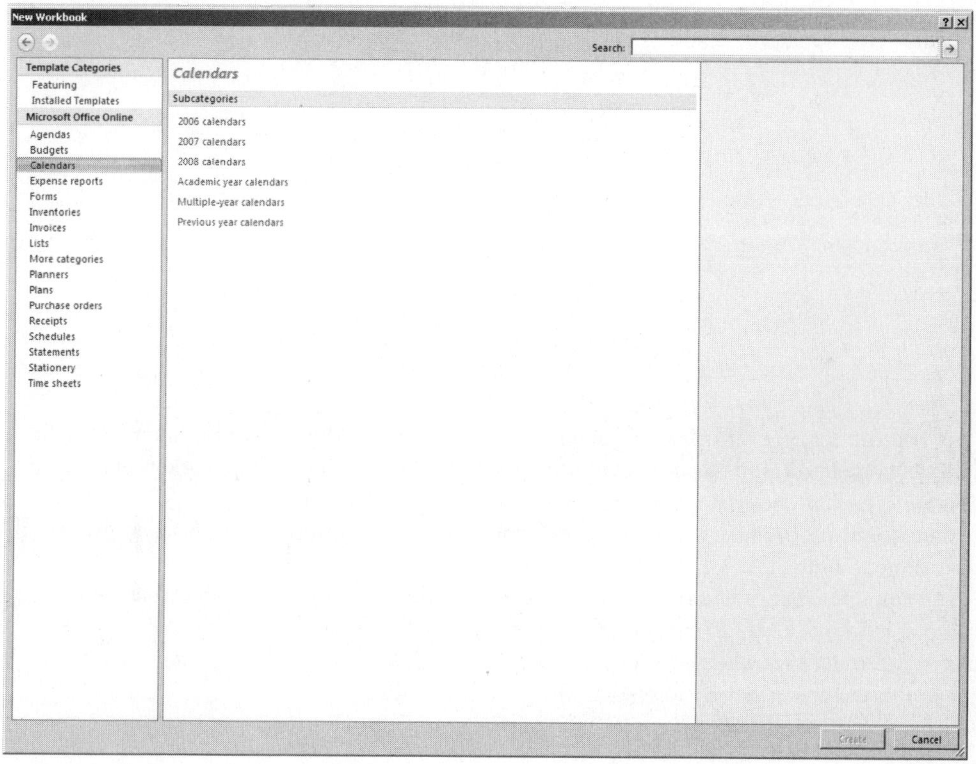

FIGURE 8.13   Calendar layout options

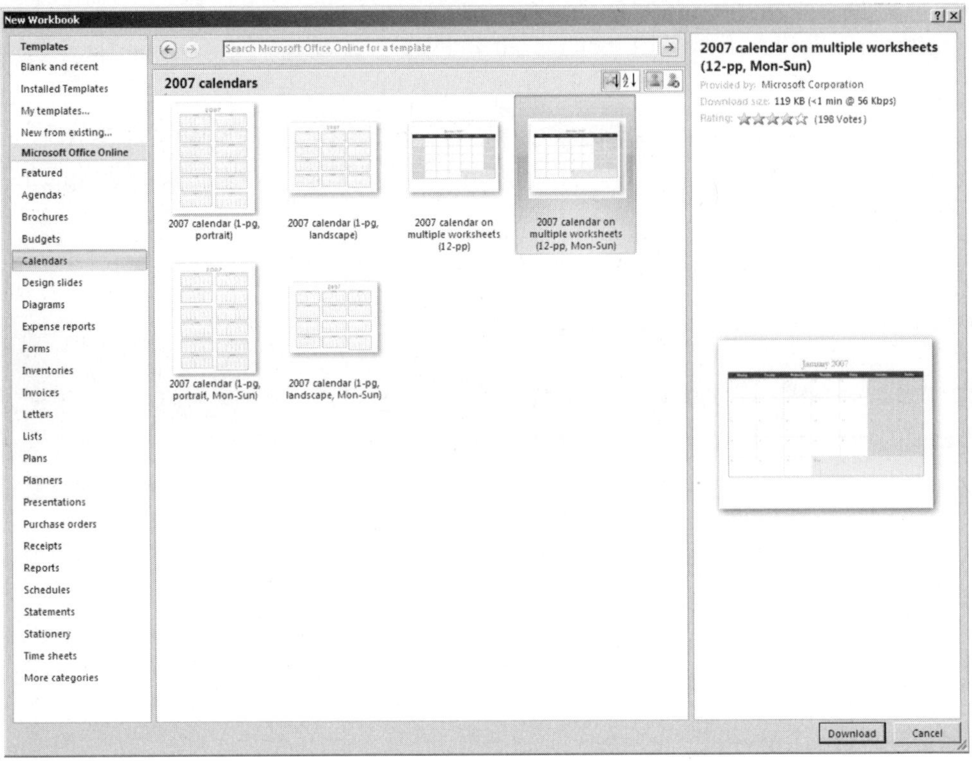

As you can see, you can choose calendars in portrait or landscape mode, calendars with multiple worksheets, and so on. We choose the 2007 calendar on multiple worksheets (12-pp, Mon-Sun). Each month is a tab along the bottom of the workbook (see Figure 8.14). Click on the date you want to make an entry to and type in the information. Figure 8.14 shows what we've done to note Steve's time off.

You could also use calendars to note dates or times that may affect the project schedule. For example, mark off all the holidays your organization observes and any other special meeting days or meeting times when project work won't occur. We'll see calendars again one more time in this chapter as a way to display the project schedule.

> **NOTE** You could also create the calendar in SharePoint using the calendar feature and then export the events to an Excel spreadsheet. Using SharePoint also gives you the advantage of creating alerts so you're notified if any of the events are updated.

FIGURE 8.14   Resource calendar

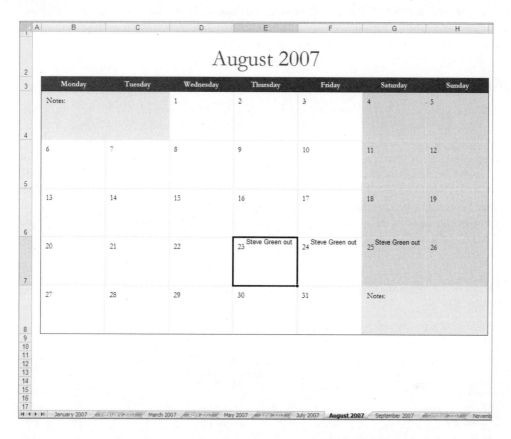

Documenting the Project Schedule

At last, we've arrived at the project schedule. By now, you should know all the tasks, duration estimates, sequencing order, and resources needed for the schedule…in a perfect world. In the real world, you may not have all the information you need yet. More often than not, the resource availability is the piece that's missing. You can still build a preliminary schedule, get the information you do have recorded on the schedule, and then fill in the resources section later.

We don't recommend publishing a preliminary schedule. It seems that once the stakeholders have seen a schedule, preliminary or not, the first project completion date they see is the one they'll hold you to.

There are several ways to display a project schedule. At this point, if you've done all your homework, it's a matter of plugging the tasks, start and end dates, and resource information in the correct sequence into the project schedule format you prefer. We'll look at four ways you can use Excel to display your project schedule in this section.

Milestone Chart

A milestone chart works well for small projects that are only expected to last a few weeks or months or for an executive overview of a large project. Milestones are key events that take place during the project or mark the completion of one or more major deliverables on the project. Milestones charts list the milestones in one column and their expected completion date in the next column. For tracking and reporting purposes, you could also show the actual completion dates of the milestones. Figure 8.15 shows an example milestone chart for some of the deliverables we identified for the Grant St. Move project.

As you can see, this template is easy to set up. List the milestone name in the first column, the dates in the next, and a place for comments in the next. You could also include a column for start dates for the milestones if you wish.

FIGURE 8.15   Milestone chart

	A	B	C	D
1		**Milestone Chart**		
2	Project Number			
3	Date			
4	Project Title			
5	Project Manager			
6				
7	Milestone	Scheduled Completion Date	Actual Completion Date	Comments
8	Perform Physical Move	Sep 30		
9	Prepare Building Security	Sep 14		
10	Setup Grant St. IT Datacenter	Sep 7		
11	Prepare Offices/Rooms	Sep 14		
12	Install Phone System	Sep 12		
13	Project Closeout	Oct 6		

Project Calendar

A project calendar is another tool that uses milestones for displaying the project schedule. Calendars usually display the start and completion dates of the milestones with a line drawn through the dates the work is taking place. You don't have to display only milestones with a calendar. If you're working on a small project of limited duration, you could also display the major tasks associated with the deliverable. Figure 8.16 shows the calendar schedule for the Perform Physical Move deliverable.

FIGURE 8.16   Calendar project schedule

Network Diagram

A network diagram looks similar to the precedence diagram we drew earlier in this chapter to determine task sequences. Again, you could draw your network diagram at the milestone or deliverable level or at the task level. You may have one network diagram at the deliverable level for stakeholder reporting purposes and have individual network diagrams for each deliverable. The size of the project and number of tasks will determine how much detail to display in the schedule.

Figure 8.17 shows a network diagram with our deliverables for the Grant St. Move project. Notice that the start and end dates are included in the boxes.

FIGURE 8.17   Network diagram

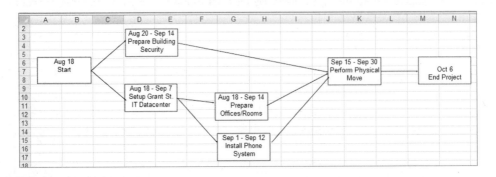

Gantt Charts

Gantt charts are typically what come to mind when most of us think about project schedules. Gantt charts can be created with all project management software packages, and you can construct one easily using Excel. Gantt charts can show whatever level of detail you'd like including: deliverables, tasks, start and end dates, duration, resources, and more. We've constructed a sample Gantt chart (Figure 8.18) that shows some of the Grant St. Move project's major milestones with a breakdown of some of the tasks for the Prepare Rooms/Offices deliverable.

FIGURE 8.18   Gantt chart

Deliverable	Duration	Start Date	End Date	Resource	18-Aug	25-Aug	1-Sep	8-Sep	15-Sep	22-Sep	29-Sep	6-Oct
Start				Project Manager								
Setup Grant St. IT Datacenter		18-Aug	7-Sep	Steve Greene								
Prepare Rooms/Offices		18-Aug	14-Sep	Contractor/Staff								
Run cable	16	18-Aug	2-Sep	Contractor								
Install and test jacks	5	3-Sep	7-Sep	Contractor								
Run wiring	8	18-Aug	25-Aug	Contractor								
Inspect and test wiring	3	26-Aug	28-Aug	Contractor								
Install cubical walls	12	3-Sep	14-Sep	Contractor								
Install desk units	7	4-Sep	10-Sep	Contractor								
Install wall units	7	4-Sep	10-Sep	Contractor								
Prepare Building Security		20-Aug	14-Sep	Facilities Team								
Install Phone System		1-Sep	12-Sep	Telecomm Staff								
Perform Physical Move		15-Sep	2-Oct	Contractor								
Project Closeout		3-Oct	6-Oct	Project Manager								

(Gantt Chart)

Project Number
Date
Project Title
Project Manager

Starting with row 11, you can see we indented the tasks that fall under the Prepare Rooms/ Offices deliverable. Alternatively, you could use the first column to list the deliverable and task numbers from the WBS or from the task list if you created one separately from the WBS. The problem we find with the WBS numbers is that they go in reverse order because of the hierarchical nature of the WBS. If you created a task list for each work package level, you could then assign task identification numbers that are more sequential.

As you can see, we listed the duration, start date, end date, and resource responsible for the task. Those entries appear as they would in a regular spreadsheet. The Gantt chart display is shown in weeks, starting with the week of Aug. 18. The time frames in which work is scheduled for the deliverables are grayed in.

As you're constructing the schedule, you may find you have resources that are overallocated. That means they're either scheduled to work on too many tasks at the same time or they have long stretches of time between tasks. Resource leveling is a technique that requires adjustment to the schedule to correct the over- or underallocation of team members. This may require that additional resources be brought onto the team or it may require that successor tasks be scheduled later than the preliminary schedule shows.

As we mentioned, you could use a combination of presentations for the project schedule, depending on the audience. Executives usually want to only see the highlights. Stakeholders may want to see more detail, and the project team members will need to see all the details.

Schedule progress should be reported at each project status meeting. Schedules for small projects are easier to monitor (and create) than schedules for large projects. It's obvious to see at a glance if the schedule dates are slipping for a small project, and you can see down to the task detail where the problem is occurring. Larger projects take a bit more investigating and are more accurately monitored by using performance measures. We'll discuss how to measure project schedule performance in the section "Determining and Monitoring Performance Measures" later in this chapter. Next, we'll examine how to create the project budget.

Creating the Project Budget

The two things on most any project that will pique the interest of the project sponsor are the schedule and the budget. More often than not, the project manager is told what the schedule and the budget will be from the start. How often have you heard a sponsor say something like this to a project manager: "This project needs to be finished by June 30 and we have $125,000 to make it happen." In our experience, most small to medium sized projects fit this scenario. Does that mean we shouldn't develop a schedule or a budget because we already know what they are? Unless the project involves only one deliverable with two or three tasks, the obvious answer is no. You'd still develop a schedule to make certain you hit the June 30 date and you'd still develop a budget to make certain you stay within the financial constraints.

The ideal situation would allow the project manager to gather all the project information and inputs and then develop a schedule and a budget that satisfies the project goals. The reality is, most organizations are constrained by dollars and time and you'll have at least the schedule if not both the schedule and the budget predetermined before the project starts.

Project budgets are a perfect application for Excel, and we'll look at some templates and examples shortly. First we'll talk about some of the documents you'll need to help determine the budget items and some elements that make up the project budget.

Budgeting Inputs

The project budget is typically the last planning document we create. We still have to cover change control, and we'll talk about that in the next chapter, but once you've set up a change control process, you can easily adapt it to new projects as needed.

Figure 8.19 is the planning portion of the project process overview you first saw in Chapter 3. As you can see, we've come a long way with our project planning documents, and this chapter should bring to light how critical the documents in the planning stage are in creating the schedule and budget.

Like the project schedule, the budget process should start with defining the elements that make up the budget and determining estimates for those elements. There are a couple of places to start. Back in Chapter 5, we started compiling a materials list in which we defined the materials needed for each requirement. Depending on when the list was compiled, the costs noted here may need updated. If estimates were obtained that have expired or the costs listed were best guesses based on previous purchases of a similar nature, they should be updated as well.

FIGURE 8.19   Planning overview

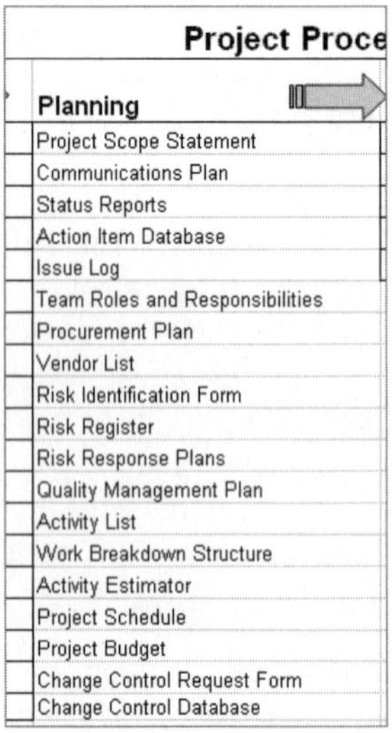

Project Proce
Planning
Project Scope Statement
Communications Plan
Status Reports
Action Item Database
Issue Log
Team Roles and Responsibilities
Procurement Plan
Vendor List
Risk Identification Form
Risk Register
Risk Response Plans
Quality Management Plan
Activity List
Work Breakdown Structure
Activity Estimator
Project Schedule
Project Budget
Change Control Request Form
Change Control Database

The information from the materials list can be easily copied into the budget. You might remember that we tied each item on the materials list to a requirement number. We could use the requirement numbers in the budget as well. This way, we can tally up the total cost for each deliverable and then sum the cost of all the deliverables to determine the overall budget.

The WBS is another document you'll want to review when creating the project budget. We talked about how the work package level, the lowest level in the WBS, allows us to easily estimate time and costs. We also talked about the tracking numbers assigned to each level of the WBS. These numbers may be used to track expenses in the project budget in place of or in conjunction with the requirements numbers.

The numbers used on the WBS often come from the company's chart of accounts. These numbers are accounting codes associated with cost accounts such as labor, equipment, training, consulting services, hardware, software, and so on. At the beginning of the project, make certain someone from the accounting department is involved on the project and gives you the chart of accounts codes to use for the WBS and/or the project budget. Backtracking after the project is complete and trying to determine how costs should be coded could prove difficult.

Other planning documents that will help you determine elements to include in the budget are the scope statement, the project schedule, resource calendars, and the contract (if applicable).

Building Project Budgets

As you've seen, deliverables, requirements numbers, charts of accounts, or other codes may be used to track the budgeted expenses against actual cost for project budgets. Project budgets may also be tracked by phases. For example, costs for the feasibility study, analysis, design, build, and implementation phases may be tracked independently. As mentioned earlier, separate categories of expenses may exist within these phases, like labor or equipment, but each phase is tracked as a separate budget.

Creating budgets by project phases or work packages has some distinct benefits. Because the budgets are broken into smaller units, or individual budgets, it's much easier to manage and control costs. And you are more likely to find problems quickly when using small budgets. That means you can fix problems quicker and have less of a chance of the budget running away from you before you realize what's happened.

The key is to work with your accounting staff to make certain you're tracking expenses and creating the budget in a way that's easy to report and fits with the organization's accounting practices.

Elements of a Project Budget

The planning documents are a great place to start to identify budget items. You can also use some of the brainstorming and sticky-backed note techniques we talked about for the requirements gathering activity to uncover all project budget items. The important thing is that you identify everything needed to complete the work of the project. This includes labor costs, equipment costs, and so on. Don't forget the indirect costs as well. Indirect costs are costs associated with the project, like the cost of the administrative support team, but not directly related or charged to the work of the project.

While it's impossible to list every possible element of a project budget, we've given you some ideas in the budget shown in Figure 8.20. These are common items you'll find on many projects. Use this list as a starting point and add your own categories of expenses.

This is a simple budget showing the tracking or identification number first followed by the budget element. The budgeted cost column is where you should record the estimate for the item. The actual cost column is where you'll track what you really spend on the item and the difference column is the variance between the budgeted cost and actual cost. Last is a column for comments, which always comes in handy.

Notice that the last two items on this list are contingency reserves and risk response costs. Contingency reserves are monies set aside to deal with risks or unforeseen events. If you find you have to implement a risk response during the course of the project, you'll be glad you accounted for the cost of the response in the budget. If you need a refresher on these topics, we talked about them in Chapter 6. Don't forget to include these in the budget.

You can create this spreadsheet as shown or you could explore the template options available in Excel as we talked about earlier in this chapter.

FIGURE 8.20   Project budget

	B	C	D	E	F
1				Project Budget	
2					
3					
4					
5					
6	Budget Item	Total Budgeted Cost	Total Actual Cost	Difference	Comments
7	Hardware				
8	Software				
9	Training				
10	Project team salaries				
11	Lease costs				
12	Utilties				
13	Administrative team salaries				
14	Labor costs				
15	Equipment				
16	Supplies				
17	Marketing costs				
18	Advertising costs				
19	Legal expenses				
20	Travel costs				
21	Consulting services				
22	Subscription charges				
23	Office supplies				
24	Legal expenses				
25	Contingency reserves				
26	Risk response costs				
27					
28	Totals	0	0		

Estimating Budget Items

Like the project schedule, the person assigned to the work package is likely the one best suited to determining cost estimates. You can use most of the same techniques we used to estimate schedule activities to estimate budget elements and the overall project budget. For example, the bottom-up technique estimates each individual element, or each phase, and then these costs are added together to come up with the overall project budget.

Interviewing techniques work well for discovering budget items and their costs. Ask your stakeholders, subject matter experts, and other project managers who've worked on similar projects in the past to help with estimates or to review the estimates you've documented. Also ask them if you've missed any costs that weren't captured.

Another method you can use that works particularly well for budgets is to ask your vendors and suppliers for prices, or put the work or item out for bid. Don't forget to ask your procurement department as well. Often they'll have a list of standard equipment and services your organization typically contracts for and they can give you an estimate on the cost.

If you have large, expensive budget items or need a substantial amount of consulting services, it's always a good idea to get bids from several vendors. Keep in mind that sometimes vendors will bid low in hopes of breaking into your industry or winning future work from your organization. That doesn't mean the vendor can't do the work or won't perform an adequate job. But make certain you understand going into the relationship that the vendor is likely already in a position of loss (that is, they won't make any profit on this project) and if things aren't going as planned or you have changes along the way, the vendor will have little flexibility to help you out of the jam.

Take a look at Figure 8.21. We've estimated the costs for some of the higher-level deliverables for the Grant St. Move project. We also added a date column to track when expenditures occurred.

FIGURE 8.21   Grant St. Move budget

	A	B	C	D	E	F	G
1			**Grant St. Project Budget**				
2	Project Number						
3	Date						
4	Project Title						
5	Project Manager						
6	ID	Date	Budget Item	Budgeted Cost	Actual Cost	Difference	Comments
7	10.1		Move Park St.	$212,000	$214,788	-$2,788	
8	20.1		Inspect building security system	$147,500	$147,500	$0	
9	30.1		Wire data center	$100,500	$100,500	$0	
10	30.2	5-Sep	**Install air conditioner**	$112,345	$117,621	-$5,276	Plumbing connection malfunctioned
11	30.2.1	2-Sep	Install wiring for air conditioner	$46,000	$49,230	-$3,230	
12	30.2.2	3-Sep	Install plumbing	$54,000	$54,000	$0	
13		20-Aug	Air conditioning units	$125,000	$125,000	$0	
14		20-Aug	Compressor unit	$190,000	$190,000	$0	
15	30.3		Install fire supression	$98,000	$97,250	$750	
16	40.1		Install electric outlets	$172,400	$171,800	$600	
17	40.2		Install patch panels	$187,900	$187,900	$0	
18	40.3		Install cubicle furniture	$164,200	$164,200	$0	
19			TOTALS	$1,609,845	$1,619,789		

Over the course of the project, your sponsor will want to see budgeted costs versus actual costs. You could report this in spreadsheet format and graph form. We broke out some of the individual tasks for the Install Air Conditioner deliverable in Figure 8.22. We developed a column chart to show the budgeted versus actual costs for these items.

We highlighted cells C10 through E14 and then chose Insert ➢ Column ➢ 2-D Column.

We used the same set of information to track costs over time in a line graph, shown in Figure 8.23.

These are only a couple examples of the graphs available to plot budget information. As we've said before, ask your sponsor and stakeholders how they prefer to see this information reported. They might want to see the budget items rolled up to the deliverable level and graphed against time or perhaps they're interested in detailed expenses for particular deliverables but summary information for others.

FIGURE 8.22   Project budget bar graph

ID	Date	Budget Item	Budgeted Cost	Actual Cost	Difference	Comments
10.1		Move Park St.	$212,000	$214,788	-$2,788	
20.1		Inspect building security system	$147,500	$147,500	$0	
30.1		Wire data center	$100,500	$100,500	$0	
30.2	5-Sep	Install air conditioner	$112,345	$117,621	-$5,276	Plumbing connection malfunctioned
30.2.1	2-Sep	Install wiring for air conditioner	$46,000	$49,230	-$3,230	
30.2.2	3-Sep	Install plumbing	$54,000	$54,000	$0	
	20-Aug	Air conditioning units	$125,000	$125,000	$0	
	20-Aug	Compressor unit	$190,000	$190,000	$0	
30.3		Install fire supression	$98,000	$97,250	$750	
40.1		Install electric outlets	$172,400	$171,800	$600	
40.2		Install patch panels	$187,900	$187,900	$0	
40.3		Install cubicle furniture	$164,200	$164,200	$0	
		TOTALS	$1,609,845	$1,619,789		

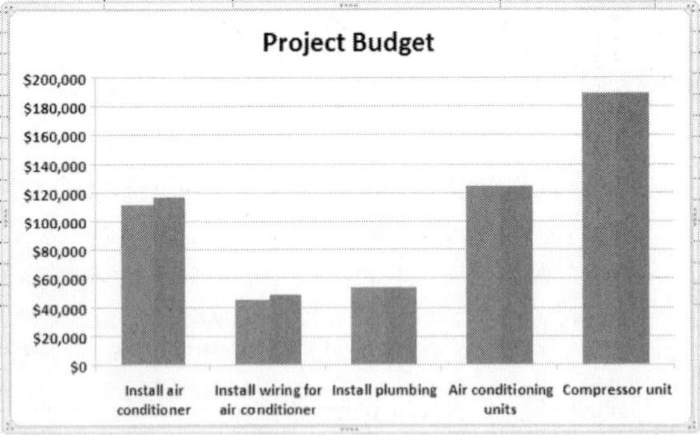

FIGURE 8.23   Project budget line graph

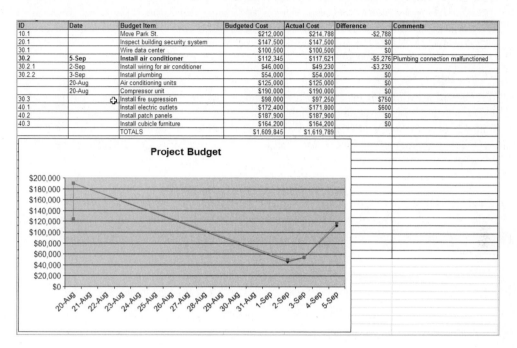

ID	Date	Budget Item	Budgeted Cost	Actual Cost	Difference	Comments
10.1		Move Park St.	$212,000	$214,788	-$2,788	
20.1		Inspect building security system	$147,500	$147,500	$0	
30.1		Wire data center	$100,500	$100,500	$0	
30.2	5-Sep	**Install air conditioner**	$112,345	$117,621	-$5,276	Plumbing connection malfunctioned
30.2.1	2-Sep	Install wiring for air conditioner	$46,000	$49,230	-$3,230	
30.2.2	3-Sep	Install plumbing	$54,000	$54,000	$0	
	20-Aug	Air conditioning units	$125,000	$125,000	$0	
	20-Aug	Compressor unit	$190,000	$190,000	$0	
30.3		Install fire supression	$98,000	$97,250	$750	
40.1		Install electric outlets	$172,400	$171,800	$600	
40.2		Install patch panels	$187,900	$187,900	$0	
40.3		Install cubicle furniture	$164,200	$164,200	$0	
		TOTALS	$1,609,845	$1,619,789		

Determining and Monitoring Performance Measures

There are several performance measurements that will help you track and monitor the performance of the project budget and the schedule. These measurements are known as the earned value technique (EVT). EVT compares what you've received to what you spent by monitoring the work planned, the value of the work completed to date, and the actual costs.

There are some definitions you need to understand before we get into the performance measure:

Earned value (EV)   Earned value is the value of the work completed to date.

Actual cost (AC)   Actual cost is the cost of completing the work or schedule activity within a given time period.

Planned value (PV)   Planned value is the cost of work that's been budgeted during a given time period.

Cost and Schedule Variance

We'll start off by looking at the two variance formulas, cost variance and schedule variance.

Cost variance (CV) tells you if the costs are higher or lower than budgeted as of the measurement date. CV is calculated as follows:

EV – AC = CV

If the result is positive, it means you're spending less than planned as of the measurement date. If it's negative, your spending is higher than planned.

Using the Install Air Conditioning task from the Grant St. Move project budget, we'll calculate CV. As of August 25, let's assume AC is 110,000 and EV is 111,500. Therefore, CV is as follows:

111,500 – 110,000 = 1,500

Our cost variance is positive, meaning we've spent less than planned as of the measurement date.

Schedule variance (SV) tells us if the schedule is ahead or behind what we planned as of the measurement date. Here is the formula for SV:

EV – PV = SV

If PV in this case is 109,000, we can plug in our numbers as follows:

111,500 – 109,000 = 2,500

Again, we have a positive result, so that means our schedule is ahead of where we planned to be on August 25.

Performance Indexes

Cost and schedule performance indexes are often used in trend analysis and to predict future performance. If the result is greater than 1, performance is better than expected, and if it's less than 1, performance is not as good as expected. If the result equals 1, performance is on target.

The cost performance index (CPI) is calculated as follows:

EV ÷ AC = CPI

111,500 ÷ 110,000 = 1.01

Our cost performance to date is on target.

The schedule performance index (SPI) is calculated as follows:

EV ÷ PV = SPI

111,500 ÷ 109,000 = 1.02

Again, schedule performance is right on track.

Variances and performance indexes are the most commonly used performance measurements. You could extend your budget worksheet to include columns to record EV, AC, and PV and add the performance measure formulas. Figure 8.24 shows our project budget with these columns added along with a column for the measurement date.

FIGURE 8.24   Project budget with performance measures

	A	B	C	D	E	F	G	H	I	J
1					Project Budget					
2	Project Number									
3	Date									
4	Project Title									
5	Project Manager									
6	ID	Budget item	Total Budgeted Cost	Total Actual Cost	Difference	Comments	Measurment Date	EV	AC	PV
7		Hardware								
8		Software								
9		Training								
10		Project team salaries								
11		Lease costs								
12		Utilities								
13		Administrative team salaries								
14		Labor costs								
15		Equipment								
16		Supplies								
17		Marketing costs								
18		Advertising costs								
19		Legal expenses								
20		Travel costs								
21		Consulting services								
22		Subscription charges								
23		Office supplies								
24		Legal expenses								
25		Contingency reserves								
26		Risk response costs								
27										
28	TOTALS:	Totals	0	0				0	0	0

Notice that at the bottom of the budget we've added a line for totals for the EV, AC, and the PV columns. Also note that we've added a new worksheet called Project Performance Measures. Figure 8.25 shows this worksheet.

Ignore the #DIV/0! errors you see in this worksheet for a moment—we'll come back to that. You probably noticed that we have the same EV, AC, and PV columns in this worksheet as the one in Figure 8.25. Cells D7, E7, and F7 hold the totals for each of these values, which are the same values as cells H28, I28, and J28 from the budget worksheet. Excel gives us a handy way to copy the information from H28 on the budget worksheet to D7 on the performance measures worksheet automatically. First, we need to go back to the budget worksheet and name these cells.

FIGURE 8.25   Project Performance Measures worksheet

	A	B	C	D	E	F
1			Project Performance Measures			
2	Project Number					
3	Date					
4	Project Title					
5	Project Manager					
6	Peformance Measure	Measurement Date	Performance Measure Result	Earned Value	Actual Cost	Planned Value
7	Cost Variance			0	0	0
8	Schedule Variance			0		
9	Cost Performance Index		#DIV/0!			
10	Schedule Performance Index		#DIV/0!			

Cell H28 on the budget worksheet is named EarnedValue. Name this cell by clicking on the name box (next to the formula bar) and typing in the name (see Figure 8.26). When your cursor is in a named cell or a named range, you'll always see the name of the range displayed in the name box.

If your cursor is in some other location on the worksheet and you want to go to a named cell, you can type the name of that cell in the name box and press Enter, and your cursor will go to the cell.

From the Home tab, you can also choose Find & Select, then Go To, and choose the cell name from the pop-up box, as shown in Figure 8.27. You can also press Ctrl+G to bring up the Go To box.

You can use this same feature to bring up any cell, even if it hasn't been named. For example, you could choose Go To and type in D10 in the Reference box.

You can also name a cell or range (and see a list of all the names) by clicking the Formulas menu tab. Then navigate to the Named Cells group and choose Name Manager. The Name Manager dialog box is shown in Figure 8.28.

You have the option to add a new name, edit the name, or delete the name. Click New Name Button and you'll see a dialog box like the one in Figure 8.29.

FIGURE 8.26 The name box

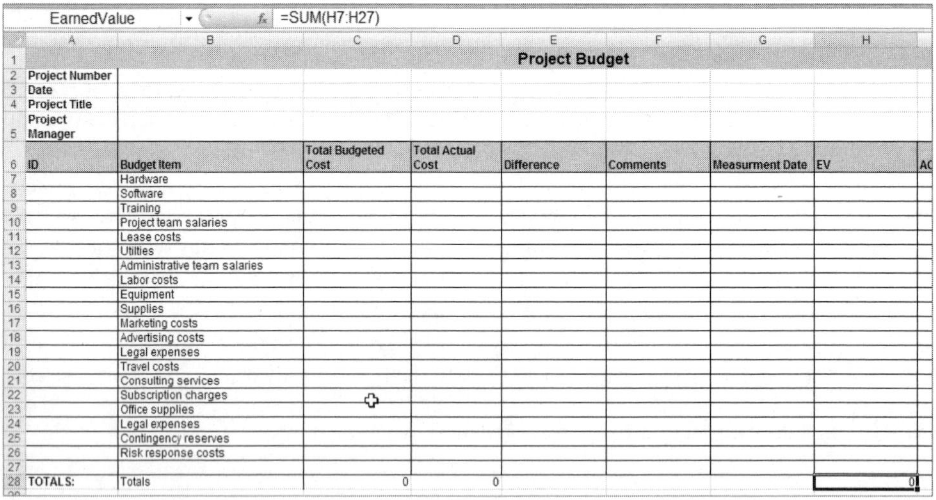

EarnedValue	▼	fx =SUM(H7:H27)						

	A	B	C	D	E	F	G	H	
1					Project Budget				
2	Project Number								
3	Date								
4	Project Title								
5	Project Manager								
6	ID	Budget Item	Total Budgeted Cost	Total Actual Cost	Difference	Comments	Measurment Date	EV	AC
7		Hardware							
8		Software							
9		Training							
10		Project team salaries							
11		Lease costs							
12		Utilities							
13		Administrative team salaries							
14		Labor costs							
15		Equipment							
16		Supplies							
17		Marketing costs							
18		Advertising costs							
19		Legal expenses							
20		Travel costs							
21		Consulting services							
22		Subscription charges							
23		Office supplies							
24		Legal expenses							
25		Contingency reserves							
26		Risk response costs							
27									
28	TOTALS:	Totals	0	0					0

FIGURE 8.27   The Go To dialog box

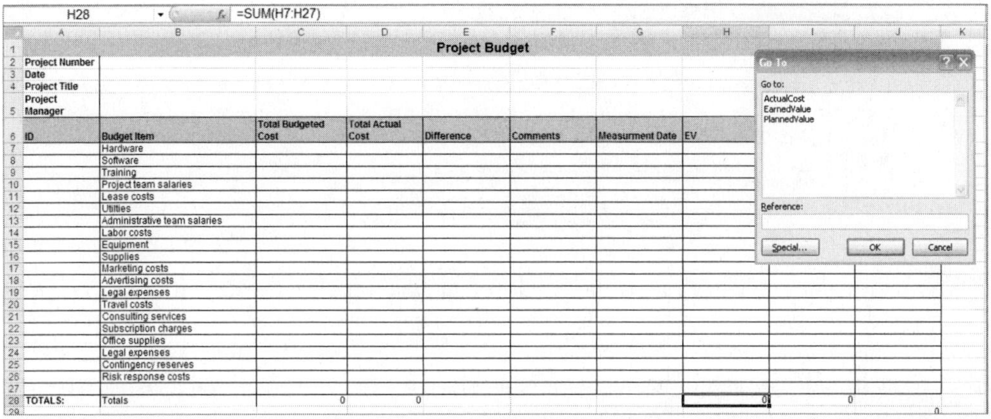

FIGURE 8.28   The Name Manager dialog box

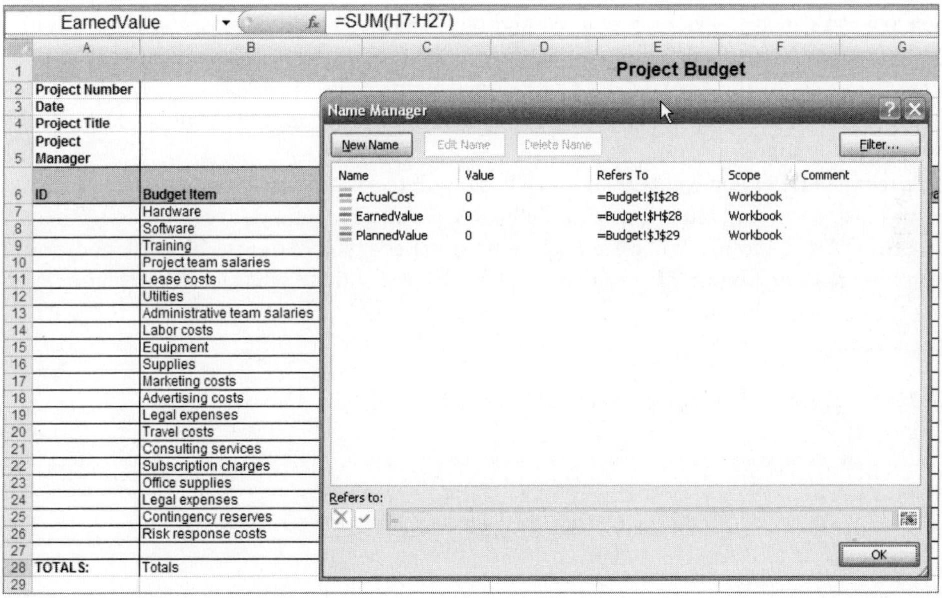

FIGURE 8.29   The New Name dialog box

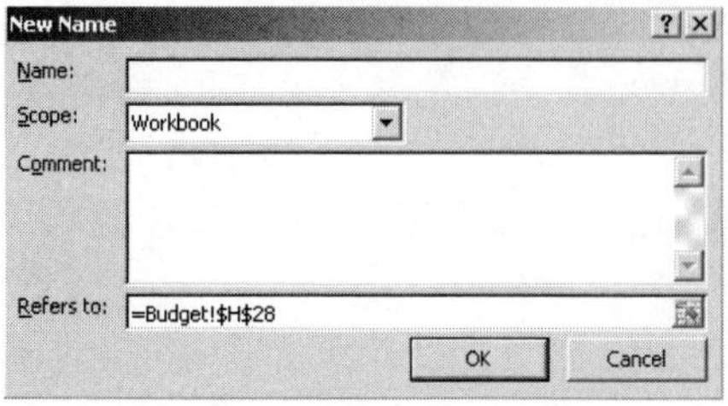

Type in the name you'd like to give the cell. If you highlight the cell before you choose Name Manager and New Name, the reference for that cell shows up in the Refers To box. Figure 8.29 shows the Budget worksheet cell H28 because that's where the cursor is sitting. You can change the reference by typing over it or highlight the contents of the Refers To box and then place your cursor where you want the reference to be.

You can delete a named cell or range by navigating to the Formulas tab and opening the Name Manager in the Named Cells group. Highlight the name you want to delete and click the Delete button.

Now that we have our cells named, switch to the performance measures worksheet. Cell D7 is the Earned Value cell. Click on this cell and type **=EarnedValue** as shown in Figure 8.30.

Now the total earned value from the budget worksheet will automatically appear in this cell. Do the same for the Actual Cost and Planned Value cells.

In the Performance Measure Result column, type in the appropriate formulas. Figure 8.31 shows the cost variance formula.

You see the #DIV/0! in cells C9 and C10 because Excel is telling you that you can't divide by zero. These formulas, like the cost and schedule variance formulas, are referencing the values in cells D7, E7, and F7, which are zero right now. Let's plug in our Install Air Conditioner measurements as of August 25 on the budget worksheet and see what happens. Figure 8.32 shows the entry on the budget worksheet and Figure 8.33 shows the results for the performance measures.

FIGURE 8.30   Naming the Earned Value cell

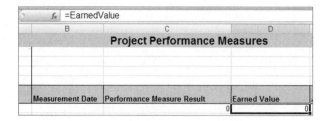

As we stated previously, the two hottest topics of interest to most project sponsors are the budget and the schedule. They'll want regular status reports regarding both, and the performance measures are a quick way to provide an at-a-glance temperature of overall project health.

We've created a sound project plan and now have the schedule and budget complete. It's important to monitor these plans and keep a close eye on changes to the schedule or budget in particular. We'll talk about change control in the next chapter.

FIGURE 8.31   Cost variance formula

C7		f_x	=$D$7-$E$7		
	A	B	C	D	E	F
1			**Project Performance Measures**			
2	Project Number					
3	Date					
4	Project Title					
5	Project Manager					
6	Peformance Measure	Measurement Date	Performance Measure Result	Earned Value	Actual Cost	Planned Value
7	Cost Variance		0	0	0	0

FIGURE 8.32   Install Air Conditioner on the budget worksheet

	A	B	C	D	E	F	G	H	I	J
1					**Project Budget**					
2	Project Number									
3	Date									
4	Project Title									
5	Project Manager									
6	ID	Budget Item	Total Budgeted Cost	Total Actual Cost	Difference	Comments	Measurment Date	EV	AC	PV
7		Hardware								
8		Software								
9		Training								
10		Project team salaries								
11		Lease costs								
12		Utilties								
13		Administrative team salaries								
14		Labor costs								
15		Equipment								
16		Supplies								
17		Marketing costs								
18		Advertising costs								
19		Legal expenses								
20		Travel costs								
21		Consulting services								
22		Subscription charges								
23		Office supplies								
24		Legal expenses								
25		Contingency reserves								
26		Risk response costs								
27	30.1	Install Air Conditioning	112,345				25-Aug	111,500	110,000	109,000
28	TOTALS:	Totals	112,345	0				111,500	110,000	109,000

FIGURE 8.33   Install Air Conditioner performance measures

	A	B	C	D	E	F
1			**Project Performance Measures**			
2	Project Number					
3	Date					
4	Project Title					
5	Project Manager					
6	Peformance Measure	Measurement Date	Performance Measure Result	Earned Value	Actual Cost	Planned Value
7	Cost Variance		5.000	115,000.00	110,000.00	109,000.00
8	Schedule Variance		2.500			
9	Cost Performance Index		1.01			
10	Schedule Performance Index		1.02			

Chapter 9

Establishing Change Control Processes

There is one thing we can guarantee will occur on almost every project you undertake—change. We'll talk about change in this chapter, why it happens, how to manage it, and how to assess its impacts. We'll also talk about how to create a change control process, including documenting the changes and tracking them for future reference.

Most effective change control processes include a change control board that reviews and approves (or denies) changes. We'll talk about establishing the change control board in this chapter as well.

When Change Occurs

Change typically gets into full swing during the Executing and the Monitoring and Controlling processes. Executing is where the work of the project occurs. Monitoring and Controlling processes are where the results of the work are measured or verified against the project plan to ensure that the correct results are being produced. Performance measures are taken and reported and actions or corrections needed to get the work of the project back on track occur now. This doesn't mean change can't occur in the Planning processes. Depending on the size and complexity of your project, you might want to institute your change control processes in the Planning processes. Figure 9.1 illustrates the Executing and Monitoring and Controlling process groups and some of the deliverables produced during these processes.

There aren't a lot of project management deliverables, as there are in the Planning group, but the work of the project is being completed, so every task, deliverable, and milestone is being worked.

FIGURE 9.1 Executing and Monitoring and Controlling process groups

Reasons for Change

Changes come about for many reasons. The following list gives you an idea of some of the sources of change. Knowing where and why changes come about will help you formulate the process for managing changes.

Stakeholders   Stakeholders are one of the biggest sources of change requests. As the work of the project proceeds, they decide they want something to look differently or behave in a different manner than originally intended.

Customer requests   Customers request changes as well. A few years after moving into our house, we decided to paint. Halfway through the job, our neighbors came running and screaming from their houses declaring we had not gotten approval from the homeowners association on the paint color or the decision to paint. We had to put in a change request with the painters to change the paint color (after a quick meeting was held on our front lawn) and have the portion of the house that was already painted completely repainted. That change cost us a pretty penny. Needless to say, we've decided to never paint again.

Project team members   Project team members are another source of change requests. As they progress on the work of the project, they may discover more efficient ways of completing the work or come up with better alternatives for the project that weren't thought of during the Planning processes.

Measurements, inspection, and acceptance   As we mentioned earlier, measurements, including the performance measurements we talked about in the Chapter 8, may bring about change requests. As deliverables are completed, they're reviewed and inspected by the customer (or stakeholder) and either accepted or rejected. If they're rejected, more than likely you'll have a change request on your hands.

Organizational changes and budget cuts   Organizational changes often bring about changes to the project, typically in the form of scope changes and/or schedule changes. Organizational changes may mean new management or a reshuffle of the existing management team or a combination of both. As the musical chairs commence, stakeholders may find themselves focused on different goals or they may discover that the new people in power don't have the same vision for the project as they do. And sometimes, organizational change results in the project being canceled.

Budget cuts usually affect both scope and schedule. You may have to break the project into phases, reduce the number of features originally requested, and/or modify the schedule to meet the revised budget.

Undocumented changes   Undocumented changes are a risk to the project and they may occur without the project manager's knowledge. Relationships between the team members and stakeholders may bring about these types of changes. Team members and vendors may also have past working relationships or personal relationships that may be used to bring about changes. And in the interest of good customer service, team members may "do a favor" for someone that requests a change without telling anyone else. It's important that all team members understand the change control process and follow it.

Also watch out for changes that may occur after implementing a risk response plan or a contingency plan. Risk responses may affect future work on the project and require changes due to the risk event or its consequences.

No matter when or where changes occur, you'll want an established process to manage them. We've seen project after project fail (or at best, delivered late) because of change requests. Project managers, wanting to please the customer, gladly take on any and all change requests and promise to incorporate them into the final result. In the end, the customer is exceedingly unhappy because the final result doesn't look much like the original scope of the project and chances are high the project was delivered behind schedule.

Dealing with Change

Nothing is more certain on a project than change. It's not a question of if, but when. Many people don't like change and will fight to keep the status quo. They may fight it because they believe the change will cause harm or because they're protecting their own interests. Or maybe they believe the final product won't work or they like their own ideas better. This is where those communication skills come in handy. Every status meeting should include time to discuss changes and why they're being implemented. Change can demotivate a team quickly if they don't believe in the purpose for the change or aren't fully aware of why the change is needed. If change after change comes their way with little communication, the project team will wonder if all their efforts are in vain.

Early on in the project, make certain everyone, including stakeholders, team members, customers, and anyone else involved with the project, understands that there is a change control process that must be followed. If you allow changes to occur unchecked and don't examine the impacts they may have, you could end up with an out-of-control project that won't meet its original goals.

Creating a Change Control Process

The change control process is a formal, documented procedure for submitting changes and managing them through the final disposition. It should document and describe the following:

- How to submit change requests
- How to process change requests
- How change requests and their status will be tracked and reported
- How to record approval levels
- How to make emergency changes
- How to escalate change request decisions

NOTE   Even if your project is small and informal, don't skip putting a change control process in place. Uncontrolled changes will quickly lead to an uncontrolled project.

The process for submitting change requests usually starts with a written submission. The project management site on MOSS is a great way to submit change requests. Stakeholders can access a copy of the form, fill it out, and have MOSS perform an email notification to the project manager that action is required. If there's only one rule you implement regarding change control, it should be that all change requests must be in writing. That way, they're easier to track and requestors won't "forget" what the details of the request are.

Level of Authority

The project manager is usually the first person to review the request on small to medium projects. Depending on the level of authority of the project manager, they will approve or disapprove the request or place it on the agenda for the next change control board meeting. We'll talk about change control boards in "Establishing a Change Control Board" later in this chapter.

We recommend that the level of authority of the project manager be documented with the change control process documents. The level of authority may be determined in a variety of ways. Here are some examples of the kinds of changes the project manager might be responsible for approving:

- Changes that impact the schedule by plus or minus 10 percent
- Changes that impact budget by plus or minus 5 percent
- Changes that impact scope by less than 5 percent

Changes that are outside of the established limits should go to the change control board. The key is to establish the level of authority for the project manager, document the levels, and communicate them. It's also not a bad idea to post these levels on the project management portal site for everyone to see. We've seen project schedules derailed because the stakeholders or project team members didn't realize the project manager had authority to disposition change requests. The team members didn't make the changes, or delayed their implementation, and the schedule was impacted as a result.

Emergency Requests

The change control process should include procedures for implementing emergency change requests. Occasionally, changes cannot wait until a formal meeting is held with the change control board. Document the processes and procedures for implementing an emergency change so that all project team members are aware of them. The emergency process should include the following:

- Notification that the change was implemented

- Description of the change
- Reason for emergency implementation

Escalation Process

Last but not least, the change control process should address how to escalate change dispositions. Hopefully it won't happen often, but there may be times when you can't reach consensus on a change decision. Or the change control board may decide on a change that the project team believes would have significant impact to the end result of the project. In these cases, the project sponsor, or another executive manager within the organization, should serve as a tiebreaker.

Creating Change Control Forms

Now that you have an idea of what the change control process looks like, let's create the forms and reporting tools you'll need to manage the process. We'll start with the change request form.

Change Request Form

First, we'll create the change request form. This is where the process begins. As we stated earlier, change requests should always be in writing, and having a form available will reinforce this rule. Figure 9.2 shows an example change request form template.

Note that in the header portion of the form we added a line for a tracking number. As with many of the other items we've numbered for easy tracking purposes, we'll want to assign numbers to the change requests. As the log of requests grows, the ID numbers help make it easier to track and report on the individual requests.

The person making the request should record the date, their name and contact information, and a description of the change. They should also document the justification for making the change. This information will be used by the change control board (CCB) to help determine whether to approve the request. The justification should emphasize the benefits to the product of the project or the organization for making the change.

The impact if the change is not made should be documented as well. This might include issues like lost opportunity, difficulty in making future enhancements, and customer satisfaction. Any alternative solutions the requestor may know of should be recorded in the last row of the requestor section.

The next section is filled out by the project manager. Here you'll document the impacts of the change if it's made, focusing on the triple constraints in particular (cost, schedule, scope).

You should also make a recommendation to the CCB about whether you believe this change should be implemented.

The last section will likely be filled out by the project manager and should record the date of the CCB meeting or review, the final disposition, and the members present at the meeting or the person who made the final decision.

FIGURE 9.2   Change request form

1	**Change Request Form**				
2	Project Number				
3	Date				
4	Project Title				
5	Project Manager				
6	Tracking Number				
7	Date				
8	Requestor				
9	Phone				
10	email				
11	Dept				
12	email				
13	Description of change				
14	Justification for the change				
15	Impact if change is not made				
16	Alternative solutions				
17	Project Manager Completes This Section				
18	Impact assessment of change				
19	Recommendation to CCB				
20	CCB Completes This Section				
21	Date of Review				
22	Disposition	Approve	Deny	Cancel	Postpone Date for re-review:
23	CCB Members				

Change Request Log

Once change requests start coming in, you'll want a way to track them and report on them. The simplest way to do that is with an Excel table. We talked about tables in Chapter 4 and in Chapter 6. We'll provide a brief recap here, but if you need a refresher, refer to these previous chapters.

Figure 9.3 shows our change control log.

To create this table, highlight A6 through H12. Click Format as Table from the Styles group and choose the table format you'd like. Once you click on the table style, a dialog box will appear like the one in Figure 9.4 that shows the range of cells included in the table. Don't forget to check the My Table Has Headers check box (because in this example, we included our header row, row 6, in the selection) or Excel will add a row of headers for you.

As you can see, in the change control log we're tracking many of the fields that you'll find on the change request form. In table format, we're able to sort on any of the data captured here. For example, sort by disposition to quickly find the number of change requests approved, denied, canceled, or postponed.

FIGURE 9.3 Change control log

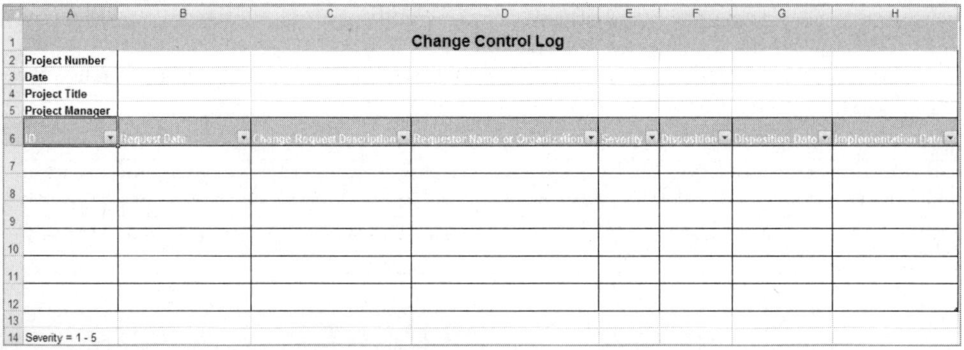

FIGURE 9.4 The Format as Table dialog box

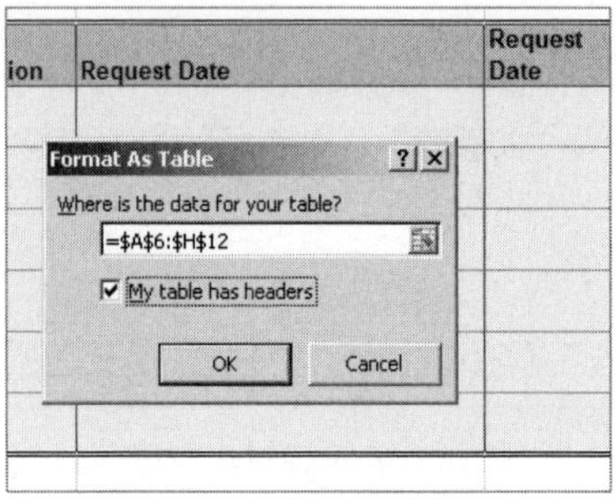

We've added a new piece of information in column E called severity. Severity is a numeric value that reflects the impact of not implementing the change request. Not all change requests may require a severity score. Scoring is helpful for projects in which a product or result is being produced—for example, a new software program—and impact is more easily determined. Severity could be expressed on a scale of 1 to 5. Example designations may look something like this:

1 = critical impact, project failure will or has occurred, work cannot progress

2 = severe impact, project failure may occur, work cannot progress

3 = medium impact, project failure may occur, work can continue

4 = low impact, project failure not likely, work can continue

5 = little to no impact, change would enhance features

Severity should be assigned by the project manager. The definitions and descriptions of scores should be determined and documented early on in the project if they aren't already defined by the project management office. Enlist your CCB members and/or team members in determining how impact should be described.

Converting Tables to Ranges

Perhaps you have a need to delete all the data in a table while keeping the table intact. Look at Figure 9.5, which shows a sample change control log for the Grant St. Move project.

The director of the Park St. office must be dreaming to think he could actually change the date of his office move, but nonetheless, he tried. But we digress.

Let's say someone has accidentally overwritten our change control log template and saved it with their project data in the table—this is one reason we may have for removing the data. Highlight the cells that contain the data you want to delete, in this case cells A7 through H8. Right-click to bring up the menu shown in Figure 9.6. Choose Clear Contents and all of the data in the table will be deleted. If you clear the contents accidentally, you can immediately press Ctrl+Z (the shortcut for Undo) to bring the data back.

Perhaps you no longer need your data in table format and want to convert the data back to normal cells. This time, highlight all the cells in the table, including the header. For our example, we would highlight cells A6 through H12. Again, right-click to bring up the submenu shown in Figure 9.7. Choose Table and then Convert to Range.

Figure 9.8 shows the result.

FIGURE 9.5 Grant St. Move change control log

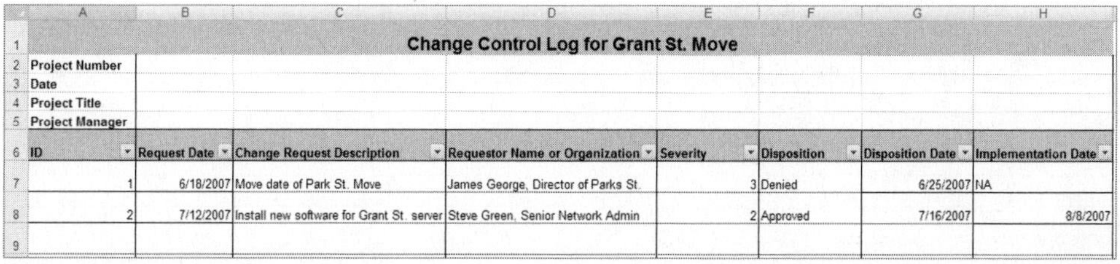

FIGURE 9.6 The Clear Contents menu option

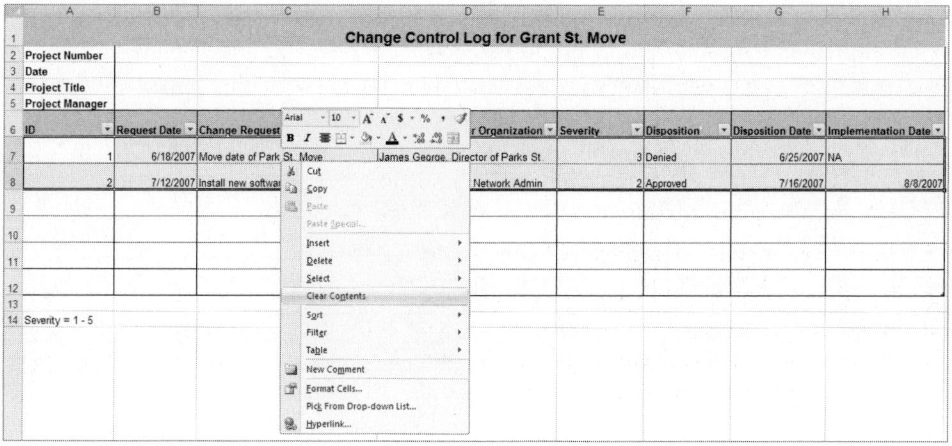

FIGURE 9.7 The Convert to Range option

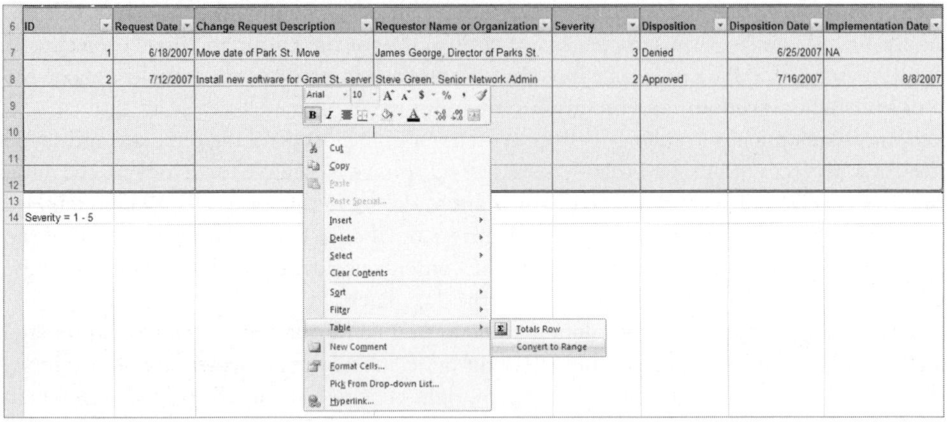

	ID	Request Date	Change Request Description	Requestor Name or Organization	Severity	Disposition	Disposition Date	Implementation Date
6								
7	1	6/18/2007	Move date of Park St. Move	James George, Director of Parks St.	3	Denied	6/25/2007	NA
8	2	7/12/2007	Install new software for Grant St. server	Steve Green, Senior Network Admin	2	Approved	7/16/2007	8/8/2007
9								
10								
11								
12								
13								
14	Severity = 1 - 5							

FIGURE 9.8 Removing table formatting

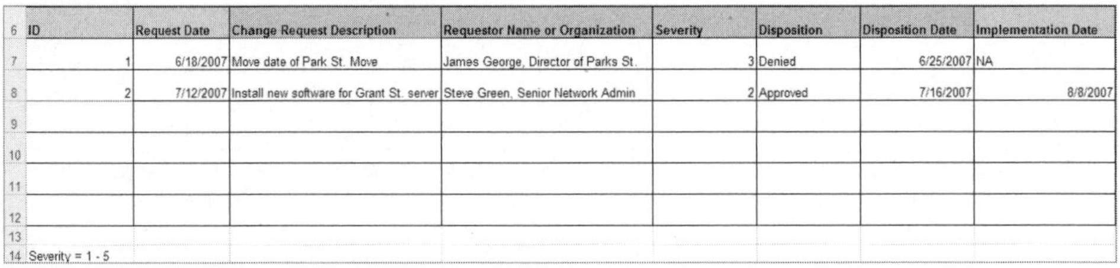

	ID	Request Date	Change Request Description	Requestor Name or Organization	Severity	Disposition	Disposition Date	Implementation Date
6								
7	1	6/18/2007	Move date of Park St. Move	James George, Director of Parks St.	3	Denied	6/25/2007	NA
8	2	7/12/2007	Install new software for Grant St. server	Steve Green, Senior Network Admin	2	Approved	7/16/2007	8/8/2007
9								
10								
11								
12								
13								
14	Severity = 1 - 5							

Reporting and Printing Change Control Data

Change requests and their disposition should be reported at each status meeting. You could print the entire log, but as more time progresses on the project, you'll have more change requests and the report could become several pages long. It's easier to filter the data and report on only the data that's been added over the last two reporting periods.

We've added two more entries on the change control log for Grant St., as shown in Figure 9.9.

FIGURE 9.9 New entries on the change control log

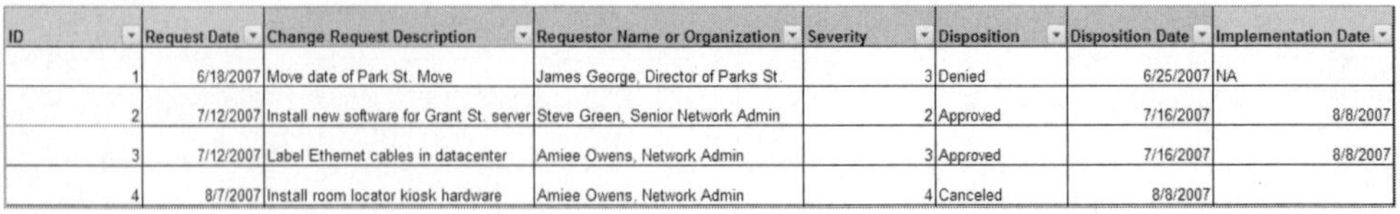

ID	Request Date	Change Request Description	Requestor Name or Organization	Severity	Disposition	Disposition Date	Implementation Date
1	6/18/2007	Move date of Park St. Move	James George, Director of Parks St.	3	Denied	6/25/2007	NA
2	7/12/2007	Install new software for Grant St. server	Steve Green, Senior Network Admin	2	Approved	7/16/2007	8/8/2007
3	7/12/2007	Label Ethernet cables in datacenter	Amiee Owens, Network Admin	3	Approved	7/16/2007	8/8/2007
4	8/7/2007	Install room locator kiosk hardware	Amiee Owens, Network Admin	4	Canceled	8/8/2007	

We now have three types of disposition: approved, denied, and canceled. For this example, we're going to report on all approved change requests. In the header column, click on the arrow next to the word *Disposition*. A drop-down menu appears (Figure 9.10).

Notice we've unchecked the Canceled, Denied, and Blanks selections so that our report will show only the approved change requests. If we wanted to further filter the data, we could click on Request Date (or another date field) and report on all approved change requests within a certain time period.

FIGURE 9.10   Sort by Selection

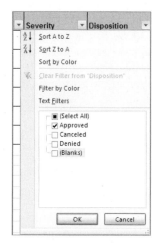

Print Settings

Next we'll print the report. The first thing we'll do is set the print area. Highlight cells A1 through H9. Then choose the Page Layout tab, and in the Page Setup group, choose Print Area. Then click the Set Print Area selection as shown in Figure 9.11.

FIGURE 9.11   The Set Print Area option

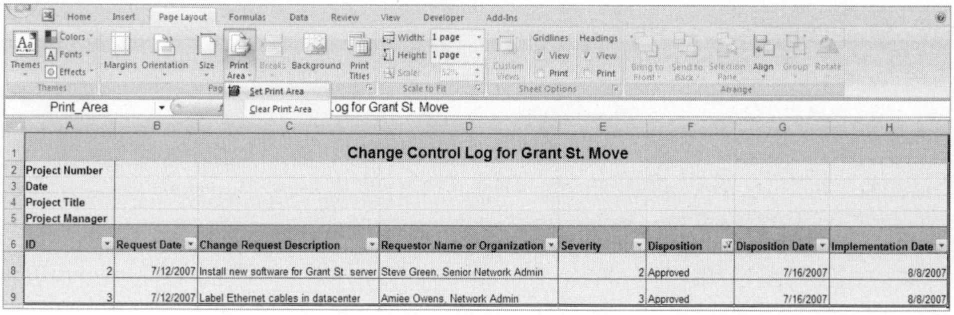

If you're like us, you want to make certain that what you think you're telling Excel to print is what's going to print. Click the Windows Office button, and from the menu choose Print and then Print preview, as we've done in Figure 9.12.

From Print Preview, as in previous versions of Excel, we have the option to make some adjustments to our page, margins, and so on. In Figure 9.13, we're in the Print Preview pane and have chosen the Page Setup selection from the Print group.

There haven't been any changes to the Page Setup dialog box from the previous version of Excel. The Page, Margins, Header/Footer, and Sheet tabs all work the same. Next we'll show you how to get to each of these tabs from the Excel ribbon.

Close out the Print Preview window and navigate to the Page Layout tab on the ribbon. You'll see several selections in the Page Setup group, including Margins, Orientation, Size, Print Area, Breaks, Background, and Print Titles. Figure 9.14 shows the Page Setup group.

We've chosen the Margins selection in Figure 9.15. You have three choices that you can choose from: Normal, Wide, and Narrow. Simply click on the selection you'd like. If none of these suits your needs, choose the Custom Margins option at the bottom of the drop-down box.

FIGURE 9.12   The Print Preview option

Orientation is the next choice in the Page Setup group. Portrait and Landscape are the choices here. Figure 9.16 shows your choices.

Size is the next option. As in previous versions of Excel, you have the standard choices Letter, Legal, Envelope, and so on. If none of these work, you can choose More at the bottom of the drop-down box and set your paper size. Figure 9.17 shows the options available in the Size selection.

FIGURE 9.13 Page Setup alterations

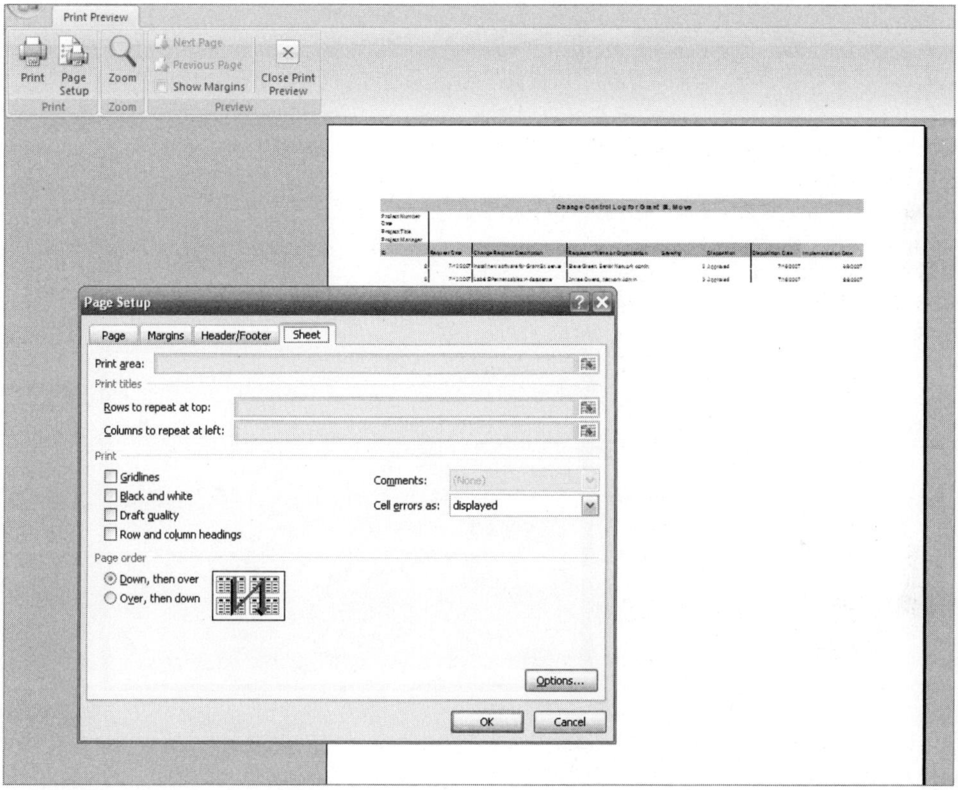

FIGURE 9.14 The Page Setup group on the Page Layout tab

FIGURE 9.15 Margins

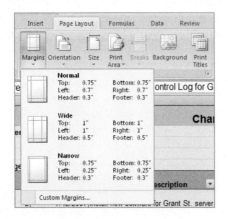

FIGURE 9.16 Orientation

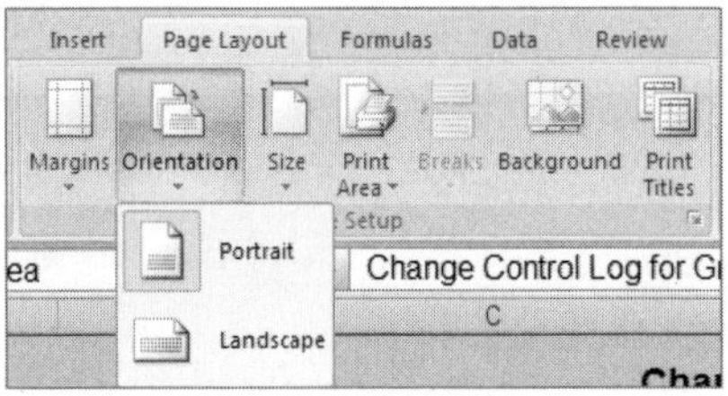

FIGURE 9.17 Size

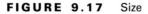

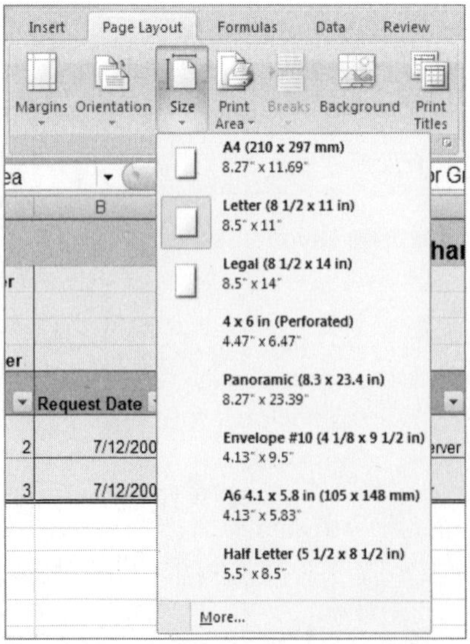

The next selection in the Page Setup group is Print Area. We covered that earlier. Breaks, the next option, gives you the ability to add page breaks at specific points in your worksheet. Place your cursor on the row where you want the page break and select this option.

Background is a new function in Excel and we love it. This selection allows you to add a customized background to your worksheet. In the beta version of Excel 2007, the background won't print with the worksheet. But if you're projecting reports on a screen to a group of stakeholders, it's a great way to squeeze in all those wonderful vacation photos that no one would take the time to look at otherwise. When you click Background, the My Pictures folder from your desktop opens and you can add any picture you have stored in this directory (or others) to the worksheet. In the worksheet shown in Figure 9.18, we added a photo from a recent Mexico vacation to the change control log worksheet. And the next three hundred figures in this book have the remaining photos of our vacation (just kidding).

FIGURE 9.18 Background

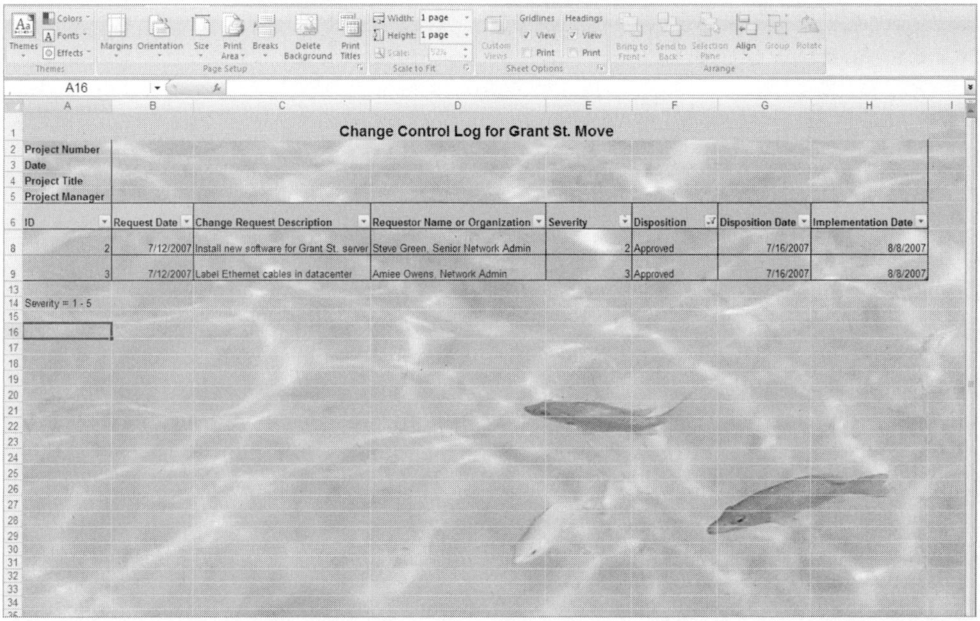

Database Lookups

Now let's imagine that our change control log is pages and pages long with too many entries to sort and count easily. How do you know how many active change requests there are, for example, without physically counting each row? Excel can help us with this task with the DCOUNTA function.

First we'll refresh your memory on Excel databases. A database in Excel consists of data laid out in tabular format. Each column represents a field of data and each row is a single database record. For example, Figure 9.19 shows a version of the change control log for the Grant St. Move project.

FIGURE 9.19   Database lookup criteria

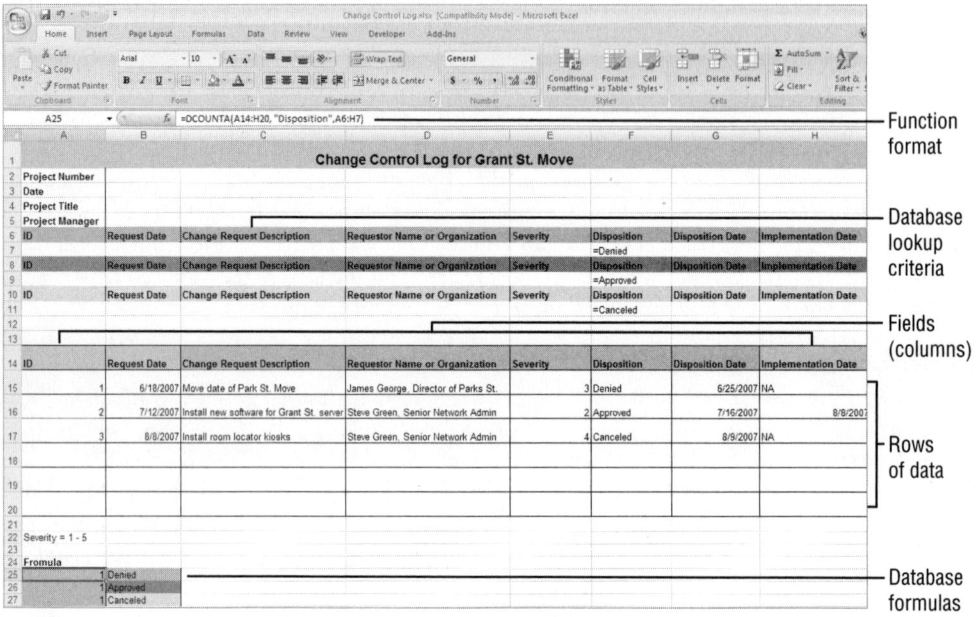

The header row in this figure is in cells A14 through I14. This row denotes the field names (or columns) for each of the data elements. Rows 15, 16, and 17 contain database records. Each row is one record. Remember, there cannot be any spaces between the rows.

We will use Excel's DCOUNTA function for our database lookup purposes. Begin by navigating to the Formulas tab. Once there, you'll see that database functions are not located within the Formulas tab, inside the Function Library group on the ribbon. Instead we have to click the Function Wizard button (see Figure 9.20 in the section "Excel Functions" later in this chapter) and then select Database from the Or Select a Category drop-down. When Database is selected, DCOUNTA will appear in the list.

In order to use the DCOUNTA function, we need to set up two rows that will act as our database lookup criteria. For example, let's say we want to count all the records in the Disposition field that have a status of Active. To do this we need two things:

1.   A set of two rows. The first row contains an exact duplicate of the header row information. The row below it holds the database lookup criteria information.

2.   The DCOUNTA formula.

Looking at Figure 9.19, you can see that we've actually created three separate database lookup criteria ranges: A6:H7, A8:H9, and A10:H11. Each of these consists of the two requisite rows that act as our database lookup criteria (as described in number 1 and 2 above). We created three separate database criteria pairs because we want to simultaneously look for three pieces of information.

Note that we also have three formula rows: A25:B25, A26:B26, and A27:B27. The DCOUNTA function (cell A25) is shown in the formula bar in Figure 9.19. Here's how the whole thing works. Criteria rows (rows 6 through 11 in the figure) tell Excel what you want to look for.

In this example, we're looking for text information. In the first criteria rows, A6:H7, we're looking for the word *Denied*. Cell F7 in Figure 9.19 looks like it says =Denied. This isn't how it's typed into the cell, however. Since we're looking for text, we need to use two equal signs like this:

    ="=Denied"

We need to type two equal signs with quotes around the second equal sign and the text. If we typed "=Denied" with one equal sign, we'd be telling Excel to place the contents of a range named denied in this cell. Case does not matter as long as the text matches the text you want to search on.

If you were looking for numbers, you'd key in only one equal sign and the number you're searching for (= 16)—no quotes or double equal signs required.

Next we'll write the DCOUNTA formula. The formula in cell A25, =DCOUNTA(A14:H20, "Disposition", A6:H7), says this: "Go into the database made up of cells A14 through H20 and look in the Disposition field for the required information. Use rows A6 through H7 for the criteria in your search. I want you to count how many of the rows you find that match the criteria and show that number."

In cell A25, Excel returns the number 1 because it found precisely one record that matched the search criteria for the word *Denied* in the Disposition column. We typed "=Denied" in cell B25, "=Approved" in cell B26 and "=Canceled" in cell B27 so that you would know which formula was which.

Note that if the disposition for the change request in row 15 was changed to approved, the count for the number of Denied records would drop to zero while the number of Approved records would increment to two.

DCOUNTA Notes

There are some notes you should consider when working with DCOUNTA and other database functions:

First, it isn't necessary for you to use the entire row of headers for the criteria. We did this for clarity, but in the example, you could just as easily use cells F6:F7 as the criteria.

Second, it isn't necessary for the criteria, database, and DCOUNTA formula to be on the same worksheet. For example, the formula itself could be on one worksheet and the references for the formula in another.

Third, you could consider linking the spreadsheet to a list in SharePoint. That way, you can create filters, groups, and custom views to accomplish the same objective without writing any formulas.

Excel Functions

To obtain help and more information on Excel's numerous functions, click the Formulas tab on the Ribbon and then any of the buttons found in the Function Library group, as shown in Figure 9.20.

Alternatively, you could click Function Wizard, which is the first button in the Function Library group. The Function Wizard is particularly helpful because you can key in what you are looking for and let Excel suggest the appropriate functions. The Function Wizard selection is shown in the top left of Figure 9.20. (The Function Wizard is the same one used in previous versions of Excel.) The Function Wizard is also listed as the last selection within all of the selections on the Formulas tab (Figure 9.20 shows Function Wizard as the last option in the Text group as an example). Figure 9.21 shows the Function Wizard dialog box.

There are numerous database functions that will work with the criteria rows set up in the worksheet. For more information simply go to Excel help and perform a search on DCOUNTA. A sample spreadsheet and a variety of database functions will be displayed and explained.

Now that you know how to report on changes and their disposition status, we'll look at how to assess their impacts.

FIGURE 9.20 Functions

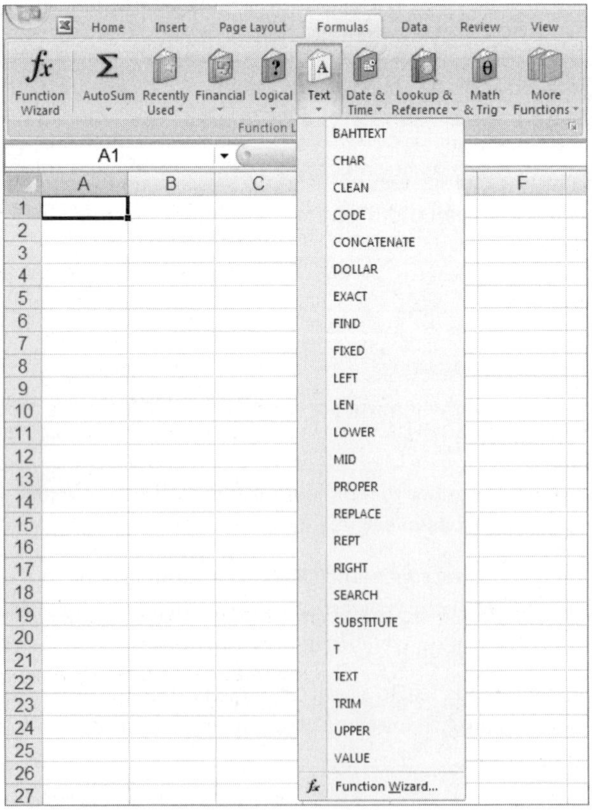

FIGURE 9.21   Function Wizard

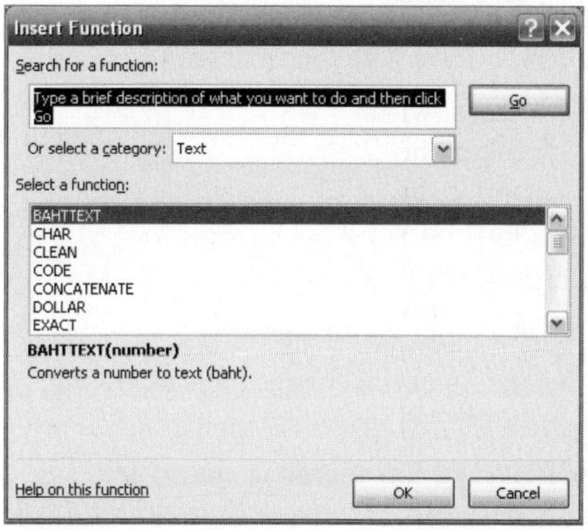

Insert Function

Search for a function:

Type a brief description of what you want to do and then click Go   [Go]

Or select a category: Text

Select a function:

> BAHTTEXT
> CHAR
> CLEAN
> CODE
> CONCATENATE
> DOLLAR
> EXACT

BAHTTEXT(number)
Converts a number to text (baht).

Help on this function   [OK]   [Cancel]

Assessing the Impacts of Change

We've all seen our share of projects in which no formal change process existed. Without a way to control change and, further, without a way to assess the impacts of change, the project probably won't succeed. Even if it reaches a successful conclusion, it will likely be over budget and late and the original scope may have long been forgotten.

The project manager, that's you, is usually the one who'll present the change requests to the change control board. We'll talk more about that in the next section. Before you get to that meeting, you'll need to perform an assessment of the changes and how they'll impact the project. The CCB members and your stakeholders will want to know how, why, when, and how much.

Many of the change requests you'll receive, if not all, will impact one or more of the triple constraints: scope, time, and budget. For example, the Grant St. Move project had a change request to change the date of the Parks St. office move. This not only impacts schedule, it could also impact budget. Resource change requests may impact the budget and probably the schedule as well. Design changes after the work of the project has started will definitely require schedule changes and may also impact the budget. It's your job to explain what these impacts are and how they affect the project.

Changes to scope always require changes to the project schedule and may require changes to the budget and/or quality. Changes to the project schedule usually require changes to the budget and may require changes to the scope and/or quality. Changes to the budget usually require changes to the schedule, scope, and/or quality.

The first step in the assessment process is to gather and review the project documents. Some of the impacts will be obvious when compared to the project plan. Others may require further analysis.

Assemble some of your key team members to assist with the analysis. Use some of the brainstorming and sticky-backed note techniques we've discussed in previous chapters to determine potential impacts of the changes. Ask a few questions to get the team thinking in the right direction. Here are some examples:

- Why is the change needed?
- Does the change impact schedule, scope, or budget?
- Are there nontangible benefits for implementing the change?
- If the change is implemented, will the results of the change have its own impacts on schedule, scope, or budget?
- If the change is implemented, will new risks be introduced to the project?
- Will the customer agree to the change?
- Are there alternatives to the change that will reduce the impact to the schedule, scope, or budget?
- Can the change be postponed to another phase without impacting the end goal of the project?
- If the change isn't made, what will the impact be to the project?

Remember that scope changes always require schedule changes. Once changes are approved, you'll need to adjust the schedule to accommodate the change. The following list includes some of the tactics you can use to help with schedule changes:

- Ask for more resources.
- Consider overtime options for existing resources.
- Hire vendors to assist with the project.
- Reduce the project scope or move the deliverable to another phase of the project.

The project budget may need adjustments as well. For example, if you hire vendors or additional resources as suggested earlier, the project budget will have to be increased. That may not be possible. Additionally, changes made as a result of other changes may require further approvals.

Don't forget to examine potential risks to the project as a result of implementing a change. The risk list might need to be updated and new response plans or updated contingency plans may need to be developed for these new risks.

As we stated, additional changes may come about as a result of an approved change. For example, an approved schedule change may require a budget change.

Next we'll look at the functions of a change control board and the project manager's role on this board.

Establishing a Change Control Board

The change control board (CCB) is made up of stakeholders, managers, customers, or others who have an interest in the project or who are serving in an oversight role. The CCB reviews and approves or denies change requests. We talked earlier in this chapter about documenting the authority level of the project manager. All change requests that fall outside of the project manager's authority are reviewed by the CCB. In addition to documenting what the project manager can disposition, you should document the criteria for CCB review with the change control process.

Change control boards are often implemented on large projects. We recommend you consider establishing a CCB for small to medium projects that fit these criteria as well:

- The project has strategic importance to the organization.

- The project is of a nature, size, and complexity never undertaken before by the organization or by this project team.

- The project impacts or involves more than one division within the organization.

- The project is politically charged either within or outside the organization or both.

Don't forget to add your CCB members to your contact list.

CCB Procedures

Change requests that impact the triple constraints—time, scope, and budget—should be reviewed by the CCB. The project manager may have authority up to a certain level for these as discussed previously. However, most stakeholders are keenly interested in how these changes may impact the project schedule and/or budget in particular.

The CCB should meet on a regularly scheduled basis. Depending on the complexity of the project and the number of change requests received, the meeting schedule could be once a week or once a month.

We recommend that the CCB meeting be conducted in a formal manner. Changes can have serious consequences to the project, and they should be examined and reviewed carefully to determine if the benefits of making the change outweigh the costs and consequences of not making it. The following is a typical progression of a CCB meeting:

- Present the change request.

- Discuss the alternatives.

- Discuss impacts if the change is not made.

- Make a recommendation.

- Take a vote and document the results.

Don't forget that emergency procedures should be documented for implementing changes that are needed in between the scheduled CCB meetings.

Project Manager's Role on the CCB

The project manager is usually the person responsible for presenting the change requests to the CCB. That means you need to be familiar with the reasons the request was made, how it will help or hinder the project, and the impact the change may have on the project. You will work with the requestor to perform assessments of the impacts of the changes prior to the CCB meeting as we described earlier. The CCB members should be briefed on this information before making a decision.

Project managers may or may not have a vote on the CCB. We've seen the process work both ways. It's possible the project manager will have some bias because of their involvement in the day-to-day activities of the project. This is one reason perhaps the project manager should not have a voting role in the CCB.

However, the argument can be made the other way as well. The project manager knows the project probably better than any other single team member. Because the project manager is so close to the project, they know which changes are beneficial to the project.

Again, the important point is that the decision about the voting rights of the project manager should occur before the project begins or very early in the planning stages.

Independent Verification and Validation

Projects that are of significant importance to the organization and are large and complex in nature may require independent verification and validation (IV&V). Just as it sounds, this is an independent, objective evaluation of the project. The person or organization responsible for IV&V examines the results of the project from an objective viewpoint and reports the results to the project steering committee and project sponsor. IV&V may be used to monitor the work of the project, specific phases of the project, the project management processes, or any combination.

IV&V is especially useful when vendors rather than an internal team are performing the work of the project. The IV&V consultant will validate the status of the project. They also validate and verify that the work performed so far meets the requirements of the project and that the work performed is in keeping with best practices. For example, you may have a vendor working on the project who wants to "leave out" some important details about the status of the project. The IV&V consultant can work with the vendor to make certain that the information makes it to the status report or that the IV&V vendor will report the missing information themselves. They will also typically assign a dashboard rating of some sort to the project as a whole as well as to the project schedule and budget.

Dashboard ratings might be Red-Yellow-Green, for example. Red means the project is in danger, Yellow means the project has problems that need immediate attention, and Green means things are progressing as planned.

The IV&V role is best filled by someone from outside of the organization (or at least outside of the business unit that's conducting the project), and they should report to someone other than the project sponsor. Often, IV&V is performed by an outside consultant. The idea is that the people responsible for IV&V are truly independent of the project and have no vested interest in it. We've seen IV&V consultants who reported to the project sponsor, and as you can imagine, once the project sponsor sensed trouble was brewing, they ordered the IV&V vendor to suppress the information. This obviously defeats the purpose of IV&V.

While IV&V is used most often for large, complex projects, you should consider using these services for projects that meet some of the same criteria listed earlier as reasons for implementing a CCB.

Windows SharePoint Services Templates

In previous chapters, we have talked some about the difference between Microsoft Office SharePoint Server (MOSS) and Windows SharePoint Services (WSS). Recall that MOSS is a product you must license and pay for. WSS is a free download (in version 2; licensing costs, if any, for version 3 have not been announced yet) for Windows Server 2003 (W2K3), installing itself as a manageable service within W2K3. MOSS is actually code that is installed *over* WSS. MOSS uses WSS as its underlying engine. MOSS also installs as a set of services. Thus, in the Services management console on a server that has both WSS and MOSS installed, administrators will see several services that pertain to WSS as well as several more that involve Office Server. Both MOSS and WSS utilize W2K3's Internet Information Services (IIS) web server software. IIS is a service that can be added at any time to any W2K3 server, allowing administrators to set up websites and administer them. Finally, it is important to note that MOSS and WSS respond to different TCP/IP ports (we say they *listen* on a given port) when a user pulls up their browser and points to a page.

Programmers can write web programs (whether using HTTP, XML, or another language) that listen on different ports. This is precisely what happens when you install MOSS (and hence WSS). Take a look at Figure 9.22.

You can see that the default website that IIS creates was stopped when we installed MOSS and WSS. Additionally, you can see that we have websites running on ports 56737 (HTTPS 56738), 3934, 48269, 7991, 80, and 24783.

So, here's a pop quiz: If you pulled up your browser and navigated to the MOSS server by typing in the command `http://server_name`, where *server_name* is the name of your MOSS machine, which website would respond? Because the default port for HTTP is port 80, your browser will ask the server to display the home page for the website on port 80. And in the case of Figure 9.22, SharePoint is using port 80. That's no help, though. Which SharePoint—WSS or MOSS? In this case, since MOSS is installed, the MOSS main page will be the port 80 reporting page and will appear when users key in the server name without a port qualifier.

In our case, the server's name is PMServer. By pulling up a browser and typing in `http://PMServer`, we get a page like the one shown in Figure 9.23.

What Is a TCP/IP Port?

The Transmission Control Protocol/Internet Protocol (TCP/IP) suite is the software protocol standard for communicating across the Internet. Without TCP/IP's invention, we would not have the Internet that we have today—we would have a hodgepodge of various proprietary protocols requiring some sort of intermediate logic to act as a translator between them. TCP/IP provides a single standardized interface that all can use.

One of TCP/IP's strong suits is the notion of a *port*. What we mean by that is a software opening, if you will, that the computer listens on for traffic and signal communications. It can get complicated (!), but to keep it simple, understand that there are numbered ports on which TCP/IP listens. Ports can be opened and closed by administrators.

There are standard ports and not-so-standard ports. For all basic web page traffic, port 80 is the standard. When you point your browser to Google, for example, you hit port 80. (There is a possibility that users hitting port 80 might be redirected to a different port once they're on the site, but initially they hit port 80.) When you're shopping on the Internet and decide to buy something, your port shifts to another standard port: 443. The Hypertext Transfer Protocol (HTTP) generally listens on port 80, while the Hypertext Transfer Protocol *Secure* (HTTPS) listens on 443. Both can be redirected to a different port.

There are other common ports. You can do some more research if you're interested at www.iana.org/assignments/port-numbers.

This is the main portal page of our MOSS site and is ready for us to begin creating subsites. Now, is there a way that we can see the other sites that IIS is currently hosting? Indeed there is! Simply point your browser to the same server, this time adding a colon after the server name and then the port number. For example, in the IIS screen shot shown in Figure 9.22, it appears that WSS may be listening on port 24783. Additionally, you can see that the SharePoint Central Administration site is listening on port 48269. All of these are ports assigned by MOSS and WSS at install time and are not necessarily the same ports you'll have with your sites—for security reasons, understandably.

By keying in `http://PMServer:24783`, we get an entirely different page, a WSS site, as shown in Figure 9.24.

FIGURE 9.22   IIS Manager

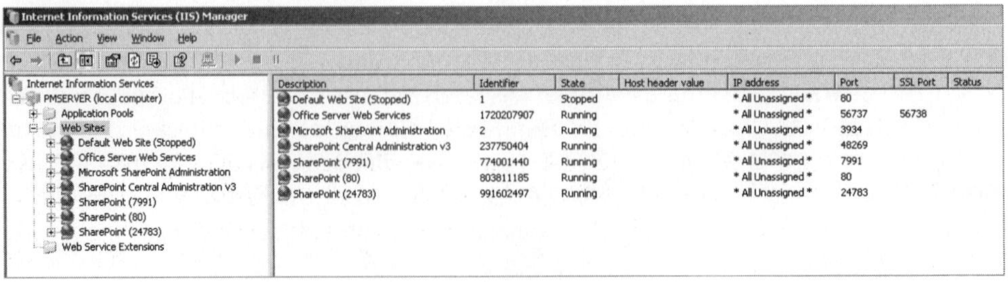

FIGURE 9.23   MOSS home site

FIGURE 9.24   WSS site

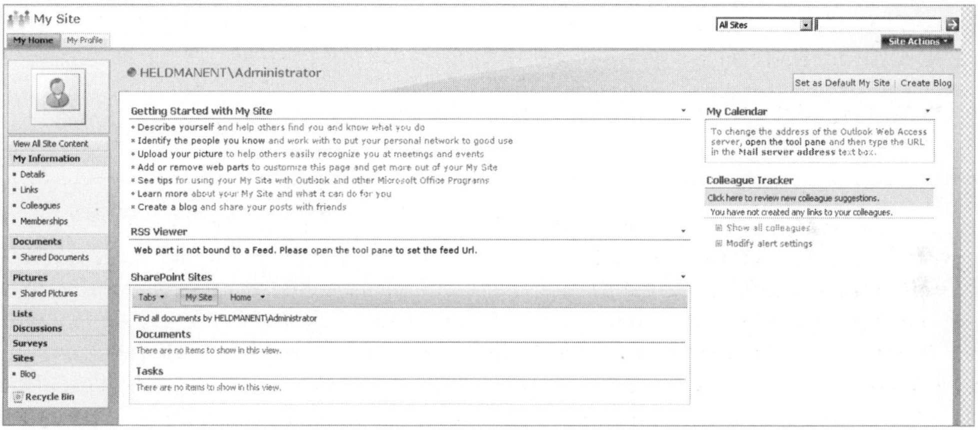

Accessing Templates in MOSS

In MOSS, when you're ready to utilize a template, you must create a subsite by going to the home page for MOSS (Figure 9.23). You click Site Actions ➤ Create Site. You'll be presented with the template gallery, as shown in Figures 9.25, 9.26, and 9.27.

Note that you have three different tabbed sections to choose from: Collaboration, which includes templates you'd use for various team-oriented efforts; Meetings, which includes templates you might use for various meetings; and Enterprise, which consists of templates that have to do with all of the users of the portal. (Recall that MOSS is really more than just a simple document repository for teams. It is a full portal server, able to provide subsite services to a wide variety of disparate teams and their needs.) Clicking any site template displays a help blurb on the left-hand side of the screen that gives you information about what the template does.

We anticipate that, as more templates are written, those specifically suited for managing projects, for example, will be available for download in the future as those currently available for WSS version 2 are.

In MOSS, when you are ready to utilize a template, you must create a subsite by going to the home page. You click Site Actions ➢ Create. Under the Web Pages tab, select Sites and Workspaces. You'll be presented with the template galleries shown earlier.

FIGURE 9.25   Enterprise templates

FIGURE 9.26   Collaboration templates

FIGURE 9.27   Meetings templates

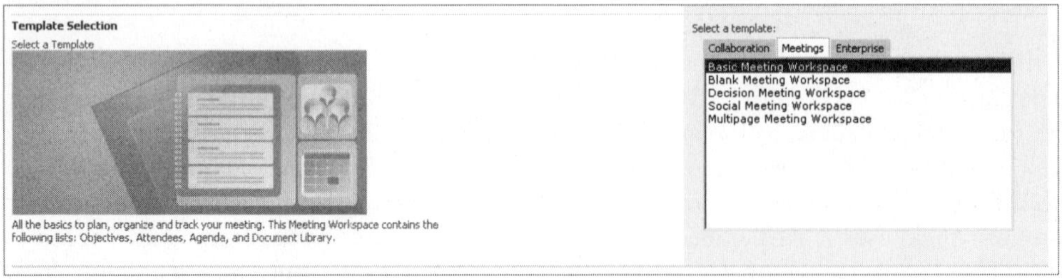

When users are ready to navigate to a subsite the first time, they must key in the primary site's name (e.g., `http://PMServer:24783` for WSS or `http://PMServer` for MOSS) as well as the subfolder's name. Let's say that you created a new team management subsite in WSS with a subfolder named TM. You would navigate to this subsite with the address of `http://PMServer:24783/TM`.

Note that the port number isn't required if you're using only WSS and you do not have MOSS installed. If you have MOSS *and* WSS installed, the port number is required to access WSS sites.

Subsite Creation

Now let's walk through a subsite creation with a new site template. First, navigate back to the MOSS home page (Figure 9.23 in our case). Next, click Site Actions ➢ Create Site, resulting in a page called New SharePoint Site, shown in Figure 9.28. We will use this page to create our Grant St. Move subsite.

Then key in a title and description for this subsite, as shown on the right side of this example.

The URL name is important—this is how you want users to be able to access this page. In this case, our users will have to navigate to `http://PMServer/GSM` in order to access the Grant St. Move subsite. We chose to utilize the same permissions as the parent site and also included a top link bar to the parent site in our new GSM site. In production environments, it would be wise to choose unique permissions rather than using the same permissions as the parent site because the parent site is the portal. Chances are you don't want everyone with access to the portal having access to the subsite.

We selected the information technology department as the division we are working in, and Local as the region. Both of these selections are options. Finally, we selected Publishing and Team Collaboration Site as the site template of choice for GSM. Clicking the Create button at the bottom of this page brings up a page similar to the one shown in Figure 9.29.

Note that the page is checked out for editing. You know this because the third menu bar from the top gives you options like Check In to Share Draft, Submit for Approval, and so on. The next line is a reminder to check this back in so that people can see your changes. You can also add Web Parts as needed at the bottom of the template.

NOTE MOSS and WSS version 3 do not currently support the WSS version 2 prebuilt site templates found at `www.microsoft.com/technet/prodtechnol/sppt/wssapps/default.mspx`. This is too bad, as there are a plethora of useful templates out there. We'll have to wait for the current WSS version 2 templates to be converted to version 3 or wait for a batch of WSS version 3 templates to be created before MOSS can be customized beyond the current site templates.

FIGURE 9.28 The New SharePoint Site page

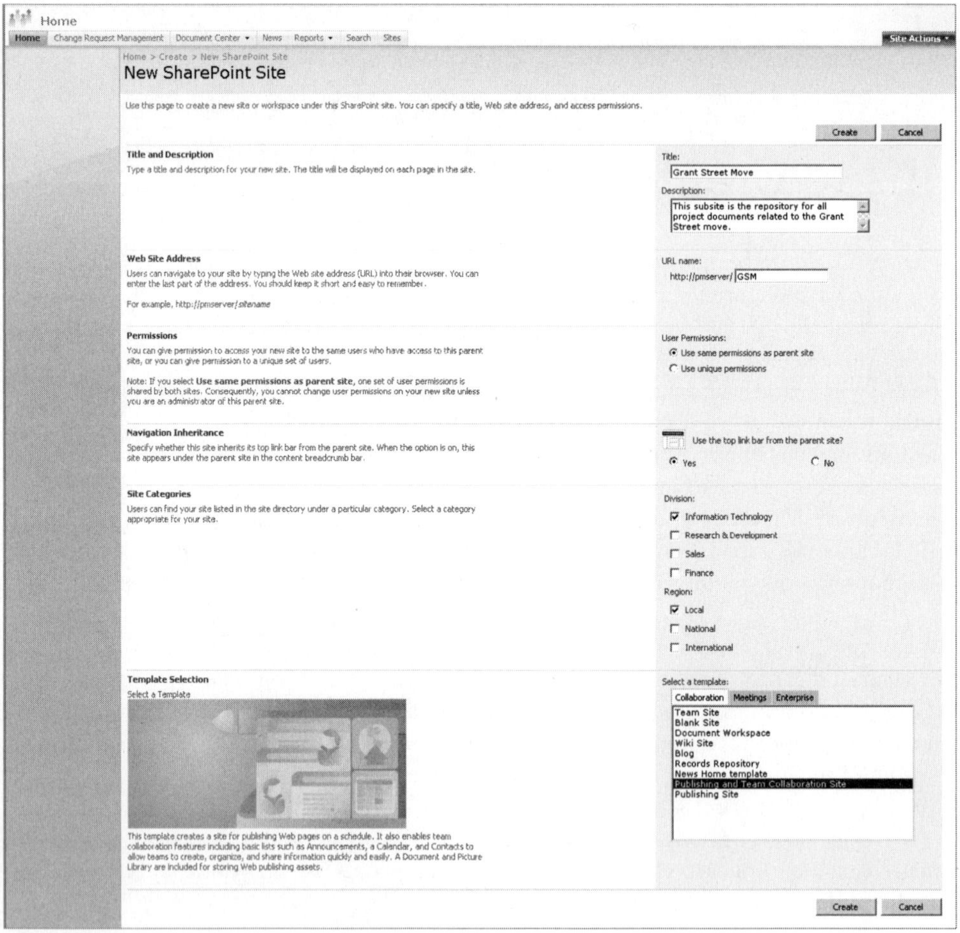
Home
Home
Change Request Management
Document Center
News
Reports
Search
Sites
Site Actions
Home > Create > New SharePoint Site
New SharePoint Site
Use this page to create a new site or workspace under this SharePoint site. You can specify a title, Web site address, and access permissions.
Create
Cancel
Title and Description
Type a title and description for your new site. The title will be displayed on each page in the site.
Title:
Grant Street Move
Description:
This subsite is the repository for all project documents related to the Grant Street move.
Web Site Address
Users can navigate to your site by typing the Web site address (URL) into their browser. You can enter the last part of the address. You should keep it short and easy to remember.
For example, http://pmserver/sitename
URL name:
http://pmserver/
GSM
Permissions
You can give permission to access your new site to the same users who have access to this parent site, or you can give permission to a unique set of users.
Note: If you select Use same permissions as parent site, one set of user permissions is shared by both sites. Consequently, you cannot change user permissions on your new site unless you are an administrator of this parent site.
User Permissions:
Use same permissions as parent site
Use unique permissions
Navigation Inheritance
Specify whether this site inherits its top link bar from the parent site. When the option is on, this site appears under the parent site in the content breadcrumb bar.
Use the top link bar from the parent site?
Yes
No
Site Categories
Users can find your site listed in the site directory under a particular category. Select a category appropriate for your site.
Division:
Information Technology
Research & Development
Sales
Finance
Region:
Local
National
International
Template Selection
Select a Template
This template creates a site for publishing Web pages on a schedule. It also enables team collaboration features including basic lists such as Announcements, a Calendar, and Contacts to allow teams to create, organize, and share information quickly and easily. A Document and Picture Library are included for storing Web publishing assets.
Select a template:
Collaboration
Meetings
Enterprise
Team Site
Blank Site
Document Workspace
Wiki Site
Blog
Records Repository
News Home template
Publishing and Team Collaboration Site
Publishing Site
Create
Cancel

FIGURE 9.29 The Grant St. Move subsite

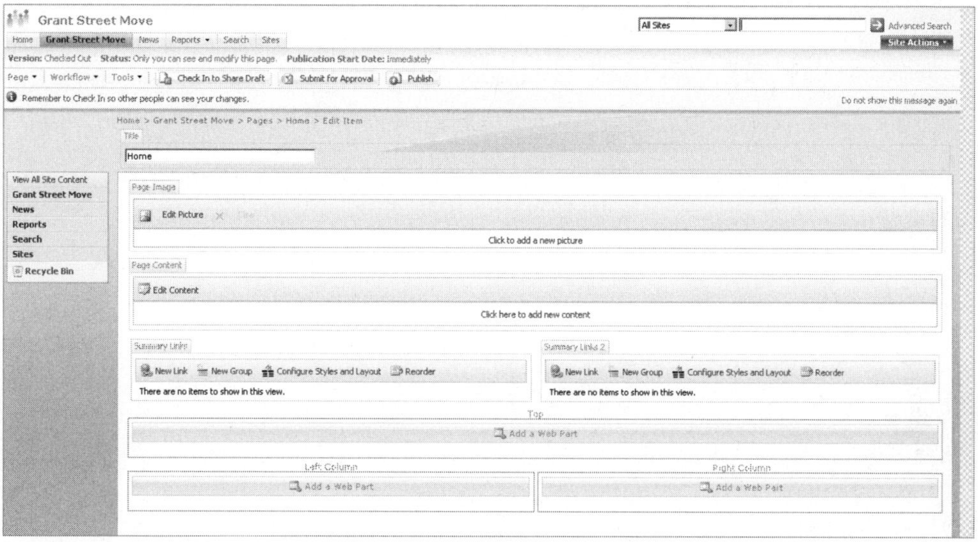

We have successfully wrapped up all the Planning process steps. As we've said before, planning is a significant effort on the project and the better your project plan is, the more likely your chances for success will be.

Once the change control processes are in place, you can easily adapt them to other projects, sometimes with little to no change. But if you change the change control process, will you need to submit a change request? We leave that to you to decide.

Chapter

10

Controlling Project Outcomes and Archiving Documents

This chapter will wrap up the work of the project and discuss the Closing processes. We'll look at performing the work of the project and what to do when things aren't going as planned. We'll also discuss deliverables acceptance and notifying stakeholders of project acceptance. The two primary functions of the Closing process are documenting lessons learned and archiving the project documents.

We'll close this chapter with a discussion of archiving project documents, backing up the MOSS project management site, and wrapping up the project with a final celebration of success.

Performing the Work of the Project

The work of the project begins when the project plan is completed and approved—in theory anyway. Often, work begins prior to approval of the project plan. Once the scope statement is agreed upon and approved, the work of the project is started at the same time the remaining Planning documents are being created. The belief is that the team is getting a jump start on the schedule. The downside of this practice is that rework may result if the team gets too far ahead of the Planning processes, budget expenditures may not be properly planned or timed, or risks that don't yet have response plans could be introduced.

The other danger in beginning the work before the plan is approved is that some deliverables or other project plans may change before they're finalized. For example, in the planning stages of the Grant St. Move project, we may decide to switch the Park St. move dates with the Elk St. move dates for a number of reasons. If we got a head start at Park St. and started packing early, we could be living out of boxes for longer than expected. The safest practice is to complete the project plan and get acceptance and approval of the plan prior to beginning work on the project.

The Executing process group is where the work of the project occurs. Most projects expend the majority of the budget during this stage. Materials are purchased, human resources are hired, space is leased, and so on. Generally speaking, the largest expense you'll have on the project is human resources. Some exceptions may include research and development projects or construction projects, which may involve as much or more spending on materials as on human resources.

The key is that during the Executing processes, spending increases, human resources are hired or brought onto the project, and work is produced. This is also where you'll likely see risks occur and the greatest number of change requests submitted. If you don't have a solid change control system in place, you could easily end up with a runaway project at this stage.

Project Plan Documents

We talked in previous chapters about approving the scope statement, schedule, budget, and project plan. The project plan includes at least all of these documents:

- Scope statement

- Communication plan

- Schedule

- Budget

- Quality plan

- Risk response plans

- Procurement plan

- Contract

- Change control system

Monitoring and Controlling the Work of the Project

A Guide to the PMBOK outlines the Executing processes and the Monitoring and Controlling processes as two distinct process groups. In reality, these processes go hand-in-hand. An almost certain guarantee of project failure is when the work of the project progresses with no inspection or control over the work results. Again, uncontrolled changes can kill a project that's made it this far.

We've discussed in previous chapters many of the plans that you'll put into action during this process. For example, project status reports and status meetings should begin sometime in the Planning processes stage. The focus of the status meetings at that point in time is obviously on the project plan and the status of the remaining components of the plan. During Monitoring and Controlling, the focus of the status meetings shifts to the progress of the work and verification of the work results. Several major components of the project plan should be monitored regularly and reported on at status meetings in order to keep the project on track with the plan, including the following:

- Schedule updates

- Budget updates

- Performance measurements

- Risk reporting
- Procurement status
- Contractor deliverables
- Contract status
- Change reports
- Team member status

Schedule and Budget Monitoring

Schedule and cost performance measures were discussed in Chapter 8. These are good indicators of project health and should be monitored regularly throughout the remainder of the project. Begin taking performance measures as soon as the work of the project begins. This helps you determine if the schedule and budget are on track. Of course, it doesn't hurt to also physically check the schedule and the budget. Ask yourself and your team some of the following questions:

Are the tasks on the schedule getting completed by their projected end date?

Are any critical path tasks behind schedule?

Are the resources originally scheduled for upcoming tasks still available and planning on performing their work on the project?

Are the task duration estimates proving to be accurate?

Have any unforeseen expenses occurred on the project?

Have any changes from outside the project team impacted the project budget so far?

Is there enough budget remaining to purchase materials not yet acquired?

Is there enough budget remaining to perform the uncompleted work?

Are budget estimates proving to be accurate?

Make certain to update your project sponsor with any adverse schedule or budget information as soon as you are aware of it. As we've talked about before, these are the two biggest project hot buttons for most sponsors and stakeholders. Don't wait until you have a crisis to deal with. If you deal with schedule and budget issues early (which you can only do if you're closely monitoring them), you'll have more of a chance for successfully resolving these issues.

Monitoring Risk

You should begin monitoring risks almost as soon as they've been identified. This should be a normal, ongoing occurrence throughout the life of the project. Team members should remain alert to risk triggers and know how to inform you of their occurrence.

Never punish team members for telling you the truth. Monitoring the project for risks, as well as other performance issues, is a process everyone on the project should be involved with. If you kill the messengers, so to speak, all you'll hear from that moment on is that their work is on track and everything looks peachy—even when it doesn't. Team members need to understand there are no negative consequences for reporting the truthful state of the project.

Review the risk list periodically at status meetings and make certain team members have a copy of it. Risk owners are responsible for monitoring the triggers for the risks assigned to them. They should report at the status meetings any trigger activity they've observed.

If a risk trigger has occurred, the response plan needs to be readied for action. The risk owner should review the response plan and update it if needed prior to implementing it. This is especially important if a lot of time has elapsed between the development of the response plan and the risk occurrence.

Once the plan is in place, it should be monitored for effectiveness. Ask the following questions to help with the risk monitoring task:

Is the response plan appropriate for the risk?

Are the impacts of the risk event still realistic?

Have new or secondary risks been introduced as a result of the response plan or the risk occurring?

Is the response plan achieving the desired results?

Have changes been examined for potential risks?

Did the implementation of the response plan require additional funds not budgeted for or not covered in the contingency budget?

Procurement Monitoring

Monitoring the purchase of equipment and supplies is done in coordination with the project schedule. It isn't usually necessary to order all the materials needed at the beginning of the project unless it's one with a short duration. As the project progresses, you'll want to time the purchase of the materials so that the team receives them as they're needed. We created a materials list back in Chapter 5 with a column labeled Date Required that you can use to monitor the proper order date.

You can also use the materials list to compare what was ordered to what was received. Depending on the types of supplies or equipment needed for the types of projects you work on, you may need additional information on the materials list. For example, the Grant St. Move project has several pieces of hardware and software to purchase for the data center build-out. You might want to note manufacture and model numbers along with any specifications (like processor speed, memory requirements, and so on) that will help identify the equipment needed.

We added some new columns to the materials list to record the specifications and the date materials were received and to check if the supplies received matched the specifications. Figure 10.1 shows the new version of the materials list.

Modify this template for the industry you work in and for the types of projects you manage and then use it to monitor purchases.

FIGURE 10.1 Expanded materials list

	A	B	C	D	E	F	G	H	I	J	K
1					Materials List						
2	Project Number										
3	Date										
4	Project Title										
5	Project Manager										
6	Description of Equipment	Manufacturer	Model or Version #	Specifications	Quantity	Cost	Total	Date Required	Requirement Number	Received Date	Match Specs? Y/N
7								0			
8								0			
9								0			
10								0			
11	SubTotal for Requirement Number:							0			
12								0			
13								0			
14								0			
15	SubTotal for Requirement Number:							0			
16	Total							0			

Monitoring Vendors and Contracts

Monitoring vendors or contractors hired to work on the project or to complete independent deliverables is straightforward if you're using a contract or purchase order (PO). The statement of work associated with the contract or PO spells out what work the vendor is expected to perform. A good monitoring practice is to tie deliverables or milestones to payment dates. That way, the project manager has an opportunity to check the work produced by the vendor at intervals throughout the project rather than all at once at the end. Once the deliverable is accepted, the contracting company can invoice you for the work performed.

This doesn't mean you have to wait for a deliverable to complete before checking on the contractor's work, however. For example, suppose you need a specific skill set for your project and the contractor has assured you that they'll send someone who is able to do the job. You'd be wise to monitor this person's work for the first week or two to make certain they really do have the skills needed. It's much easier to get the person replaced early on than to wait for weeks or months to go by and then try to explain that the person isn't working out and you need the vendor to send someone else.

Contracts should also include dated milestones. This makes the job of monitoring what's been accomplished easier and more efficient than checking all the work at the end of the contract. If you're using a time and materials contract, require your contractors to fill out timesheets and check them weekly or biweekly. Review all materials invoices and periodically check prices for accuracy. Also check that the materials they're charging you for were actually received and used on the project.

If you discover a problem with the contracting organization, contact them immediately. Most reputable firms want to go out of their way to satisfy the terms of the contract and to make sure you're happy (they want you as a reference on future contracts). If you don't get satisfaction, put your concerns in writing.

Document the work performed by contractors throughout the project. If you do get into an issue with the vendor, having a written trail will help bolster your case if you have to press the matter. Your legal department will likely thank you as well.

If you're working on a large project, some of the contract monitoring tasks may fall to the procurement department. They will still need your help in determining if the work is completed and if it's satisfactory. Don't forget that you can also enlist other team members or assistant project managers to assist with the procurement, vendor, and contract monitoring tasks.

Change Request Monitoring

As we discussed in Chapter 9, change requests can get out of hand on a project if there aren't proper controls and processes in place to monitor them.

The further along you are with the work of the project, the larger the impact the change request can have. If the majority of the project work is complete, changes may dramatically increase the budget or delay the schedule. And changes introduced at any time during the project can bring about new risks.

Every change request comes with a price. The project manager must analyze each request for its impact, cost, and potential delay to the project. In addition, the team must review the request and estimate how much work is needed to implement the change. Every change request the project manager and the team reviews involves time taken away from the work of the project. If there are a significant number of changes, the act of reviewing alone will cause delays to the other work of the project.

Team Member Monitoring

Team member status is something we don't always think about monitoring. Knowing the condition of your team and establishing good relationships with them will help give you an inside glimpse of the project status and the team's health.

If your team is small enough, consider having one-on-one discussions occasionally with each team member to determine their perceptions of the project. This also gives you some insight into whether there are troubles brewing on the project team or with stakeholders or if other problems exist that haven't been reported.

A significant risk to any project occurs when key team members leave before the work is finished. If you're meeting regularly with your team members, you have a better chance of recognizing when they're not happy. You may also have an advanced opportunity to correct the situation before it gets so bad it's beyond repair. At the very least, you're prepared to think about replacing this person earlier than you would have been had you not been meeting with them.

We can't encourage you enough to have open and honest communication with your team members and stakeholders. Once you've established a level of trust, they'll go out of their way to alert you to project issues and keep you informed of problems, including problems within the team.

Communication between you and the project team is one of the most important monitoring tools you have at your disposal. It's amazing what people will tell you when you take the time to ask and listen.

There will be times during the project when you may have nothing more than your reputation to lean on—use it wisely. You build your reputation through success, honesty, and doing what you say you'll do. If you don't follow through with these qualities, you won't have the ability to convince others of your line of thinking when questionable issues come up. We've all seen project managers with less than admirable reputations. What tends to happen is the team huddles on their own to make decisions without input from the project manager and lots of covert action takes place.

Your reputation is your best asset. Use it wisely.

Successful projects meet the requirements of the project, are delivered on time and on budget, and satisfy the expectations of the stakeholders. Monitoring the work of the project helps assure that each of these criteria is met. Many of these monitoring techniques use measurements to determine status. Remember that while the measurements occur in the monitoring stage, determining what to measure and how to measure it occur during the Planning processes.

Taking Corrective Action

The reason we monitor project outcomes is to assure that the work performed is in keeping with the project plan. If we're producing deliverables that aren't needed or don't fulfill the requirements the stakeholders outlined in the scope statement, we won't have a successful project when we're finished. Monitoring the project work at regular intervals gives us an opportunity to take action when variances occur.

Once the Executing processes have started, 80 percent of the project manager's time should be spent monitoring "right now" issues. But you can sometimes avoid future issues by using the remainder of your time thinking about potential future problems, alternative possibilities, risks, and so on.

Corrective actions are actions taken to align project performance with the project plan. Nearly all projects have issues that arise and need correcting. This might mean adding resources when the schedule is behind, for example, or postponing purchases when the budget is overextended. The corrective action you take depends on the problem you're facing. We'll look at some specific corrective actions in the following sections.

Schedule Actions

Schedule problems may require changes to the resource pool, postponement of deliverables to later phases in the project, or eliminating some deliverables.

Schedule compression techniques such as fast-tracking and crashing are corrective actions that can help get the schedule back on track. Fast-tracking is starting two tasks simultaneously that were originally scheduled to start sequentially. For example, on the Grant St. Move project, the company we're hiring to install the cubes and office furniture needs to finish roughly a week earlier than they originally told us. (Never mind they're under contract to perform this work as originally requested. Pretend we're nice people and we'll do what we can to accommodate a change.) We could fast-track some of the tasks in the Prepare Rooms/Offices deliverable. Figure 10.2 is the original Gantt chart for the Grant St. Move project. Figure 10.3 shows the Install Cubicle Walls tasks starting at the same time as the Inspect and Test Wiring task. This allows us to start the Install Desk Units and Install Wall Units tasks earlier than originally scheduled as well.

FIGURE 10.2   Grant St. Move Gantt chart

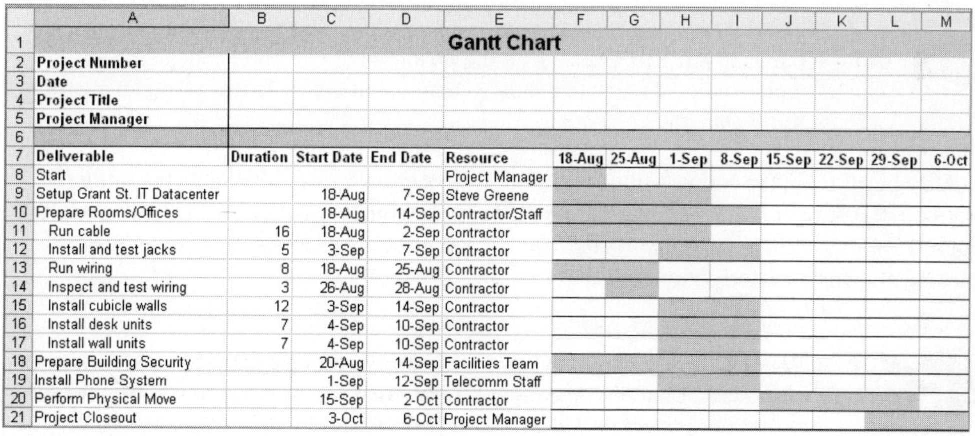

	A	B	C	D	E	F	G	H	I	J	K	L	M
1					**Gantt Chart**								
2	Project Number												
3	Date												
4	Project Title												
5	Project Manager												
6													
7	Deliverable	Duration	Start Date	End Date	Resource	18-Aug	25-Aug	1-Sep	8-Sep	15-Sep	22-Sep	29-Sep	6-Oct
8	Start				Project Manager								
9	Setup Grant St. IT Datacenter		18-Aug	7-Sep	Steve Greene								
10	Prepare Rooms/Offices		18-Aug	14-Sep	Contractor/Staff								
11	Run cable	16	18-Aug	2-Sep	Contractor								
12	Install and test jacks	5	3-Sep	7-Sep	Contractor								
13	Run wiring	8	18-Aug	25-Aug	Contractor								
14	Inspect and test wiring	3	26-Aug	28-Aug	Contractor								
15	Install cubicle walls	12	3-Sep	14-Sep	Contractor								
16	Install desk units	7	4-Sep	10-Sep	Contractor								
17	Install wall units	7	4-Sep	10-Sep	Contractor								
18	Prepare Building Security		20-Aug	14-Sep	Facilities Team								
19	Install Phone System		1-Sep	12-Sep	Telecomm Staff								
20	Perform Physical Move		15-Sep	2-Oct	Contractor								
21	Project Closeout		3-Oct	6-Oct	Project Manager								

FIGURE 10.3   Grant St. Move fast-tracked tasks

7	Fast Track Technique												
8	**Deliverable**	**Duration**	**Start Date**	**End Date**	**Resource**	**18-Aug**	**25-Aug**	**1-Sep**	**8-Sep**	**15-Sep**	**22-Sep**	**29-Sep**	**6-Oct**
9	Start				Project Manager								
10	Setup Grant St. IT Datacenter		18-Aug	7-Sep	Steve Greene								
11	Prepare Rooms/Offices		18-Aug	14-Sep	Contractor/Staff								
12	Run cable	16	18-Aug	2-Sep	Contractor								
13	Install and test jacks	5	3-Sep	7-Sep	Contractor								
14	Run wiring	8	18-Aug	25-Aug	Contractor								
15	Inspect and test wiring	3	26-Aug	28-Aug	Contractor								
16	Install cubicle walls	12	3-Sep	14-Sep	Contractor								
17	Install desk units	7	31-Aug	6-Sep	Contractor								
18	Install wall units	7	31-Aug	6-Sep	Contractor								
19	Prepare Building Security		20-Aug	14-Sep	Facilities Team								
20	Install Phone System		1-Sep	12-Sep	Telecomm Staff								
21	Perform Physical Move		15-Sep	2-Oct	Contractor								
22	Project Closeout		3-Oct	6-Oct	Project Manager								

Now we finish the Prepare Rooms/Offices deliverable four days earlier than the original schedule shows. That helps out the contractor but doesn't change the end date of the project. What if we had a reason to finish the project earlier than scheduled? We could use fast-tracking on other tasks as well, or we could compress the schedule further using the crashing technique. For example, the Prepare Building Security task on the original schedule takes 25 days (we're not including weekends in this calculation). We could compress this by contracting with the security company to help us with the install to shorten the time frame to 18 days. We could compress the Install Phone System deliverable as well so that the Perform Physical Move task could begin on September 7 rather than September 15.

The changes we're suggesting in this example require that the phone, alarm system, and security system vendors, along with the moving company, all agree to the date changes. In real life, it isn't likely all the vendors would or could agree to the date change, but please follow along for example purposes.

After performing the compressions techniques, we've now moved the final end date of the project from October 6 to September 27 (again, we're not counting weekends in these examples). Figure 10.4 shows the revised Gantt chart for the Grant St. Move project using both the fast-tracking and compression techniques.

Remember that schedule compression techniques should be used on critical path tasks. Changing the dates of non-critical path tasks won't change the project end date.

FIGURE 10.4   Revised Grant St. Move Gantt chart

		Duration	Start Date	End Date	Resource	18-Aug	25-Aug	1-Sep	8-Sep	15-Sep	22-Sep	29-Sep	6-Oct
7	Compression Technique												
8	**Deliverable**												
9	Start				Project Manager								
10	Setup Grant St. IT Datacenter	21	18-Aug	7-Sep	Steve Greene								
11	Prepare Rooms/Offices	28	18-Aug	14-Sep	Contractor/Staff								
12	Run cable	16	18-Aug	2-Sep	Contractor								
13	Install and test jacks	5	3-Sep	7-Sep	Contractor								
14	Run wiring	8	18-Aug	25-Aug	Contractor								
15	Inspect and test wiring	3	26-Aug	28-Aug	Contractor								
16	Install cubicle walls	12	26-Aug	6-Sep	Contractor								
17	Install desk units	7	31-Aug	6-Sep	Contractor								
18	Install wall units	7	31-Aug	6-Sep	Contractor								
19	Prepare Building Security	18	20-Aug	6-Sep	Facilities Team								
20	Install Phone System	10	28-Aug	6-Sep	Telecomm Staff								
21	Perform Physical Move	18	7-Sep	24-Sep	Contractor								
22	Project Closeout	4	24-Sep	27-Sep	Project Manager								

Adding and Subtracting Dates in Excel

As you've seen in previous examples, Excel easily adds and subtracts dates. If you look at the revised Grant St. Move Gantt chart, we could find the difference in start dates between the Perform Physical Move deliverable and the start of the Project Closeout task by entering the following formula in a blank cell:

   =C55-C54

The cells you're adding and subtracting must be formatted as dates, not text, for this to work. Excel should recognize you've entered dates, but just in case, here's how to format a cell as a date. From the Cells group on the Home tab, choose Format and select Cells from the bottom of the drop-down menu, as shown in Figure 10.5.

FIGURE 10.5   Format cells as dates

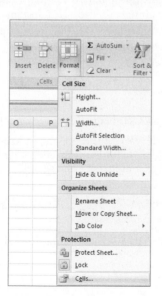

FIGURE 10.6 Choosing the Date format

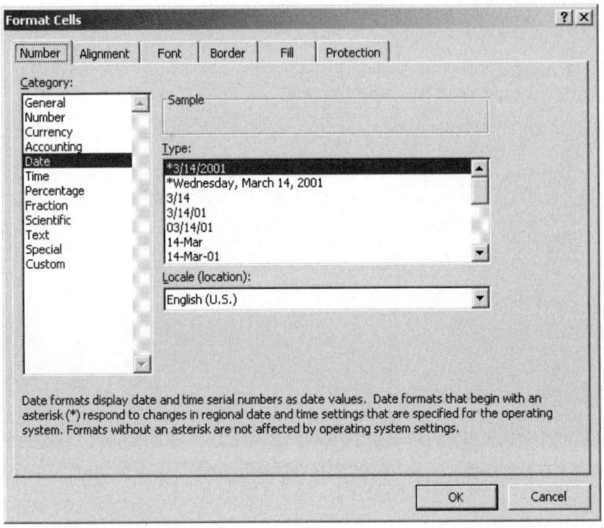

Once you click Cells, you'll get the screen shown in Figure 10.6. You can see we have Date highlighted in the Category scroll box and we can choose from among several formats in the Type box.

Serial Number Calculations

Excel can calculate differences in dates because it's using and storing serial numbers for the dates behind the scenes. The serial numbers start with the number 1, which represents January 1, 1900. The numbers progress sequentially so that January 2, 1900 is 2, and January 1, 2010 is number 40,179, and so on. So when you're subtracting August 18, 2007 from August 26, 2007, for example, Excel is really subtracting the serial numbers that represent these dates. Here's a quick way to find out today's serial number. Pick a blank cell and type in the following function:

=Today()

This will return today's date formatted as a date. If today is October 6, 2007, for example, the Today function will display 10/6/2007 (or whatever format you've chosen from the Type box to display dates). Now, go to Format in the Cells group on the Home ribbon and choose Cells from the bottom of the drop-down list. Format this cell as a number. The cell will change to a serial number. In our example, you should see 39,361.

The Now function will return both today's date and time. Type the following in a blank cell:

=Now()

This time, you should see something similar to 10/6/2007 14:57 displayed in the cell.

There's another handy date function in Excel that tells you the number of workdays between dates. It's called NETWORKDAYS. The formula looks like this:

=NETWORKDAYS(start_date, end_date, holidays)

This is a great function to use when you need to know the number of days between the start of a project and the end. Figure 10.7 shows NETWORKDAYS in the formula bar and 29 workdays as the result for the revised Grant St. Move project. Workdays in this case are Monday through Friday.

You can also exclude holidays from this formula. In Figure 10.8, we added a section for holidays and included those references in the formula. We realize Aug 31 isn't a typical holiday but wanted to show you the format for a range of holiday dates.

FIGURE 10.7 NETWORKDAYS for Grant St. Move

FIGURE 10.8 NETWORKDAYS with holidays

Sometimes schedule problems are due to poor estimating techniques. Another corrective action you can take is to recalculate your estimates if you're finding they are off. If you have a lot of work remaining on the project, consider reestimating the critical path tasks and adjusting the schedule once to accommodate the new estimates rather than having to readjust each time measurements are taken.

Budget Actions

Budget problems may require some of the same actions as schedule problems—postponing deliverables, cutting resources, and so on. You also may have the ability to ask the sponsor for more money. If this is the case, be prepared to tell the sponsor how the budget problem occurred. Perhaps the cost of materials increased after the estimates were prepared but before the order was placed. Maybe change requests were introduced that required additional expense. Perhaps budget items were missed in the planning stage. If you missed it or someone on the team should have known about the budget item, don't hide your mistakes; fess up to them. This helps you build your reputation as well.

Finances and project budgets can be touchy subjects. Remember that your project budget consists of funds that could have been used for someone else's project or for other organizational needs. You'll always have to compete for project funding—unless you happen to be the CEO of the organization. Stakeholders won't let you forget that your project was approved while their need was denied.

Here's another way to look at it. If your organization runs at a 12 percent profit margin, it takes approximately $835,000 in sales to fund a $100,000 project. Let's take this to one more level. Imagine your salary is $83,500 per year. After housing and food expenses, you're left with 12 percent, or about $835 per month, for car payments, savings, entertainment, and extras (like those yearly license plate tags and quarterly insurance bills). Your dream is to take your spouse on a two-week European vacation, but the reality is your grade-schooler needs braces. The point is no matter how many zeros are behind the project budget, funding is always hard to come by. Priorities must be set and choices made about where the money goes just as with our own personal finances. Use your organization's money wisely and stick to the budget—the executives will notice.

> **NOTE**   Corrective actions to schedule and budgets often require updates to the project plans and a repeat of the Executing processes.

Personnel Actions

We could write an entire book on the topic of managing personnel. We'll stick with some of the most important reminders. The most important of all is the one you've heard all your life: Treat others the way you want to be treated.

This author (Kim) once had a boss who called the project team into his office for a lecture—he was fond of lecturing. At the end of his, um, speech, he informed the team that the organization wasn't in business to provide them with jobs and if they didn't like what they heard they could go elsewhere. Needless to say, some of them did. Afterward, Kim asked the boss two things. First, didn't he know he just killed the team's morale, and second, why did he do it? (Kim's all in favor of the direct approach—even with bosses.) His answers were: no one is irreplaceable, and he said it because he could. You have to ask yourself, If he were told the same thing by his boss, wouldn't he feel as dejected as his team felt?

When you have personnel problems with team members—perhaps they're not performing their job or they're showing up late—admonish them in private. Never call a team member on the carpet in front of their peers.

Always hit problems (personnel or otherwise) head on as soon as they arise. If you wait, it will be harder to bring up the subject, and the longer you allow the behavior to occur without correction, the more difficult it will be to change the behavior. We're not attorneys and don't pretend to give legal advice, but you should keep in mind that it's possible you could make firing the employee more difficult as well if you allow the issue to drag on. Their argument could be that you allowed their behavior to go on for some length of time without correction and now all of a sudden it isn't acceptable.

Gather all the facts. We know it's a cliché, but there are two sides to every story. Don't make a judgment call or decide on a course of action until you've heard from everyone involved in the situation. Sometimes the facts are muddy and it's difficult to determine what happened. Keep digging and discover as much as you can, use your powers of deduction for what you can't determine, and follow your instinct.

Stakeholders can sometimes cause you problems as well. You aren't usually in authority over stakeholders, but that doesn't mean you can't take action. Again, deal with the issues as soon as they surface. Talk to the stakeholder one-on-one. Understand what their issue is and then turn it into a win-win by telling them what you'll do for them and asking for their help.

Here's another great technique to use with both stakeholders and team members to avoid problems in meetings: Gain consensus before going into the meeting. Prior to the meeting date, meet with each of the key stakeholders and explain your issue and the reasons for the solution you'd like to propose. If you get a majority of the key stakeholders on your side in individual discussions, when you get to the meeting they'll show support for you and your solution and the remaining stakeholders will probably follow suit.

> **NOTE** Another way of avoiding problems in meetings is never ask a question in a meeting setting that you don't know the answer to. Find out the facts before you go to the meeting so that you're fully prepared for questions or issues that may come up publicly.

Your best offense and defense for monitoring project work and taking corrective action is regularly gathering information on project status; staying in communication with the team, the stakeholders, and the sponsor; and knowing where the schedule and budget stand.

Contract Actions

Problems with contractors can be a real time drain and the actions needed aren't much different than dealing with employee issues. It requires extra diligence on your part to monitor and verify work results and to meet with the vendor regularly to discuss action plans.

We mentioned earlier in this chapter that contract concerns should be put in writing. Use a deficiency notice to record the deliverable, the problem you've discovered, a requested resolution and reinspection date, and any additional instructions regarding the deficiency. Figure 10.9 is an example deficiency notice form.

If you're finding even after issuing a deficiency notice that the vendor cannot or will not resolve the issue, you should consider issuing a stop work order. This demands that the vendor stop working on the deliverable (or the project) until you've both come to agreement on a course of action. Stop work actions are carried out according to the terms of the contract. Figure 10.10 is an example stop work form.

Stop work orders should be sent return receipt requested or classified mail so that a signature of the recipient is required.

If you have a procurement department, they probably already have their own notices and stop work actions. Again, document the problems you're having with the vendor so that your contract officer has the information they need to fill out the notices. Then let them handle it.

FIGURE 10.9 Deficiency notice

	A	B	C	D	E	F
1			**Deficiency Notice**			
2	Project Number					
3	Contract Title/Number					
4	Date					
5	Project Title					
6	Project Manager					
7						
8	Reference Number	Deliverable or Work Package Component	Problem or Deficiency Description	Resolution Date	Re-inspection Date	Additional Instructions
9						
10						
11						
12						
13						
14						
15						
16						
17						
18						
19						
20						
21						
22						
23	Signature of Project Manager					
24	Date					

FIGURE 10.10   Stop work form

	A	B
1		**Stop Work Order**
2	Project Number	
3	Contract Title/Number	
4	Date	
5	Project Title	
6	Project Manager	
7		
8	Work Stop Instructions	
9	Description of work	
10	Location of work	
11	Reason for Work Stoppage	
12	Duration of Order	
13	Conditions for Resuming Work	
14	Additional Instuctions	
15		
16		
17	Signature of Project Manager	
18	Date	

Signs of Project Trouble

Time and again, these authors have seen projects reach the stage where work is in progress, a portion of the budget has been spent, and resources are fully engaged when in reality the project shouldn't proceed one step further but the sponsor refuses to make a kill decision. They argue that since so much time and money have already been invested, you should press ahead to the end. That isn't a valid reason for prolonging a project that's long since died. Cut your losses and move on to the next project.

Killing a project doesn't necessarily mean you or the team have failed. Changes in management, budget cuts, downsizing, and a host of other reasons may bring about the end of a project. If you've done a great job managing the project and your plans are sound, you have nothing to be ashamed of if the project is killed for reasons outside of your control. If the reasons were because of mismanagement, well, that's another topic—we're going to assume that isn't the reason.

There are warning signs of a project in trouble. We've listed some of them here. Periodically review this list throughout the project to check if action should be taken to get the project back on track or if it's time to make the kill decision. Again, we're going to hope the first two aren't ever a reason to kill one of your projects.

- Poor project planning
- Poor project management techniques
- Poor estimating techniques or the wrong personnel developed the estimates
- Stakeholders or sponsors who don't want to hear bad news

- Sponsor or key stakeholders leaving the organization during the project
- Budget cuts prior to or during the project
- Delaying the project start but expecting the original schedule to be met
- Project team lacking important skills
- Inexperienced project team
- Dishonest team members
- Uncontrolled or too many changes
- Unforeseen catastrophic risk
- The organization being sold or acquired during the project
- Project that shouldn't have been undertaken in the first place

Accepting Project Deliverables

Acceptance of project deliverables should be a formalized process that requires the sponsor and/or stakeholders to sign off indicating they are satisfied with the work results. You should review the scope statement, requirements, and acceptance criteria when verifying deliverables.

Acceptance criteria is documented with the deliverables when you write the scope statement. For example, we said back in Chapter 4 that the acceptance criteria for the Prepare Building Security deliverable might look like this: Card-reader systems will be installed, tested, and functioning at least three days prior to the Park St. employees move date. All alarm systems will be tested and functioning at least two weeks prior to the Park St. employees move date.

Our Gantt chart shows this deliverable finishing one day prior to the start of the first physical office move. We don't have the breakdown of all the tasks listed on this example Gantt chart, so we can assume there are cleanup tasks that occur for the last two days of this deliverable. But what if when we crashed the schedule, we ended up with the last of the testing occurring on September 6 and the physical move starting on September 7? That would violate our acceptance criteria.

We have two choices. We could modify the schedule one more time to meet the acceptance criteria of the "three-day" limit, or we could modify the acceptance criteria. Since we've already changed the schedule once to accommodate other issues, we're probably left with modifying the acceptance criteria. This type of change should go through the change control process so that you have a written record of the reasons for the change. No one may remember later on in the project why the acceptance criteria was changed and finger-pointing could occur. Following change control processes and documenting the reasons will help prevent accusations from starting.

You can create an acceptance form like the one shown in Figure 10.11. At a minimum, you should include the following fields on the form:

- WBS or other reference number of the deliverable
- Deliverable description

- Acceptance criteria including attributes like quantity, appearance, performance, capacity, user acceptance, and so on
- Comments
- Signature section

FIGURE 10.11   Deliverables acceptance form

	A	B
1		**Deliverable Acceptance**
2	Project Number	
3	Date	
4	Project Title	
5	Project Manager	
6		
7	Description of Deliverable	
8	Accept/Reject	
9	Comments	
10	Reason for Rejection	
11		
12	Signature	
13	Date	

Notifying Stakeholders of Project Acceptance

When all the deliverables of the project have been accepted and the work is completed, it's time to get project sign-off and notify the stakeholders that the project has been accepted.

The final sign-off should be written (electronic signatures work as well). This ensures that the sponsor, customers, and the stakeholders have formally accepted the product or service of the project and they are satisfied with the results.

The form can be straightforward and simple by including the standard header (the project name, project manager's name, date, and so forth) and text like the following:

> The final product or service of the _____ project meets the requirements outlined in the project scope statement (including revisions and updates) and the project plan. All deliverables have been satisfactorily accepted and implemented.

Then include lines for signatures of the sponsor, key stakeholders, and customers, or require electronic signatures.

Part of the sign-off process includes the distribution of a final status report. This report should document the resolution of any outstanding issues and indicate that all deliverables have been accepted and implemented.

The last step in the sign-off process is the notification to stakeholders that the project has been accepted. Again, this might be a simple email (and/or notice posted on the MOSS project site) that the project has been accepted and signed off. If the project has become an ongoing operation, let the stakeholders know it's been implemented and turned over to the business unit. Include contact information for the people responsible for the ongoing day-to-day operations so you don't get the support calls. Also include where to find the project documentation in the notice and how long the documentation will be available.

Closing Out the Contract

If your project, or portions of it, was completed under contract, you'll need to close out the contract and formally notify the seller that the contract is complete, that the product or service is satisfactory, and that you accept the product or service. If there are outstanding issues to resolve, don't close out the contract until they're completed. Notify the vendor of the remaining issues that need wrapped up and agree on a resolution date. Let them know the contract will not be closed out until the issues are finalized.

Closing out the contract involves many of the same activities as closing out the project. You'll verify that the deliverables meet the requirements and accept them. Any knowledge transfer or training required should take place before the contract is closed out. And if the product or service comes with a warranty, review the warranty information with the vendor before the contract is wrapped up.

Documenting Lessons Learned

We've mentioned lessons learned several times throughout the course of this book. Lessons learned are those things you've learned during the project that can help you or other project managers have greater success on future projects. Lessons learned include both good and not so good processes or outcomes that led to the success (or dare we say failure) of the project.

Both authors have worked in political organizations where the executive-level staff changes frequently. Too often we've seen the new administration come in with great ideas and high expectations and, unfortunately, a refusal to listen to the cautions of the experienced staff. The new administration often attempts to conduct a project in the same manner a previous project that went down in flames was conducted. It's a lot easier to approach an executive with written documentation on why the project didn't succeed using the methods they're proposing than it is to try to recount from memory all the things that went wrong.

Lessons learned are helpful when embarking on a new project of similar size and scope. After all, why not copy what worked well and avoid repeating what didn't?

Let's look at an example where lessons learned will benefit a future project. Imagine that you've completed the Grant St. Move project and everything went smoothly according to plan. The company is sold and merges with another company six months after the move. Guess what—you get to move again to a new location. But you're feeling confident about the upcoming move because almost everything you learned from the first move can be applied to the next move project because you documented the lessons learned.

Capture lessons learned as the work of the project progresses. At the end of each phase of the project (or at end of the project if it's a small project), hold a brainstorming session with team members and key stakeholders to make certain you've documented everything. It's important to emphasize to all participants that lessons learned is not an exercise in blame. This process is for the benefit of future projects and is not meant to punish team members or pass judgment on anyone's work. If you've built relationships and trust with the team members throughout the life of the project, they'll know they can trust you with lessons learned information as well and should be forthcoming with the good, the bad, and the ugly.

The following is a list of some of the items you should document as lessons learned. This is by no means an exhaustive list. Make certain to record anything that helped the project succeed and write down those things that could have been done better.

- Project management processes used on the project
- Communication techniques
- Accuracy of the project schedule
- Accuracy of the project budget
- Accuracy of the estimates
- Experience level of those providing estimates
- Reasons corrective actions were taken
- Results of corrective actions
- A review of the action item and issues log
- The reasons for performance measurement variances
- Occurrence of unplanned risk events
- Team performance and morale
- Vendor performance
- Meeting effectiveness
- Stakeholder issues and concerns
- Contract issues
- Deficiencies in materials or supplies

There are several ways you could record lessons learned information. You could construct a table with category headings to make it easier to search. It could be written in narrative form with headings indicating the project phase discussed or topic, such as project management processes, team performance, contract issues, and so on. Figure 10.12 is a sample lessons learned template.

FIGURE 10.12   Lessons learned

	A	B
1		**Lessons Learned**
2	Project Number	
3	Date	
4	Project Title	
5	Project Manager	
6		
7	Project Phase	
8	Project Management Group	
9	Topic or Category	
10	Description of Lesson Learned	
11	Positive or Negative Effect	
12	Impact or Effect of Lesson Learned to Project	
13	Suggestions for Future Projects	

Let's walk through an example from the Grant St. Move project to get an idea of how to use the template. In Chapter 4 we discovered that three employees at the Main St. location need extra assistance in packing and unpacking their offices and also require special work area accommodations. Both of these situations should be recorded as lessons learned.

First, capture the project phase in which you discovered the issue. In this case, we were in the Executing process group because we were performing the work of the project when we discovered the problem. (Alternatively, or in addition, you could note the project phase itself, such as build, design, implement, or in this case Move Park St.)

The project management Group responsible for this phase is recorded next.

The Topic or Category entry helps you to group the types of lessons learned according to commonality. At the end of the project, you can group all the lessons learned from each category and determine if there were common misunderstandings or missed steps in that category that could be prevented in the future. The Grant St. Move project might have categories such as physical move, data center build-out, and contractor performance.

The description of the lesson comes next. Include enough information here so that someone who is not familiar with the project and reading this at a future date will understand what happened.

Positive or negative impact should be described next followed by how this lesson learned affected the project. Finding out we had three employees who needed special assistance for the Grant St. Move project after we started the work had a negative impact on the project budget. We had to hire consultants who specialize in workplace ergonomics to examine the needs for these employees and design work area accommodations for them.

Suggestions for future projects should describe what you would do differently if you had the chance. In our case, we would include special needs assessments in the requirements gathering process.

Modify the lessons learned template to fit your needs and remember to fill it in as you go; don't wait to try to remember everything at the end of the project.

Releasing Team Members

If you're working in a functional organizational structure, you'll need to release team members back to their original work units at the end of the project or when their work is completed. Good communications are required during this transition, with both the team members and their functional managers. Team members can become anxious toward the close of the project and wonder what they'll be doing next or if their old position is still open. Open communication will help answer their questions before they boil over into anxiety.

Another thing to watch out for toward the end of the project is a work slowdown. Cohesive, productive teams are sometimes reluctant to move on. They've experienced great success and synergy with their fellow workers and don't want the fun to stop. That's understandable, but slowing down the work to drag out their time together will ultimately delay the project delivery date. Keep reinforcing the goals of the project all the way to the end, and remind your team of the schedule due dates. Let them know if there's a possibility of them working together again on an upcoming project. Their functional managers can also help by familiarizing them with the tasks or operations waiting for them on their return.

Archiving Project Documents

The project has been successfully concluded, approved, and accepted. That's great news and cause for celebration. However, you're not quite done with the project management pieces of the project.

First, you'll want to close out the budget and code of accounts so no more charges are logged against the project. If you have a contract in place, you or your contract administrator should close out the contract. Review the terms of the contract because there may be specific steps or provisions outlined for closure. Finalize all outstanding issues with vendors, team members, and others.

You've spent a great deal of time documenting project plans, change reports, lessons learned, and more throughout the project. You've also collected signatures for the project plan, deliverables acceptance, and final project acceptance. On rare occasions, you may need to access these signatures after the project has been implemented to remind the stakeholders of what they agreed to.

Some of the planning documents may save you a great deal of time on the preparation and planning for a future project. Scope statements, schedules, WBSs, risk plans, and others may require only moderate changes for projects of a similar nature. That means you'll want easy access to these documents in the future. The easiest way to accomplish this is by creating an archived project site in SharePoint. Develop a policy that allows for the project documents to remain on the active project directory site for some specified time frame after completion and then move them to the archived site. It would be a good idea at this point to make all documents read-only so that no modifications can be made to the documentation after the project has been closed out. At some point, you may find you need to move archived documents off the archive site as well. You could back them up to disk or tape or other storage medium. Check your organization's document retention policy before removing or deleting any documents from your server.

Backing Up the MOSS Server

Since we're on the topic of archiving, we'll take some time to discuss backing up the MOSS server. Backups are your insurance policy against loss of data. Eventually, all computers get old and break down. But even before that inevitable breakdown occurs, other misfortunes can occur, like fire or water damage in the computer room, inadvertent deletion of files, sabotage, theft, and the list goes on.

Most of the time, backup functions are performed by your network administrator. Check with them to make certain these backups are occurring.

As with all other Microsoft server products, a backup utility is provided with MOSS for backing up the portal and associated subsites. From the Central Administration screen, select the Operations button to bring up the Operations page, shown in Figure 10.13.

FIGURE 10.13   MOSS Central Administration Operations Page

![MOSS Central Administration Operations Page screenshot]

The Operations page contains sections for Topology and Services, Security Configuration, Logging and Reporting, Upgrade and Migration, Global Configuration, Backup and Restore, and Data Configuration.

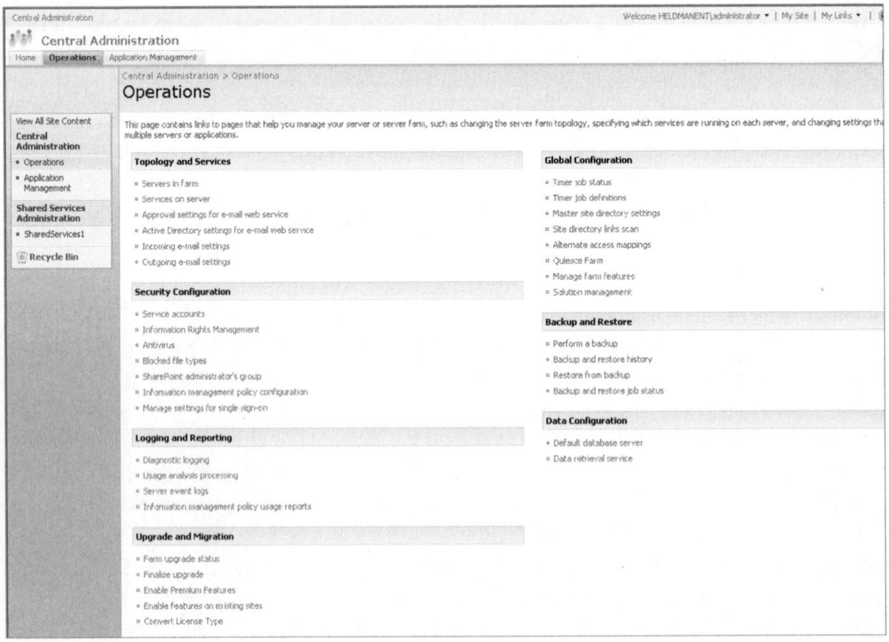

From the Backup and Restore section, select Perform a Backup. The Perform a Backup page appears (Figure 10.14), offering you different portions of the portal to select for backup. Note that if you check the Farm check box, the entire farm will be backed up. Alternatively, you can select any portion of the portal you'd like to back up.

Select those sections of the portal you want to back up and then click Start Backup Process. Clicking this button brings up a Start Backup page, shown in Figure 10.15. Note that the page shows the backup component(s) selection we chose as well as the type of backup we want to perform and the location in which the backup file should be stored.

FIGURE 10.14 The Perform a Backup page

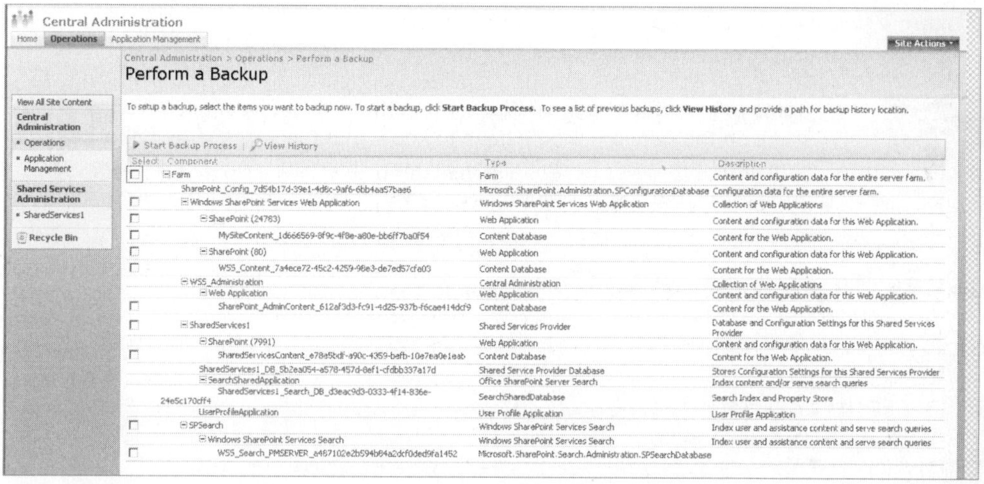

FIGURE 10.15 The Start Backup page

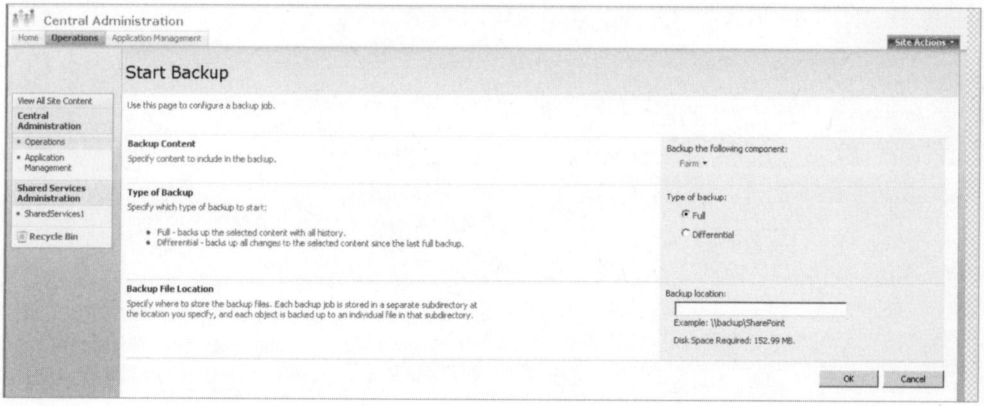

An incremental backup differs from a full because it backs up only the changes made since the last backup. Thus, the very first incremental you run will be a full backup. After that, only those elements that have changed will be backed up, saving you time.

We suggest you use the Universal Naming Convention (UNC) methodology for your backups. Suppose that you have a backup server or device—such as a Storage Area Network (SAN) or Network Attached Storage (NAS)—that has a NetBIOS or Common Internet File System (CIFS) sharename associated with it. For example, let's say you have a NAS named CorpNAS, and it has a folder on it that has been shared out as BACKUP. Assuming you have sufficient rights to that folder, you can key in the UNC name \\CorpNAS\BACKUP as the location for the backup file. Check with your system administrator for correct server and sharename nomenclature for your company.

Figure 10.16 shows the output of the backup process.

 Some sharenames have a dollar sign ($) after them. This hides visibility of the share on the network. You'll have to know that the sharename has a dollar sign after it in order to facilitate a backup. The result will be the same—the point is that the share is hidden from view to keep people from discovering it.

FIGURE 10.16 Status of backup process

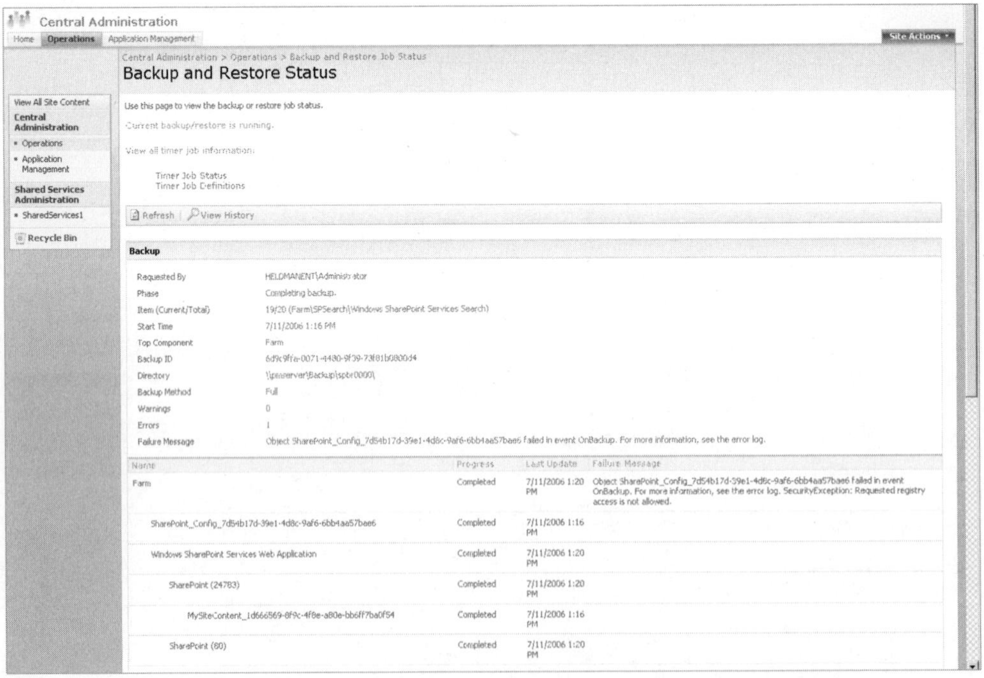

Name	Progress	Last Update	Failure Message
Farm	Completed	7/11/2006 1:20 PM	Object SharePoint_Config_7d54b17d-39e1-4d8c-9af6-6bb4aa57bae6 failed in event OnBackup. For more information, see the error log. SecurityException: Requested registry access is not allowed.
SharePoint_Config_7d54b17d-39e1-4d8c-9af6-6bb4aa57bae6	Completed	7/11/2006 1:16 PM	
Windows SharePoint Services Web Application	Completed	7/11/2006 1:20 PM	
SharePoint (24783)	Completed	7/11/2006 1:20 PM	
MySiteContent_1d666569-0f9c-4f8e-a80e-bb6ff7ba0f54	Completed	7/11/2006 1:16 PM	
SharePoint (60)	Completed	7/11/2006 1:20 PM	

Please be aware that if a computer has a local firewall installed on it, it is quite possible that you cannot connect to a sharename associated with that computer to begin backing up content because the firewall is restricting you. If Windows firewall, or another brand of firewall (such as McAfee) is enabled, chances are that you won't be able to connect to it without either disabling the firewall altogether, or setting it up so that it allows you to connect to it.

Celebrate

Now that the project is completed, the documents archived, and the contract is closed out, celebrate your success. You and the team have worked hard to bring in a successful project. Celebrating is a way to formally bring closure to the project and allows you to recognize the team and individual efforts in a public manner. The project sponsor should also do their part to share the success story with the executive team. Success is one of the factors that helps build your reputation—enjoy it.

Appendix A

Excel Function Junction

Excel is an extraordinarily powerful tool. Spreadsheets are a breeze to create and use. And with Office 2007, formatting chores are easier than ever to handle. Calculations are simple to create and to copy and paste.

But few people venture beyond the confines of creating routine spreadsheets toward harnessing Excel's amazing complex function powers. (Note that the two terms *formulas* and *functions* are used interchangeably. We'll use the word *functions* from here on out.) Further, integration with the new Excel Services in a Windows Server 2003 implementation running MOSS expands on the ability to leverage worksheet formulas and numbers so that they're accessible by a diverse array of people.

In this appendix, we'll examine several of Excel's features, including Excel Services, publishing to MOSS, and Excel functions. We'll also show you how to automate Excel and consolidate worksheets and give you some tips on pivot tables.

Leveraging Excel Functions Using Excel Services

In this section, we'll talk about Excel functions and using Excel Services to allow others to view and manipulate data.

Begin by making sure you understand that Excel Services, an installed feature of MOSS, doesn't have any out-of-box *trusted locations* to which Excel sheets can be published. You or your friendly neighborhood administrator must add trusted locations to MOSS. At the MOSS server, click Start ➢ Microsoft Office Server ➢ SharePoint 3.0 Central Administration to access the main administration page for MOSS, shown in Figure A.1.

Click the Add Excel Services Trusted Locations link to bring up a new page, shown in Figure A.2. Next to the Action heading, select Add Excel Services Trusted Locations to bring up the Trusted File Locations page, shown in Figure A.3. On this page, click the Add Trusted File Location link to bring up your final destination, the Add Trusted File Location page, shown in Figure A.4.

FIGURE A.1   Accessing the MOSS Central Administration page

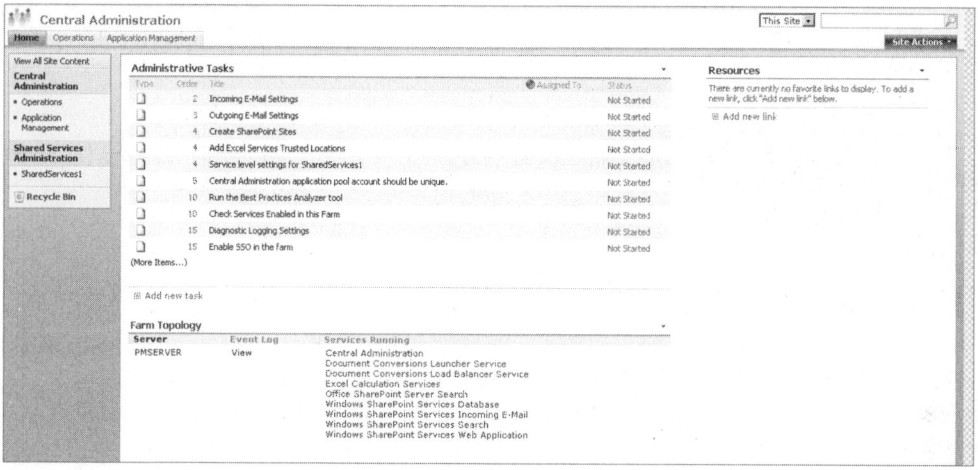

FIGURE A.2   Adding Excel Services trusted locations

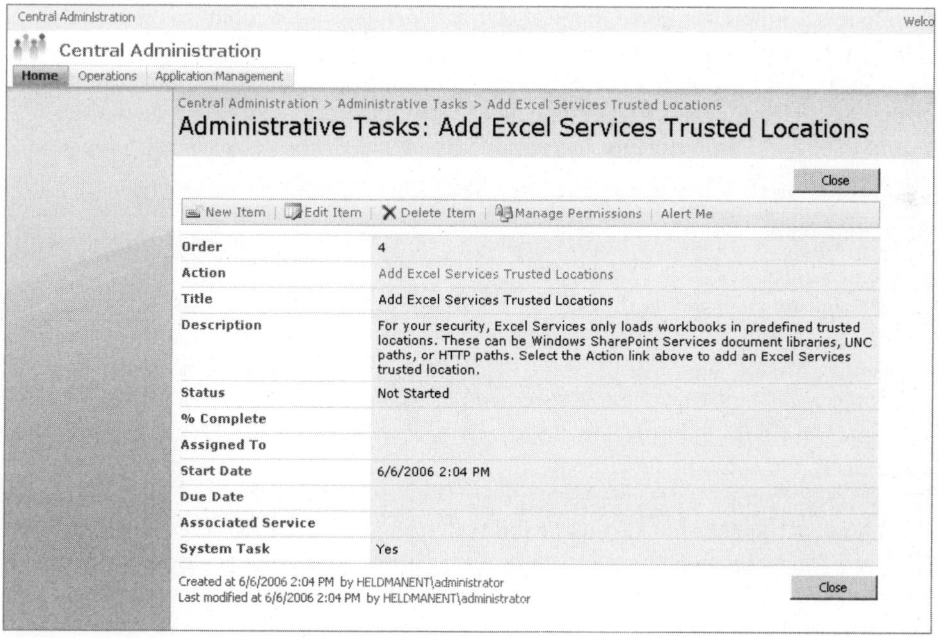

FIGURE A.3   The Trusted File Locations page

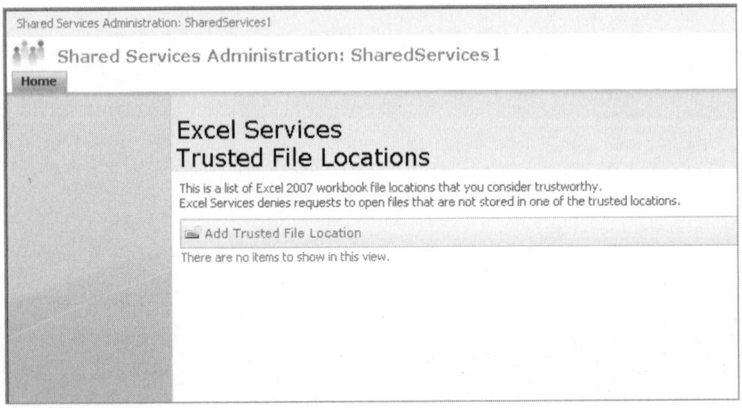

Shared Services Administration: SharedServices1

🎎 Shared Services Administration: SharedServices1

Home

Excel Services
Trusted File Locations

This is a list of Excel 2007 workbook file locations that you consider trustworthy.
Excel Services denies requests to open files that are not stored in one of the trusted locations.

📇 Add Trusted File Location

There are no items to show in this view.

In our case, we'll add the address of the entire MOSS portal. However, in a production environment, this may not be such a good idea. There may be other locations that you'd want to add instead of the entire portal. Note in Figure A.4 that you can choose from Windows SharePoint Services locations such as a shared directory, Universal Naming Convention (UNC) shares such as a Windows share on a network (in the form of *server_name**share_name*), or an HTTP address. In this example, we keyed in the URL http://PMServer to point to the entire portal as a source for trusted locations and selected the HTTP location type button.

Suppose you didn't want to enable the entire portal for Excel Services. For example, suppose you had a subsite called PMs. You could enable Excel Services by keying in the HTTP address of http://PMServer/PMs, or you could reference the Windows SharePoint Services directory PMs.

Figure A.4 also shows the Children Trusted check box. This is important. If checked, it means that any child libraries or folders created underneath the current folder you are setting up for Excel Services will also be included.

All other options will stay at the default. However, take a look at the Allow User-Defined Functions setting at the bottom of Figure A.4. This option allows workbooks that contain functions not normally a part of Excel—custom functions that someone has created—to be included. The problem with including these isn't necessarily that the user who created a user-defined function (UDF) didn't create it correctly, it is a security issue. By allowing UDFs in Excel Services, you could be unwittingly allowing scurrilous functions to be uploaded to MOSS—a serious action with potentially devastating consequences. The likelihood? Low. The likelihood of someone having the capability of bringing harm to a server via a malformed UDF? High. The recommendation would be to *not* allow UDFs unless absolutely necessary.

After you click OK, Excel Services has a trusted location to which Excel workbooks can be published, as shown in Figure A.5.

FIGURE A.4   Adding a new trusted file location

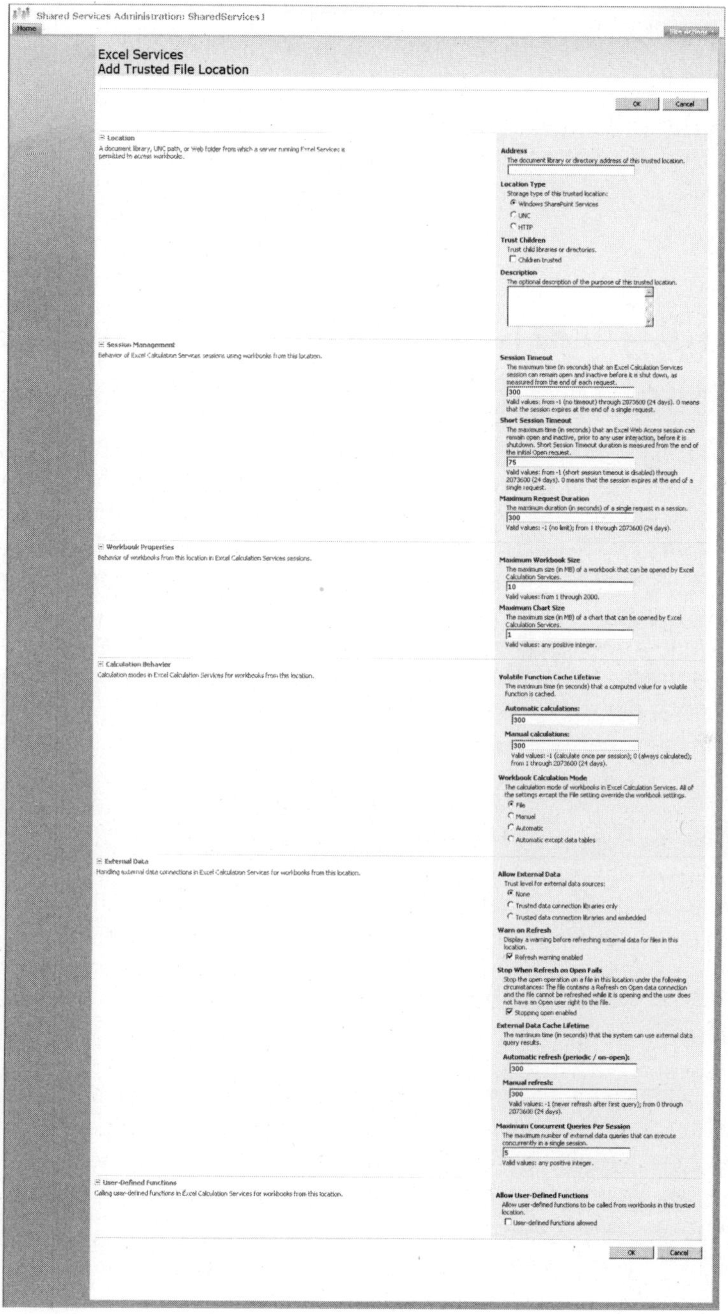

FIGURE A.5 New trusted services location

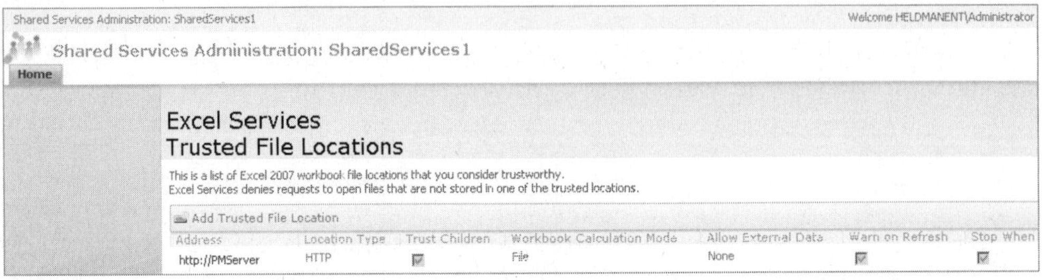

Calculating Various Workbook Elements and Publishing to MOSS

Now let's turn our attention to some typical spreadsheet work you might be involved with—information that you'll want to share with others via MOSS. We'll then turn back to Excel Services running under MOSS to see how these spreadsheets are shared.

Consider, for example, a Grant St. Move quality-control effort in which you must ascertain the rated CPU speeds, in gigahertz (GHz), among all 2,500 user PCs in the organization, along with how many are over- or underclocked. You obtain a report from the system administrators—who have used standard system management software to obtain their numbers—and compile a spreadsheet, shown in Figure A.6.

FIGURE A.6 User CPUs

	A	B	C	D
1	CPU GHZ	# Computers	# Overclocked	# Underclocked
2	0.9	71	30	2
3	1.0	96	13	2
4	1.1	0	0	0
5	1.2	74	17	3
6	1.3	71	0	0
7	1.4	75	1	3
8	1.5	55	3	3
9	1.6	176	1	12
10	1.7	133	7	14
11	1.8	207	2	15
12	1.9	154	4	11
13	2.0	213	10	33
14	2.2	255	4	23
15	2.4	276	5	17
16	2.6	130	2	21
17	2.8	121	1	40
18	3.0	119	0	6
19	3.1	110	0	8
20	3.2	74	0	4
21	3.4	37	1	3
22	3.6	29	0	7
23	3.8	24	1	2
24		2500	102	229

This sheet is easily published to MOSS. We first start by naming the range. We highlight the entire set of cells, then right-click and select Name a Range from the ensuing menu. Figure A.7 shows the pop-up dialog box, with a suggested name of CPU_GHZ, along with the highlighted cell range. The named range is important to us because we want to save the named range, *not* the entire workbook, to MOSS. There is no point in making the entire workbook accessible when we merely want to show people a named range.

The round "flag" key at the northwest corner of Office is called the *Office button* by MicrosoftNext; from Excel, click the Office button ➤ Publish ➤ Excel Services, as shown in Figure A.8.

From the resulting Save As menu, select Excel Services Options to change the save process from the entire workbook to a named range. Figure A.9 shows the selection.

FIGURE A.7   Naming a range

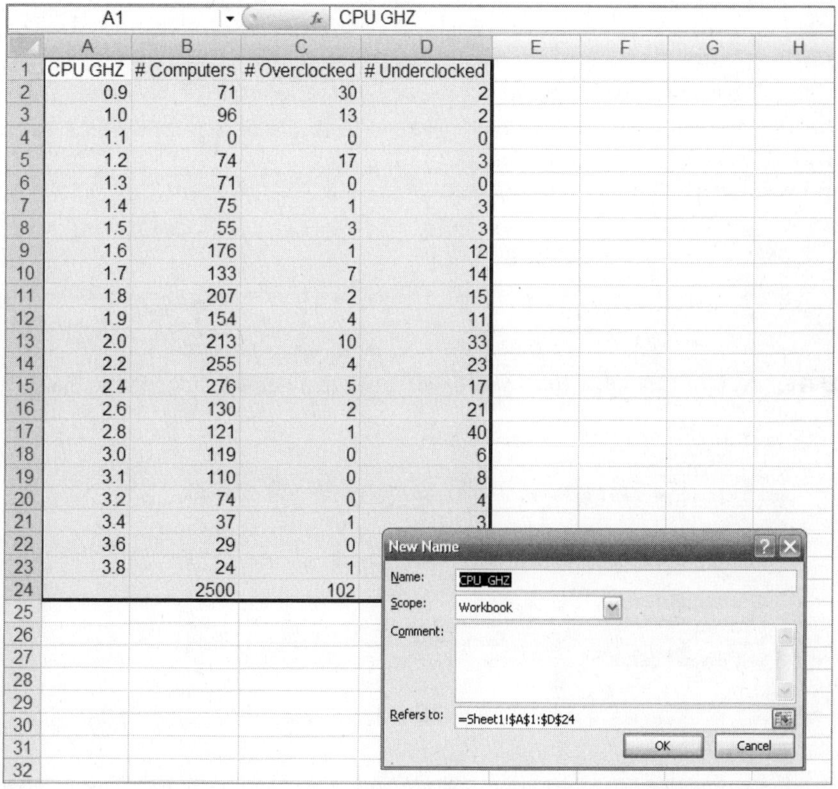

	A	B	C	D
	A1			f_x CPU GHZ
1	CPU GHZ	# Computers	# Overclocked	# Underclocked
2	0.9	71	30	2
3	1.0	96	13	2
4	1.1	0	0	0
5	1.2	74	17	3
6	1.3	71	0	0
7	1.4	75	1	3
8	1.5	55	3	3
9	1.6	176	1	12
10	1.7	133	7	14
11	1.8	207	2	15
12	1.9	154	4	11
13	2.0	213	10	33
14	2.2	255	4	23
15	2.4	276	5	17
16	2.6	130	2	21
17	2.8	121	1	40
18	3.0	119	0	6
19	3.1	110	0	8
20	3.2	74	0	4
21	3.4	37	1	3
22	3.6	29	0	
23	3.8	24	1	
24		2500	102	

New Name

Name: CPU_GHZ

Scope: Workbook

Comment:

Refers to: =Sheet1!$A$1:$D$24

OK   Cancel

Select Items in the Workbook from the drop-down list and the CPU_GHZ named range appears. Select it, as shown in Figure A.10. (The All Named Ranges check box is automatically checked. If you had more than one named range, you would have to be careful to *deselect* all but the named ranges you really wanted to save to MOSS.)

FIGURE A.8   Publishing to Excel Services

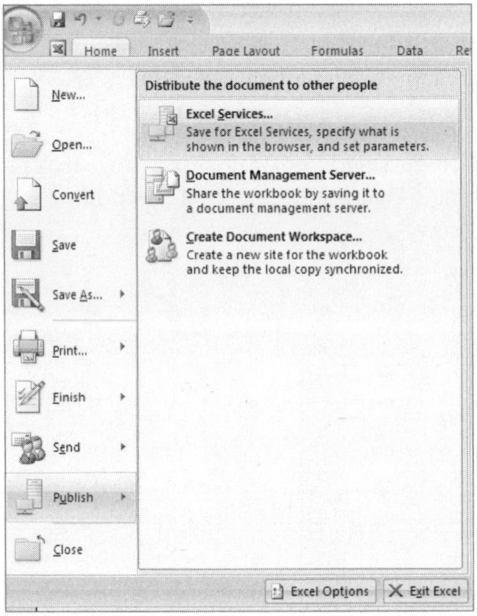

FIGURE A.9   Changing from entire workbook to a named range in the Excel Services dialog box

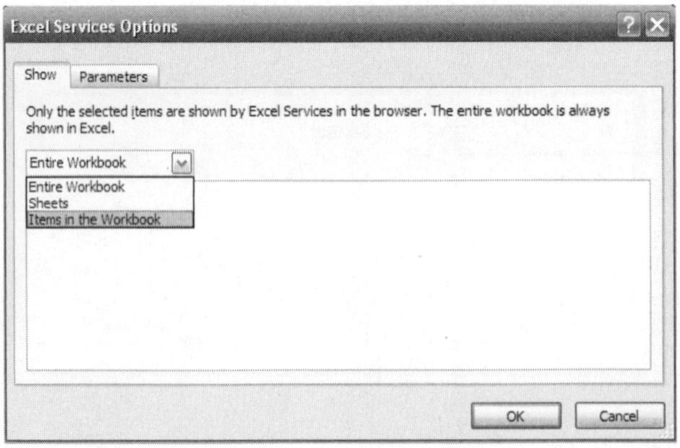

You could select single cells with named values from the Parameters tab of the Excel Services Options dialog box as shown in Figure A.11. This effectively reduces other readers' ability to alter all but those cells you choose upon publishing to MOSS. In our case, we have no single cell references and will leave this menu alone.

Next, from the Save As menu, navigate to My Network Places and select PMServer, then Grant Street Move from the list of available sites (Figure A.12). Note in Figure A.12 that we have navigated to a subsite folder on PMServer called GSM and it is within this subsite we are going to place CPUs.xlsx.

FIGURE A.10   Selecting a named range in the Excel Services dialog box

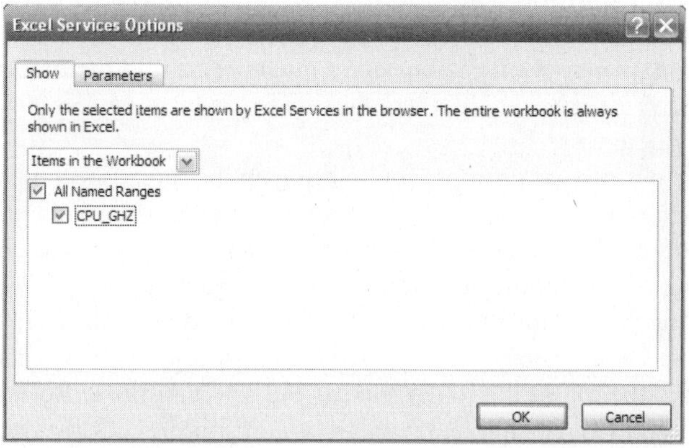

FIGURE A.11   Parameters tab of the Excel Services menu

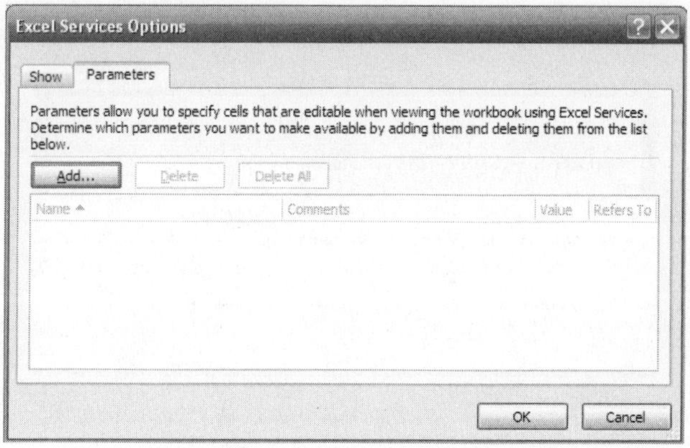

Note that in larger production networks, you may not have the MOSS server in your My Network Places listings. If you've never accessed the server using Web folders, chances are you probably won't. In a case like this, you can paste the URL of the site in the filename box. When you click Save, your computer will browse the site and the site is also added to your My Network Places.

We'll drill down into the Documents folder and get ready to save the named range of this spreadsheet. Our choices are to save as an ordinary Excel workbook (with an .xlsx extension) or as a binary (i.e., encrypted) workbook with an .xlsb extension. Since we're on a local intranet, we trust the embedded authentication of MOSS (and W2K3), so we do not require a binary workbook format. You may want to consider a binary format in the case of, say, a vendor who uses a virtual private network (VPN) connection to log on to MOSS. Figure A.13 shows us ready to save the document.

Provided you checked the button that prompts you to bring up the spreadsheet in a browser after completing the save operation, you'll see the named range appear, as shown in Figure A.14. No one can edit it in the browser. Nor can they directly edit it using Excel until it is checked in and approved. Until that time, a local copy must be saved and worked on.

Checking in and approving the document is straightforward (but does require Home Member rights.) If you are the site Owner, simply navigate to the appropriate folder, click the All Documents button located at the top of the folder listing, and select Approve/Reject Items from the menu. Figure A.15 shows an example. If you are a contributor, click the document's drop-down and select Check In.

FIGURE A.12   Navigating to the Grant St. Move folder location

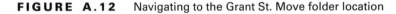

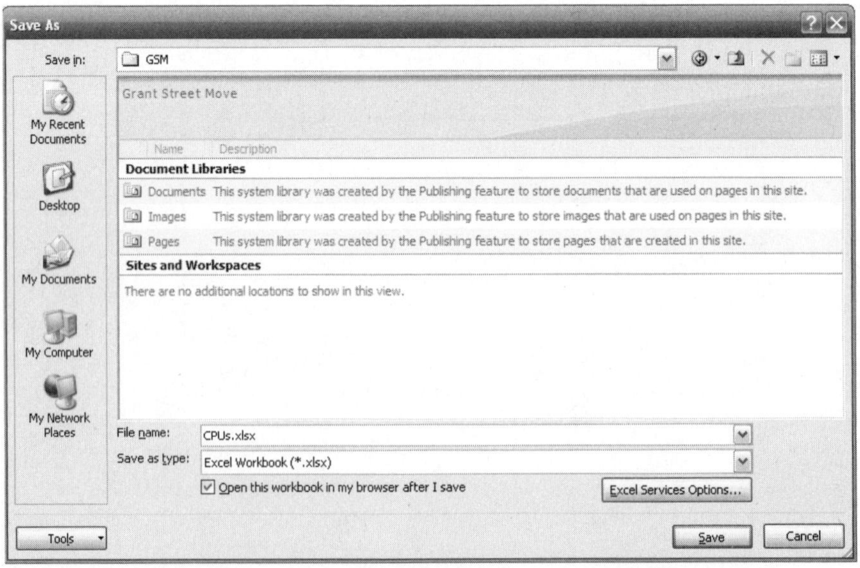

FIGURE A.13   Saving CPUs.xlsx to the Documents folder of PMServer/GSM (Grant Street Move) Subsite

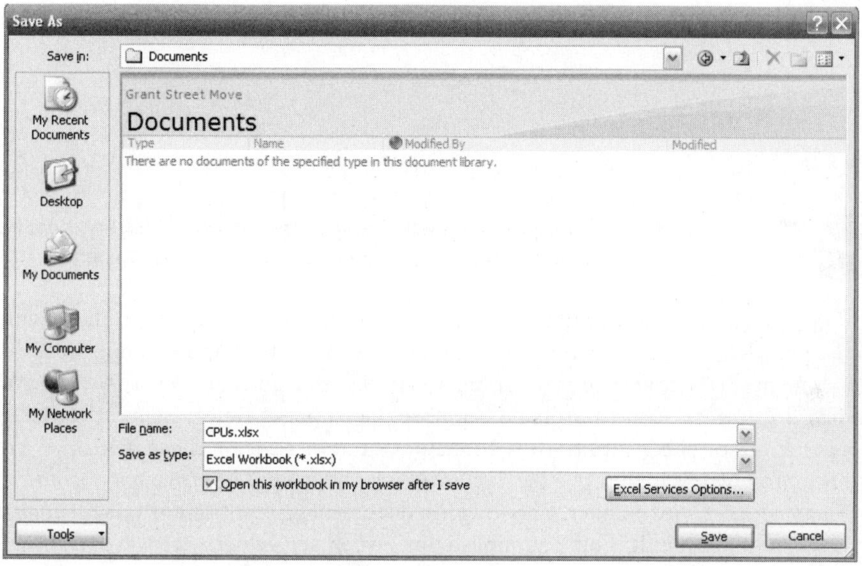

FIGURE A.14   Viewing CPUs.xlsx in a browser

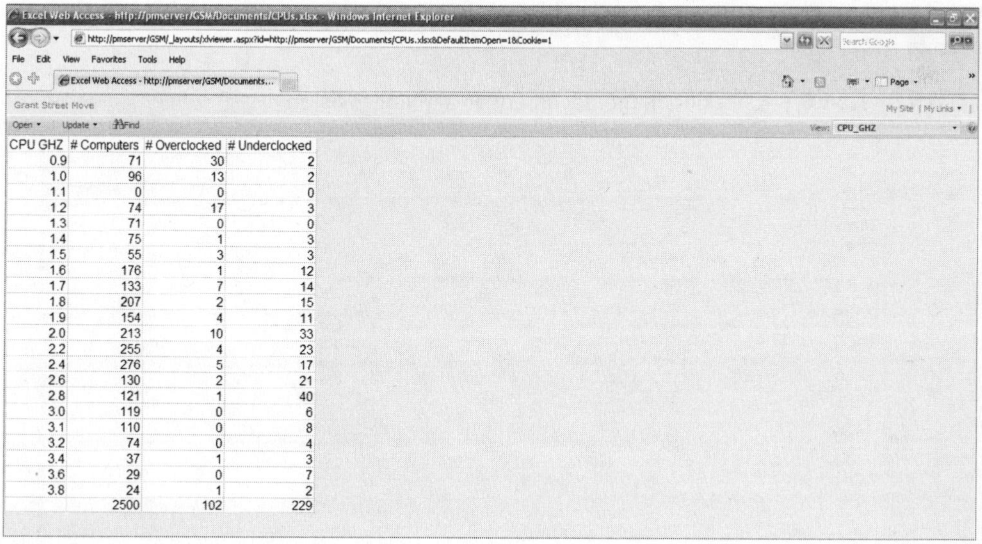

CPU GHZ	# Computers	# Overclocked	# Underclocked
0.9	71	30	2
1.0	96	13	2
1.1	0	0	0
1.2	74	17	3
1.3	71	0	0
1.4	75	1	3
1.5	55	3	3
1.6	176	1	12
1.7	133	7	14
1.8	207	2	15
1.9	154	4	11
2.0	213	10	33
2.2	255	4	23
2.4	276	5	17
2.6	130	2	21
2.8	121	1	40
3.0	119	0	6
3.1	110	0	8
3.2	74	0	4
3.4	37	1	3
3.6	29	0	7
3.8	24	1	2
	2500	102	229

FIGURE A.15   Approve/Reject Items

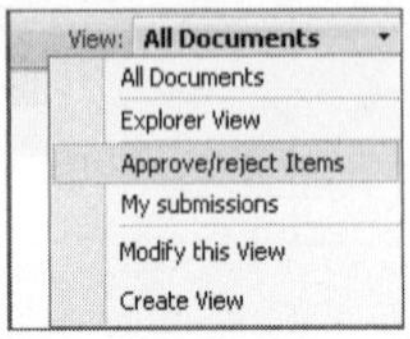

View:	**All Documents**	▼
	All Documents	
	Explorer View	
	Approve/reject Items	
	My submissions	
	Modify this View	
	Create View	

As we've mentioned in earlier chapters, the document library must be configured for versioning and content approval in order for you to perform these tasks.

Note that Approve/Reject Items is a special selection available only to those with site Owner permissions. This button provides an Owner with a grouping of approval statuses for *all* documents in the folder, thus providing Owners with a quick, easy way to approve or reject pending documents. Contributors do not have the Approve/Reject Items selection and may only check out or check into draft with major or minor revision those items they created.

It is up to Owners to approve the document for publishing. Approving a document *always* gives it a major revision number. Checking in a document gives it a minor version number update but does not publish it. It is only at publish time, when an Owner approves the document, that a major revision number is given to it. All document version information is available for viewing by anyone with permissions to the site—whether Owner, contributor, or reader.

Whether one has Owner or Member status, there is a two-step process involved in getting the document to a place where it is visible by all those who will be reading the documents. First, one must check in the document, as shown in Figure A.16. Then an Owner must approve, as shown in Figure A.17.

FIGURE A.16   Checking in the document as a major revision

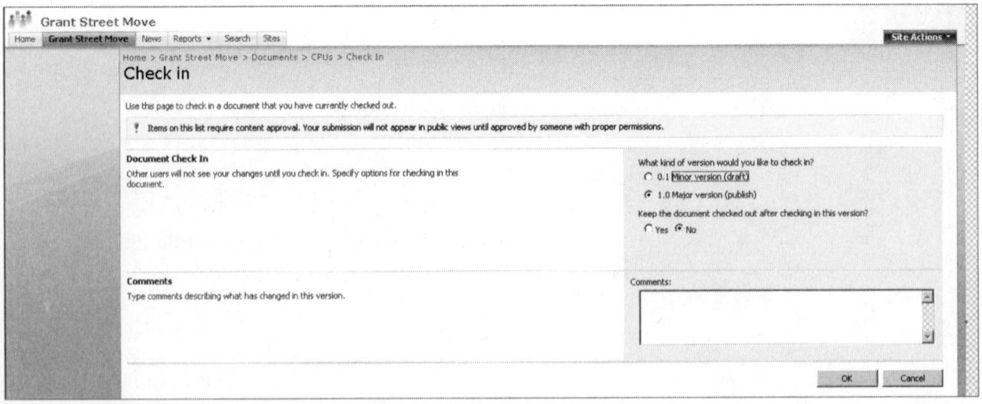

Grant Street Move

Home | Grant Street Move | News | Reports ▼ | Search | Sites | Site Actions ▼

Home > Grant Street Move > Documents > CPUs > Check In

Check in

Use this page to check in a document that you have currently checked out.

⚠ Items on this list require content approval. Your submission will not appear in public views until approved by someone with proper permissions.

Document Check In
Other users will not see your changes until you check in. Specify options for checking in this document.

What kind of version would you like to check in?
○ 0.1 Minor version (draft)
◉ 1.0 Major version (publish)

Keep the document checked out after checking in this version?
○ Yes ◉ No

Comments
Type comments describing what has changed in this version.

Comments:

[OK]   [Cancel]

FIGURE A.17   Approving the document

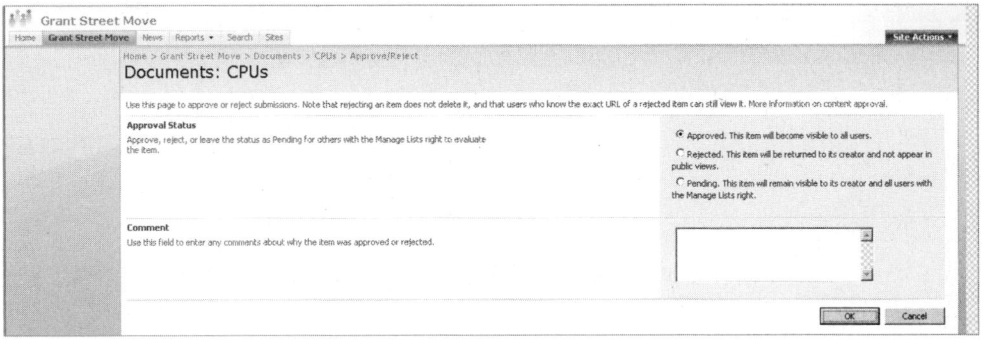

When a Member contributor simply checks in the document with a minor or major revision number, *it is not published*, nor can the Member publish (i.e., approve) the document, even though they may see an Approve/Reject Item selection on the drop-down menu for the document.

Owners *must* be the approvers and also possess contributor permissions. Note that both Member and Owners working with document check-in will see a screen similar to the one shown in Figure A.16.

Owners approve a document by clicking the document's drop-down arrow and selecting Approve/Reject from the list. They are then presented a screen similar to the one shown in Figure A.17.

MOSS wants to know if the check-in is to be considered a minor revision (a number on the right-hand side of the decimal usually indicates a draft of the document or a minor revision to the draft) or a major revision (an increase on the left-hand side of the decimal is considered to be a finalized document and represents a major change in the document contents). Since we're finished with the document, we select major revision. MOSS gives this document version 1.0 because it is our first major saved revision. After the document is approved, it is available for others to view and utilize.

Now suppose that the PC technicians at the company take at look at the spreadsheet and question some of the numbers. After going through an onsite audit of some of the PCs, they come back and provide some new figures. For example, in the 1.7 GHz range, they count 113, not 133, PCs, only 3 of which are overclocked.

The lead for the PC technicians navigates to `http://PMServer/GSM` (recall that we selected GSM as short for Grant St. Move to avoid having to type long URLs) and then clicks All Site Content ➢ Documents. Figure A.18 illustrates this. Alternatively, the lead could have simply keyed in `http://PMServer/GSM/Documents/` to find his way to the folder.

FIGURE A.18 Navigating to the http://PMServer.GSM/Documents folder

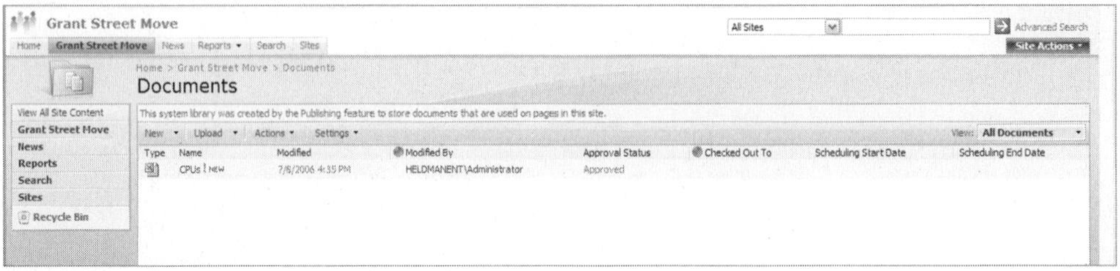

FIGURE A.19 Document options

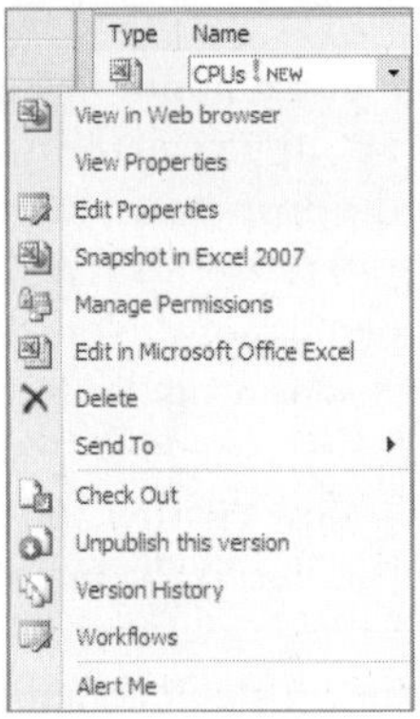

At this point, depending on the level of permissions, the user has options regarding what to do with this document, as shown in Figure A.19.

View in Web Browser allows the user to view the document content in a web browser—not edit its content. The user will not be able to use Excel edit and update options without first checking the document out. Thus the changes cannot be registered for all to see. First the user must check out the document and then work on it. When ready to republish, the user must go through the act of checking in, approving, and publishing the document again (provided, of course, they have the correct permissions—if not, someone with Owner privileges must do the final work). When extensive changes like this are made and the document is republished in final form, it will be given a new version number, 2.0 in this case.

Snapshot in Excel 2007 and Edit in Microsoft Office Excel both launch Excel for editing. Snapshot in Excel 2007 takes a copy of the spreadsheet and moves it into Excel for editing. This is a *local* copy—you *are not* editing the server document at this juncture. Edit in Microsoft Office Excel prompts you first to check out the document and then loads Excel so you can edit it. The check-out notification is shown in Figure A.20.

Excel Web Services handles the responsibility of displaying this information inside a web browser for others to view. The Excel Web Services engine can also be used to display dashboards (using an optional Microsoft product called Business Scorecard Manager) and provide a number of business analysis services.

FIGURE A.20 Checking out the document

![Screenshot of the Grant Street Move document library with a Microsoft Internet Explorer dialog box for checking out the document]

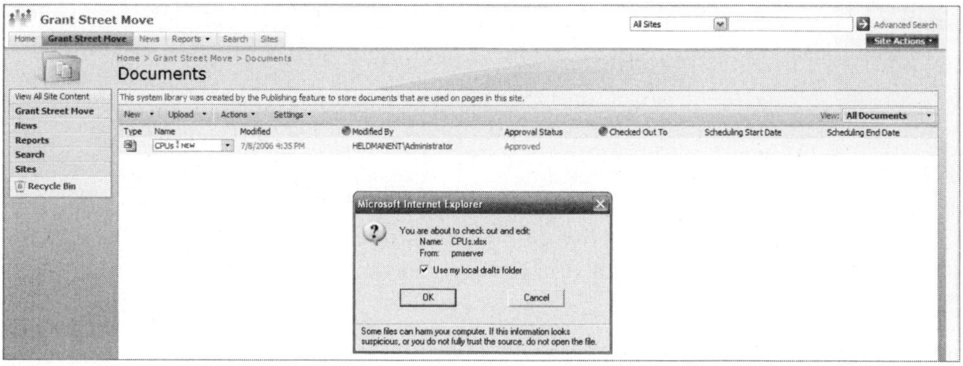

Using Excel Functions to Enhance Project Management Productivity

There are numerous functions in Excel 2007 that you can utilize to enhance Excel's calculation capabilities. Functions are grouped into several different categories and usually, but not always, take on the form of =*Function_Name(parameter1, parameter2…)*. The equal sign always precedes the name of a function in a cell. Depending on what the function requires as input, there may be one or more parameters that you'll have to pass into the function to get it to work. Functions range from very easy to use to quite obscure. If you have a calculation to perform that is not an ordinary addition, subtraction, multiplication, and division problem, there is likely a function you can use to accomplish your task.

Formulas are found by clicking the Formulas tab on the ribbon.

When performing calculations in Excel, remember the phrase we all learned in grade school concerning basic math rules: My Dear Aunt Sally. This stands for: Multiply and divide before adding and subtracting. For example, the formula 2 + 3 * 2 is not the same as (2 + 3) * 2.

Many of the functions are the ones you saw in Office XP and 2003, but there are some new ones. For example, the CUBE functions are new. They allow you to manipulate pivot tables or Online Analytical Processing (OLAP) against a SQL Server database.

The function groupings are listed in the next section. We'll talk about some of the functions you'll likely find most useful in your project management efforts and give you some examples of how to use them.

Function Groups

Functions in Excel are logically grouped into categories that may be useful for the task at hand. We will now take a few moments to review the function categories.

Cube A new category, this group of functions is provided to help you manipulate cubes, also known as pivot tables.

Date/Time These functions are provided to help you manipulate dates and times. You can turn text or numbers into a date or time and vice versa. Excel keeps track of dates and times using a serial number. Number one in the serial set is January 1, 1900 and the counting moves upward from there. Using serial numbers to represent specific dates makes it easy to perform date arithmetic.

Engineering A robust set of engineering-centric functions is provided. For example, to convert a decimal to hexadecimal, the DEC2HEX function can be used.

Financial There probably isn't an accountant, financial officer, auditor, actuary, or other individual in the financial services arena who does not utilize Excel's financial calculation capabilities on a daily basis. Everything from Net Present Value (NPV) to currency conversion is provided.

Information This group of functions exists to help you determine what a cell contains—what it *has in it* and what it *does not*. For example, does a cell contain text? A number? Is it empty? These are questions the Information category of functions helps you answer. These are mostly used programmatically (Visual Basic for Applications, or VBA) or in macros.

Logical The logical function group helps you determine if something elsewhere in the workbook is true and, if so, perform some operation. If you're familiar with programming, the standard IF-THEN-ELSE construct typifies the style of logical function operations. Also, error detection can occur using the functions in this group.

Lookup/Reference Used with Excel's tremendous database capabilities, the lookup/reference functions allow you to perform various database lookup operations against your workbook data. For example, HLOOKUP is a horizontal lookup function that allows you to find data within rows.

Math/Trigonometry Excel includes a tremendous array of math and trigonometry functions you can use for more complicated calculations. For example, the Excel FACT function can create a factorial ($n * n+1 * n+2...$), which is useful in certain kinds of scientific calculations. The ROUNDDOWN function rounds a number toward zero, while the ROUNDUP rounds away from zero, and so forth.

Statistical Because statistics are such a large part of many math operations, Excel comes with an even larger group of statistical functions than the math functions it includes. If you need to calculate a standard deviation (STDEV) or find the skew or slope (SKEW, SLOPE) of a data distribution, among other things, Excel can handle the job.

Text Manipulating text, whether for data lookup purposes, formatting the worksheet, or other uses, is an integral part of spreadsheet work. For example, text functions such as UPPER can convert all text to uppercase.

Functions for the Project Manager

There are some Excel functions a PM will likely never touch. But others will be your bread and butter. Next we'll detail some of the more useful functions that you might use in a project management role. At the end of this section we'll explain how to use some of the functions so you have a feel for them. Note that with any given function, there may be one or more parameters required to make it work correctly. If you're curious about the syntax for a given function, navigate to www.microsoft.com and search on "Excel functions" for a full explanation of what the functions are, their syntax, and an example of their usage.

Text Functions

- DOLLAR() converts a number to text format and then applies a currency symbol.

- LOWER() converts text to all lowercase letters.

- PROPER() formats a sentence in proper case (first letter capitalized, all others lowercase).

- TEXT() changes a number to text.

- UPPER() converts text to all uppercase letters.

Logical Functions

- IF() evaluates a parameter, does one thing if true, does another if false.

Date/Time

- DATE() returns the date serial number for a given date.

- DAY() returns that part of a date serial number that represents the day. MONTH() and YEAR() perform the same function for their respective parts of the serial number.

- DAYS360() calculates the number of days between two dates based on a 360-day year. Many organizations' financial departments utilize a 360-day calendar year for their work.

- NETWORKDAYS() allows the calculation of the number of days between two dates and includes the option to include holidays.

- NOW() yields the current date and time. Especially useful for registering the exact date and time of an entry into the spreadsheet.

- TIME() provides the decimal number for a specific time. (SECOND(), MINUTE(), and HOUR() yield their respective portions of that time.)

- WEEKDAY() returns the day of the week corresponding to a certain date. However, it is given in integer form (1 = Sunday, 2 = Monday, and so on).

- WEEKNUM() tells you the number of a week—where it falls within the year.

- WORKDAY() yields a date that represents the number of working days after a certain date. Excludes any holidays you give it and weekends.

Lookup/Reference

- HLOOKUP() is used to find something you're looking for within a row of data.

- HYPERLINK() allows you to create a link to a website within a cell. When users click on it, they are taken there.
- VLOOKUP() is used to find something you're looking for within a column of data.

Math/Trig

- COUNT() counts the number of cells that contain *numbers*. (Note that COUNT() does not work with text data.)
- COUNTA() counts the number of cells that are not empty (i.e., works with text data).
- EVEN() returns a number rounded up to the nearest even integer.
- FLOOR() rounds a number downward to the nearest point of significance.
- GCD() can be used to find the greatest common divisor, extremely useful in algebraic manipulations.
- LCM() returns the least common multiple of integers, also useful for algebraic calculations.
- MAX() brings back the largest number in the data group. (Note that MAX() does not work with text data.)
- MIN() brings back the smallest number in the data group. (Note that MIN() does not work with text data.)
- MOD() returns the modulus of a number when divided by another number. This is useful for logic determinations; for example, if MOD2 (a number divided by 2) has no modulus, then we know we have an even number.
- PRODUCT() multiplies all of the numbers given and returns the product.
- QUOTIENT() returns the *non-remainder* portion of a division operation. Remainders are not included. Note the difference between this function and MOD().
- ROUND() rounds a number to a specified number of digits.
- SUBTOTAL() provides a subtotal in a list or a database. SUBTOTAL() is an unusual function in that it requires the *function number* for the associated function you would like for it to run. For example, suppose that you want to run a subtotal on a column but you simply want the sum of the numbers in that column. The code for SUM() is 109. For a range B2:B23, your SUBTOTAL() function would be formulated as follows: =SUBTOTAL(109, B2:B23). The function numbers you'll need to go along with SUBTOTAL() pop up for you as you're formulating the parameters of the function, but they are included here for your reference:
  - 1 – AVERAGE
  - 2 – COUNT
  - 3 – COUNTA
  - 4 – MAX
  - 5 – MIN
  - 6 – PRODUCT
  - 7 – STDEV

- 8 – STDEVP
- 9 – SUM
- 10 – VAR
- 11 - VARP
- 101 – AVERAGE
- 102 – COUNT
- 103 – COUNTA
- 104 – MAX
- 105 – MIN
- 106 – PRODUCT
- 107 – STDEV
- 108 – STDEVP
- 109 – SUM
- 110 – VAR
- 111 – VARP

You're probably asking yourself, "Why are each of the functions repeating?" The answer is that function numbers 1 through 11 will carry out their function even with hidden rows. Function numbers 101 through 111 will *not* consider hidden rows.

- SUM() is the workhorse of Excel and is included as an Autosum (with a picture of capital Epsilon) button on the ribbon. Sum adds up a row or column of numbers.
- TRUNC() truncates a number by removing its fractional part, leaving only the integer part of the number.

Engineering

- CONVERT() can be used to translate a table of numbers from one measurement system to another (e.g., miles to kilometers, degrees Fahrenheit to Celsius, etc.).
- DEC2BIN() converts a decimal number to binary.
- DELTA() tests to see if two numbers are equal and returns 1 for equal, 0 for inequality.

Statistical

- AVERAGE() returns the arithmetic mean of a list of numbers.
- MODE() returns the most repetitively occurring value in an array of data.
- QUARTILE() is used to find population representations for a given group of data.
- STDEV() gives you the standard deviation of an array of data. The data group can be only a sample of the group, not the entire array.
- STDEVP() gives you the standard deviation of an array of data. Must represent the entire data group.

- TDIST() can be used to test Student-t probability data groups. Used for hypothesis testing.
- VAR() provides the variance based upon a sample of data.
- VARP() provides the variance based upon the entire data group.

Information

- CELL() gives you the formatting information for a given cell.
- ISEVEN() returns true if the value in the cell is even.
- ISODD() returns true if the value in the cell is odd.
- There are other IS functions, such as ISBLANK, ISNUMBER and so forth

Next we'll take a look at a couple of examples of how to use these functions.

Date Functions   Using the DATE() function can be confusing if you don't understand the underlying formatting that is applied to the worksheet. By default, all Excel cells are set for what is called General formatting. That is, they have no specific number formatting. Until you alter a cell, the cell's formatting is set to General.

When the DATE() function is used, if Excel sees that the cell is formatted as General, it will convert the cell to a Date format. Thus, even though you're promised the serial representation of the date, you won't see it—you'll see its date representation instead. Figure A.21 shows this. In cell C3 in the figure, we've purposely formatted the cell as Numeric with two decimal places. You can see that the date 12/25/2007 was used in the function and the function returns serial 39441.00. In cell C4, we left the formatting untouched. Excel calculated the date serial number and inserted it in Date format.

To illustrate the serial number date math, in Figure A.22 you can see that we've keyed New Year's Day of 2008 in cell D3, which is serial 39448. Using Excel's ordinary arithmetic capabilities, it is quite easy to subtract C3 from D3 to yield the number of days between 12/25/2007 and 1/1/2008, which is 7 days as shown in cell D5. However, note in cells C7 and D7 that when we allow Excel to provide the date formatting (that is, we did not purposely change the formatting to Numeric, nor did we enter these dates as a DATE function), the date arithmetic in cell D8 returns an erroneous date.

This is where the DATEVALUE() function comes in handy. This function returns the serial number of a date that has been keyed in as text. You need quotes around the date entry, as shown in Figure A.23, to make certain you get the serial number as the result.

FIGURE A.21   Using the DATE() function

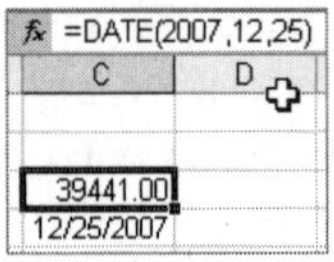

FIGURE A.22   Using the DATE() function in date arithmetic

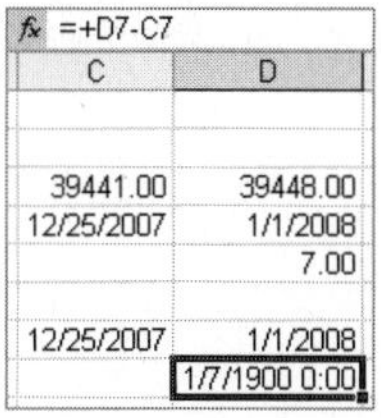

C	D
fx =+D7-C7	
39441.00	39448.00
12/25/2007	1/1/2008
	7.00
12/25/2007	1/1/2008
	1/7/1900 0:00

FIGURE A.23   Using the DATEVALUE() function

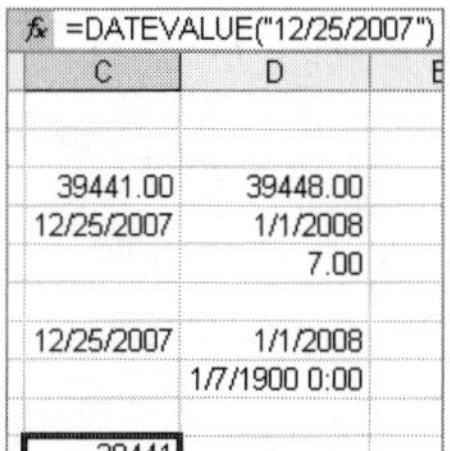

C	D	E
fx =DATEVALUE("12/25/2007")		
39441.00	39448.00	
12/25/2007	1/1/2008	
	7.00	
12/25/2007	1/1/2008	
	1/7/1900 0:00	
39441		

Statistical Functions   Another useful set of functions belongs to the statistical group. The standard deviation measures how widely members of a data group vary from the average. The average (arithmetic mean) returns the average value for a given data group. The median brings back a number that is exactly in the middle of a given set of numbers. The mode gives you the most frequently occurring value in a data group.

Figure A.24 shows the CPU spreadsheet we dealt with in an earlier example with the changes the PC technician lead recommended, as well as the standard deviation, mean, median, and mode added for each of the pertinent data columns.

In this figure, you can see that the number of computers within any given GHz rating varies by 75. The average number of computers is approximately 113. The exact middle of the number of computers is 103. And the most frequently occurring value is 71. Simply copying these formulas to columns C and D yields the same kind of information for over- and underclocked CPUs, respectively.

You can also *nest* one function within another. For example, we don't really need the two-decimal-place accuracy in our calculations. We can use the ROUND() function to make rounding decisions for us. In Figure A.25, you can see that we started out with our original STDEV() function. In the next cell below, we just keyed in a formula to round whatever was in cell B26, with zero decimal places. In the bottom cell, we nested STDEV() inside of ROUND() to simultaneously calculate the standard deviation and round the result to two decimal places.

FIGURE A.24   Statistical functions to analyze data

	A	B	C	D	E	F
1	CPU GHZ	# Computers	# Overclocked	# Underclocked		
2	0.9	71	30	2		
3	1.0	96	13	2		
4	1.1	0	0	0		
5	1.2	74	17	3		
6	1.3	71	0	0		
7	1.4	75	1	3		
8	1.5	55	3	3		
9	1.6	176	1	12		
10	1.7	113	3	14		
11	1.8	207	2	15		
12	1.9	154	4	11		
13	2.0	213	10	33		
14	2.2	255	4	23		
15	2.4	276	5	17		
16	2.6	130	2	21		
17	2.8	121	1	40		
18	3.0	119	0	6		
19	3.1	110	0	8		
20	3.2	74	0	4		
21	3.4	37	1	3		
22	3.6	29	0	7		
23	3.8	24	1	2		
24		2480	98	229		
25						
26	Standard Deviation	74.579572	7.268505268	10.83055242	=STDEV(*range*)	
27	Mean (Average)	112.727273	4.454545455	10.40909091	=AVERAGE(*range*)	
28	Median	103	1.5	6.5	=MEDIAN(*range*)	
29	Mode	71	0	3	=MODE(*range*)	

FIGURE A.25   Nesting functions

25			
26	Standard Deviation	74.579572	=STDEV(B2:B23)
27		75	=ROUND(B26,0)
28		75	=ROUND(STDEV(B2:B23),0)

VBA, Macros, and Other Ways to Automate Excel

Many of the functions are not the type you'd natively use. What we mean by that is you're not likely to use the UPPER() function to convert something to uppercase while typing text into a worksheet. Most of the time, you'll probably just hit the Caps Lock key and type in the text. So what good are functions like this?

Functions that have no apparent direct interaction with the user are likely meant to be used programmatically, whether in a macro or a Visual Basic for Applications (VBA) program. For example, let's say you've built a form in VBA that allows users to type in various project information, but you want to guard against getting different text cases (uppercase, lowercase). You would use the UPPER() function in the VBA code as a way of assuring uniform data.

There are now five ways of automating your work in Excel:

- The first is VBA. Provided you're familiar with the Visual Basic (VB) language, you can write an application that directly interacts with your spreadsheet. This is a great in-workbook way of dramatically extending the power of Excel.

- Macros are another method for automating your work. Think of macros as scripts that store common keystrokes you make when editing a workbook. Once it's recorded, you can launch the macro to type the keys for you. For someone who doesn't have programming experience, this is a good way to avoid the confusion of the VB language structure and syntax and still get some benefits of automation. However, macros are limited in the capabilities you can apply to your spreadsheets.

- If you have Microsoft's Visual Studio 2005 Tools for Office, you can create Visual Studio (VS) applications with Excel running inside the VS framework. That is, you open a workbook you want to automate right within VS. This is the most sophisticated of all techniques and brings you the full power of VS, including database manipulation capabilities and the ability to lock down cell named ranges and other elements. This tool is recommended for experienced software developers who want to extend Excel's power.

- You can import XML files directly into your workbook, or edit those already linked in the workbook.

- Finally, you can add simple controls directly to the spreadsheet using the Developer tools within Excel.

Before you can create a VBA module or macro, import or modify XML files, or install custom controls, you have to enable the Developer tab on the Excel ribbon. Here's how: Click Office Button ➤ Excel Options. Under the Personalize section of Excel Options you'll see a Show Developer Tab in the Ribbon box, as shown in Figure A.26.

Check Show Developer Tab in the Ribbon and exit the Excel Options window. Now a Developer tab with several groups is made available for you, as shown in Figure A.27.

Clicking the Macros button in the Code group allows you to name a macro, and the smaller tools to its right allows you to record, play back, set security for, and edit relative references for a macro.

Clicking the Visual Basic button in the Code group brings up a separate window where you create your VB code. Figure A.28 shows this screen.

Click the Insert menu item to insert a control such as a drop-down or list box, as shown in Figure A.29.

FIGURE A.26   Enabling the Developer tab

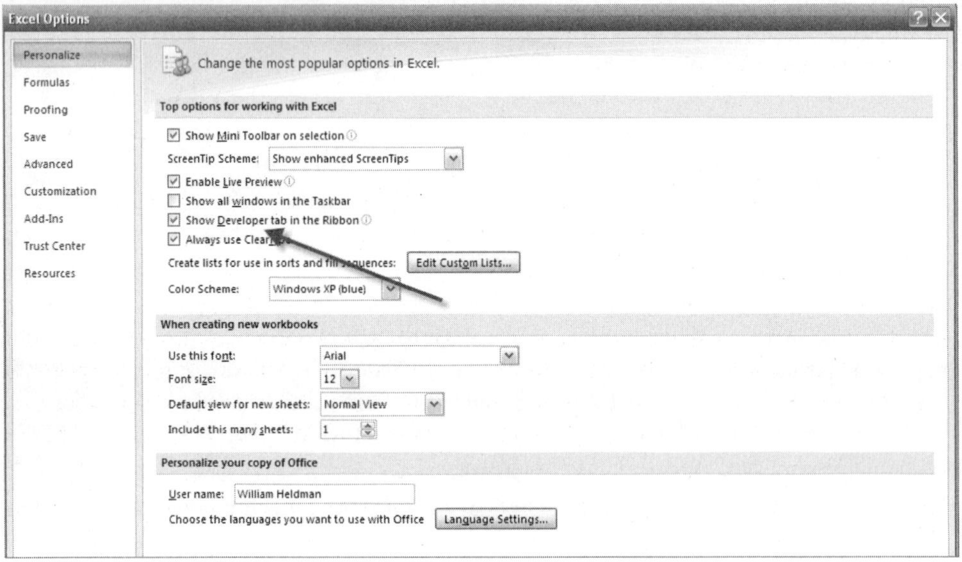

FIGURE A.27   Developer tab

FIGURE A.28   VBA screen within Excel

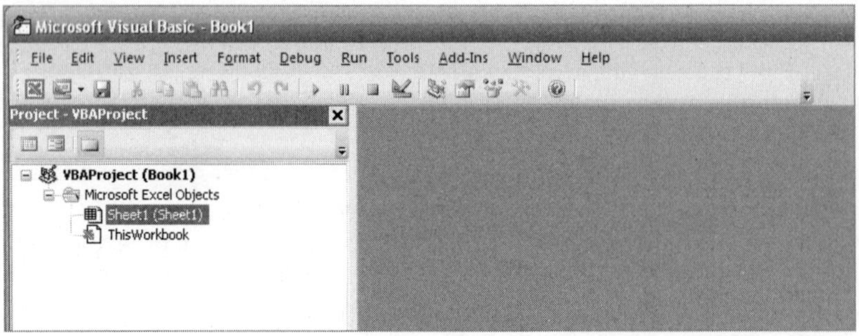

FIGURE A.29   Inserting controls into the workbook

There is no code associated with the control, even though you're able to successfully place it on the screen. You'll need to click View Code to add VB code to the control object. However, this isn't necessary if all you want is a simple pick-from-the-list box to simplify user choices.

Here's how to create a basic drop-down:

1. Choose an out-of-the-way place for your drop-down text. For example, in cells AA1 through AA8, add some text as shown in Figure A.30. These are the choices you are giving to the people that will utilize your spreadsheet. Excel will take the choices keyed into AA1:AA8 and utilize them in your combo box (drop-down) control.

2. Click Insert and select the combo box from the list of control choices. (See Figure A.29. The combo box is the second button from the left, top row, under the Form Controls heading).

3. Place the combo box so that it straddles cells B1 and C1, as shown in Figure A.31. (This is where the combo box will appear.) The combo box is currently empty—we have not yet told it where to get its list information.

FIGURE A.30   Drop-down text keyed into a remote part of the workbook

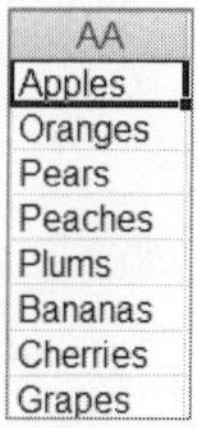

AA
Apples
Oranges
Pears
Peaches
Plums
Bananas
Cherries
Grapes

FIGURE A.31   Inserting a combo box into the workbook

4. With the combo box highlighted, right-click with your mouse and choose Properties. Figure A.32 illustrates the remainder of the steps.

5. In the Input Range field, key in the range of cells you made back in step 1.

6. In the Cell Link field, key in **A1**. This is the place where Excel will put the choice the user made.

7. You have the ability to determine how many drop-down lines are available. We have eight choices in our input range. If you want to include a blank as a selection option, expand the Input Range value by one cell to capture a blank cell.

8. You can opt to apply 3D shading to the drop-down box if you wish.

Now all you need to do is pick out a choice from the drop-down and watch Excel pop it into Cell B1 as shown in Figure A.33.

FIGURE A.32   Format control

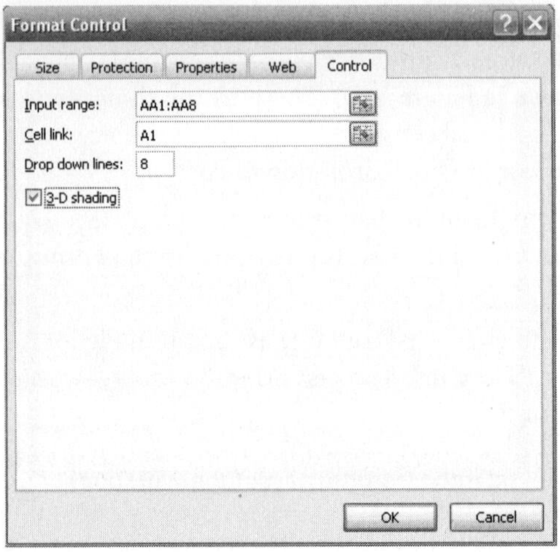

FIGURE A.33   Selecting from the combo box

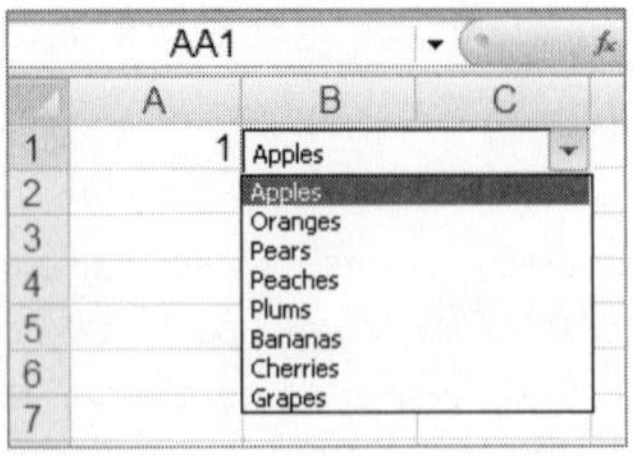

If the user chooses Apples from the drop-down list, Excel puts a 1 in cell A1 because Apples is the first member of the list. If you choose Cherries from the list, the number 7 would appear in cell A1. If you want to go beyond this capability, you'll have to write VB code. To do this, click the View Code button on the Developer tab (in the Controls group, see Figure A.27 for reference) to bring up the VB module window, as shown in Figure A.34.

FIGURE A.34 Viewing the VB module for the combo box

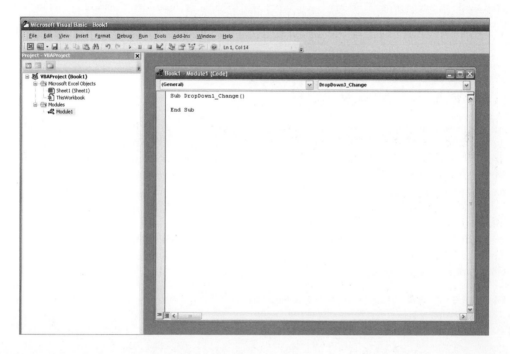

The New Visual Studio Express Editions—Right For The Pocket-Book

VS 2005 Professional contains all of the out-of-box languages that VS supports (C++, C#, VB, and J#). This is great for a shop that utilizes these tools on a daily basis to create software either for resale or for in-house custom applications.

But what if you just want to learn software development and don't want to get into the expense of buying VS? Microsoft now offers its Visual Studio 2005 software development packages in what it calls *Express Editions*. Novice and hobby use is where the VS Express packages come in. They are free for the download, they are language specific, and there are a number of tutorials included on Microsoft's website and within the package itself to help you get up and functional very quickly. Visual C# 2005 Express Edition, for example, comes with the VS tools needed to create VS applications and includes some sample projects you can learn from, such as a screen-saver builder.

You'll have to download an Express Edition for each language you're interested in learning. There is a separate download for Microsoft SQL Server Express Edition so you can create applications that extract records from an enterprise-class database.

Additionally, there are numerous books and classes available for VS. If you're genuinely interested in learning to develop software, VS Express Editions are a great starting place.

To download the Express Editions, navigate to www.microsoft.com/vstudio and follow the prompts from there.

Consolidating Sheets

Another useful feature of Excel is its ability to consolidate data from various worksheets or workbooks into a single *consolidation sheet*. The purpose of the Consolidate feature is to bring together data from disparate locations and perform common functions (like SUM() or MAX(), for example) to yield information about the data collectively. Consolidation is a comparison of at least two data sources, whether from within the same workbook or from different workbooks. Let's walk through how to perform a consolidation worksheet that averages information from our CPUs data worksheets.

Highlight a cell in a blank worksheet and then click the Consolidate button in the Data Tools group under the Data tab, shown in Figure A.35. We'll examine the input boxes in the Consolidate dialog box from the bottom up.

FIGURE A.35   Consolidate Dialog Box

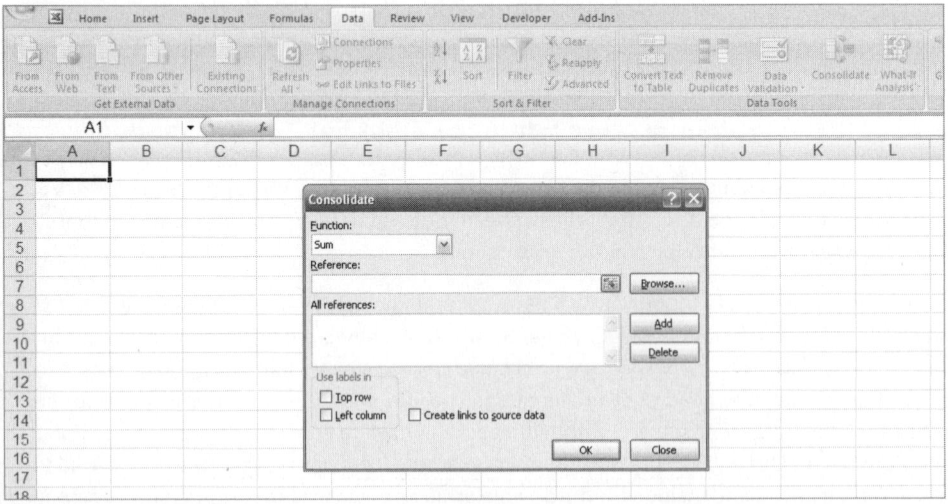

First, you can bring together cells or entire worksheets. You can type in the references in the All References box starting with the name of the worksheet followed by what we geeks call the "bang" symbol, more lovingly referred to as the exclamation point. Next you'll need to know the range of cells (or range names) in order to add the references—for example, $A$1:$D$21.

The easiest way to add worksheets to your range is to use the Browse button and click Add when you find the one you're looking for. In our example, we've added two: CPUs2005 and CPUs2006. Figure A.36 shows the ranges included within these worksheets. The blank worksheet we opened originally has been renamed to Data Consolidation.

From the Function drop-down, select the function you'd like Excel to perform. Your choices include SUM(), COUNT(), AVERAGE(), MAX(), MIN(), PRODUCT(), COUNT NUMBERS, STDEV(), STDEVP(), VAR(), and VARP(). Note that STDEVP() is like STDEV() only it assumes that you're including the *entire* data group as the population sample. In large data groups, this might not be the case. If you're using only a *sample* of your population, utilize STDEV(). If you're using the entire population, use STDEVP(). You have a similar choice with the variance functions VAR() and VARP(). There is no actual COUNT NUMBERS function. COUNT NUMBERS is a variance of Autosum, where only cells with numbers are counted using the COUNT function.

FIGURE A.36 Consolidation screen In the left-hand pane of the Excel sheet, alongside the Consolidate dialog box, and initial Excel data with data entries

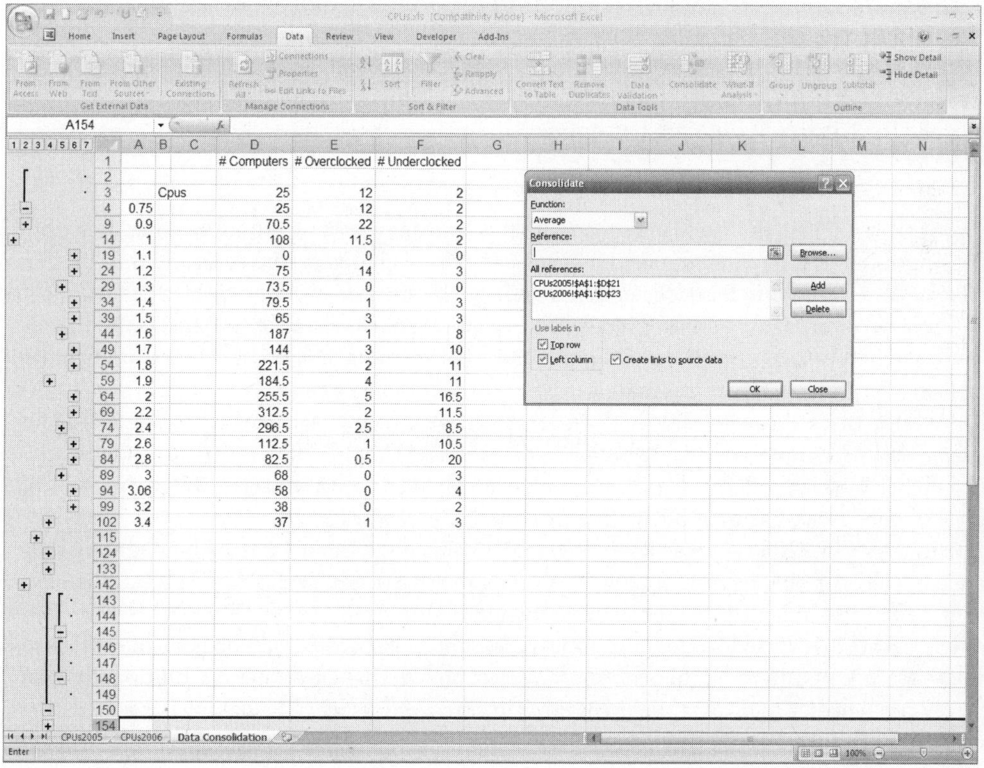

We chose AVERAGE() as our consolidate function. You'll notice there is a series of + marks in seven columns to the left of the data. When you click the plus sign, you'll see the information behind the calculation. For example, if you click the + on row 4 and row 9, you'll see the information Excel collected from the CPUs2005 and CPUs2006 worksheets to perform the average (Figure A.37).

Rows 3 and 4 show the data for 0.75 GHz entries. In this case, only one of the worksheets has an entry for 0.75 GHz (the CPUs2005 worksheet) and it's displayed in row 3. Row 4 is the resulting average. The same is true for rows 7 through 9. Row 7 shows the data for the CPUs2005 entries for 0.9 GHz CPUs and row 8 is the CPUs2006 information. Row 9 shows the averages.

FIGURE A.37   Revealing the calculations

1 2 3 4 5 6 7	A	B	C	D # Computers	E # Overclocked	F # Underclocked
1				# Computers	# Overclocked	# Underclocked
2						
3			Cpus	25	12	2
4	0.75			25	12	2
5						
6						
7			Cpus	71	15	2
8			Cpus	70	29	2
9	0.9			70.5	22	2

Cubes/Pivot Tables

A pivot table is a data mining feature that allows you to analyze large groups of data. By simply dragging columns into different positions, you can obtain unique perspectives and thus be able to make better decisions about the data at hand.

A cube is simply a pivot table that consists of more than two elements of data—sales figures by sales region by salesperson, for example. In a project management scenario, you might be interested in projects by project manager by percent completed.

In a lot of cases, the pivot table or cube data is derived from a variety of sources. Excel again has the ability to link to disparate data resources. Excel supplies the needed connection software under the Data tab of the ribbon. As previously mentioned, Excel 2007 provides a full range of cube functions to assist with your data analysis work.

Using the CPUs2006 worksheet, let's create a basic pivot table. Start by highlighting the range of cells you're interested in, and then from the Insert tab, click Pivot Table and select Pivot Table from the resulting menu, as shown in Figure A.38.

The Create Pivot Table dialog box appears (Figure A.39). Note that you have the ability to choose a range of cells or a table, or you can select an external data source. Additionally, you can choose whether to display the pivot table in a new worksheet (the default) or an existing worksheet.

FIGURE A.38   Pivot Table menu

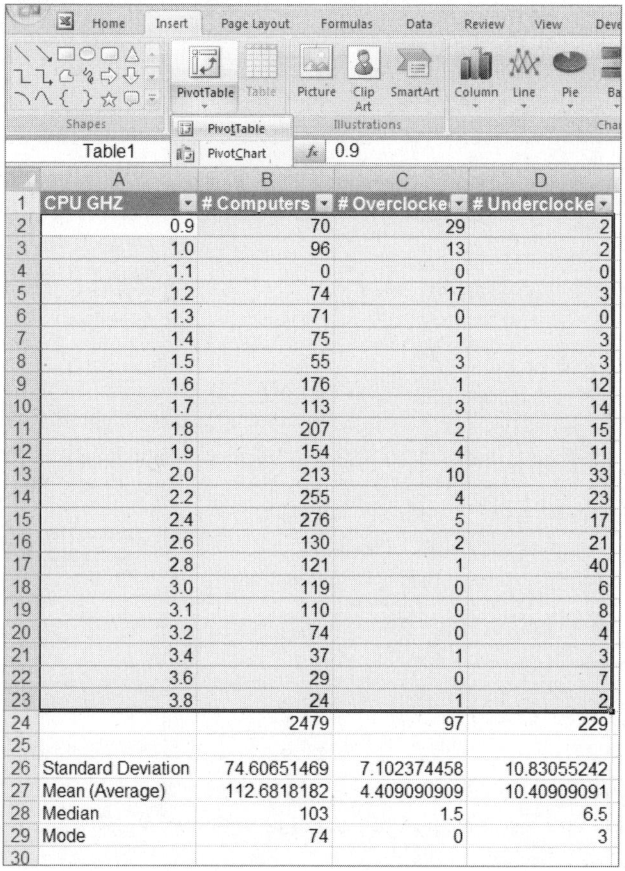

	A	B	C	D
1	CPU GHZ	# Computers	# Overclocke	# Underclocke
2	0.9	70	29	2
3	1.0	96	13	2
4	1.1	0	0	0
5	1.2	74	17	3
6	1.3	71	0	0
7	1.4	75	1	3
8	1.5	55	3	3
9	1.6	176	1	12
10	1.7	113	3	14
11	1.8	207	2	15
12	1.9	154	4	11
13	2.0	213	10	33
14	2.2	255	4	23
15	2.4	276	5	17
16	2.6	130	2	21
17	2.8	121	1	40
18	3.0	119	0	6
19	3.1	110	0	8
20	3.2	74	0	4
21	3.4	37	1	3
22	3.6	29	0	7
23	3.8	24	1	2
24		2479	97	229
25				
26	Standard Deviation	74.60651469	7.102374458	10.83055242
27	Mean (Average)	112.6818182	4.409090909	10.40909091
28	Median	103	1.5	6.5
29	Mode	74	0	3
30				

FIGURE A.39   Create Pivot Table dialog box

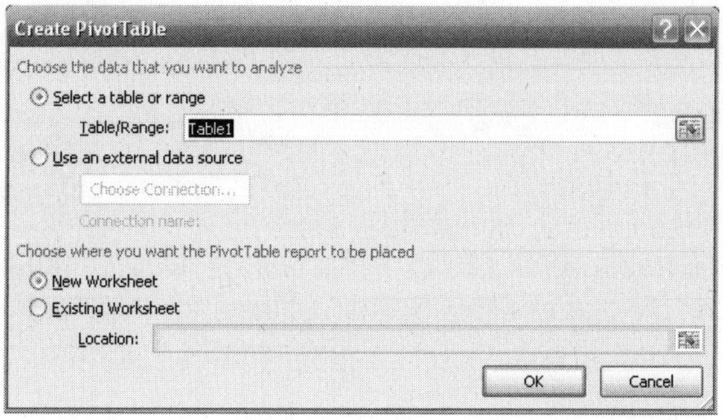

We've covered the resulting pivot table in previous chapters, but Figure A.40 shows the output of the CPUs2007 range. It's a snap to drag columns into the different boxes in order to obtain different viewpoints on the data.

FIGURE A.40   Resulting CPUs2005 pivot table

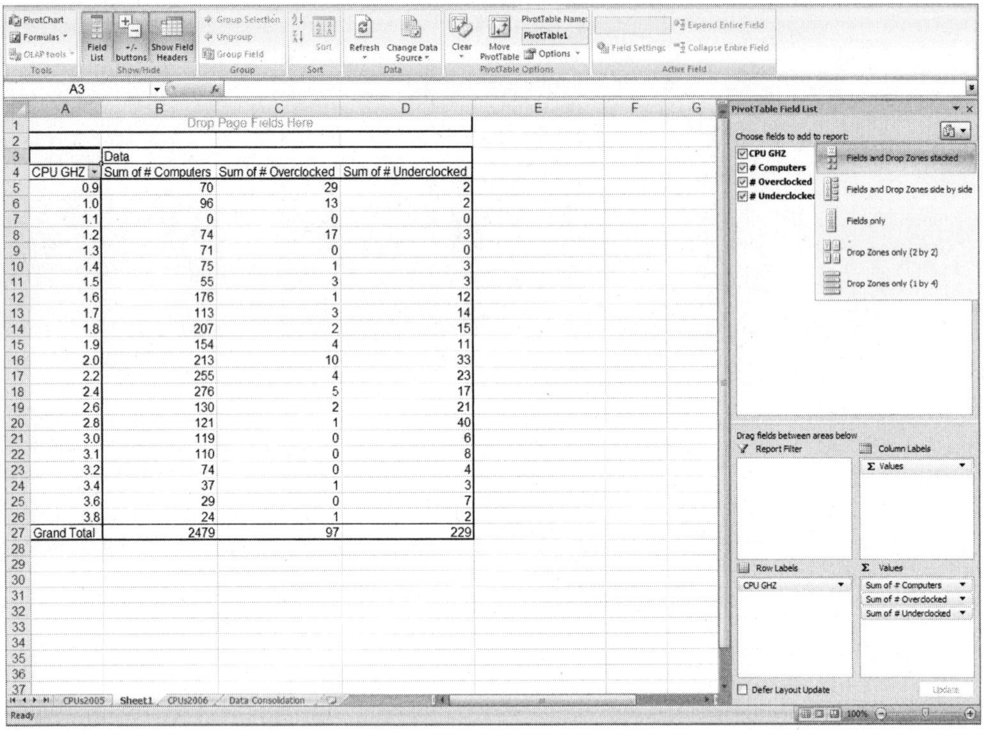

Index

Note to the Reader: Throughout this index **boldfaced** page numbers indicate primary discussions of a topic. *Italicized* page numbers indicate illustrations.